Irish Imperial Networks

This is an innovative study of the role of Ireland and the Irish in the British Empire, which examines the intellectual, cultural and political interconnections between nineteenth-century British imperial, Irish and Indian history. Barry Crosbie argues that Ireland was a crucial sub-imperial centre for the British Empire in South Asia that provided a significant amount of the manpower, intellectual and financial capital that fuelled Britain's drive into Asia from the 1750s onward. He shows the important role that Ireland played as a centre for recruitment for the armed forces, the medical and civil services, and the many missionary and scientific bodies established in South Asia during the colonial period. In doing so, the book also reveals the important part that the Empire played in shaping Ireland's domestic institutions, family life and identity in equally significant ways.

BARRY CROSBIE is Assistant Professor of European History in the Department of History at the University of Macau.

Irish Imperial Networks
*Migration, Social Communication
and Exchange in Nineteenth-Century India*

Barry Crosbie

CAMBRIDGE
UNIVERSITY PRESS

University Printing House, Cambridge CB2 8BS, United Kingdom

One Liberty Plaza, 20th Floor, New York, NY 10006, USA

477 Williamstown Road, Port Melbourne, VIC 3207, Australia

314-321, 3rd Floor, Plot 3, Splendor Forum, Jasola District Centre, New Delhi - 110025, India

79 Anson Road, #06-04/06, Singapore 079906

Cambridge University Press is part of the University of Cambridge.

It furthers the University's mission by disseminating knowledge in the pursuit of education, learning and research at the highest international levels of excellence.

www.cambridge.org
Information on this title: www.cambridge.org/9780521119375

© Barry Crosbie 2012

This publication is in copyright. Subject to statutory exception and to the provisions of relevant collective licensing agreements, no reproduction of any part may take place without the written permission of Cambridge University Press.

First published 2012

A catalogue record for this publication is available from the British Library

Library of Congress Cataloging in Publication data
Crosbie, Barry.
  Irish imperial networks / Barry Crosbie.
    p.   cm.
  Includes bibliographical references and index.
  ISBN 978-0-521-11937-5 (hardback)
  1. Ireland–Relations–India.   2. India–Relations–Ireland.
  3. Irish–India–History.   4. Great Britain–Colonies–History.
  5. Imperialism–History.   I. Title.
  DA964.I4C76 2011
  954´.0049162–dc23
  2011029846

ISBN 978-0-521-11937-5 Hardback

Cambridge University Press has no responsibility for the persistence or accuracy of URLs for external or third-party internet websites referred to in this publication, and does not guarantee that any content on such websites is, or will remain, accurate or appropriate.

This book is dedicated to my wife and family

Contents

Preface	*page* ix	
Acknowledgements	xi	
List of abbreviations	xiii	
1	**Introduction: networks of empire – Ireland and India**	1
	Introduction	1
	Colony, nation and empire	3
	Transnational histories of empire	11
	Networks and empire	14
	Irish imperial networks	17
2	**The business of empire**	24
	Introduction	24
	Colonial trade and Ireland in the eighteenth century	26
	The extension of Irish Atlantic networks eastward: Ireland and the East Indian trade	31
	'In the road of the chiefest trade in the world': East India Company agencies and 'colonial' ports in eighteenth-century Ireland	42
	East Indian trade and the Irish Sulivan connection	44
	London and the fashioning of Irish business networks in South Asia	49
	East India Company patronage networks and Ireland	51
	Smuggling, private trade and commercial links between Ireland and India in the late eighteenth century	57
	Conclusion	62
3	**British overseas expansion, Ireland and the sinews of colonial power**	64
	Introduction	64
	Atlantic isolation and the birth of the second British Empire	66
	The East India Company, Ireland and the Seven Years War	68
	Robert Brooke's army of 'idle natives' and 'dissolute mechanics'	75
	Union for Ireland, union for the Empire	81
	The fashioning of an Irish imperial identity in India	85
	Localised networks and patterns of exchange	94
	Conclusion	97

vii

viii Contents

4	**From trade to dominion**	99
	Introduction	99
	Ireland and the shaping of imperial science	101
	The Irish Ordnance Survey and the Great Trigonometrical Survey of India	106
	Surveying and colonial power in Ireland and India	111
	Thomas Oldham and the Geological Survey of India	117
	Conclusion	126
5	**Religion, civil society and imperial authority**	129
	Introduction	129
	The Catholic Church in Ireland after the Union	131
	Roman Catholicism and the East India Company	136
	Catholic priests and Irish soldiers in India's military cantonments	141
	Irish Catholicism and Indian caste: Daniel O'Connor and the Madras mission	145
	The East India Company and the growth of Irish Catholic networks	154
	Fenian agitation in India	163
	Conclusion	167
6	**From Company to Crown rule**	169
	Introduction	169
	Medicine and the modernising state: Ireland and India	171
	Irishmen and the East India Company's Medical Services, pre 1840s	177
	The Great Famine and the Irish School of Medicine	185
	Irish doctors and the Crown Raj	193
	Irish universities and the growth of professional networks	199
	Conclusion	202
7	**Imperial crisis and the age of reform**	205
	Introduction	205
	Irish recruitment and the Indian Civil Service, 1855–1900	207
	Social and intellectual origins of Irish civil servants in British India	211
	Irish 'Orientalists', the Gaelic revival and the Indian Civil Service after 1858	216
	Land, tenancy and nationalist thought: Irish and Indian connections	224
	'*L'enfant terrible* of the ICS': C. J. O'Donnell and the British administration of Bengal, 1872–82	228
	Emergent Irish and Indian nationalisms	246
	Conclusion	250
8	**Conclusion**	253
	Glossary	263
	Bibliography	266
	Index	291

Preface

This book examines the historical interconnections between Ireland, India and the British Empire in the late eighteenth and nineteenth centuries, a greatly overlooked subject in the scholarship of modern Irish, British imperial and South Asian history. Specifically, the book focuses on the role of imperial networks and how Irish people in India set about circulating their own ideas, practices and material goods across the Empire during the colonial period. Indeed, the geographical connections and networks linking different parts of the world traced in this book reflect my own personal journey and career path to date that has taken me back and forth across what was once the British Empire.

My earliest encounter with the Empire and its long, complex history began as a child growing up in County Wexford, an important site of Cromwellian conquest and English colonisation in Ireland during the late 1640s. It was in Wexford, where my parents' house lay in close proximity to the walled, mysterious environs of 'Cromwell's Fort', that I first became interested in the idea of colonialism and in developing an understanding of how Ireland's past has been shaped by it. Later, as a student of history my studies took me to Cambridge, for so long one of the great intellectual centres of the Empire, where I learned to appreciate how colonial histories were seldom isolated, individual histories, but were in fact closely interwoven narratives whose common themes were replicated across different parts of the globe.

Subsequent spells spent researching and writing this book in many former British colonies, including India, Sri Lanka and Trinidad and Tobago, have served to further develop my understanding of colonial histories, where I have been fortunate enough to appreciate first hand the diverse manifestations of the Empire's profound impact on the lives and spaces of those involved in it.

Today, teaching in Macau, a former Portuguese colony neighbouring Hong Kong, whose university's language of instruction is English,

ix

x   Preface

it appears the legacy and global impact of the British Empire endures. Given the relatively recent phenomenon of British decolonisation in East Asia with the reversion of Hong Kong to Chinese sovereignty, it is perhaps fitting that the book now reaches the end of its journey with me on the China coast.

Acknowledgements

Throughout my time spent as a doctoral student at the University of Cambridge, my supervisor, Professor Sir Christopher Bayly, was an immensely important mentor who provided me with much of the necessary framework for thinking about the connections between Ireland, India and the British Empire. Through his stimulating discussions, insightful commentaries and friendly counsel, he not only helped to encourage my spirit of academic enquiry but has been a tremendous source of inspiration at all times. I wish to express my sincere gratitude to Professor Roy Foster, Dr Timothy Harper, Dr Eugenio Biagini and Professor John MacKenzie for their very generous support, suggestions and encouragement throughout this project. I would also like to thank several colleagues at the National University of Ireland, Galway, especially Professor Gearóid Ó Tuathaigh, without whom my PhD thesis would probably never have assumed the form of a book. His constant encouragement, characteristic wit and humour, as well as his uncanny ability to identify the crux of an argument, contributed enormously to the successful completion of this book. Professor Nicholas Canny, Professor Steven Ellis, Dr Simon Potter and Dr Jason McHugh also deserve special mention. They have each made positive contributions to my experience in Galway by involving me in conferences and other academic pursuits, commenting on my work and offering precious advice.

I wish to offer the Master, Fellows, students and staff of Darwin College great thanks for providing me with excellent facilities, accommodation and a warm, supportive environment in which to study, write and socialise during my time in Cambridge. I must also acknowledge the help and the kind assistance that I have received from the staff of libraries and research centres in Cambridge, including the Centre of South Asian Studies, the Cambridge University Library, the Faculty of Oriental Studies Library, the Seeley Historical Library and Trinity College's Wren Library. In London, the staff of the following libraries and archives have been most helpful: the Asia, Pacific and Africa Collections in the British Library; the Royal Botanical Gardens

xii   Acknowledgements

Archives, Kew; the National Army Museum; and the Imperial College Archives, University of London. In particular, I would like to express my gratitude to Timothy Thomas for providing me with much valuable information concerning material of Irish interest in the British Library. In Ireland, I received much valuable and kind assistance from the librarians and archivists at the National Library of Ireland, St Patrick's College, Maynooth and All Hallows College, Drumcondra.

I would also like to gratefully acknowledge the following funding bodies and institutions for their generous financial support: the Arts and Humanities Research Council (AHRC) for a three-year doctoral scholarship; the Cambridge European Trust Bursary; the Holland Rose Studentship, Christ's College, University of Cambridge; the Prince Consort and Thirlwall Prize, Faculty of History, University of Cambridge; and the Smuts Memorial Research Fund, University of Cambridge; an Irish Research Council for the Humanities and Social Sciences Government of Ireland Postdoctoral Research Fellowship; and a Start-Up Research Fund from the University of Macau.

During regular visits to the South Asian subcontinent I experienced outstanding hospitality, warmth and friendship, all of which made each journey joyful and edifying. I owe an enormous debt of gratitude to my parents-in-law, Nihal and Sarojini Jayawickrama, whose generosity, goodwill and knowledge has taught me much about the subcontinent and life in South Asia.

This book would not have been possible without the help, support and love of my family. My wonderful parents, Derek and Sheila Crosbie, have been models for me both in terms of personal and academic integrity. From them I have learned the value of commitment, hard work and perseverance. Their unwavering love, support and belief in what I was doing at all times have been essential to the completion of this book. My sisters, Diane and Genevieve, and brothers-in-law, Jamie and Jeremy, have also been incredibly supportive. I cannot thank them enough for the friendship and kindness they have shown me throughout the time spent researching and writing this book.

Finally, I would like to thank my wife, Sharanya. Not only has she provided immense practical support in the form of reading and editing the manuscript, but she has also been one of the key contributors in helping me to define both the overall form and structure of the book. Her keen understanding and knowledge of postcolonial theory and literature and willingness to impart this knowledge to me at all times has allowed me to reflect upon history from points of view that otherwise would have been unfamiliar to me. Not only has she been my special 'editor-in-chief', but she has long been my best friend, my travelling companion and the person who has stood by me throughout.

Abbreviations

BL	British Library
BMC	British Military Consultations
Bod. Lib.	Bodleian Library, Oxford
CUL	Cambridge University Library
GMC	General Medical Council
GSI	Geological Survey of India
GTS	Great Trigonometrical Survey of Ireland
ICS	Indian Civil Service
IMS	Indian Medical Service
NAM	National Army Museum
OIOC	Oriental and India Office Collection (British Library)
PP	Parliamentary Papers
PRONI	Public Record Office Northern Ireland
SMS	Subordinate Medical Service
TCD	Trinity College Dublin
UCC	University College Cork
UCG	University College Galway

1 Introduction: Networks of empire – Ireland and India

Introduction

The narrow, atavistic and reactionary section of the Ireland of to-day will, doubtless, sneer at us 'Shawneens' and 'West-Britons,' but at the time we regarded ourselves as Irish Europeans, cosmopolitans and citizens of the world, who hoped to find in a liberalised and democratised British empire, in which Ireland occupied her worthy place, a *metier* in which we could live satisfying lives, and perhaps contribute a share, great or small, to human progress and human civilisation.[1]

Patrick Heffernan, a former Irish member of the Indian Medical Service, made these comments in 1958, almost ten years after the Taoiseach, John A. Costello, had unexpectedly announced to a Canadian reporter that Ireland was to leave the British Commonwealth of Nations and become a republic. Heffernan, who had been brought up on the outskirts of Cahir, Co. Tipperary and had received a Catholic education in Cork and Dublin, held the conviction that Ireland and Irish people (irrespective of religious creed or class) had played significant roles in the wider British imperial system. At a time when Éamon de Valera and the Fianna Fáil party had just returned to power following the Irish General Election in 1957, Heffernan's comments had a particular resonance. His sense that an Irish Catholic background was not incompatible with British imperial service, and therefore did not diminish his Irishness, was not uncommon, even during the heyday of Irish nationalism in the 1950s.

Heffernan's 'cosmopolitans and citizens of the world' emerged from the distinct cultural, economic and political conditions of nineteenth-century Ireland, yet were joined together with their English, Scottish and Welsh colleagues within the British Empire, a legitimate arena for work where they could improve the material condition of their own lives as well as contribute to the welfare of others. As one astute Indian civil

---

[1] Major P. Heffernan, *An Irish Doctor's Memories* (Dublin: Clonmore & Reynolds, 1958), pp. 1–3.

2   Introduction

servant, A. G. Haggard, a Sub-Divisional Officer in Buxar, commented in the late nineteenth century:

The Irish members [of the Indian Civil Service] have mostly known each other in Ireland, the Scotch in Scotland and the English in England. During their long preparatory studies and their subsequent training the whole body have met (Irish, English and Scotch) time after time; they have formed intimacies and friendships; have worked, resided, and travelled together; have been united in a common end and occupation; have given material assistance and shared in mutual rivalries.[2]

Like Heffernan, Haggard emphasises shared collaborative experiences, popular beliefs and cultural mentalities which have nevertheless become somewhat obscured within Irish historiography over the past fifty years.

In its attempts to recover these everyday mentalities and restore nineteenth-century Ireland to its proper imperial context under the Act of Union (1801–1922), this book focuses on the cross-cultural experiences, ideologies, institutions and personnel at the centre of imperial networks that were fashioned through Ireland's involvement with the British colonial project in India during the 'long' nineteenth century. In doing so, it examines the complex historical processes that brought these two very different communities of the Empire into systems of contact, collaboration and conflict long before the development of modern communications technology and the so-called contemporary 'age of globalisation'. From the mid eighteenth century until the late nineteenth century, Ireland and India were joined together by an intricate series of networks of military recruitment, intellectual exchange and political interdependence. These networks were imperial in nature and were borne out of direct Irish involvement in British territorial expansion into South Asia during the Seven Years War. Although Ireland was never a homogeneous economic, political or religious entity during the nineteenth century, Irish men and women (both Catholic and Protestant, from the north and south) nevertheless served as soldiers, missionaries, educators, doctors, scientists and administrators within the imperial system, where they played an important part in the formation of the colonial state and in defining the expanding roles and responsibilities of the modern British state in its Indian environment. Yet, despite occupying central roles within this process, the Irish have never been the subject of a detailed, contextualised study

---

[2] Memorandum by A. G. Haggard to the Secretary to the Government of Bengal, d. Buxar, 12 August 1875. Papers Relating to the Selection and Training of Candidates for the Indian Civil Service: *Parliamentary Papers*, Vol. LV (1876), p. 333.

Colony, nation and empire

that charts their movements, shifting concerns and significance within the numerous global networks forged through British imperialism in India. Equally, despite recent isolated studies examining the plethora of connections that existed between nineteenth-century Ireland and India, Ireland's role in facilitating British imperial expansion in the East has yet to be sufficiently considered by historians.[3] Indeed, the reticence of scholars to examine the Irish within an imperial context in India is almost certainly attributable to the nature of much written history in both Britain and Ireland during the second half of the twentieth century.

Colony, nation and empire

Historical interpretations of the role of Ireland and the Irish in the nineteenth-century British Empire have traditionally been dominated by several contradictory developments. Among the widely varying responses to the establishment of British hegemony in Ireland under the Act of Union are those ranging from accommodation and apathy to statements of resistance and armed struggle.[4] In evaluating these responses, however, scholars have been somewhat hindered in their investigations by perceived notions of exclusivity and exceptionality in relation to Ireland's status under British rule. Although not officially a 'colony' of the British Empire per se, Ireland was nevertheless subjected to Tudor colonisation during the sixteenth and seventeenth centuries, and was joined legislatively to Great Britain under the Act of Union between 1801 and 1922.[5] Owing to the existence of various constitutional anomalies lying at the heart of the Union, Ireland, at once, was not perceived to be a 'colony' in the same sense that India, for example, was.[6] Conversely, despite supplying a disproportionate number of soldiers and administrators for British overseas service, the Irish, unlike the Scots, were not fully integrated into the sinews of metropolitan power. Rather, the Irish occupied an anomalous position of being 'imperial' and 'colonial' at the same time, 'coloniser' but

---

[3] For a recent example of the substantial personal connections linking Ireland, India and the British Empire, see Tadhg Foley and Maureen O'Connor (eds.), *Ireland and India: Colonies, Culture and Empire* (Dublin: Irish Academic Press, 2006).

[4] C. Brady, *Interpreting Irish History: The Debate on Historical Revisionism, 1938–1994* (Dublin: Irish Academic Press, 1994).

[5] D. Fitzpatrick, 'Ireland and Empire', in *The Oxford History of the British Empire: The Nineteenth Century* (Oxford University Press, 1999), pp. 494–521.

[6] See T. Bartlett, '"This Famous Island Set in a Virginian Sea": Ireland in the Eighteenth-Century British Empire', in P. Marshall (ed.), *The Oxford History of the British Empire, Vol. 2, The Eighteenth Century* (Oxford University Press, 1998), pp. 254–76.

4   Introduction

also 'colonised'.[7] Although there have been plenty of recent studies on aspects of 'Scotland's Empire' – most notably on the influence of the Scottish Enlightenment and Scottish Presbyterianism on the manner in which the Scots circulated their ideas and cultivated distinctive relationships with indigenous peoples abroad – the case of Ireland and empire is still very much a new field of enquiry.[8] To a significant degree, the reticence of Irish scholars to write about Ireland's engagement with the Empire was further reinforced by a developing nationalist mode of historical writing that took hold in Ireland in the aftermath of decolonisation. This tradition – encouraged initially by the process of state-building and state-reform movements in Europe during the nineteenth century – has remained the dominant mode of history writing for almost 150 years. As a result of the mainstream practice of writing history within national boundaries, historians have tended to focus upon domestic concerns and issues at the expense of international influences in order to explain the origins of national development as well as the formation of national identities.[9] To the detriment of empire studies in Ireland, nationalism during this period was generally equated with anti-imperialism and as a result the role that Ireland played in British overseas expansion was largely omitted from Irish history books.[10]

Moreover, given the heterogeneous nature of nineteenth-century Ireland and the presence of multiple ethnic and religious divisions within it, a single unifying sense of Irishness was never really a defining feature of the Irish in the Empire. Rather, it becomes important to thoroughly nuance the notion of Irishness to recognise that the Irish comprised a multiplicity of communities, often with very different, sometimes contradictory or competing sets of aims and imperatives. Indeed, it is this very difficulty in framing a discussion around the Irish as a distinct migrant community that goes some way towards explaining why nationalist historiography has struggled to accommodate the role of Ireland in the Empire in general. Indeed, the persistence of the nation state as the traditional framework of historical analysis has meant that many histories of modern Ireland in fact belie the significance of

---

[7] A. Jackson, 'Ireland, the Union, and the Empire, 1800–1960', in K. Kenny (ed.), *Ireland and the British Empire: Oxford History of the British Empire Companion Series* (Oxford University Press, 2004), pp. 123–52.

[8] See, for example, T. M. Devine, *Scotland's Empire, 1600–1815* (London: Allen Lane, 2003) and M. McLaren, *British India and British Scotland, 1780–1830: Career Building, Empire Building and a Scottish School of Thought on Indian Governance* (University of Akron Press, 2001).

[9] See A. G. Hopkins, 'Back to the Future: From National History to Imperial History', *Past and Present*, 164 (1999), 198–243.

[10] Brady, *Interpreting Irish History*, p. 210.

Colony, nation and empire

Ireland's imperial past by producing narratives that have traced the historical course of the nation from the onset of colonialism through to independence, while virtually ignoring Ireland's substantial involvement in the Empire.

In recent years, an increasing number of scholars have begun to consider more fully the distinct experiences of separate Irish, English, Scottish and Welsh relationships with the British Empire.[11] For over two decades, proponents of the 'New British History' have attempted to view the domestic history of Britain and Ireland in the context of the experiences of the four primary ethnic groups that constituted these lands, namely, Irish, English, Scottish and Welsh.[12] Yet, the history of the British Empire (integral to the unfolding of the history in each of these locations) has until recently been treated separately. Traditional accounts of metropolitan-focused imperial history, for example, have tended to view the history of the British Empire almost exclusively from the perspective of England, or more specifically, from London. By focusing upon the binary interactions between 'metropole' and 'periphery', such accounts have helped consign the history of Irish, Scottish and Welsh involvement in the British Empire to the margins of imperial history, while simultaneously obscuring the crucial role of indigenous peoples and the colonies themselves in the imperial process.

A failure to pluralise the imperial experience at a domestic level implicitly recognises the centrality (and thus singular importance) of England as the centre of the Empire from where ideas, capital and power were all transmitted to the colonies in the periphery. It was precisely because Ireland, England, Scotland and Wales were never homogeneous economic, political or religious entities that the Empire was designed to act as a powerful solvent for the different ethnicities and identities of these regions, binding them together and finding a common purpose through a distinctly 'British' endeavour. However, recent research has demonstrated that far from dissolving regional particularisms and unifying the diverse peoples of the 'British Isles' under the imperial umbrella, the Empire actually worked in a manner whereby separate relationships between each were formed and national identities reinforced. Increasingly, historians are now moving away from a study of the simple bilateral relations involving 'metropole' and 'periphery' to the more complex multilateral relationships engendered

[11] See J. M. MacKenzie, 'Irish, Scottish, Welsh and English Worlds? A Four-Nation Approach to the History of the British Empire', *History Compass*, 6/5 (2008), 1244–63.

[12] H. Kearney, *The British Isles: A History of Four Nations* (Cambridge University Press, 1989).

6   Introduction

through separate Irish, English, Scottish and Welsh involvement with the Empire. Many studies typical of the 'new imperial history', for example, have demonstrated that Irish, English, Scottish and Welsh personnel in fact viewed the Empire in different ways and interacted with indigenous people and culture accordingly.[13] By charting a myriad of these responses, historians of the British Empire are now beginning to piece together a fuller explanation for the timing and development of overseas expansion as well as the complex factors leading towards decolonisation.

Certainly, histories of other former colonies of the British Empire have demonstrated similar preoccupations with the nation. The historiography of Australia, for example, has long abandoned an imperial framework with its emphasis on tracing constitutional, political and administrative progress from crown colony through to limited self-government, Federation and eventual full national autonomy. Australian history now views the process of 'white' settlement as a violent incursion upon a peaceful and rich indigenous culture and upon a fragile land unable to cope with the introduction of Western agricultural norms and practices. What was once a historiography that recognised the British Empire as a reciprocal movement of peoples and energies as part of a broader global phenomenon has now yielded to more pressing national concerns.[14] The same may also be said of South Asian historiography with its continued emphasis on nationalism, separatism, communal conflict and partition.[15] Even in India, where the 'Subaltern Studies' school has done much to advance our understanding of 'history from below', there remains a strong focus on the nation and elite constructions of nationalism.[16] Such a focus on the nation-state as a neatly bounded, excisable dimension fails to recognise the essentially

---

[13] See, for example, K. Jeffery (ed.), 'An Irish Empire'? Aspects of Ireland and the British Empire (Manchester University Press, 1996); J. M. MacKenzie and N. R. Dalziel (eds.), The Scots in South Africa: Ethnicity, Identity, Gender and Race, 1772–1914 (Manchester University Press, 2007); and A. Jones and B. Jones, 'The Welsh World and the British Empire, c. 1851–1939: An Exploration', Journal of Imperial and Commonwealth History, 31, 2 (May 2003), 57–81.

[14] See, for example, S. MacIntyre, 'Australia and the Empire', in R. W. Winks (ed.), The Oxford History of the British Empire: Vol. V, Historiography (Oxford University Press, 1999), pp. 163–81.

[15] See, for example, I. Talbot, 'Pakistan's Emergence', in Winks (ed.), The Oxford History of the British Empire, pp. 253–63.

[16] R. Guha, 'On Some Aspects of the Historiography of Colonial India', in R. Guha, Subaltern Studies I (Delhi: Oxford University Press, 1982), pp. 1–8; D. A. Washbrook, 'Orients and Occidents: Colonial Discourse Theory and the Historiography of the British Empire', in Winks (ed.), The Oxford History of the British Empire, pp. 596–611.

Colony, nation and empire

dispersive and permeable nature of all national boundaries.[17] As a consequence, studies that treat the nation as a discrete body of historical analysis do not sufficiently take into consideration the broader global currents fashioned through involvement in imperialism that have helped shape the course of national development and national identities.[18] This is not to say, of course, that one needs to dispense with the idea of the nation entirely. On the contrary, many important aspects of national histories remain integral to the process of tracing links and reciprocity between nineteenth-century Irish and Indian history. However, if such links are to be thoroughly examined in the future there is clearly a need to look beyond the limited framework of national histories and boundaries to the broader connections that tied Ireland and India together to a wider imperial system.

Indeed, in recent years the limited framework of national histories has come under increased scrutiny. Following the pioneering work of Nicholas Mansergh and the subsequent 'revisionist' debates that infused Irish scholarship in the 1970s and 1980s, historians working on placing British overseas expansion in the context of world history began pointing to the central role played by Ireland in facilitating British imperialism during the late eighteenth and nineteenth centuries.[19] In *Imperial Meridian*, C. A. Bayly, for example, observes how British imperial history had been continually 'straitjacketed by the "English" and "nationalist" views of Irish history'.[20] Teleological narratives, Bayly argues, failed to take into account 'the extent to which Ireland was the colonial society where the mechanics and ideology of imperial rule were first implemented'.[21] In their attempt to create a national history of Ireland, Irish historians continually 'downplayed their rôle in the military and political service of the British Empire' despite the fact that 'Irish patriots were desperate to reap the benefits of imperial expansion' and 'Irish soldiers and savants were in the front line of empire-

---

[17] A. Burton, 'Who Needs the Nation? Interrogating "British" History', *Journal of Historical Sociology*, 10, 3 (September 1997), 227–48 and 'When Was Britain? Nostalgia for the Nation at the End of the "American Century"', *The Journal of Modern History*, 75, 2 (June 2003), 359–74.

[18] F. Cooper, *Colonialism in Question: Theory, Knowledge, History* (Berkeley; London: University of California Press, 2005), p. 18.

[19] See N. Mansergh, *Commonwealth Perspectives* (London, 1958); N. Mansergh, *Survey of British Commonwealth Affairs: Problems of Wartime Co-operation and Post-war Change, 1939–1952* (Oxford University Press, 1958); N. Mansergh, *The Commonwealth Experience* (London, 1969); and N. Mansergh, *The Prelude to Partition: Concepts and Aims in Ireland and India* (Cambridge University Press, 1978).

[20] C. A. Bayly, *Imperial Meridian: The British Empire and the World, 1780–1830* (London: Longman, 1989), p. 12.

[21] Ibid.

8   Introduction

building'.[22] Notwithstanding a renewed interest by scholars in Ireland's interaction with the British Empire, however, surprisingly very little has been written exploring the various ways in which Ireland and Irish people impacted upon the Empire and vice versa.

Unlike historians of the nineteenth and twentieth centuries, scholars of early modern Ireland have long recognised the need to move beyond employing simple 'national' or 'coloniser–colonised' models in their analysis to more enabling cross-cultural or transnational approaches. The work of Steven G. Ellis on late-fifteenth- and sixteenth-century Tudor Ireland has stimulated an ongoing academic debate because of its positioning of Ireland as a focal point in the construction of contemporary Tudor politics and state-building. Far from a separate political or geographical entity, Ellis insisted that the history of Ireland at this time could only be properly understood in the context of a wider 'British Isles' framework.[23] Other historians of this period, most notably Nicholas Canny, have instead preferred to locate early modern Ireland within the broader global context of a 'British Atlantic world'. Building on the work of D. B. Quinn, Canny was among the first of his generation of scholars that sought to merge the histories of English (later British) settlement in Ireland with colonial expansion in North America.[24] For Canny, sixteenth- and seventeenth-century Ireland was central in the construction and maintenance of the 'first British empire'. As Britain's 'oldest colony', Ireland was an important site from where ideas, capital and personnel all moved with great fluidity westward to Britain's colonies in North America, the Caribbean and beyond.[25]

Although historians have called for similar research on Ireland's multifaceted imperial role for the modern period, contemporary debates surrounding the nature of Ireland's historical relationship with the Empire have remained largely centred on the character of its constitutional and political ties with Britain.[26] Moreover, such attempts have tended to focus almost exclusively on the colonies of 'white settlement' or in North America, overlooking Ireland's significant presence in Britain's Eastern Empire. Kevin Kenny's edited volume of essays on *Ireland and the British Empire*, for example, has sought 'to determine the

---

[22] Ibid., pp. 12–13.

[23] S. G. Ellis, *Ireland in the Age of the Tudors, 1447–1603: English Expansion and the End of Gaelic Rule* (London: Longman, 1998).

[24] For an example of Quinn's early work on this subject, see D. B. Quinn, *The Elizabethans and the Irish* (Ithaca, NY: Cornell University Press, 1966).

[25] N. Canny, *Kingdom and Colony: Ireland in the Atlantic World 1560–1800* (Baltimore: Johns Hopkins University Press, 1988).

[26] S. Howe, *Ireland and Empire: Colonial Legacies in Irish History and Culture* (Oxford University Press, 2000).

Colony, nation and empire 9

shifting meanings of empire, imperialism and colonialism in Irish history over time'.[27] Beginning with the Tudor conquests and colonisation of Ireland in the sixteenth and seventeenth centuries, Kenny's book attempts to demonstrate how 'modern Irish history was largely determined by the rise, expansion, and decline of the British empire' and equally how 'the course of British imperial history…was moulded in part by Irish experience'.[28] Although several authors in the volume venture to 'examine the participation of Irish people in the empire overseas', important questions regarding the identity of Irish imperial savants and settlers, their relationship with the colonial state, other 'colonisers' and 'colonised' peoples, as well as the exchange of ideas, practices, material objects and styles fashioned through these encounters, remain largely unanswered. Despite offering fascinating glimpses into these issues at times, the recurring theme that dominates the majority of essays in this volume concerns whether Ireland's historical relationship with England (later Britain) could be characterised as being specifically 'colonial' in nature, and at what point in that relationship was Ireland's colonial status established and who was responsible for it.[29]

While ongoing debates concerning the exact nature of Ireland's colonial status persist, its role as an important supplier of goods and commodities, personnel, ideas and finance for the British Empire is only beginning to be explored.[30] As the work of Clive Dewey, Howard Brasted and S. B. Cook has demonstrated, British legislation, systems of governance and methods of control were all frequently 'tried and tested' in Ireland before being 'exported' to other parts of the Eastern Empire.[31] At various points over the past thirty years, these scholars have demonstrated persuasively that owing to its close geographical proximity to Britain and given the central role that it commanded in domestic British politics, Ireland served as a 'laboratory' or testing-ground for numerous social, administrative and constitutional policies for imperial matters in the East.[32] Furthermore, taking into account the sheer volume of

---

[27] Kenny, *Ireland and the British Empire*, p. xix.   [28] Ibid.

[29] Ibid; see also T. McDonough (ed.), *Was Ireland a Colony? Economics, Politics and Culture in Nineteenth-Century Ireland* (Dublin: Irish Academic Press, 2005).

[30] See, for example, Howe, *Ireland and Empire*; Kenny, *Ireland and the British Empire*.

[31] See, for example, C. Dewey, 'Celtic Agrarian Legislation and the Celtic Revival: Historicist Implications of Gladstone's Irish and Scottish Land Acts, 1870–1886', *Past and Present*, 64 (1974), 30–70; H. V. Brasted, 'Indian Nationalist Development and the Influence of Irish Home Rule, 1870–1886', *Modern Asia Studies*, 12 (1980), 37–63; S. B. Cook, *Imperial Affinities: Nineteenth Century Analogies and Exchanges Between India and Ireland* (New Delhi: Oxford University Press, 1993); C. A. Bayly, 'Ireland, India and Empire: 1870–1914', *Transactions of the Royal Historical Society*, X (sixth series) (2000), 377–97.

[32] Cook, *Imperial Affinities*, pp. 29–30.

10   Introduction

Irish people involved in imperial service overseas, Ireland, like Scotland, played an integral role in the construction of a 'British' national identity. In recent times, Linda Colley, among others, has pointed to the need for a comprehensive study of the origins of 'Britishness' that takes into account the vast number of Catholic Irish soldiers who served in the British army both at home and abroad.[33] In equal ways, historians of Ireland have been at pains to demonstrate how the Empire played a crucial role in informing the varieties of Irishness that emerged under British rule. R. F. Foster, Gearóid Ó Tuathaigh and Peter Gray have all recently argued that Irish identity in the nineteenth century was not only constructed within the framework of the Act of Union, but also that British and Irish identity were closely connected with a favourable view of the Empire, as an arena within which the Irish could prosper.[34]

Although there are signs that historians are now beginning to give more serious attention to Ireland's historical relationship with the British Empire, Keith Jeffery has recently pointed out the need to move beyond simply recalling the achievements or deeds of those Irish who rose to prominence in the Empire, if we are to truly advance our understanding of this relationship.[35] Jeffery's call that scholars begin to consider more fully the implications of various Irish backgrounds, forms of education, religious, political or moral viewpoints on imperial affairs in different parts of the Empire assumes all the more relevance at a time when an increasing number of historians, postcolonial theorists and literary critics are beginning to frame their narratives in broader global and transnational contexts.[36] One very important development in this regard has been the rise to prominence in recent years of the 'new imperial history' that emerged in the wake of earlier debates involving the Subaltern Studies Collective and the Cambridge school of historians.[37] Proponents of the 'new imperial history' have attempted to shift the focus of colonial studies away from the metropolitan domain of

[33] See L. Colley, *Britons: Forging the Nation, 1707–1837* (New Haven, CT: Yale University Press, 1992).
[34] R. F. Foster, *Paddy and Mr Punch: Connections in Irish and English History* (London: Allen Lane, 1993); G. Ó Tuathaigh, 'Religion, Identity, State and Society', in J. Cleary (ed.), *The Cambridge Companion to Modern Irish Culture* (Cambridge University Press, 2004); and P. Gray (ed.), *Victoria's Ireland? Irishness and Britishness, 1837–1901* (Dublin: Four Courts Press, 2004).
[35] Jeffery, *'An Irish Empire'?*, Introduction.
[36] J. Cleary, 'Amongst Empires: A Short History of Ireland and Empire Studies in International Context', *Éire-Ireland*, 42, 1–2 (2007), 11–57.
[37] See R. Guha and G. Chakravorty Spivak (eds.), *Selected Subaltern Studies* (New York: Oxford University Press, 1988). For an overview of some of the debates involving Subaltern Studies, see V. Lal, 'Subaltern Studies and Its Critics: Debates over Indian History', *History and Theory*, 40, 1 (February 2001), 135–48.

Transnational histories of empire

elites and high politics to the reciprocal encounters between empire and culture. Foremost among these encounters is the movement of various different peoples (particularly the subaltern, non-Western and non-elite people), practices and ideas affected by mass migration, slavery and other direct consequences of British imperial hegemony.[38] Moreover, within the past ten years these types of studies have been encouraged by a growing desire among imperial historians to understand how the British first appropriated and interpreted aspects of indigenous culture and society before modifying them and eventually transmitting them throughout the globe.[39] Following Frederick Cooper and Ann Laura Stoker's call for 'metropole' and 'periphery' to be placed in the same analytical framework in the late 1990s, a greater number of colonial and imperial historians began producing studies of a comparative nature that focused not only upon the interaction between the 'metropole' and the 'periphery', but also on the critical series of connections that bound overseas colonies and dependencies to one another.[40] This developing interest in examining how the colonies shaped the experience of the Empire is attributable to a more general revival of imperial history and empire studies over the past two decades, brought about in part by the growing influence of postcolonial studies as well as the publication of the voluminous *Oxford History of the British Empire* and by the work of the 'British World' historians.[41]

Transnational histories of empire

More recently still, scholars such as A. G. Hopkins and Bayly have taken this approach a step further to highlight both the complexity of the Empire as a transnational phenomenon and the history of globalised

---

[38] See K. Whelan (ed.), *A New Imperial History: Culture, Identity and Modernity in Britain and the Empire, 1660–1840* (Cambridge University Press, 2004). This body of work is perhaps best reflected in J. M. Mackenzie's ongoing 'Studies in Imperialism' series published by Manchester University Press.

[39] See C. A. Bayly, *Empire and Information: Intelligence Gathering and Social Communication in India, 1780–1870* (Cambridge University Press, 1996); R. Drayton, *Nature's Government: Science, Imperial Britain and the 'Improvement' of the World* (New Haven, CT; London: Yale University Press, 2000); C. Hall, *Civilising Subjects: Metropole and Colony in the English Imagination 1830–1867* (Cambridge University Press, 2002).

[40] F. Cooper and A. L. Stoler (eds.), *Tensions of Empire: Colonial Cultures in a Bourgeois World* (Berkeley: University of California Press, 1997), p. 15.

[41] For example, see N. Lazarus (ed.), *The Cambridge Companion to Postcolonial Literary Studies* (Cambridge University Press, 2004); A. Porter (ed.), *The Oxford History of the British Empire: Vol. III, The Nineteenth Century* (Oxford University Press, 1999); C. Bridge and K. Fedorowich (eds.), *The British World: Diaspora, Culture and Identity* (London; Portland, OR: F. Cass, 2003).

12   Introduction

relations as something whose roots can be traced much further back in time. In recent years their work has contributed enormously to the rise of an influential scholarly discourse that has stressed the importance of sketching 'connective' and 'comparative' histories as a means of demonstrating the truly global nature of the modern world. Although historians have for a long time recognised how the experience of empire was central to the creation and form of nation states, it is only latterly that scholars have attempted to use globalisation as a theme of serious historical analysis.[42] By transcending national boundaries and examining the multifarious interdependencies and interconnections that linked political and social movements across the globe, we can learn more about the complex and shifting nature of imperial relations as they evolved over centuries, traversed many lands and cultures and encompassed enormous degrees of economic, religious and social change.[43] What were once thought of as separate and discrete national histories are now being brought together, woven into a broader narrative of 'interconnectedness' and 'interdependence' and are read as global history.[44]

Bayly, for example, has recently traced the rise of global uniformities in the ways in which states, religions, political ideologies and economic activity developed during the 'long' nineteenth century. For Bayly, the ruptures to the world order caused by increased conflict between the rivalling imperial states of Europe after 1780 contributed in no small measure to this rapid period of growth in global uniformity. As increased levels of overseas expansion, warfare and migration tied world events together, so too did the ways in which people began to see one another and how they began to define themselves. According to Bayly, this became evident not only in the way powerful institutions such as churches and systems of education and justice were organised and run, but also in the manner in which different peoples began to relate to one another, how they dressed, what they ate, for instance, as well as how they communicated.[45] Nor was this simply a story of the 'rise of the West and the fall of the rest'. Hans van de Ven and Amira K. Bennison have recently highlighted the non-Western dimensions of globalisation by exploring its origins, historical forms and sequences in the context of both Chinese and Islamic history.[46] Their work points to

[42] A. G. Hopkins (ed.), *Globalization in World History* (London: Pimlico, 2002).
[43] See, for example, ibid. and C. A. Bayly, *The Birth of the Modern World, 1780–1914: Global Connections and Comparisons* (Oxford University Press, 2004).
[44] Bayly, *Birth of the Modern World*.
[45] Ibid., pp. 1–21.
[46] H. van de Ven, 'The Onrush of Modern Globalization in China' and A. K. Bennison, 'Muslim Universalism and Western Globalization', in Hopkins (ed.), *Globalization*, pp. 167–94, 74–98.

Transnational histories of empire

certain degrees of convergence and interaction between the economic and political spheres of Europe, Asia and Africa from as early as the seventeenth century, and demonstrates how state systems, early financial institutions and forms of pre-industrial manufacturing in each were linked.

Other scholars, such as Tony Ballantyne and Richard Drayton, have emphasised in equal measure the importance of the historical, cultural and intellectual dimensions of globalisation.[47] Ballantyne has argued that the 1760s, in particular, represented a form of 'globalising decade' when a whole host of new imperial states, fronted by Britain, embarked upon voyages of exploration, commercial development and territorial expansion. As imperial powers consolidated their newfound colonial possessions and negotiated a whole series of informal economic arrangements and relationships with non-colonised lands, resultant warfare, scientific activity and commerce fashioned the emergence of new bodies of knowledge and cultural networks.[48] Within these networks, the encounters between imperial agents and indigenous peoples generated an entirely new system of global information gathering and exchange that eventually underpinned alternate conceptions of race, language and religion.[49] Of course information, ideas and knowledge were not all that flowed through these increasingly globalised networks. Drayton, for example, has demonstrated how improved efficiency in the transactions sector led to a wider circulation of goods and commodities between almost every continent between 1500 and 1900. Increased circulation of bullion, sugar, tobacco, cotton, opium and labour brought about by multiple cycles of colonial expansion and European settlement created complex webs of trading mechanisms and encouraged greater uniformity throughout the world in terms of driving consumer taste and demand.[50]

Rising levels of global 'interconnectedness' generated by the growth and expansion of European imperial states after the 1760s had several profound implications. Foremost among these was the notion that areas of the world previously unconnected were now brought into regular contact with one another through what Ballantyne has described as

---

[47] See T. Ballantyne, *Orientalism and Race: Aryanism in the British Empire* (Basingstoke: Palgrave, 2002); T. Ballantyne and A. Burton (eds.), *Bodies in Contact: Rethinking Colonial Encounters in World History* (Durham, NC: Duke University Press, 2005); Drayton, *Nature's Government*.

[48] T. Ballantyne, 'Empire, Knowledge and Culture: From Proto-Globalization to Modern Globalization', in Hopkins (ed.), *Globalization*, pp. 115–40.

[49] Ballantyne, *Orientalism and Race*, p. 4.

[50] R. Drayton, 'The Collaboration of Labour: Slaves, Empires and Globalizations in the Atlantic World, *c*.1600–1850', in Hopkins (ed.) *Globalization*, pp. 98–115.

14   Introduction

'systems of mobility and exchange'.[51] These encounters, although highly uneven given the unequal nature of the power relations of colonialism, in turn played an important part in changing the way people both in the imperial sphere and in the colonies began to view themselves and their roles in the wider world around them. One of the most successful and illuminating means of tracing narratives of linkage and reciprocity in imperial/global history in recent years has been the employment of 'networks', 'webs' and 'systems' as methodological tools of analysis. For more than a decade, a range of scholars across the humanities and social sciences have been drawing on the study of social network analysis in order to understand more clearly how sets of individuals or organisations were historically interdependent, often tied together by a set of common values, ideas, friendship, conflict, financial exchange or trade. Resulting social networks borne out of these ties operated on many different levels – ranging from families up to the level of nations – and played critical roles in determining the way problems were solved, organisations were run and the degree to which individuals succeeded in achieving their goals.[52]

Networks and empire

An increasing number of imperial historians have now begun to draw on the study of networks in an attempt to examine more fully the critical connections and structures that bound the nineteenth-century British Empire together. Alan Lester, for example, has demonstrated how imperial networks in the Cape Colony in southern Africa played fundamental roles in shaping thinking about race, Britishness and identity within Britain and across the Empire during the nineteenth century.[53] His work is further developed by that of Ballantyne, who has stressed the importance of conceiving of the British Empire as a 'series of historically contingent networks' that connected disparate regions together 'through dynamic systems of mobility and exchange' as part of a wider process of 'imperial globalization'.[54] Similar to Lester, Ballantyne's work is distinguished by its emphasis on connections between more than two

---

[51] Ballantyne, *Orientalism and Race*, p. 3.
[52] See, for example, S. Wasserman, *Social Network Analysis: Methods and Applications* (Cambridge University Press, 1997); L. J. Griffin, *New Methods for Social History* (Cambridge University Press, 1999); and J. Scott, *Social Network Analysis: A Handbook* (London: SAGE, 2000).
[53] A. Lester, *Imperial Networks: Creating Identities in Nineteenth-Century South Africa and Britain* (London: Routledge, 2001).
[54] Ballantyne, *Orientalism and Race*, pp. 3–5.

Networks and empire

sites of British imperialism in the nineteenth century, establishing links of intellectual exchange between regions as disparate as New Zealand, India and Ireland. In a recent study examining the connections that linked Celticism and Orientalism as discourses of governance and cultural analysis in Ireland and India, and the role of Irish antiquarians, folklorists and linguists in the British imperial system, Ballantyne explores some of the more subtle, nuanced issues surrounding Ireland's interaction with the Empire.[55] For example, by placing the ethnology of the Celticist Charles Vallency in a wider imperial context, Ballantyne explores the interrelatedness between two supposedly discrete bodies of knowledge (Celticism and Orientalism) and how they were used as discourses of governance 'grounded in the desire to understand a (subject) people who were...under British authority'.[56]

Zoe Laidlaw's work on colonial connections investigates the sinews of imperial power in Britain, the Cape Colony and New South Wales in the first half of the nineteenth century. Through its focus on elaborate 'networks' and 'webs' that linked these metropolitan and colonial spheres, Laidlaw investigates the nature of imperial authority, seeking to find out where such power lay and how it was exercised, influenced and perceived, while at the same time suggesting that the 'study of networks of personal communication' adds new depth 'to the question of colonial governance'. Significantly, Laidlaw's study makes clear the existence of further networks in operation in the Empire based on ethnic affiliation. On more than one occasion she points to the importance of Irish and Scottish networks on professionals and their associations, on missionary societies and within the colonial administrative framework itself.[57]

More recently still, a study by Gary B. Magee and Andrew S. Thompson of the types of networks and movement of people, goods and capital that helped tie the wider British world together during the nineteenth century has emphasised how such networks were in fact both transnational and national in nature. Through increased migration these networks at once bridged British communities throughout the Empire while simultaneously constituting a nationality-based web of patronage and support for migrant groups overseas.[58] According to Magee and

---

[55] T. Ballantyne, 'The Sinews of Empire: Ireland, India and the Construction of British Colonial Knowledge', in McDonough (ed.), *Was Ireland a Colony?*, pp. 145–65.

[56] Ibid., p. 151.

[57] Z. Laidlaw, *Colonial Connections 1815–1845: Patronage, the Information Revolution and Colonial Government* (Manchester University Press, 2005).

[58] G. B. Magee and A. S. Thompson, *Empire and Globalisation: Networks of People, Goods and Capital in the British World, 1850–1914* (Cambridge University Press, 2010), pp. 13–20.

16   Introduction

Thompson, the supra-national migrant networks – 'built upon kinship structures, religious institutions, ethnic societies and fraternal organizations' – that connected private, official and provincial interests in Britain to its colonial outposts at this time functioned as a kind of 'software of empire'. This software enabled the operation of a vast system through which ideas and information, trust and contracts, commodities and people ricocheted from one point of contact to another, producing 'complex circuits of exchange' in a thoroughly 'interconnected zone'.[59] To a significant degree then, the types of traffic that navigated imperial networks was thus defined by location, and in this sense it is important to recognise the central role of Britain and London in the creation and sustenance of many of these networks and how they functioned as crucial nodes through which much imperial traffic flowed. However, as Magee and Thompson note, and as this book demonstrates, 'it would be wrong to think of the British world simply in terms of the spokes of a bicycle wheel; connections were not simply radial, connecting different parts of the so-called "periphery" with the "core"'.[60] Throughout the 'long' nineteenth century, a multitude of connections and linkages were established between the colonies themselves, at times by-passing the metropolitan core entirely, establishing their own complex circuits of exchange in the process. At the same time, though, and as Magee and Thompson recognise, we must be careful not to 'sanitise' imperial networks, which were, after all, undergirded by superior British military, legal and political structures of authority and that effectively privileged British networks over non-British counterparts.[61]

Certainly, there are some problems with employing a thoroughly networked conception of the British Empire during this period, and this study recognises that 'networks' do have their limitations. Foremost among these limitations is a recognition that not all imperial connections operated in a loosely defined manner, and that certain impulses transmitted along networks between the metropole and the colony tended to be stronger in the main than those travelling directly between the colonies themselves. Moreover, certain areas of the Empire tended to be more developed and sophisticated in terms of communications technology and infrastructure and therefore enjoyed stronger imperial connections (with the metropole and other colonies) than did others in the nineteenth century.[62] Despite their shortcomings, networks

---

[59] Ibid., p. 16.   [60] Ibid., p. 18.
[61] Ibid., p. 20.
[62] S. Potter, 'Networks, Webs and Systems: Globalization and the Mass Media in the Nineteenth- and Twentieth-Century British Empire', *Journal of British Studies*, 46 (July 2007), 621–46.

Irish imperial networks 17

nevertheless offer the historian a useful tool to think more thoroughly about the range and scope of connections that once bound the constituent parts of the British Empire together. In the case of Ireland this is important as it helps the historian evade the narrowly national focus of earlier (and very limited) accounts of Ireland's imperial role.

Irish imperial networks

Although the chronology of this book extends from the early 1700s through to the early 1900s, it concentrates principally on the nineteenth century – a time when imperial linkages and connections between Ireland and India appeared to be operating most noticeably and effectively. This study follows Lester, Ballantyne, Laidlaw and Magee and Thompson in the use of 'imperial networks' and supports the work of historians such as Bayly and Hopkins who recognise the multiplicity of connections that existed between the various sites of British imperialism and their importance in terms of our understanding of global history. By offering a contextualised account of the role of Ireland and Irish people in India during the 'long' nineteenth century, this book focuses particularly on Ireland's role as a crucial sub-imperial centre that supplied the Empire with a vital repository of manpower, knowledge and skill that fuelled Britain's drive into South Asia from the 1750s onward. The first such book written, it is based on a thorough examination of contemporaneous published works and private papers of Irish migrants and settlers, India office manuscript archives and the wider social, political and intellectual worlds they inhabited, and is aimed at audiences in British and Irish history, imperial and colonial history, the history of science, as well as diaspora and migration studies.

By tracing the relationships between the various types of networks engendered through Irish involvement in the colonial project in India during the nineteenth century, it arrives at a radically revised understanding of their significance and importance in terms of how historians view the British Empire and its history. It demonstrates how Irish military, commercial, missionary, civil, scientific and political networks in India functioned in ways which recognised the crucial role of Ireland in imperial affairs. Far from a straightforward, homogeneous group of people who worked to conspire against the 'evils' of the Empire (as is so often depicted in national or nationalist-focused histories, or indeed not at all as in the case of more traditional accounts of metropolitan-focused imperial history), the Irish were distinguished by their complexity and heterogeneity, and were very much rooted in – and respondent to – he political and economic conditions of nineteenth-century Ireland, drawing heavily on their experiences and education, and were loyal

18   Introduction

and committed servants of an 'improving' Empire. As the book will demonstrate, it is impossible to make sense of the Irish without first understanding their background, education and politics. Indeed, past attempts to isolate their contributions in narrow terms, reducing their significance to so many formulas (some very negative), have ended up missing the very things – some intellectual, some not – that make them one of the most interesting groups during this period. By focusing upon a cross-section of nineteenth-century Irish society in India (Irish elites and the less well-connected alike), *Irish Imperial Networks* uncovers Ireland's multidirectional involvement in the British Empire.

In tracing the origins and impact of Irish imperial networks in nineteenth-century India, the book pays equal attention to the early experiences and education of Irish colonial servants in Ireland, their intellectual influences, their political endeavour, and their engagement with contemporary work on economic, political and social questions in India. In doing so it examines the context for Irish Empire-building and how this process adapted and changed within the shifting political circumstances of the 'long' nineteenth century. The book pays close attention to the emergence of variegated Irish imperial networks at different points in time during the colonial period in India and demonstrates how they circulated their ideas, practices and material goods through carefully cultivated networks of friends, contacts and patrons in the British, Irish and imperial administrations. The work of individuals – each responsible for forging their own personal networks through the manipulation of social, familial, education and other connections in India – demonstrates the manner in which the Empire was central to the promotion of their concerns and how at times it worked to energise and provide impetus to their interests.

Central to the book – as it was to their own lives and careers in India – is the notion that Irish people operated within carefully constructed imperial personnel networks, in some cases based explicitly along ethnic lines. This is usually taken to mean that sets of individuals or organisations within the Empire were historically interdependent, often tied together through kinship or a set of common values, ideas, friendships, conflicts, financial exchange or trading mechanisms which were all central in the construction of the modern British imperial state, and more fundamentally still, continue to underpin our understanding of modern government, science, and social and political debate. Imperial networks, as a new way of thinking about groups of individuals who shared similar ideas and outlooks and influenced policy, played pivotal roles in the transition from an early modern to a modern world order. Yet what has never really been appreciated, and what the sources make especially clear, is that Ireland and the Irish were deeply implicated in this process. At once metropolitan and colonial, they were, in fact, an extremely important group (both numerically and influentially) that drew on their own religious, medical, politico-economic, philosophical training and interests – which were in part informed by the experience of English colonisation in Ireland – and played vital roles in the various intellectual networks and values that tied the Empire together. Understanding them and their concerns, in other words, means understanding the nineteenth-century Empire in its proper 'four nations' context – a time when the peoples of Ireland, Scotland, England and Wales were united as a supposedly unified 'British' people. More fundamentally still, the book attempts to change the way we see the history of the British Empire during this period, by challenging the privileged place of England, or more specifically London, as the nexus of empire – a way of seeing things familiar to postcolonial scholars and the 'new imperial historians', but so far little practised in mainstream British or Irish historiography.

The book offers not only an original contextualised account of the role of Ireland and the Irish in the Empire, but also new biographical accounts of less well-known Irish figures involved in India. In tracing the origins and impact of Irish imperial networks in nineteenth-century India, this book takes us through a fascinating series of interconnected worlds: the small towns and villages of Cork and Limerick where Irish soldiers were recruited by East India Company crimps; the Court of Proprietors and Directors in London where Laurence Sulivan wielded his extensive civil and commercial lines of patronage; the intellectual ferment of Protestant universities in Dublin, Belfast and Edinburgh during the Irish and Scottish enlightenments; the world of Catholic learning in the seminaries of Maynooth and Carlow; the mysterious realm of quacks, faith-healers, homeopathic medicine, herbal remedies, folklore and myth of the west of Ireland; not to mention the revolutionary social and nationalist ideas of Irish and Indian radicals in Calcutta, Delhi, London and Dublin. Some of these figures that climbed socially from modest backgrounds to knighthoods or to the status of imperial virtuosi were matched by an ever-expanding social network, and among their friends included some of the most prominent figures of the period in British and Irish history. Their interests often reflected those of their patrons, sponsors and peers. Yet they were by no means a homogeneous group that advocated one particular political or cultural agenda. Divergent responses to British hegemony were as much present within specific Irish networks in India as of course they were in particular individual responses.

20   Introduction

This book will thoroughly revise our understanding of the crucial role of Ireland and the Irish in imperial affairs in the nineteenth century, and therefore increase the significance of the relationship between Ireland and empire for several different audiences. From the perspective of Irish history, it will present an alternative approach to understanding Ireland's past by situating Ireland in its wider imperial and global context. By moving outside the nation-state framework, it demonstrates the distinctive and unique contribution of the Irish in constructing and sustaining British colonial rule in India, while at the same time stressing how Ireland's Indian experience shaped domestic institutions and Irish identities in equally significant ways. From the perspective of the history of ideas, this book will emphasise the central role of the so-called 'peripheries' in negotiating and shaping the development of 'colonial knowledge' within the nineteenth-century Empire. In this regard, it considers Ireland as an important site where new ideas, technologies, methods of scientific practice and organisation – largely distinct from metropolitan trends – were developed and then 'exported' to India. For historians of modern Britain, it will turn the Irish from an occasional source of interest into a coherent intellectual body and political grouping, whose complicated lives and work within the Empire illuminate the politics and possibilities of this era in unsuspected ways. For historians of South Asia, it will offer a thorough examination of Ireland's (as distinct from England's, Scotland's or Wales') complicated and sometimes controversial role in India, while contributing to a debate on the use of recent concepts in the study of imperial history, such as 'networking' and the role of 'knowledge communities' on the sources and influence of colonial knowledge. For a wider audience, this book provides a fascinating account of groups whose social networks included many of the greatest names of the nineteenth century, whose interests covered the spectrum of religion, science, politics and economics, and whose engagement with the nineteenth-century world has shaped the way we see our own.

Chapter 2 begins by examining the early encounters and experiences of Irish merchants and entrepreneurs involved in colonial trade in the East in the eighteenth century. It explores how Irish people, from a variety of social, religious and economic backgrounds, came to wield great commercial and political influence within the Empire, establishing important lines of trade and finance between late-eighteenth-century Ireland, England and India, owing in part to the considerable degree of influence that was exercised by the dominant Irish Sulivan connection in the Court of Directors and of the growing importance of Ireland to the East India Company at this time. Chapter 3 develops

Irish imperial networks 21

the theme of the increasing penetration of the East India Company into Irish society during the second half of the eighteenth century by exploring how Ireland became an important recruiting ground for the Company's armed forces in India during the Seven Years War. While Irish soldiers provided a crucial surplus of manpower that effectively facilitated the Company's expanding territorial ambitions on the sub-continent in the second half of the eighteenth century, the presence of a large body of Roman Catholics had important implications for the ways in which the Company exercised imperial authority and control in India. It argues that the specific Gaelic-Irish culture introduced by Irish-speaking Roman Catholic soldiers in India played key roles in debates over the exercise of imperial authority and provided an important reference point for the East India Company in its attempts to understand and make sense of the indigenous cultures of South Asia. Irish soldiering networks acted as important conduits of cultural, financial and political interchange between Irish, Indian and Eurasian communities. In addition to its role as recruiting ground for South Asian military service and provider of religious personnel, Ireland also supplied a certain amount of intellectual capital around which British rule in India was constructed. Chapter 4 examines how from 1801 Ireland served as an important testing ground or 'laboratory' for colonial science to be adopted and utilised, albeit in modified forms in India. Irish people, both Catholic and Protestant, from the north and south, who had participated in these colonial initiatives at home, were at the forefront of transferring these systems of scientific knowledge and practice to India. During the 1850s scientific networks were formed, sometimes based along ethnic affiliation. Within certain Irish scientific networks, specimens, samples, theories, ideas and agendas (scientific and political) were transmitted across the Empire, from Calcutta to London mainly, but also between the colonies themselves (Calcutta–Dublin/Dublin–Calcutta). Devoid of any cultural dependence upon the metropole, Irish scientific networks promoted the education of Indians and were prominent in forging alliances with other scientific networks eager to promote the autonomy of science in the colonies. Chapter 5 examines how Irish religious networks came to dominate various Indian Catholic communities and sometimes presented serious challenges to Company authority in the first half of the nineteenth century. From the 1830s onward, Irish chaplains and bishops travelled to India where they formed close alliances with Catholic soldiers and their families within the various British military cantonments and accumulated substantial bases of revenue from soldiers' wills, donations and monetary contributions. In turn, remittances conveyed through these religious networks

22   Introduction

played important roles in establishing reconstructed parochial systems across the Empire – building churches, schools, hospitals and other ecclesiastical structures in both Ireland and India.

Chapters 6 and 7 examine how, alongside the Scottish and English schools, Irish universities, learned societies and institutions served as the great imperial powerhouses of the mid nineteenth century in terms of supplying the civil and medical colonial services with a critical base of personnel, expertise and knowledge around which later colonial rule in India was based. A growing desire among the rising Irish middle classes (Catholics and Protestants, north and south) to obtain careers in the Empire gradually gave rise to more sophisticated networks of intellectual exchange – including anthropological, ethnographical and medical – between various 'Irish knowledge communities' constructed within the parameters of the colonial civil and medical services in South Asia. Their collective writings demonstrated a common anthropological mission that set about preserving the culture of rural Indian life before it disappeared through increased contact and exposure to Western scientific thought and appliances of civilisation. Significantly, this concern with celebrating and preserving rural and folk traditions in India reflected the prominence of Irish antiquarian debates in their education and the influence of the Great Famine in informing modern medical and therapeutic practice in Irish universities and medical schools after the 1850s. These amateur anthropologists and ethnographers and medical doctors' collective intellectual pursuits were largely consistent with the legislative and politico-economic concerns of their fellow Irish civil servants in India during the same period. They recorded and circulated revealing views on religious antagonisms, economic and agrarian malformations and were particularly forceful in their demands for tenancy legislation.

Other Irish imperial networks worked to further more radical political agendas and ideologies and were motivated by a desire to bring about reform and change within the Empire. In the late nineteenth century, an elaborate web of contact, dialogue and exchange was fashioned between the nationalist spokesmen of Ireland and India who gradually became aware of each other's calls for economic reform and national self-determination. This interaction drew considerable publicity and attention to the perceived failings of the British imperial administration and stimulated further nationalist criticism throughout the Empire. Approaches to the study of Ireland's imperial past that facilitate such connections allow us to move beyond the old 'coloniser–colonised' debate (a persistent feature of many previous works on 'Ireland and the Empire') to address the key issue of whether Ireland or the varieties of

Irishness of its imperial servants and settlers made a specific difference to the experience of the Empire.

In describing the multiplicity of Irish connections within the context of the nineteenth-century British Empire in India, the networks discussed in this book are intrinsically interesting. Because such networks (and the relationships they generated) were always subject to constant change and flux – thus rendering any definitive judgements on their structure or configuration at any one point in time problematic – their most significant historical relevance is the way in which they were used by their contemporaries (settlers, migrants and indigenous agents) as mechanisms for the exchange of a whole set of ideas, practices and goods during the colonial era. Irish imperial networks in nineteenth-century India were dynamic and constantly shifting vectors of cultural interaction, rather than frozen channels of an imperial 'centre'. An examination of the colonial connections that bound nineteenth-century Ireland and India together in a shared analytical space can help highlight the central role played by Ireland and Irish people in the wider British imperial system. As an alternative to the existing historiography on the Irish diaspora that focuses almost exclusively on Irish settlement and migration to North America and Australasia, a study of these networks stresses the ubiquitous influence and distinctiveness of Irish presence in constructing and maintaining almost two centuries of British colonial rule in South Asia. Moreover, the persistence of Irish networks in India throughout this period demonstrates just how important both Ireland and India were in the discourses and practice of modern British empire-building and 'imperial globalisation'. By positioning Irish history within the complex global currents fashioned through Ireland's involvement in British imperialism, we can understand more fully how Irish national development was shaped during this period, while simultaneously situating the history of the nineteenth-century British Empire in a broader, more dynamic 'four nations' context.

2 The business of empire

Introduction

By the early eighteenth century the British Empire was already proving to be a great resource for Irish commerce and military entrepreneurs in the Atlantic world – an important economic platform that was used to foster and expand Irish mercantile activity in the burgeoning East Indian trade later in the century. This chapter examines a series of business connections and commercial exchanges between Ireland and India that have so far been elided by historians of empire as well as being neglected within the broader historiography of Ireland. The chapter begins by examining Irish involvement in colonial trade in the British Atlantic world in the eighteenth century before demonstrating how such links expanded eastward in tandem with a rapidly growing Empire. Irish involvement in colonial trade and commerce in the East was ultimately bound up in the evolving structure and shifting responsibilities of the East India Company over the eighteenth century, a critical period which witnessed a fundamental transition in the Company's organisational structure from trading power to imperial authority on the subcontinent. The gradual transformation of the Company's administrative role and function in India was in part reflected in the nature of much Irish participation at a commercial and business level.

Initially, Irish merchants – much like their English, Scottish and Welsh counterparts – were subject to the same restrictions imposed upon private trade by the laws protecting the Company's monopoly and exclusive right to trade in the East. This was mirrored in the relative number of private traders and free merchants from Ireland who attempted to establish legitimate business interests in the Indian Ocean region in defiance of the Company. However, as an increasingly militarised East India Company began extending the boundaries of its political sovereignty in the second half of the eighteenth century, acquiring more Indian territory and in doing so developing more sophisticated commercial links both inland and throughout the Indian Ocean region,

Introduction 25

it began drawing on Irish resources, personnel and experience as an important means of facilitating its new administrative and commercial responsibilities. As the Company evolved into a more complex organisation during this period, it was brought into increased contact with a whole host of communities outside of metropolitan London and centres of trade on the Indian subcontinent, particularly in Ireland where it became reliant upon a series of representative agents or business houses in Cork and Limerick to act on its behalf and to secure its particular commercial interests in a region. These agencies were established primarily because of the strategic and commercial significance of Ireland in facilitating long-distance trade, but also because of the need to protect the Company's interests during a period of almost constant international conflict.

The chapter then turns to an examination of the powerful Irish Sulivan network that originated in early eighteenth-century Cork, where initial maritime and naval links with the East India Company gradually gave rise to important Irish merchant and family business connections in Bombay and Calcutta. From the mid eighteenth century, members of the Irish Protestant Ascendancy and landed gentry families, including a few associates of the Catholic gentry, followed their fathers into the Company's service where they perpetuated a variety of Irish military and business dynasties in India. These men closely resembled the political elite at home and formed close alliances between land, overseas trade and finance. Irish presence among the 'official caste' – the military and civil officials – of Anglo-Indian society during the second half of the eighteenth century was, for the most part, controlled by influential Irish patrons, such as the Irish Sulivan connection in the Court of Directors, and its extensive patronage networks in India. The career of Laurence Sulivan in India was typical of many successful eighteenth-century Company servants and indicative of patterns of upward social mobility, as he rose from factory writer and small merchant to wealthy entrepreneur. Sulivan was further distinguished by his ability to cultivate several successful business interests in insurance, banking, speculation and money-lending in Bombay in the 1740s and 1750s that saw him rise to Company Director in London later in the century. At this time he was particularly visible among the powerful shipping circles where his involvement in freighting activities harnessed numerous contacts in the Company's marine service. During his time in India, Sulivan forged important shipping alliances and was one of a number of key members of dominant Charter parties who controlled the terms and conditions of ships being hired for Company service. Together with the 'Bombay Faction', the Irish Sulivan network dominated the various shipping

26   The business of empire

Committees of the East India Company and commanded a large voting strength in the Court of Proprietors and Directors in London for over thirty years, a position that facilitated much Irish movement and opportunity within Britain's Eastern Empire.

By the time these links began to wane somewhat in the 1780s, Protestant radicals in Ireland were already demanding greater Irish integration within the wider British world. The political motivation behind the Irish patriot movement of the late eighteenth century was directly related to developments happening within the wider imperial system and was based on a growing resentment of the restrictions imposed by Britain on Irish trade and the perceived dearth of opportunities that existed for Irish Protestants in British and imperial service at the time. Irish patriots, inspired by recent developments in North America and France, wanted better constitutional rights for Irish Protestants and greater cultural respect from Britain, but also a greater share in the riches of empire for Ireland. Irish Protestants looked to the new opportunities in the East as a means of securing better access to colonial trade and mounted a challenge to the Company's monopoly during the 1790s. Irish involvement in the Company's commercial expansion on the subcontinent – in terms of patronage, shipping and supplying personnel, maritime expertise and knowledge, commodities as well as access to Irish ports – highlights the extent to which Ireland functioned as an important sub-imperial centre at this juncture.

Colonial trade and Ireland in the eighteenth century

Thomas Bartlett's claims that Ireland's poor economic performance in the nineteenth century may more 'legitimately be attributed to those insidious colonial legacies of cultural conflict, religious disharmony, and political division, than to the effects of the Laws of Trade and Navigation' raise several important questions relating to Ireland's broader economic role in the British Empire. To what extent, for example, did the responses created by the onset of colonialism in Ireland under the Act of Union – a term that Andrew Porter has described as 'empires in the mind'[1] – obfuscate the reality of the growing number of economic opportunities at hand for many Irish people in Britain's overseas colonies? How far did the restrictions imposed upon Irish colonial trade contribute to the pauperisation of a large majority of the Irish population by the 1840s? The evidence thus far is unclear. During the

---

[1] A. Porter, 'Empires in the Mind', in P. J. Marshall (ed.), *The Cambridge Illustrated History of the British Empire* (Cambridge University Press, 1996), pp. 185–224.

Colonial trade and Ireland in the eighteenth century 27

late eighteenth and early nineteenth centuries, many contemporary commentators cited the restrictions imposed upon Irish colonial trade as evidence of Britain's determination to keep a potential economic rival in check and to maintain its dominance over 'poor' Ireland at all cost. For example, Thomas Newenham, an MP from Clonmel, Co. Tipperary, and leading authority on the Irish economy, endorsed the idea that British economic policy in Ireland in the late eighteenth and early nineteenth centuries was destructive. From Newenham's point of view, the explicit objective of imposing stringent imperial trade regulations was 'to cramp, obstruct and render abortive the industry of the Irish...to gratify commercial avarice, to secure Britain at the expense of Ireland...and to facilitate the government of the latter'.[2] A vociferous opponent of the Act of Union, Newenham believed that English ignorance of Ireland would lead to injustice under the Union and would continue to undermine Ireland's attempts to carry out profitable foreign and colonial trade.

Although Newenham's observations broadly reveal the level of frustration felt by sections of the Irish Protestant community with the British administration at this time, his views are interesting in that they reflect a popular contemporary belief that English self-interest was at the heart of much of Ireland's economic problems. Anti-Union sentiment as espoused by people such as Newenham was taken up in later years by nationalist-focused historians who cited such evidence as irrevocable proof that the imperial trade regulations imposed by Britain on Ireland had effectively brought about the ruin of a potentially dynamic Irish plantation trade. Yet recent research has made clear that the forces of British mercantilism in operation in Ireland in the eighteenth century were actually mitigated much in the same way as they were in Britain's other colonies in North America and the Caribbean. Moreover, Irish people, far from being excluded from the Atlantic trade, actually took an active role in it.

In the early seventeenth century, Ireland, in most respects, was treated as a foreign country outside the protective carapace of the Empire, yet at the same time a dependent state subject to English control. Initially, English authority in Ireland rested largely upon religious considerations and had for the most part been guided by a concern for English political security rather than seeking economic advantage. Indeed, following successive Tudor Plantations in Ireland during the sixteenth and seventeenth centuries, it was hoped that Ireland would enjoy a

---

[2] T. Newenham, *View of the Natural, Political, and Commercial Circumstances of Ireland* (London: T. Cadell and W. Davies, 1809), p. 97.

28   The business of empire

relatively productive relationship within the Atlantic world where its strategic geographical location astride the main Atlantic trade routes would afford its merchants a share in the rapidly expanding commercial world of North America and the West Indies. As early as 1673, Sir William Petty, the English economist, scientist and philosopher, had confidently asserted that owing to its close geographical proximity to North America, Ireland was most certainly 'fit for [colonial] Trade'. The island, he observed, 'lieth Commodiously for the Trade of the new American world; which we see every day to Grow and Flourish...It lyeth well for sending Butter, Cheese, Beef, Fish, to their proper Markets...to the Southward, and the Plantations of America'.[3]

Indeed, for a brief period, Petty's vision of an industrious and profitable Irish colonial venture operating alongside England appeared to ring true. The first Navigation Acts of 1651 and 1660 treated Ireland on a par with England, permitting Irish trade with the colonies and conferring equal status on Irish ships along with English vessels. It was only later, when certain vested interests in England began complaining of Irish competition and Irish encroachment upon what they perceived to be England's exclusive right to the American plantation trade, that the Laws of Trade and Navigation gradually became more restrictive and sought to squeeze Irish merchants out. In 1667, for example, the English Parliament prohibited the importation of Irish cattle to England, a measure designed to weaken one of Ireland's principal sources of annual income.[4] This was closely followed by the Navigation Act of 1671 that sought to place restrictions on certain enumerated goods from the American colonies (principally sugar, tobacco and indigo) arriving in Ireland. Soon after, most goods being exported from the New World were required by law to be shipped from the colonies exclusively to England and Scotland from where they could only then be re-exported to Ireland and sold on by Irish merchants for a much reduced profit.[5]

The impact of this new legislation had the effect of severely limiting the potential profit that Ireland could harness from colonial trade. By the end of the seventeenth century the value of Irish exports to the

---

[3] C. H. Hull (ed.), *The Economic Writings of Sir William Petty, Together with the Observations upon Bills of Mortality, More Probably by Captain John Graunt* (Cambridge University Press, 1899), p. 31.

[4] F. G. James, *Ireland in the Empire, 1688–1770: A History of Ireland from the Williamite Wars to the Eve of the American Revolution* (Cambridge, MA: Harvard University Press, 1973), p. 192.

[5] R. C. Nash, 'Irish Atlantic Trade in the Seventeenth and Eighteenth Centuries', *William & Mary Quarterly*, 3rd series, XLIII (July 1985), 329–56.

Colonial trade and Ireland in the eighteenth century

West Indies and the British colonies in North America (mostly linen and salted provisions: beef, pork and butter) was adversely affected because the majority of Irish goods destined for colonial markets either had to be sent via England first, or were handled by third-party agents of London firms before being shipped overseas. While there were many small individual Irish merchant houses operating out of the principal trading ports in the Empire, the Atlantic plantation trade of the eighteenth century was largely dominated by English merchant houses based in the City of London and financed by English capital. In this way, a large proportion of the profit derived from all Irish overseas trade during the eighteenth century was siphoned off to England and into the pockets of English intermediaries. In marked contrast to Scotland – which had secured unrestricted access to colonial markets as part of the terms and conditions agreed under the Anglo-Scottish Act of Union in 1707, and had subsequently benefited from the profits derived from the re-exportation of colonial-produced tobacco and sugar – Ireland had its hands tied.[6] The resultant economic relationship between Ireland and Britain's colonies forged by later Laws of Trade and Navigation, in turn, produced only a modest return for the Irish economy, thereby failing to stimulate any meaningful self-sustaining development in the eighteenth century.[7] Although it is true that colonial trade accounted for only a small proportion of all Irish overseas trade during this period, the restrictions imposed by Britain were enough to blunt Ireland's competitive edge on the international scene and impede economic growth.

While there is little doubt that Ireland's involvement in colonial trade in the eighteenth century was subject to certain checks by the British government in the defence of English self-interest, it is nonetheless important to recognise that Ireland was never thoroughly excluded from this process either. In evaluating Ireland's imperial role during the eighteenth century, F. G. James once remarked that when put into a wider context, 'Ireland's place in the British empire was second only to that of England itself'. According to James, despite the proscriptive nature of the Laws of Trade and Navigation governing Irish colonial trade, Ireland was compensated by its imperial connection. Throughout the first half of the eighteenth century, Ireland enjoyed 'a significant share in imperial defence' while 'Irish trade and communications with the colonies expanded rapidly' to such a degree that

[6] L. M. Cullen and T. M. Smout (eds.), *Comparative Aspects of Scottish and Irish Economic and Social History, 1600–1900* (Edinburgh: J. Donald, 1977).
[7] L. M. Cullen, *Anglo-Irish Trade, 1660–1800* (Manchester University Press, 1968), p. 44.

30   The business of empire

'Ireland...ranked second among all the political units under [British] dominion in population, in revenue and expenditures, and in volume of trade' by 1760.[8] The fact remained that because of the explicit 'English' origins of the British Empire, coupled with the obvious cultural, political and religious differences that existed between the two neighbouring islands, Ireland would never be allowed to become a dominant or, for that matter, even an equal partner in the imperial process; protecting colonial trade simply meant taking another step in defining more fully the parameters of eighteenth-century Ireland's subordinate status to England, and to England's Empire.

Despite the obvious constraints that Irish merchants had to operate in outside of the protective walls of the Empire, there were some very tangible benefits to be had through Ireland's direct imperial connection with Britain. Recent research, for example, has demonstrated that on balance eighteenth-century Ireland enjoyed a modest surplus in profit from its participation in transatlantic trade.[9] By gaining access to colonial markets and exposure to ever-widening trading networks, Irish producers and manufacturers were provided with important outlets to sell their goods and commodities. Perhaps more significantly still, Irish merchants were able to forge important connections that enabled them to expand their businesses elsewhere and position themselves advantageously within the broader global networks being forged through renewed British expansion into Asia and the Pacific during the second half of the eighteenth century. To be sure, the 'half-in half-out' status that was effectively conferred upon Irish entrepreneurs and merchants through the exacting nature of British legislation affecting Irish colonial trade presented a whole host of new opportunities further afield.

By the time the British had successfully imposed stringent trade regulations carefully protecting the lucrative plantation trade of the Atlantic world, many Irish merchants had already begun to turn their attention to imperial markets in the East. As British trade regulations gradually became more entrenched and competition from North American and West Indian competitors increased during the eighteenth century, the volume of Irish exports to, and thus merchant activity in, the Caribbean correspondingly declined. Many of those who had previously been involved in the exportation of Irish food provisions or Irish-produced linen to the West Indies, and who now found themselves being increasingly squeezed out of these marketplaces, attempted to extend the reach

[8] James, *Ireland in the Empire*, p. 1.
[9] T. M. Truxes, *Irish-American Trade, 1660–1783*, App. II (Cambridge University Press, 1988), pp. 260–1, 282–3.

The extension of Irish Atlantic networks eastward in an attempt to engage in the burgeoning East India trade. As an early centre of the Irish provisions trade, Cork City played a leading role in forging some of the earliest, and subsequently most enduring, Irish commercial networks that operated in South Asia. Experienced merchant families such as the O'Sullivans and Irwins who had long been engaged in shipping and naval enterprises in Ireland, for example, provided critical knowledge and expertise at an early stage of the development of the East India Company's shipping and marine service, building successful Indian careers along the way and opening lines of patronage for generations of young Irish entrepreneurs eager to forge careers in the imperial services.

The extension of Irish Atlantic networks eastward: Ireland and the East Indian trade

Irish involvement in the East Indian trade can be traced back to the origins of the East India Company in the seventeenth century where a small number of Irish Protestants are recorded as travelling aboard East Indiamen, generally as surgeon mates attached to the Company's maritime service, as agents stationed within Company factories, or later as writers with the Company's covenanted civil service. In the main, Irish migration to India differed fundamentally from that to North America or later to the colonies of settlement. Irish migration to India was neither seasonal nor permanent, instead encompassing the careers of individuals of ten to twenty years in duration. In the context of Irish commercial contact with South Asia, links in the main tended to be even more transitory than those forged through the military or the covenanted services. These links generally involved relatively shorter periods of time spent in India – three to four years, perhaps – though many did stay longer either by managing to assimilate into Anglo-Indian society, or by simply evading the strict regulations governing British-Asian trade at the time, operating as free merchants and private traders.

As in the Atlantic world, British trade in South Asia was carefully regulated during the eighteenth century. From the outset, the mercantilist system of trade afforded a considerable degree of protection to the many chartered European trading companies operating in the Indian Ocean region.[10] Initially, the English East India Company, much like other European trading ventures, developed an interest in the East

---

[10] O. Prakash, 'The English East India Company and India', in H. V. Bowen, M. Lincoln and N. Rigby (eds.), *The Worlds of the East India Company* (Woodenbridge: The Boydell Press, 2002), pp. 1–19.

32   The business of empire

because of the availability of large quantities of pepper and other spices to sell in Europe.[11] From its origins as purely a commercial entity, one of the enduring qualities of the Company lay in its organisation as a joint-stock enterprise. The adoption of this structure effectively enabled a collective body of merchants and investors to share the risk of long-distance trade while also ensuring a steady reserve of capital and other resources from which to draw upon if and when required.[12] What really set the English East India Company apart from many of its European rivals operating in the same region and thereby giving it a strong competitive edge in its dealings with India's indigenous merchant families, though, was the dynamic nature of its internal organisation. In addition to its joint-stock origins, the Company drew much of its strength from a streamlined, centralised bureaucracy, fronted by a twenty-four-man Court of Directors with accompanying specialised staff based at the Company's headquarters in Leadenhall St, London.[13]

Granted a monopoly by the Crown over Britain's Asian trade, along with the privilege of arming its vessels to protect itself from interlopers, the Company initially sought entry into the profitable arena of the spice trade in Southeast Asia. As a relative latecomer onto the scene, however, the Company found itself competing against a far superior rival in the form of the Dutch East India Company (VOC), whose greater financial resources and long-established trade networks curbed Britain's activity in the region. As a result, the Company quickly made the decision to re-centre its commercial activities on the Indian subcontinent. Instead of spices, the Company turned to Indian-produced textiles centred on the Coromandel Coast (muslin, calico and chintz), to satisfy a growing demand in European markets for fine clothing from the late seventeenth century onward. By the beginning of the eighteenth century, Bengal emerged as the single largest provider of Indian textiles for the Company's Euro-Asian trade, thus laying its foundation as the most important theatre of British activity on the subcontinent.[14]

---

[11] For a general account of European trading companies in Mughal and eighteenth-century India, see O. Prakash, *European Commercial Enterprise in Pre-colonial India*, vol. 2.5 of *The New Cambridge History of India* (Cambridge University Press, 1998).

[12] P. J. Marshall, *East Indian Fortunes: The British in Bengal in the Eighteenth Century* (Oxford: Clarendon Press, 1976).

[13] For a concise general history of the East India Company, see P. Lawson, *The East India Company: A History* (London: Longman, 1993).

[14] On the Company's commercial expansion and the importance of Bengal, see K. N. Chaudhuri, *The Trading World of Asia and the English East India Company, 1660–1760* (Cambridge University Press, 1978).

The extension of Irish Atlantic networks eastward   33

For much of its existence the English East India Company enjoyed sole monopoly over trade from India to Europe and for the most part all private merchants (those not officially employed by the Company) from both Britain and Ireland were officially prohibited from taking part in it. Instead, private traders, along with some speculating senior Company employees, were forced to engage in the much more competitive and unpredictable arena of the intra-Asian or 'country' trade on their own account.[15] In this respect, at least, Irish merchants operating outside of the employ of the East India Company were no more disadvantaged than their English, Scottish and Welsh counterparts, who were equally obliged to operate within the carefully regulated systems of European chartered monopolies and state protection that dominated much of the East Indian trade at the time.

The forces of British mercantilism at work in Asia were, however, offset by a number of compensating advantages for marginalised groups, particularly by way of evasion. Throughout the eighteenth century, successive English, Irish and Scottish merchants engaged in illegal trade with their Indian counterparts as a means of countering the restrictions imposed on British-Asian trade. In turn, their activities contributed to the emergence of a series of illicit trade networks that presented a serious challenge to the authority and monopoly of the East India Company at a crucial stage of its development in the early eighteenth century.[16] During the 1720s and 1730s, some of the most influential free merchants and traders operating within the Indian Ocean region were of Irish origin. Although they were disproportionately Protestant in number, Irish Catholic merchants and émigrés, especially those with important links to the Jacobite court in France, sought to exploit the rather indeterminate position of Ireland within the Empire's expanding commercial sphere.

For example, in 1717, William Morgan and Andrew Galwey, an uncle and nephew from Co. Galway, led a syndicate of free merchants and privateers who approached the King of Sweden for help in their attempts to legitimise communal business interests that centred on the exportation of Indian cotton from Bombay and along the Malabar Coast to pay for West African slaves. At the close of the seventeenth century, the

---

[15] P. J. Marshall, 'Private British Trade in the Indian Ocean before 1800', in A. Das Gupta and M. N. Pearson (eds.), *India and the Indian Ocean, 1500–1800* (Calcutta: Oxford University Press, 1987), pp. 276–300.

[16] See, for example, L. Müller, 'Scottish and Irish Entrepreneurs in Eighteenth-Century Sweden', in D. Dickson, J. Parmentier and J. Ohlmeyer (eds.), *Irish and Scottish Mercantile Networks in Europe and Overseas in the Seventeenth and Eighteenth Centuries* (Gent: Academia Press, 2007), pp. 147–75.

34   The business of empire

interconnections between the East Indian trade and the Atlantic slave trade were significant.[17] During this period, a whole host of European trading companies developed an interest in two particular facets of the African slave trade. The first of these involved the lucrative re-export trade in cotton-piece goods to pay for African slaves. The expansion of sugar plantations in the West Indies during the sixteenth and seventeenth centuries increased the market for the coarse type of Indian cotton that was used to barter for slaves on the West African coast. At the time these goods could only legally reach Africa by being trans-shipped in Europe and loaded aboard the smaller vessels used by many of the African companies. The slaves that were procured under these circumstances were used to supply the growing demand for domestic servants within the numerous trading factories being established by the British East India Company in India.[18] Instead of purchasing slaves directly through East African or Arabian intermediaries, the British preferred to buy slaves independently through their own established contacts. This was the trade that Morgan, Galwey and a small band of Irish Jacobite privateers-turned-merchants were trying to take advantage of.

Most privateering was confined to the West Indies, where successive European governments sought to employ the services of privateers as a means of disrupting enemy trade and plundering rival merchant vessels during times of war.[19] In the wake of the War of the Spanish Succession (1701–14), however, many privateers who were harried out of the Caribbean began turning their attention to exploiting the growing importance of the East Indian trade to Atlantic commerce. In defiance of the monopoly of Indian trade by the East India Company, Morgan, Galwey and some of their closest business associates sought a form of collaboration in an attempt to effect a direct trade with East Indian merchants themselves.[20] With the help of a Swedish diplomat, Baron de Höpken, and a Danish nobleman, Jean Henri Hugaetan, who was charged with bringing the scheme to the attention of the Swedish royal court, Morgan and Galwey travelled to Strömstad in 1717 to negotiate on behalf of the group. Central to their plans was the assurance of protection by the Swedish monarch, King Charles XII, who,

---

[17] See K. Ward, *Networks of Empire: Forced Migration in the Dutch East India Company* (Cambridge University Press, 2009).

[18] F. A. Logan, 'The British East India Company and African Slaves in Bunkulen, Sumatra, 1687–1792', *The Journal of Negro History*, 41, 4 (October 1956), 339–48.

[19] J. C. Appleby, 'War Politics and Colonization, 1558–1625', in Porter (ed.), *The Oxford History of the British Empire*, pp. 55–79.

[20] H. Furber, *Private Fortunes and Company Profits in the India Trade in the Eighteenth Century*, ed. R. Rocher (Aldershot: Variorum, 1997).

The extension of Irish Atlantic networks eastward 35

in return for an initial capital investment of 540,000 French pounds and the use of two armed vessels registered in St Malo, would provide a base for a consortium of European privateers-turned-merchants to form a Swedish East India Company.[21] The privateers' ability to raise the necessary funds was to a large degree attributable to Morgan and Galwey's contacts in France where they used their extensive network of Irish Jacobite allies in Paris to finance the business venture. Upon arrival in Sweden, Morgan and Galwey proposed that Charles XII send out a number of colonists along with Swedish technical and commercial expertise in order to assist in the establishment of the new colonial venture which was to be based on the island of Madagascar, an ideal geographical location in close proximity to India with no established European power in situ. As colonisers in Madagascar or directors of the new East India Company based in Sweden, Morgan and Galwey argued that the new venture would not only provide a certain degree of legitimacy and protection to free traders in their commercial dealings in India, but it would present a timely challenge to the trading monopoly currently being established by the British East India Company on the subcontinent.

Morgan and Galwey, it appears, were persuasive. By September 1718, Charles XII approved the plan and initial orders were sent out to prepare ships to sail to Madagascar later in the year. It was only when Charles XII died suddenly three months later that the proposed Irish Jacobite mission to establish a Swedish East India Company received its first setback.[22] Undeterred, Morgan and Galwey soon secured fresh authority from the new King of Sweden, Frederick I. With his approval, Galwey travelled to London in 1720 under the assumed name of Andrew Gardiner where he petitioned several prominent figures with East Indian connections – 'persons of distinction, all established in London' – to participate in the venture. With the backing of Captain Lane, formerly a Director of the East India Company, and Captains Coward and Sanderson, former captains of Company ships, Galwey had two new ships of fifty-two and twenty-six guns built in the Thames to replace those that had been disarmed and sold on the orders of the French government in 1718. Under the terms of the agreement, Galwey's London associates were to be made proprietors of the

---

[21] The following account is based on MSS in Stockholm, Rigsarkivet: Handel och Sjöfart, 192. See also Furber, *Private Fortunes and Company Profits*, pp. 12–18.
[22] For the role of Irish entrepreneurs in the history of Sweden's industrialisation, see S. Murdoch, 'Irish Entrepreneurs and Sweden in the First Half of the Eighteenth Century', in T. O'Connor and M. A. Lyons (eds.), *Irish Communities in Early-Modern Europe* (Dublin: Four Courts Press, 2006), pp. 348–66.

36   The business of empire

new Swedish East India Company with the proviso that they would insure the new vessels for 600,000 crowns in Amsterdam and help the Company recruit some fifty English-speaking sailors with experience of voyages to the East Indies.

However, despite the interest that Galwey managed to generate among potential investors among London's merchant community, the scheme quickly ran aground. Shorn of adequate funding and hindered by almost constant speculation that their activities had aroused suspicion among the British authorities – including the involvement of Galwey whom the British suspected was involved in a separate Jacobite plot to restore James III to the throne – Galwey was forced to relocate to Madrid in 1723, where he remained in exile for almost twenty years. Frustrated that his plans to establish a trading company to rival the dominance of the British in India did not come to fruition, Galwey wrote to the King of Sweden describing how his involvement in the affair had exhausted his family fortune and reaffirming his belief that if the venture had succeeded Sweden would not only have brought the entire island of Madagascar under colonial rule, but that control of 'the greater part of the commerce of the two Indies' would almost certainly have followed.

The scheme, though ultimately a failure, nevertheless demonstrates how Irish colonial trade networks, originally focused upon Britain's colonies in North America and the West Indies, gradually began to extend eastward from the early eighteenth century in tandem with an expanding British Empire. Despite the restrictions imposed upon them, Irish merchants operating outside of the protective walls of the Empire were compensated to a certain degree by the ambiguous nature of their status under British rule. As neither wholly foreign subject nor domestic partner, many Irish were able to operate around the fringes of the Empire, seeking alternate means of trading, identifying potential openings in imperial markets and positioning themselves advantageously in relation to them. These networks were largely non-hierarchical and personal in form, functioning loosely in accordance to custom and tradition rather than adhering rigidly to a series of prescribed legal requirements. Moreover, early Irish commercial networks in operation in the East were relatively fluid in movement and multifaceted in direction. By taking advantage of unrestricted access to the metropole, they were able to draw upon an established network of contacts and patrons as well as prominent figures among London's extensive Irish merchant community.[23] The sophisticated finance mechanisms and institutions that

[23] T. M. Truxes, 'London's Irish Merchant Community and North Atlantic Commerce in the Mid-Eighteenth Century', in Dickson *et al.* (eds.), *Irish and Scottish Mercantile*

The extension of Irish Atlantic networks eastward 37

these contacts had access to in London at times provided the necessary capital or raw materials for undertaking such colonial ventures. At the same time, Irish trading towns and cities further fuelled such enterprises by providing key personnel and manpower to add cohesion and stability to these networks. Recent research has demonstrated that for much of the eighteenth century Irish commercial networks were based almost exclusively on kinship; a common strand in overseas trade that provided the necessary ingredients of trust, reliability and determination to establish an effective Irish presence in global commerce.[24]

This determination and resolve was heightened all the more by the fact that some of the families involved in these trading networks (such as those with Jacobite links) were politically compromised at home and perhaps would have shared some sense of common grievance or spirit of community with other political exiles with whom they operated. To a considerable degree, Irish commercial activity in early-eighteenth-century India rested upon the ability of individual merchants and entrepreneurs to develop kinship networks, which in turn served as a platform from which to establish other kinds of business and trade alliances in the East. Recognition of this multidirectional movement emphasises the centrality of London as a hub for colonial trade, but also stresses the significance of trading towns and ports in Ireland as subordinate centres of these networks. Indeed, such networks – often extending beyond Ireland or England to include the involvement of other Irish merchant communities in France, Spain, the West Indies and North America – facilitated Irish merchant engagement in East Indian trade.[25]

Networks, pp. 271–309. See also D. Hancock, *Citizens of the World: London Merchants and the Integration of the British Atlantic Community, 1735–1785* (Cambridge University Press, 1995).

[24] For examples of Irish mercantile networks in the early modern period, see L. M. Cullen, 'Galway Merchants in the Outside World, 1650–1800', in D. O'Cearbhaill, *Galway, Town and Crown, 1484–1984* (Dublin: Gill and Macmillan, 1984), pp. 63–89; L. M. Cullen, 'The Blackwater Catholics and County Cork Society and Politics in the Eighteenth Century', in P. O'Flanagan and C. G. Buttimer (eds.), *Cork History and Society: Interdisciplinary Essays on the History of an Irish County* (Dublin: Geography Publications, 1993), pp. 535–84; L. M. Cullen, 'The Dublin Merchant Community in the Eighteenth Century', in L. M. Cullen and P. Butel (eds.), *Cities and Merchants: French and Irish Perspectives on Urban Development, 1600–1800* (Dublin: Department of Modern History, Trinity College Dublin, 1986), pp. 195–209; L. M. Cullen, 'The Smuggling Trade in Ireland in the Eighteenth Century', *Proceedings of the Royal Irish Academy*, 67, 5 (1969), 149–75; David Dickson, 'The Cork Merchant Community in the Eighteenth Century: A Regional Perspective', in P. Butel and L. M. Cullen (eds.), *Négoce et Industrie en France et en Irlande au XVIIIe et XIX siècles* (Paris: Éditions du Centre National de la Recherche Scientifique, 1980), pp. 45–50.

[25] See D. Bracken, 'Piracy and Poverty: Aspects of the Irish Jacobite Experience in France, 1691–1720', in T. O'Connor (ed.), *The Irish in Europe, 1580–1815* (Dublin: Four Courts Press, 2001), pp. 127–42.

38   The business of empire

Furthermore, the existence of Irish commercial networks in South Asia calls into question the common assumption that those located on the geographical margins, or placed outside of the political heartland of the metropolis, found vastly fewer opportunities to profit from the growth of international trade within an expanding Empire. It was precisely because Irish mercantile activity was officially curtailed that alternate methods of trade and commerce were pursued, thereby facilitating a measure of inclusion. Irish merchants in the eighteenth century, for example, often migrated in search of work to the great European entrepôts of long-distance trade – such as Seville, Amsterdam or London – and in doing so frequently infiltrated important merchant communities or established networks of their own in the process.[26] Their experiences show how Irish merchants were able to operate across political boundaries in the early eighteenth century. By positioning themselves in order to be able to exploit new commercial opportunities and by not necessarily restricting themselves to one sphere of operation, Irish commercial networks were fluid enough to adapt to the shifting trading patterns and structures of global commerce. As the geographical focus of trade within the British Empire gradually shifted eastward in the eighteenth century, as new markets were entered, new commodities traded and new possessions and territories acquired, Irish commercial networks realigned themselves accordingly.

This early engagement of Irish merchants and entrepreneurs in South Asian trade in part reflected the relatively indeterminate position of the East India Company in relation to both British and Indian politics at the time. Before war with France broke out in India in the mid 1740s, the activities of British merchants operating in and out of South Asian ports rarely attracted the attention of parliament or even the interest of the British press. Although the Company had experienced a period of relative growth and surplus in trade in the first half of the eighteenth century, its long-term viability in India was far from guaranteed. Despite some early commercial success, there remained much uncertainty over the direction in which the Company was headed. As a commercial venture, the Company had harboured little thought of territorial conquest

---

[26] J. Parmentier, 'The Irish Connection: The Irish Merchant Community in Ostend and Bruges during the Late Seventeenth and Eighteenth Centuries', *Eighteenth-Century Ireland*, 20 (2005), 31–54; J. Parmentier, 'The Ray Dynasty: Irish Mercantile Empire Builders in Ostend, 1690–1790', in O'Connor and Lyons (eds.), *Irish Communities in Early-Modern Europe*, pp. 367–82; T. M. Truxes, 'New York City's Irish Merchants and Trade with the Enemy during the Seven Years War', in D. Dickson and C. Ó Gráda (eds.), *Refiguring Ireland: Essays in Honour of L. M. Cullen* (Dublin: Lilliput Press, 2003), pp. 147–64; A. B. Acedos, *The Irish Community in the Basque Country, c.1700–1800* (Dublin: Geography Publications, 2003).

on the subcontinent in its early years, but recent political developments had complicated matters somewhat. Mughal imperial authority, which for years had rested upon a hierarchical distribution of power among different levels of Indian society, was now being severely challenged by the rise to prominence of various princely rulers, local magnates and *zamindar*s (landlords) who were eager to establish their independence of the Mughal Emperor.[27] Traditionally, the Company occupied a largely subordinate status in relation to both the British and Indian state. From the outset, the Company was dependent upon the approval of the Crown and the English parliament for the periodic renewal of its Charter, a series of laws that ultimately determined the nature of trading privileges and extent of military powers granted to them to trade in the East. Moreover, to carry out trade on the subcontinent, the Company had to humbly petition the Mughal Emperor whose royal consent was needed before Company servants could trade with India's merchant families or Company factories built on Indian soil. As a new system of regional states emerged in India in the first half of the eighteenth century, the Company was forced to reassess its entire commercial strategy; a fundamental reappraisal of its role in India that led the Company into direct conflict with both its Indian and European rivals alike.

By the 1760s, a very different East India Company emerged compared to the institution that had been operating on the subcontinent during the first half of the eighteenth century. Political rivalry with France had spilled over onto the subcontinent in the mid 1740s, further fuelling an already bitter power struggle between the two countries for European commercial supremacy in India. For the Company, a desire to assert its dominance over France as well as other European East India companies and local rivals meant investing heavily in armed vessels, the erection of fortified buildings and, above all, amassing a powerful private army to fight its battles. As the Company became increasingly militarised in the 1740s and 1750s, the frequency with which it confronted its enemies rose exponentially. In particular, the Company's position in north-eastern India underwent a dramatic transformation. Following the catastrophic loss of Calcutta to the Nawab of Bengal, Siraj-ud-daula, in 1756, the Company responded by sanctioning a prolonged military campaign in Bengal, culminating in the establishment of political authority over Bengal's Indian rulers in the wake of Robert Clive's victory at Plassey in 1757. Several other military successes by the Company quickly followed, most notably at Buxar in 1764, which

---

[27] M. Alam, *The Crisis of Empire in Mughal North India* (Oxford University Press, 1986).

40   The business of empire

further strengthened the Company's growing commercial and political dominance in India.

Under the terms of the Treaty of Allahabad in 1765 the Company secured the *diwani* or 'right' to collect the land revenues for Bengal, Bihar and Orissa, a vast annual income – worth an estimated two to four million pounds – which meant that the Company was now able to pay for its own armed forces and consolidate Indian territories under its control. Indeed, much to the chagrin of politicians in London, the Company continued to pursue its policy of expansion and undertaking military operations against its enemies in the years following the conquest of Bengal. The Company was particularly concerned with confronting the powerful state of Mysore and the Maratha Confederacy, both of which were receiving support from France.[28] Above all other regions, however, it was in Bengal – the commercial heartland of India – where the Company drew most of its newfound confidence and strength.[29] Although the north-eastern provinces continued to be governed in the name of the Nawab of Bengal in the second half of the eighteenth century, the East India Company was now the real power-broker and de facto sovereign of the region.

Along with the immediate implications that the assumption of British colonial 'rule' had for Indian society from the 1760s onward, the actual changes wrought upon the East India Company itself were manifold.[30] In terms of the vast resources that were now placed at its disposal – land, money and people – there was a growing awareness among the Company's hierarchy that they were 'no longer mere traders' in India and that their responsibility lay not only to shareholders but increasingly to the British nation.[31] In addition to maintaining the core commercial and maritime nature of its activities, the mid-eighteenth-century Company, then, adopted many features characteristic of a colonial government. No longer simply a private trading organisation, the Company sought to develop a range of measures and policies suitable

[28] M. R. Kantak, *The First Anglo-Maratha War, 1774–1783: A Military Study of Major Battles, 1774–1783* (Bombay: Popular Prakashan, 1993), p. 61.

[29] On the importance of Bengal for the British, see, for example, P. J. Marshall, *Bengal: The British Bridgehead – Eastern India, 1740–1828*, vol. 2.2 of *The New Cambridge History of India* (Cambridge University Press, 1987).

[30] For a discussion of recent debates surrounding the changes to Indian society following the onset of British colonial rule, see P. J. Marshall (ed.), *The Eighteenth Century in Indian History: Evolution or Revolution?* (New Delhi: Oxford University Press, 2003), pp. 1–49.

[31] H. V. Bowen, '"No Longer Mere Traders": Continuities and Change in the Metropolitan Development of the East India Company, 1600–1834', in H. V. Bowen, M. Lincoln and N. Rigby (eds.), *The Worlds of the East India Company* (Woodbridge: Boydell, 2002), p. 27.

The extension of Irish Atlantic networks eastward   41

for the support of a powerful army, the exercise of control and authority over new people and territories and the collection of revenues.

As Britain slowly tightened its grip on India and began to assert supremacy over its European and Indian rivals, commercial networks correspondingly became more formal and systematised. Benefiting from greater access to indigenous commercial facilities and availing of loans from a number of wealthy north Indian banking houses, the Company was able to tap into lucrative new trade networks from which it had been previously excluded.[32] At the same time, war with France as well as the ongoing difficulties that Britain was experiencing with its North American colonies led to a sharp increase in public scrutiny of Company affairs in the second half of the eighteenth century. Concerned by the high level of corruption and private wealth that was being amassed by individuals involved in East Indian trade, the British parliament began demanding greater accountability from Company servants, more thorough regulation of trading practices and curbs on the activity of those engaged in illicit trade.

As more and more Indian territory began to fall under Company rule and as the size of its armed forces grew in tandem, British trade networks gradually became more regular, secure and stable. In part, this was a result of the increased number of full-time staff being employed in Company service to fill the growing number of vacancies in its expanding bureaucracy. As it did for the Company's military organisation at this time, Ireland played an equally important role in facilitating the expansion of British commercial interest on the subcontinent. From the 1740s onward, many Irish people – and particularly those from the south of Ireland with existing commercial ties to colonial trade networks in the West Indies and North America – were, in fact, integrated into the formal structures of the Company's shipping services which were keen to draw on Irish maritime knowledge and expertise. As a result, Irish commercial networks in operation in India gradually became more formal and established in nature. As the Company extended its operations across the subcontinent and opened up new avenues of trade, many former interlopers who had once acted in defiance of the Company's monopoly found themselves drawn into more formal relationships and structures of business in the East Indian country trade. As these networks became more closely linked to official Company affairs – operating by and large within the law and therefore benefiting from a certain measure of protection from the British government – they

---

[32] C. A. Bayly, *Rulers, Townsmen and Bazaars: North Indian Society in the Age of British Expansion, 1770–1870* (Cambridge University Press, 1983), pp. 229–39.

42   The business of empire

became more robust in form, tended to endure longer and had a greater impact upon the lives of those drawn into them.

'In the road of the chiefest trade in the world': East India Company agencies and 'colonial' ports in eighteenth-century Ireland

As the Company evolved into a more complex organisation during the eighteenth century, it was brought into increased contact with a whole host of communities outside of metropolitan London and centres of trade on the Indian subcontinent, particularly on the domestic front in Britain and Ireland. By extending the nature and geographical reach of its operations, the Company became increasingly reliant upon a series of representative agents or business houses stationed at certain domestic ports and towns within the British Isles to act on its behalf and secure its particular commercial interests in a region.[33] In addition to the numerous military recruitment centres that were founded by the East India Company in Ireland in the eighteenth century, the Company established commercial agencies in Cork (1706), Kinsale (1708) and Limerick (1758). These agencies were established primarily because of the strategic and commercial significance of these regions in facilitating long-distance trade, but also because of the need to protect Company interests during periods of war. The port of Kinsale with its strategic fort at Castlenye Park, garrison and Governor, for example, was considered an ideal location by the Company to establish one of its first commercial agencies in Ireland. Benefiting from a small supply store and victualling depot under the supervision of a naval agent, Kinsale was used to replenish Indiamen or carry out light refit work to Company vessels en route to – or returning from – the East Indies.[34]

Limerick, too, figured prominently in the Company's early plans to expand its operations in Ireland. Located partly on an island, in the south-west of the country next to the Atlantic Ocean, Limerick was a thriving, busy commercial town that benefited from the brisk trade generated by free-spending troops and merchants entering and exiting the city on a daily basis. Eager to avail itself of Limerick's natural defensive location at the head of the Shannon estuary, the Company established its first agency there during the Seven Years War in 1758. As with Kinsale, Limerick was of immense strategic and military importance to

[33] J. H. Thomas, 'East India Company Agency Work in the British Isles, 1700–1800', in Bowen et al. (eds.), The Worlds of the East India Company, pp. 33–47.
[34] R. D. Merriman (ed.), Queen Anne's Navy: Documents Concerning the Administration of the Navy of Queen Anne 1702–1714 (London: Navy Records Society, 1961), p. 102.

'In the road of the chiefest trade in the world'   43

the Company, which valued the ability to sail its ships in the enclosed channel approaches in bad weather or when exposed to possible attack from European privateers or North African corsairs.[35] By far the most important of the Company's commercial agencies in Ireland, however, was the agency that was established in Cork during the War of the Spanish Succession.

Cork's engagement with overseas and colonial trade, of course, pre-dated Company involvement in Ireland, where it had emerged much earlier as the centre of a burgeoning Irish provisions trade with the New World in the 1640s. As early as 1620, the Virginia Company began using Cork's ports to ship livestock and salted provisions directly from Ireland to North America.[36] Contemporary observers noted how Cork's ideal geographical make-up – boasting as it did a multitude of natural deep-water harbours and inlets – could provide essential shelter and protection for merchant vessels engaged in transatlantic trade. According to Richard Boyle, the Earl of Orrery, the great 'ox-slaying city of Cork'[37] was foremost 'in the road of the chiefest trade in the world', an ideal location for the development of the Irish victualling trade and lading of vessels with cargoes of beef, hides, tallow and butter bound for France and the Caribbean.[38] Boasting a long lineage of overseas trade, Cork had developed a strong commercial infrastructure replete with a thriving manufacturing sector specialising in the production of maritime wares and military clothing. Indeed, Cork's close relationship with the sea was mirrored in its physical appearance. With an abundance of canals, quays and townhouses, Cork, as one contemporary observer commented, resembled more a typical 'Dutch town' than a traditional Irish port.[39]

By 1702 Company vessels were already using Cork to ship Irish provisions to India, a process that quickly gathered pace after the Company established its first agency in the city in 1706.[40] While the establishment of East India Company agencies in Ireland reflect the

[35] Ibid., pp. 102–3.
[36] Patrick O'Sullivan, *The Economic History of Cork from the Earliest Times to the Act of Union* (Cork University Press, 1937), p. 106.
[37] See Emily Charlotte Boyle, Countess of Cork and Orrery (ed.), *The Orrery Papers* (London: Duckworth & Company, 1903), Vol. I, pp. 204–6. Orrery to Swift, Mar. 1736–1737; Orrery to Southerne, Mar. 1736–1737.
[38] *Orrery State Letters*, Vol. 1, p. 210.
[39] A. Young, 'A Tour in Ireland;...with General Observations...Made in 1776, 1777 and 1778 and Brought Down to the End of 1779', in J. Pinkerton (ed.), *A General Collection of the Best and Most Interesting Voyages and Travels in All Parts of the World*, Vol. III (London: Longman, Hurst, Rees and Orme, 1808–14), p. 835.
[40] Cal. Treas. Papers (1702–7), p. 195. H. MSS. Com., Ormond MSS. (New series), Vol. 8, p. 261.

44   The business of empire

relative status of Irish port towns and maritime cities as important sub-centres of British colonial trade during this period, such developments draw further attention to the increasing penetration of the East India Company into Irish society from the early eighteenth century onward. Moreover, recognition of the growing importance of such areas outside of the 'metropole' to the machinations of the Company highlights how London, which acted as a focal point for Irish patronage networks, was not always considered to be the hub of British colonial commerce in the eighteenth century.

East Indian trade and the Irish Sulivan connection

One such example of the type of network that connected Irish port towns and harbours to East Indian trade during this period was that associated with the Irish entrepreneur, financier and Company Director, Laurence Sulivan. Sulivan had travelled from Cork City to Bombay in the late 1730s, where several members of his family had already established successful business links as free traders or Company servants. Sulivan's commercial and financial operations in India were numerous. He was involved in shipping, banking and speculating enterprises in various capacities for the East India Company's Bombay operation before retiring and establishing a successful business in London and gaining election to the Court of Directors. Great political influence in London subsequently gave Sulivan the power to grant favours that benefited the economic interests of Irish business associates trading between Britain, Ireland and India and facilitated his own patronage network that had important implications for generations of Irishmen eager to pursue careers in the East.

The Sulivan family followed a typical route of upward social mobility for many Irish people in the eighteenth century, converting from Catholicism to Protestantism and moving from an interest in trade to the professions. Sulivan's career was testament to the manner in which many Irish families without substantial connections and status identified the East India Company as being central to their prospects of rising in late-eighteenth-century British and Irish society. Moreover, Sullivan's career was all the more significant because it coincided with a particularly turbulent period in the Company's history between 1757 and 1786. As a successful London businessman, director and proprietor, he was a fundamental part of the Company's governing nexus for almost thirty years, responsible for shaping future developments in both Britain and India at a time when the Company's new relationship with the state was being redefined. Throughout his career Sulivan

East Indian trade and the Irish Sulivan connection 45

retained a strong commitment to his Irish roots and was a key component of a network of prominent Irish merchants, businessmen and professionals who between them were able to control and redirect flows of capital, goods and personnel from different parts of the Empire in order to service British campaigns in North America, the West Indies and the Indian subcontinent.

Before embarking upon his career in India, Laurence Sulivan was engaged in the blossoming Cork provisions trade, focusing his attention on the commercial networks that at the time linked Ireland with continental Europe and the Atlantic world. Sulivan's origins in Cork were relatively humble. His father, Philip O'Sullivan, was a Roman Catholic who had married into a local Protestant family, the Irwins, who, although by no means wealthy, had ties to local government and maritime circles in counties Roscommon and Cork, with some Indian connections. These connections served Sulivan and his family well. Sulivan's younger brother, Benjamin, for example, served as attorney-at-law and clerk of the Crown for counties Cork and Waterford in the 1740s and 1750s, before transferring to India in 1777, where he later rose to become a judge of the High Court in Calcutta. Captain James Irwin, Laurence Sulivan's uncle, was a free trader before securing a position as a Company servant in Bengal, while another of Sulivan's brothers, John Sulivan, was a naval captain who frequently travelled on commercial voyages to Bombay.[41]

In Cork, Sulivan began his career as a free trader before his fortunes changed when he followed the expansion of family business interests into South Asia during the boom in private trade in India during the late 1730s.[42] He first arrived in Bombay in 1738 having secured his passage aboard an Irish-owned brig, named the *Mary*, which had been purchased by his uncle, James Irwin, and a friend, Anthony Upson, to participate in the country trade in Bombay and the Malabar coast.[43] Irwin and Upson had also benefited from earlier Cork connections in India established through a family relation, Captain Robert Irwin, who was employed as supercargo aboard merchant vessels sailing between Ireland and India in the 1720s. By the time Sulivan embarked upon his career in India, James Irwin was already quite established in private trading circles. He had been involved in commercial activity at

---

[41] Bombay Abstract Letters Received, Vol. 1, p. 92, No.49, Oriental and India Office Collection, British Library (hereafter, OIOC, BL).

[42] Court Book 53, p. 410, OIOC, BL; see also L. Sutherland, *The East India Company in Eighteenth-Century Politics* (Oxford: Clarendon Press, 1962), p. 60.

[43] S.G.O. GD/Sect.1/464/(c), ff. 25–7, Scottish Records Office, Register House, Edinburgh.

46   The business of empire

St Helena and Java before receiving direct employment by the Company in the 1740s.[44]

In Bombay, Sulivan followed his Irish relatives into the family business where he began a career as a free merchant before entering the East India Company in an official capacity. One of the earliest records of Sulivan in Bombay lists him as secretary to Governor John Horne, where he was employed in the accounts department alongside another Bombay civil servant, Edward Owen, in 1739.[45] It was Stephen Law, however, who succeeded John Horne as Governor of Bombay in April 1739, who became Sulivan's patron and confidant in India, and provided him with a critical understanding of the machinery of the East India Company's government. As Sulivan later admitted to his son Stephen, without Law's friendship he had lacked sufficient patronage to rise in the Company's ranks, and without anyone in England with sufficient influence to speed his promotion his 'line was marked, unknown to all, and its success depended upon resolution and perseverance' alone.[46]

As a servant of the Company, Sulivan held every rank within its civil branch apart from that of writer. He kept records, organised Company business, administered justice and kept 'well informed of the intricate power politics of the "country powers" with whom Company servants were in contact'.[47] Benefiting from Law's patronage, Sulivan obtained his first official appointment from the Directors as a Company Factor in Bombay in February 1741. He held the post of Company Factor for over six years before he was promoted to the position of Junior Merchant in 1747, and later Senior Merchant and Collector of Revenues in 1752.[48] As a Company servant in Bombay during the 1740s and 1750s, Sulivan distinguished himself through a combination of diligence and hard work. In no small part, his Cork connections and involvement in Irish shipping circles proved significant in helping to propel him up the ranks of the Company's marine service.

At an early stage in his Company career in Bombay, for example, Sulivan displayed a critical understanding of the Company's shipping business, specialising in a thorough knowledge of ship insurance and the lading of cargoes. As he became more established, his peers commented

---

[44] Bengal Diary, Vol.1, n.p., 24 February 1752; Petitions, Vol. 6, p. 279, OIOC, BL.

[45] Bombay Public Consultations, 27 August 1739, Vol. 10, p. 350, OIOC, BL.

[46] Laurence Sulivan's Letterbook to his son, Stephen, d. April 1778, Sulivan Mss. Eng. Hist. c.269, f. 7.h. Bod. Lib., Oxford.

[47] Sutherland, *East India Company*, p. 53.

[48] Sulivan's energy in collecting rents and revenues and other monies to be paid to the Company was remarkable. From June to November 1752 he collected 74,723 rupees in his official role as Collector. See Bombay Public Consultations, Vol. 18, ff. 266, 285, 381, 423. OIOC, BL.

East Indian trade and the Irish Sulivan connection 47

on his ability to measure profit margins from freight transfers and were particularly impressed by how he could easily assess potential shipping costs and work out associated distribution dues. Sulivan's early maritime schooling in Cork meant that he was already well attuned to the interplay between ships' captains, entrepreneurs and merchants by the time he began his Indian career; an advantage that may have predisposed him to the types of problems then facing a rapidly expanding Company marine service. It appears Sulivan was also highly skilled in legal and public notary techniques prior to his employment in the East India Company. As Alderman in the Bombay Mayor's Court from 1739 to 1743, he attended court regularly, handling clients' wills and administrations, and participated in settling legal disputes and wrangles involving Company business. His work at the Mayor's Court led to him earning a seat on the Bombay Council in 1751.[49]

Through the various legal and commercial appointments he held in Bombay during the 1740s and 1750s, Sulivan cultivated a substantial network of contacts and business associates in India with whom he was closely connected, including the prominent Bombay financier, Servaji Dharmasath, and Governors Stephen Law and William Wake. His knowledge of the intricacies of the country trade and local commerce, in particular, brought him to the attention of both Horne and Wake who entrusted Sulivan to act on their behalf as a participant in the country trade – trading in indigo, saltpetre and cotton on his own account – and then sharing the profits accordingly. In this way – through his involvement in East Indian private trade along with his business activities in Bombay as an attorney, executor, trustee and remittance agent – Sulivan made a considerable sum of money and subsequently forged powerful connections in the early 1750s, before returning to England where he was intent upon establishing a political career.[50]

While Sulivan's early experiences in India were perhaps similar to other eighteenth-century *nabobs*,[51] he was quite unique in that he was very much a self-made man. Irish connections had provided him with a platform from which to make money in India, but the greater development of his career and subsequent impact on Irish concerns occurred in London during the Seven Years War, when he first became involved in the central administration of Company affairs at Leadenhall St. During his early years in London, Sulivan built up a successful

---

[49] Bombay Diary, 1752, f. 127, OIOC, BL.
[50] Bombay Public Consultations, Vol. 18, ff. 395, 397. OIOC, BL.
[51] See T. W. Nechtman, *Nabobs: Empire and Identity in Eighteenth-Century Britain* (Cambridge University Press, 2010).

48   The business of empire

business before securing election to the Company's Court of Directors in 1757. Through his Bombay connections Sulivan became involved in various business interests including insurance, banking, speculation and money-lending.[52] He was particularly interested in shipping circles where his involvement in freighting activities harnessed numerous contacts in the Company's marine service. Through these connections, Sulivan forged important shipping alliances in London where he became a key member of a number of dominant Charter parties who controlled the terms and conditions of ships being hired for Company service.

In forging these alliances, Sulivan operated across class divides and made friendships among men of apparent lesser social standing, including ordinary Company servants, 'Country' captains, free traders and some of the Company's Indian employees. Religious, class or ethnic differences, for example, did not appear to get in the way of Sulivan's business dealings. In advising his son, Stephen, in the proper way to conduct business relations in later years, he noted that: 'Black clerics and Dubashes are in general a set of artful, plausible scoundrels...however, at the same time, under a proper curb, with care that you are drawn into no scrapes, they may often be extremely useful.' Such an attitude allowed Sulivan to cultivate a close network of ex-Company colleagues, which included Governors Horne and Law, John Spencer, Thomas Lane and Timothy Tullie in the civil service, while Captain Hough, William Jones and James Barton remained close contacts from Sulivan's dealings with the Marine service.

From 1757, under the guidance of Sulivan as Company Director and proprietor, this network of returned expatriates formed what became known as the 'Bombay Faction' within the Court of Directors in London. It was Sulivan's control of this powerful pressure group that was responsible for overseeing a large proportion of the everyday business of Company affairs – planning and executing of naval and military strategies; supplying adequate manpower, equipment and supplies for war; liaising with officials and governments – and whose influence was to dominate Company politics until Pitt's India Act of 1784. Invariably these activities and broad network of associates brought Sulivan into contact with some of the largest London-based firms, such as the Colebrookes – an international commercial house with multiple trading and business interests in India.

[52] See Sulivan's Accounts d. 1755–6. He issued, for example, a band to a Thomas Ramnet and Mary Reynolds, his sister, at a high rate of interest. Sulivan Mss. Eng. Hist. c.472, f. 40 et seq., Bodl. Lib., Oxford.

London and the fashioning of Irish business networks in South Asia

As the commercial core of the eighteenth-century British world, London remained integral to Irish business interests in India. Given its status as one of the biggest markets for the Company's Asian exports, London-based institutions and personnel played vital roles in facilitating East Indian trade. Access to English banks, merchant houses and legal firms whose contacts were responsible for furnishing financial services to a broad spectrum of clients across the Empire made London an indispensible location for all those involved in colonial trade. Establishing alliances with the influential brokers in London who made East Indian trade possible was essential in the maintenance and appreciation of one's wealth and social status. However, as the importance of Ireland to the East India Company grew – in a commercial as well as military recruiting sense – during the second half of the eighteenth century, locations such as Cork, Limerick and Dublin came to join London as cardinal points on the Irish–East Indies compass. Over time, business trips to London to source venture capital became opportunities for many Irish businessmen and entrepreneurs with interests in India to reinforce contacts and old friendships from shared localities or educational institutions in Ireland. The increasing significance of social capital – through the writing of letters of introduction, recommendation or nominating each other's relatives for positions – impacted upon the type of people who travelled to, settled or took important positions in India. Their particular educational experiences or background, in turn, helped shape colonial policy as Britain's imperial services in India gradually opened themselves up to more Irish members in the nineteenth century.

Membership of an Irish network remained at the core of much of Laurence Sulivan's dealings in London during his career as Director and proprietor with the East India Company. These networks in turn greatly influenced the direction and flow of Irish goods and people to Britain's Indian empire. Yet these networks were by no means closed systems or defined exclusively by ethnicity. In Sulivan's case, Irish networks operated within a much broader co-ethnic network of Company officials, politicians and business professionals based in the City of London. The Irish element provided critical support for Sulivan at a time when communications were poor and when there was no real distinct Irish commercial community operating in London that he could rely upon.

50 The business of empire

To be sure, recent scholarship has suggested that because there was no distinct Irish commercial community operating in London during the eighteenth century – an anomaly given the presence of many different ethnic trading communities in the commercial heartland of the British Empire at the time – the Irish were actually able to cultivate more far-reaching and sustainable business networks. Lying in close proximity to England, enjoying parallel systems of law and following similar customs and commercial procedures, eighteenth-century Irish merchants were very much integrated into metropolitan commercial life. Moreover, the majority of merchant communities in Irish port towns and cities spoke English and counted among them many descendants of English and Scottish families who had settled in Ireland during the Plantations. What is more, it appears that there was simply no need for Irish merchants to form a collective grouping – a distinctive Irish ethnic commercial community in London – because of the fact that the Irish also enjoyed relatively unrestricted access to London's non-commercial sectors.[53] Although there were certain curbs placed on the movement of Irish Catholics and Presbyterians, Irish Protestants, at least, were able to participate in the same political and professional institutions of the metropolis as their English, Scottish or Welsh counterparts. By being able to penetrate such professions as law, medicine or government, those who would otherwise have been confined to mercantile networks were able to extend the boundaries of their affairs beyond purely commercial concerns to a multitude of related business interests.

The ability to establish linkages with compatriots who were not simply limited to commerce was of great significance to Sulivan and at least played a part in keeping intact the broader global networks in which he operated. To a certain degree, greater Irish access to London, the professions and the machinery of power enabled the formation of such networks and in part ensured their longevity. London had particular significance for Irish professionals in the eighteenth century. For one, it had much better credit facilities and financial services than Ireland did and thus attracted many merchants eager to raise the necessary capital to fund overseas commercial ventures. Furthermore, as the centre of the British political and legal system, of which Ireland was a part, London and its associated educational and political institutions were vital to those seeking careers in the legal profession. Irish connections among these circles were certainly vital to Sulivan's power base. The need for access to Irish markets, ports and personnel by the East India Company – particularly during times of war – were factors that

---

[53] Cullen, *Anglo-Irish Trade*, pp. 91–119.

East India Company patronage networks and Ireland 51

kept powerful individuals such as Sulivan as key participants in ethnic networks.

Although Ireland was relatively impoverished during the late eighteenth century, the Ascendancy landed interest were still an important economic group who held peerages and wielded considerable influence in both Britain and Ireland at the time. Indeed, many of the larger London-based Irish firms were linked directly to the Irish gentry who frequently sent their sons to England with a view to using pre-existing family links to establish new business interests in London. The granting of social and political favours by Ascendancy figures or their contacts in London were thus of critical importance to those with commercial aspirations in Ireland and also played a part in determining whether or not a particular individual remained committed to Irish circles. Sustaining powerful Irish connections was advantageous to both sides. On the one hand, it provided Sulivan with support to establish and maintain his political and economic interests in London, while on the other it benefited family and friends in Ireland by providing connections to the metropolis and the possibility of a career in India.

East India Company patronage networks and Ireland

Once ensconced in Leadenhall St, Sulivan, together with 'the Bombay Faction', gradually began to exert control over the Company's shipping committees, allowing them in the process to amass a large voting strength in the Court of Proprietors as well as exerting a strong influence in the Direction. Sulivan's immediate power base within the Company itself was based upon a close series of friendships and a broad network of colleagues that he had marshalled during his time as a Company servant in Bombay. Colleagues such as Thomas Lane and Peter Godfrey, for example, were of critical importance in Sulivan's rise to become Chairman of the East India Company. Lane formed part of an elite body of shipowners whose interests were closely allied to those of Sulivan, while Edmund and Thomas Godfrey, two senior Company shipping authorities, were involved with Sulivan in remitting money from Bombay and appear to have influenced his progress in the Company.[54] By February 1755 he had accumulated enough earnings to purchase £2,000 worth of Company stock and in April 1757 he was

---

[54] Peter Godfrey bought land in Co. Kerry during the period 1754–8 from Laurence Sulivan's brother Benjamin, who was resident in Cork, and from Sulivan's uncle, Cornelius. See *Register of Deeds* (Dublin), Vol. 170, p. 411, Memorial 114454 and Vol. 175, p. 317, Memorial 117207.

52   The business of empire

elected Deputy Chairman of the Company. One of the most significant consequences of Sulivan's rise to power in the India House was the extraordinary degree of influence that he exerted over the Company's lucrative patronage networks.

During the late eighteenth century, issues of patronage pervaded almost every facet of the East India Company's activities. It was the principal means by which family members obtained commissions in the Company's army, membership of the Court of Directors and ownership of East India stock.[55] The administration of the multifarious aspects of the patronage system occupied the bulk of the Director's time and energy and its conferral or withdrawal played a significant role in determining the course of political influence and social power in both Britain and Ireland. While Company Directors frequently bestowed their patronage with self-interest in mind, there was also a surprising element of generosity and humanity that accompanied it. Patrons found the claims of 'friendship' a potent influence while deciding on their distribution of patronage. Being somebody's patron carried immense social and psychological implications where the reward for dispensing patronage boosted one's self-esteem and acted as a reminder of one's worldly success and social importance.[56]

Moreover, patronage operated as a process of social exchange. Through this process Company servants, directors, proprietors, parliamentarians, commercial entrepreneurs and their respective families came together and found common ground. Through collective action, patronage provided the means necessary to prevail over certain social, economic and political barriers operating within eighteenth-century British and Irish society. Acts of patronage tied members of particular groups together through bonds of honour and loyalty, in turn reinforcing the idea of personal obligation and duty between each individual concerned. The dispensation of patronage, however, was not without risks. In an era when communications were poor and laws difficult to enforce in overseas colonies, patrons had to be mindful of to whom and where their reputation and good name extended. One of the most effective ways of countering the risks of patronage was through ethnicity.[57]

---

[55] L. Sutherland, 'Lord Shelburne and East India Company Politics, 1766–9', *The English Historical Review*, 49, 195 (July 1934), 450–86.

[56] B. S. Cohn, 'Recruitment and Training of British Civil Servants in India, 1800–1860', in R. Braibanti (ed.), *Asian Bureaucratic Systems Emergent from the British Imperial Tradition* (Durham, NC: Duke University Press 1966), p. 105.

[57] On the subject of ethnicity and patronage, see, for example, J. M. Bourne, *Patronage and Society in Nineteenth-Century England* (London: Edward Arnold, 1986); S. Fenton, *Ethnicity* (Cambridge: Polity Press, 2010).

East India Company patronage networks and Ireland 53

By granting patronage to those from a shared geographical region, socio-economic background or with similar cultural experiences and interests, patrons were in better positions to make surer judgements on character and on the likelihood of reciprocation. Ethnicity in this regard often facilitated the process of social exchange and was an important element in eighteenth-century patronage networks.[58]

For long periods of his career in London, Sulivan controlled Company patronage. He used the Irish networks he was a part of in conjunction with his non-Irish connections to facilitate his wider interests in the world of the East Indies. Key members of the Irish Sulivan network included Joseph Hickey, who in the late eighteenth century was a prominent Irish lawyer and business entrepreneur. Like Sulivan, Hickey was very much a self-made man. He was born in rural Cashel, Co. Tipperary, of Catholic lineage, but his family had converted to Protestantism in the seventeenth century. While attending Trinity College Dublin, Hickey became acquainted with Richard Burke, father of Edmund Burke, who later secured an apprenticeship for Hickey at a London-based law firm before he worked his way up to become attorney at court for the King's Bench and solicitor at the Court of Chancery. Hickey's apparent abilities and 'respectable connections' in the metropole soon procured him an abundance of private business where he went on to establish successful legal practices in Dublin and London. During the second half of the eighteenth century, Hickey established himself as one of the leading legal practitioners in Britain and although he was based in London much of his actual business came from clients in Ireland.

To avail himself of the multiple business opportunities of the metropolis but yet to retain clients and source business opportunities in Ireland, Hickey forged strategic alliances with other Irish professionals. He worked closely with such figures as Thomas Hicky, 'an old acquaintance' from Ireland and 'an opulent merchant' who secured apprenticeships for Hickey's sons in Dublin. In addition to the Burkes, with whom he and 'all his family...lived upon the most familiar terms', Joseph Hickey was a long-time friend and business associate of Laurence Sulivan and Company Chairman, Sir George Colebrooke. Both Colebrooke and Sulivan variously nominated and wrote letters of introduction and recommendation for several of Hickey's sons, particularly William Hickey who later recalled how 'with all my father's friends and acquaintances

---

[58] On recent debates on social network analysis, see P. V. Marsden and N. Lin (eds.), *Social Structure and Network Analysis* (Beverly Hills, CA: Sage, 1982); B. Wellman and S. D. Berkowitz (eds.), *Social Structures: A Network Approach* (Cambridge University Press, 1988); and T. Schweizer and D. R. White (eds.), *Kinship, Networks and Exchange* (Cambridge University Press, 1998).

54   The business of empire

[in the Company] I was a great favourite'. Sulivan was an especially generous patron who Hickey noted was 'very kind, and promised to give letters' to 'his Asiatic friends' that 'would be of essential service' to him after he had received a commission in the Company's army in Madras during the first Anglo-Mysore war in 1768.

Also operating within this Irish network were the Nesbitts, eminent merchants in Bishopsgate St in London.[59] The Nesbitt family were prominent Irish Quaker merchants whose business interests in London were both commercial and financial.[60] They were involved in banking and shipping circles and had risen to prominence as government contractors during the Seven Years War, exploiting the Irish market by outfitting British vessels with Irish salted provisions to supply British troops abroad from Cork.[61] The expansion of their business across the Empire during the Seven Years War brought them into increased contact with more established commercial houses in London, particularly those connected to Sulivan, Colebrooke and the East India Company. Joseph Hickey and Arnold Nesbitt were also closely connected due in no small part to their shared business concerns in London and Cork. They frequently called upon one another for favours and used each other's connections to further the interests of family members.

In 1770, for example, Hickey approached Arnold Nesbitt about the possibility of obtaining a position for his son, William (who had subsequently left the Company's Madras army) in one of his merchant houses in the West Indies. Edmund Burke this time provided letters of recommendation and put Hickey in contact with Sir Basil Keith, the Governor of Jamaica and a relation of his, Richard Burke, then Collector of the Customs for Grenada. After a failed career in the Company's Madras army and as a prospective West Indian planter in Jamaica, William Hickey eventually returned to England where he once again solicited the assistance of Laurence Sulivan in London to return to India and begin a new career as a Company writer. Shortly after entering the Bengal Civil Service in 1773, with Sulivan's help, Hickey recorded how at the time he believed that 'there never was a man better recommended' than himself. In Bengal, Sulivan arranged for his brother, Stephen Sulivan, and his wife to help Hickey to settle in and introduce him to some of the most prominent figures in the Company's service. Among those whom Sulivan later put Hickey in contact with included

---

[59] R. B. Sheridan, *Sugar and Slavery: An Economic History of the British West Indies, 1623–1775* (Baltimore: Johns Hopkins University Press, 1974), p. 62.

[60] Truxes, *Irish-American Trade*, p. 60.

[61] C. Bailey, 'The Nesbitts of London and their Networks', in Dickson *et al.* (eds.), *Irish and Scottish Mercantile Networks*, pp. 231–46.

East India Company patronage networks and Ireland   55

the Governor of Madras, and fellow compatriot, George Macartney. Macartney was an 'old friend' and 'fellow collegian' of Hickey's father, Joseph, at Trinity College Dublin, whom Joseph had provided financial aid to when Macartney was based in St Petersburg and worked as British Envoy to Russia.[62] Macartney had come to India following brief spells as Chief Secretary of Ireland and Governor of the British West Indies. As a fellow Irishman and close acquaintance of Lady Ossory, he had enjoyed the aristocratic patronage of Lord Shelburne in the British parliament and had secured Sulivan's backing in the Court of Directors upon putting his candidacy forward for the vacant Governorship of the Madras Presidency in 1780.[63] Alongside his trusted secretary, George Staunton (another Irishman and family friend of Joseph Hickey), Macartney was entrusted by Sulivan and the Court of Directors with regulating the Company's financial affairs in Madras following the controversy over the debts of the Nawab of Arcot.[64]

Although most of the patronage Sulivan dispensed was rewarded by support at the annual election of the Court of Directors, he nevertheless did much to advance the careers of family and friends in Ireland.[65] This was something that his colleagues and political opponents complained about bitterly. In writing to Henry Dundas – one of Sulivan's opponents within the Court of Directors – in 1784, Richard Atkinson noted that 'the ruling passion with him [Sulivan] is the vanity of being supposed the head of the India Company and the power of giving protection to his friends in the Company's service'.[66] Indeed, Sulivan helped launch the careers of his brother's three eldest sons, Benjamin, John and Richard Joseph Sulivan, in India where they subsequently rose to positions of power and influence in the Company's employ.[67] From 1801 to his death in 1810, Benjamin Sulivan served as Puisne Judge of the Supreme

---

[62] For Macartney's Irish background, see P. Roebuck (ed.), *Macartney of Lisanoure, 1737–1806: Essays in Biography* (Belfast: Ulster Historial Foundation, 1983), pp. 1–22.

[63] L. Sutherland, 'Lord Macartney's Appointment as Governor of Madras, 1780: The Treasury in East India Company Elections', *The English Historical Review*, 90, 356 (July 1975), 523–35.

[64] Sulivan to Macartney, 8 January 1781, Mic. 407/2, PRONI. For detail on the nature of the problems Macartney faced in Madras in the 1780s, see B. D. Metcalfe and T. R. Metcalfe, *A Concise History of India* (Cambridge University Press, 2002), pp. 28–54.

[65] George K. McGilvary, *Guardian of the East India Company: The Life of Laurence Sulivan* (London: Tauras, 2006), p. 51.

[66] R. Atkinson to H. Dundas, d. 22 July 1784. Quoted in H. Furber, 'The East India Directors 1784', *Journal of Modern History*, V (1933), 483.

[67] Francis Sykes to Warren Hastings, d. 16 May 1779. 'Mr Sulivan's nephew (Henry Boyle Sulivan, youngest son of Benjamin Sulivan of Cork) proceeding immediately overland'. BL. Add. Mss. 29143, f. 344. See also John Sulivan to Laurence Sulivan, d. 19 September 1784, Sulivan Mss. Eng. Hist. b.190, f. 53. Bodl. Lib., Oxford.

56   The business of empire

Court of Judicature at Madras. John Sulivan became Under-secretary at War from 1801 to 1805, while Richard Sulivan obtained a writership in the Company's service before returning to England where he successfully embarked upon a political career as MP for New Romney in 1787.[68] In addition, several of Sulivan's family relatives from Cork also directly benefited from his extensive patronage in the Court of Directors. His cousin Eyles Irwin, for instance, obtained a writership in the Company's service in 1766 and with Sulivan's influence had secured the appointment of 'superintendent of the company's grounds within the boundaries of Madras' by 1771. Later, Eyles Irwin was employed as a member of the Committee of Assigned Revenue by Lord Macartney and rose to become the superintendent of revenue in the Tinnevelly and Madura districts in the Madras Presidency.[69]

The Sulivan network outlined here thus traces a fragment of a much larger Irish network that operated in the context of the political and professional world of Britain during the second half of the eighteenth century. On many occasions, such networks helped fuse so-called 'peripheral' locations like Cork, Limerick and Dublin to London and the wider British Empire beyond. Moreover, Sulivan's network stresses the importance of British institutions such as the East India Company as a critical structural node within these networks that facilitated exchange and mobilised Irish resources across vast distances. The role of ethnicity in the organisation and structure of these networks was significant. The idea of creating a system of mutual dependency within this web of contact was itself a key factor in preserving an 'Irish' identity among this core group of figures as well as securing their commitment to networks based on ethnic affiliation. At a time when much long-distance trade rested upon complex systems of credit arrangements involving agents in multiple locations, the collaboration of trusted local contacts was essential to ensure relatively smooth financial transactions and the fluid movement of people, capital and goods through mercantile networks. A key characteristic of such activity was the ability of Irish merchants and entrepreneurs to form networks of kinship in order to tie a

---

[68] On the career of John Sulivan, see Letters to Warren Hastings and others d.1779–1814, BL Add. Mss. 29143–89 passim; Correspondence with Lord Macartney, d.1782–83, Mss. Eng Hist c.111, Bodl. Lib., Oxford; Letters to Sir Thomas Munro, d.1815–1819, Eur Mss. F.151, OIOC, BL. On the career of Sir Richard Joseph, see Correspondence with Warren Hastings etc., d.1777–1301, BL Add. Mss. 29138–78 passim; see also Sir R. J. Sulivan, *An Analysis of the Political History of India* (London, 1779).

[69] For more on Irwin's Indian career, see Ms. Eng. Poet d.37, Bodl. Lib., Oxford; Letters to William Hayley d.1780–1806, Hayley IX 43–67, Cambridge University, Fitzwilliam Museum; Correspondence with Lord Macartney, d.1794–98, Mss. Eng. Hist. b 242, c 1123, Bodl. Lib., Oxford.

diverse group of individuals and family members together into bonds of trust and reliance.[70]

Establishing, maintaining and ensuring the longevity of networks based on bonds of trust were particularly relevant in the eighteenth century when legal sanctions were weak and difficult to enforce, and when poorer communications technology meant that commercial transactions took longer to complete. One of the critical elements to the success and long-term viability of these business networks then was reputation. Establishing a good reputation among peers was not only vital for the survival of those engaged in pre-industrial maritime trade, but was also deemed necessary in order to encourage greater cooperation and foster confidence in shared commercial ventures. Networks of kinship thus enabled Irish merchants and businessmen to pursue communal family interests while at the same time afforded them a certain measure of protection and stability when operating within the volatile markets of the Indian Ocean region. In such a competitive environment, trading or business networks whose foundations were built firmly upon existing family ties and group solidarity stood a greater chance of survival. Family ties and friendships provided essential financial, emotional and cultural support for the participants in the network. Moreover, owing to the diverse professional backgrounds and expertise of members of this network, individuals were able to exchange knowledge, resources and skills with each other.[71]

Smuggling, private trade and commercial links between Ireland and India in the late eighteenth century

The East India Company that emerged under the Direction of Laurence Sulivan in the decades after 1756 was profoundly different from the one that had existed in the first half of the eighteenth century. The political and economic influences that so radically affected the world of the Indian subcontinent initiated a corresponding transformation in the domestic world of the East India Company itself, changing the course of its development as an institution in the process. During the late eighteenth century general shifts in attitude towards the Empire combined powerfully with a renewed commitment and vigour to deal

---

[70] See Magee and Thompson, *Empire and Globalisation*, pp. 45–56.

[71] See, for example, P. J. Corfield, *Power and the Professions in Britain, 1700–1850* (New York: Routledge, 1995) and F. G. James, 'The Irish Lobby in the Early Eighteenth Century', *The English Historical Review*, 82 (July 1966), 543–57.

58   The business of empire

with the old issue of corruption within the Company. In particular, popular movements in metropolitan thought – including the advance of economic ideas by intellectuals such as Adam Smith and others who advocated free trade – began to challenge what were being viewed as increasingly outmoded mercantilist ideas of trading monopolies and state protectionism.[72] Moreover, the late eighteenth century witnessed a rise in the stock market and a parallel growth in the system of public finance in England, a development that presented a serious challenge to the Company's status and privilege as one of Britain's premier financial institutions.[73] The combination of these issues, in turn, led to a much tighter regulation of imperial affairs from the 1780s onward.[74] As parliament introduced reform to Company practices and the government gradually began to assert greater control over Company affairs, the East Indian market, in turn, was opened up to more competition from private traders in Britain.

In Ireland, Protestant radicals, sensing the increased economic significance of India to Ireland and more generally the opportunities that the wider Empire held, began demanding a greater share in the wealth of the Empire and access to imperial posts. Perhaps conscious of the dominant Irish Sulivan connection in the Court of Directors and its extensive patronage network in India, prominent Irish patriots such as Wolfe Tone, whose brother William worked for the East India Company and later for the Maratha rulers of Western India,[75] increasingly looked to India as an important outlet for frustrated Irish imperial ambition.[76] While the Company was prepared to open its doors to Irish personnel – and did so enthusiastically through Sulivan's influence in the Court of Directors – it was not, however, about to alter its position on the extent to which Ireland and its merchants could participate in East Indian trade directly. Under Grattan's parliament, attempts were made to ameliorate trading restrictions between Ireland and Britain, and Irish merchants did enjoy a brief period of free trade in the 1780s, but in the face of mounting opposition from the British mercantile classes this proved relatively short-lived. Nevertheless, as pressure mounted during this period to assert its political autonomy at home and keep private

[72] P. J. Cain, 'Economics and Empire: The Metropolitan Context', in Porter (ed.), *The Oxford History of the British Empire: Vol. III, The Nineteenth Century*, pp. 31–53.
[73] H. Bowen, *The Business of Empire: The East India Company and Imperial Britain, 1756–1833* (Cambridge University Press, 2006), pp. 53–84.
[74] These themes are explored in Bayly, *Imperial Meridian*, pp. 100–63.
[75] T. W. Tone, *The Autobiography of Theobald Wolfe Tone, 1763–1798*, vol. I, ed. R. B. O'Brien (London: T. Fisher Unwin, 1893), p. 2; see also W. H. Tone, *Some Institutions of the Maratha People* (London: D. Lankheet, 1799).
[76] Tone, *Autobiography*, vol. I, pp. 18–20.

Smuggling, private trade and commercial links

merchants at bay in India, the Company became ever more concerned about the anomalous position of Ireland – and the growing demands of Irish Protestant merchants – in relation to the imperial trade system. Prior to the enactment of Pitt's India Act (1784), which made provisions to bring the administration of the East India Company under the control of the British parliament, the Board of Directors wrote to the Home Secretary, Thomas Townshend, in March 1783 outlining their concerns over certain 'rumours' that Ireland and the newly formed United States were attempting to breach the monopoly of the East India Company and participate in the East Indian and China trade directly. Concerned over the possible future use of Irish ports in either supplying or refitting American ships bound for India, the Directors wanted to know what measures the government would put in place in order 'to prevent any disagreeable consequences from such a trade, either to the Company or to the [British] State'.[77]

The impending threat posed by Irish demands for greater access to British markets in the East gathered pace in the early 1790s. Sensing an opportunity to challenge the Company at a critical point in its development, the Irish parliament offered its unequivocal support to those looking to secure certain rights and privileges in Ireland to participate directly in East Indian trade. In January 1793, for example, the Irish parliament passed a bill, without seeking the consent of Westminster or Leadenhall St, entitled 'Heads of the Act of Parliament of Ireland for regulating the trade of that kingdom with the East Indies', calling for equal rights to be granted to Irish merchants as citizens of the Empire. It asserted that 'any of his majesty's subjects may export from Cork, to the coasts of Coromandel and Malabar or to Bengal and Sumatra in the Company's ships, any merchandise of the growth, product or manufacture of the King's Dominions in Europe' and that 'if an export trade in those articles shall be open to British subjects, it shall be open to Irish'. Furthermore, the bill stipulated that 'any new possession acquired in China' by the East India Company, would in future be of benefit to Irish merchants, too; 'Irish subjects', the bill declared, were 'to receive reciprocal benefits of export trade as British subjects'.[78]

These claims were all the more significant as they were put forward at a time when the East India Company was in the process of having

---

[77] Board of Directors to Lord Sydney, 12 March 1783, 'Intentions of Ireland and the USA to Trade in the East Indies', Home Miscellaneous Series IOR/H/169 (East India Series 77), 18, p. 635. OIOC, BL.

[78] 'Claim of Ireland to Participation in the Indian and China Trade', Bill from the Irish Parliament to the Court of the Directors of the East India Company, d. 22 January 1793. IOR/A/2/11 (1793), OIOC, BL.

60   The business of empire

its charter renewed for a further twenty years.[79] During this period, Irish vested interests joined calls from lobbyists and pressure groups in Britain, to try to persuade the Secretary of State, Henry Dundas, to separate the management of the Company's commercial interests from that of their territorial and political affairs in India. Prior to the renewal of the charter in 1793, the central issue concerning these groups involved whether or not the new charter should confer an exclusive right of trading beyond the Cape of Good Hope to the Company and thus a monopoly on all trade between Britain and India.[80] Owing to the fact that South Asia was becoming an increasingly British 'colonial' sphere of influence, private traders argued that they had a right to benefit from access to imperial markets in the East, as an important outlet for British and Irish manufacturers and a source of public revenue. 'It will become the grand aim of the enlightened and prudent political reformers', one petition proclaimed,

to reconcile as much as possible, the public good and the interests of the great commercial bodies in this, as well as in the Kingdom of Ireland...by granting to those commercial bodies such a participation in the East Indies trade, as ought in all reason, to satisfy them...by an increasing outlet to manufacturers, yield and increasing revenue to the public.[81]

Irish merchants were unequivocal in their demands for inclusion. The petition noted that it was 'to be understood' that Ireland was 'to possess the same privileges in our East India commerce that are granted to British subjects, and that the term "British," in all that concerns our trade with India, is to extend to the Irish nation, as well as to England and Scotland'.[82]

Ever mindful of Ireland's disadvantaged past in relation to the restrictions imposed upon Irish trade by the British government, the petitioners of the 1790s were prepared to use history as sanction as a means of applying pressure on Dundas and the Directors to review the Company's stance on Ireland. It was brought to Dundas' attention that petitioners acting on behalf of Irish merchants had 'attempted on this subject to agitate the passions of Ireland', stating that in the past 'her interests' had been 'sacrificed to a trading Company; that the

---

[79] See 'Bill for Settling the Trade of Ireland to the East Indies and Confirming the Exclusive Rights of the United Company 1793', Home Miscellaneous Series, IOR/ H/64 (1678–1793), 15, pp. 721–839. APAC, BL.

[80] Composite volume of papers addressed mainly to Henry Dundas relating to the renewal of the East India Company's charter in 1793, IOR/A/2/11 (1793), 221. APAC, BL.

[81] IOR/A/2/11 (1793), 222. OIOC, BL.

[82] IOR/A/2/11 (1793), 235. OIOC, BL.

Smuggling, private trade and commercial links 61

independence of her legislature was violated; that the freedom of trade which she had lately acquired was done away'. Aware that previous experience had shown 'that questions on the rights of Ireland inflame the most', the British government felt it prudent to properly address the issue, fearing that a failure to do so may mean that similar questions were 'likely to be revived' again in the future. Moreover, given the growth in popularity of the Irish Volunteer movement and its increasing links with revolutionary France which had declared war on Britain in February 1793, the government was convinced that the claims being put forward by Irish merchants were being supported 'by those who wish to disturb the public tranquility' in Ireland and that, at very least, they should warrant proper consideration.

After much debate in parliament, Dundas wrote to the MP for Armagh, Henry Hobart, in May 1793 informing him that despite his memo 'respecting the expectations of Ireland in relation to India', the government had determined that 'any attempt on the part of Ireland to carry on a rival trade with the East India Company would be nugatory'. Dundas expressed particular concern over the sale of Indian goods in Ireland, something that the government believed would contravene the principal notion that England had to remain at the centre of imperial trade. He reminded Hobart that it was the 'policy of government to keep the India trade concentrated in one place', and that above all others had to be 'the port of London'. He believed that the sale of Indian goods in Irish ports would 'give rise to a multitude of claims, a compliance with which would be attended with the utmost inconvenience' to the British government and the East India Company authorities. As a portent of things to come under the Union, Dundas was dismissive of the whole appeal, claiming that direct Irish access to East Indian trade would not only 'be very inconvenient to this country [England]' but in the long term would really be 'of very little importance to Ireland'. Eager to establish some sort of compromise, however, Dundas assured Hobart that Ireland remained central to British planning 'in the preservation of the Indian Empire' and that their 'common interest' should be reflected 'in a situation as similar as circumstances will admit'.[83]

In the end, it was decided that Irish merchants who desired to participate in the East Indian trade would be afforded the same benefits as their English and Scottish counterparts, but with some important conditions. All future private Irish trade with the East Indies was conditional 'that no individual should engage in the exportation of masts,

[83] Letter from Henry Dundas to Rt Hon. Robert Hobart, d. Whitehall 23 May 1793, IOR/A/2/11 (1793), 453. OIOC, BL.

62   The business of empire

spars, cordage, anchors, pitch and tar...by any individual, in the ships of the...Company, or employed in their service'. As part of the new arrangement, the Company agreed that 'in the proper season of every year' – between October and February – it would 'provide and appropriate eight hundred tons of shipping at the least for the specific purposes of carrying from the port of Cork to the East Indies such goods, wares' as supplied by Irish merchants. In addition, Irish merchants were permitted to send items to Britain first before being loaded aboard Company ships and then exported to India. Likewise, Company traders were allowed to send goods back to Britain from India and then re-export to Ireland.[84]

Conclusion

Thus, on the eve of Union, it appeared that Ireland was moving towards a gradual transformation in terms of its wider role and responsibilities within the Empire, from colonial outpost for much of the eighteenth century to sub-imperial centre by the beginning of the nineteenth. As Britain gradually moved towards a policy of free trade and as Irish patriots increased their demands and calls for greater imperial inclusion, the restrictions imposed upon Irish involvement in the business of empire became ever more relaxed. Moreover, the geographical reorientation of the Empire eastward from the mid eighteenth century onward appeared to facilitate a more dynamic and integrated role for Irish merchants and entrepreneurs in imperial commerce. The combined variegated factors of distance and poor communications involved in trade between Britain and South Asia meant that the East India Company became reliant on greater numbers of experienced, reliable staff and knowledge to carry out effective and profitable trade. The growing significance of Ireland to British imperial ambitions in the second half of the eighteenth century was reflected in the degree to which Ireland was bound up in the evolving structure and shifting responsibilities of the East India Company. As the Company evolved into a more complex organisation during the second half of the eighteenth century, conquering and annexing Indian territory and in doing so developing more sophisticated commercial links throughout South Asia, it began drawing on Irish resources, personnel and experience as an important means of facilitating its new administrative and commercial responsibilities. Greater responsibilities   .

---

[84] 'Claim of Ireland to Participation in the Indian and China Trade', Bill from the Irish Parliament to the Court of the Directors of the East India Company, d. 22 Jan 1793. IOR/A/2/11 (1793), f. 30. OIOC, BL.

Conclusion

brought the Company into increased contact with a whole host of communities outside of metropolitan London and centres of trade on the Indian subcontinent, particularly in Ireland where it became reliant upon a series of representative agents or business houses in Cork and Limerick to act on its behalf and secure its particular naval and commercial interests in a region. These agencies were established primarily because of the strategic and commercial significance of Ireland in facilitating long-distance trade, but also because of the need to protect the Company's interests during a period of almost constant international conflict. Here, direct Irish involvement – in terms of patronage, shipping and supplying personnel, maritime expertise and knowledge and commodities, as well as access to Irish ports – greatly assisted the Company's commercial expansion on the subcontinent. Not only this, but within the expanding administrative structures of the Company itself, Irish merchants and entrepreneurs found numerous opportunities to forge careers and further business opportunities tying Britain, Ireland and India together, a development that ultimately facilitated greater Irish movement and opportunities within the Empire.

3 British overseas expansion, Ireland and the sinews of colonial power

Introduction

Since the 1780s, agrarian inequality had become a common feature of both Irish and Indian life. Lord Cornwallis' Permanent Settlement Act of 1793 had served to entrench the power of *zamindars* or landlords in India against both the state and the peasantry in the expectation of securing fixed revenue to fund Britain's imperial wars.[1] The Revolutionary and Napoleonic War years witnessed a highpoint for landlords and the Ascendancy interest in Ireland too. Having long benefited from access to British and colonial markets in North America and the Caribbean, they consolidated their power and wealth in Ireland by the mid eighteenth century, imposing greater financial regulations on their estates at the expense of peasants and poor tenant farmers alike.[2] Irish Catholics, on the other hand, long restricted from owning land, obtaining commissions in the army or entering the professions, and suffering from high wartime taxation, escalating food prices and a rapid growth of population, were increasingly driven into the hands of East India Company recruiting sergeants or 'crimps'.[3] As Britain expanded its commercial influence and political authority in South Asia during this period, Ireland came to be seen by contemporaries as being an integral part of this drive. This chapter examines the role of what I term the 'subaltern Irish' or Irish people of humble origins from poor or modest backgrounds who seized the opportunities afforded to them through imperial migration and made careers in the various British military and commercial ventures in India during this critical period when the sinews of colonial power in the East were strengthening.

---

[1] S. Bose, *Peasant Labour and Colonial Capital: Rural Bengal since 1770* (Cambridge University Press, 1993).

[2] R. D. C. Black, *Economic Thought and the Irish Question 1817–1870* (Cambridge University Press, 1960), pp. 55–8.

[3] T. Bartlett, 'The Irish Soldier in India', in M. Holmes and D. Holmes (eds.), *Ireland and India: Connections, Comparison and Contrasts* (Dublin: Folens, 1997), pp. 12–29.

Introduction   65

From the mid 1750s poor Catholic families in the south and west of
the country were targeted by old East Indian 'hands' (many with Irish
connections) who were contracted by the Company to tap into the rich
reserves of personnel at hand to shore up depleted Company regiments,
which at the time were being decimated by exposure to the tropical
Indian climate, disease and warfare.[4] While several historians have ven-
tured to explore the Irish in India, insufficient attention has been paid
to the profound economic, demographic and political shifts within both
Ireland and the Empire during the late eighteenth century that ultimately facilitated Irish imperial service. Rather than focusing narrowly
on familiar representations of the Irish soldier abroad, this chapter
attempts to locate Irish military service in India more robustly within
contemporary imperial ideology and changing patterns of economic
and political thought in Britain and Ireland. By foregrounding the centrality of Ireland to British imperial expansion in the East, this chapter
aims to deepen an understanding of the multifaceted and essentially
pluralised nature of the 'British' imperial experience by embedding the
experiences of Irish people in the broader context of the shifting nature
of the East India Company's role in India. From this starting point, the
chapter examines changing understandings of the value and importance of the Irish to Britain's imperial project in nineteenth-century
India, focusing on specific points in time when changes to that relationship became apparent.

Turning to the exchanges of people between Ireland and India, the
chapter examines the close, informal bonds that existed between individuals within the imperial armed forces in South Asia and how this
gradually gave rise to personnel soldiering networks formed along ethnic
lines, bolstered by the presence of Irish Catholic chaplains, stationed in
British military cantonments. As methods of communication improved
during the nineteenth century, these networks acted as important conduits of cultural, financial and political interchange between Irish,
Indian and Eurasian communities. Material items and remittances
were transmitted across the Empire – almost always back to Ireland
from India – and used for educating siblings or in support of Catholic
agencies such as the rebuilding of churches or the reconstruction of
a new parochial system and infrastructure following emancipation.
Other goods travelled between different military cantonments, villages,
towns and cities in India, while money from the wills of Irish soldiers
provided critical financial support for Eurasians and 'poor whites' in

---

[4] A. N. Gilbert, 'Recruitment and Reform in the East India Company Army, 1760–
1800', *Journal of British Studies*, 15, 1 (1975), 89–111.

66 Ireland and the sinews of colonial power

the form of trustee bonds and savings accounts. Although much has been made of the mutiny of the Connaught Rangers in 1920 – particularly in contemporary press accounts – this was more a reflection of the general crisis in British–Irish relations during this period than a proper gauge of Irish attitudes to empire.[5] On the whole, Irish soldiers and their families were loyal servants of the Raj who held an intense interest in, and profited from, South Asian military service. Moreover, an understanding of their movements tells us much about the reception, behaviour and loyalty of Irish people from poor or modest backgrounds in the service of the British Empire during this period.

Atlantic isolation and the birth of the second British Empire

Although Irish involvement in the Empire can be traced back to the establishment of the plantation colonies in the West Indies and North America during the seventeenth and eighteenth centuries, the emergence of what Jeffery has termed 'an Irish Empire' should be viewed more as the product of important economic and political shifts arising from the birth of British colonialism in South Asia after 1765.[6] Until the second half of the eighteenth century, Ireland occupied a sustained though somewhat limited connection with Britain's Atlantic Empire. Occupying a strategic geographical location across the main Atlantic trade routes, its role as one of the principal suppliers of linen, provisions (salted beef, pork and butter) and people (passengers, convicts and indentured servants) promised a bright future for Ireland in the burgeoning plantation trade. However, unlike other British colonies in the Atlantic world, Ireland's close proximity to Britain meant that its capacity to trade independently was severely hindered. Irish access to colonial trade during the seventeenth and early eighteenth centuries was ultimately determined by England (later, Britain, from 1707) who through an amalgamation of constitutional and legislative decrees (some dating back to the fifteenth century) restricted the flow of both people and material goods between Ireland and the rest of the Empire.[7]

The rationale behind this lay in an inherent belief among officials in Protestant Britain that Ireland, a predominantly Catholic country, could be used as a base for foreign enemies or a haven for domestic

---

[5] M. Silvestri, *Ireland and India: Nationalism, Empire and Memory* (Basingstoke: Palgrave Macmillan, 2009), pp. 176–208.

[6] Jeffery, '*An Irish Empire*'?, p. 1.

[7] T. Bartlett, 'Ireland, Empire and Union, 1690–1801', in K. Kenny (ed.), *Ireland and the British Empire* (Oxford University Press, 2004), pp. 61–89.

Atlantic isolation and the second British Empire 67

rebels or malcontents.[8] Through the enactment of a series of prescriptive legislation including Poynings' Law (1494) and the Declaratory Act (1720), the Irish parliament was effectively rendered subordinate to the British government who exercised informal control over Irish affairs and retained the power to appoint officials to the Irish government from London. Moreover, penal legislation dating back to the seventeenth century prohibited Irish Catholics (and Presbyterians) from all public office, intermarriage with Protestants, owning land or holding commissions in the British army or navy. British concern over Ireland's potentially adverse geopolitical status fed into debates over the extent to which Ireland was to be formally integrated into British trade networks in the Caribbean and the mainland colonies.

From the 1660s onward, a series of Navigation Acts, designed to restrict the use of 'foreign' shipping for trade between England and its colonies, worked to keep the Irish plantation trade in check, while offering a certain measure of protection to English and Scottish merchants. Although these laws were sporadically relaxed throughout the eighteenth century, and Irish merchants for the most part enjoyed an active role in the Empire's commercial networks, profits from colonial trade always accounted for only a small percentage of the annual value of Irish overseas trade during this period. Moreover, because the 'first British Empire' was based largely upon the principles of mercantilism and revolved solely around trade, Irish involvement in the Atlantic world tended to be commercially oriented and was driven primarily by sections of the privileged Anglo-Irish community – Ireland's Protestant ruling elite – who dominated the small number of Irish merchant houses and financial institutions.[9]

While emigration was a persistent feature of Irish involvement in the Atlantic Empire, it was both numerically and demographically disproportionate to Ireland's population at the time. An estimated 165,000 Irish, consisting mainly of convicts, indentured servants and passengers, made their way to North America between 1630 and 1775. However, the majority of these were Ulster Presbyterian settlers of Scottish descent, who fled to British colonies to escape religious persecution in Ireland.[10] Large-scale Irish Catholic emigration to North America occurred much later in the nineteenth century. Indeed, at the very centre of Ireland's relationship with the Atlantic

[8] R. B. McDowell, *Ireland in the Age of Imperialism and Revolution, 1760–1801* (Oxford: Clarendon Press, 1979).
[9] Bartlett, 'Ireland, Empire and Union', p. 62.
[10] P. Griffin, *The People with No Name: Ireland's Ulster Scots, America's Scots Irish, and the Creation of a British Atlantic World, 1689–1764* (Princeton University Press, 2001).

68   Ireland and the sinews of colonial power

Empire lay a series of problems created by the inherent religious divisions within Irish society. Throughout the seventeenth and eighteenth centuries, Irish Roman Catholics (who constituted the majority of Ireland's population), Protestant members of the Established Church of Ireland and Presbyterians vied with one another for political representation and power.[11] As such, Ireland, unlike other colonies in the Atlantic world, developed a central administration that over time evolved into a curious hybrid of metropolitan legislature and local assembly.[12] Rather than a sister kingdom engaged in a joint imperial venture, Ireland was viewed by successive British officials as an increasingly anomalous state, located at the centre of the Empire but perennially peripheral.

The East India Company, Ireland and the Seven Years War

The turning point in the relationship between Ireland and the British Empire came in the aftermath of the Seven Years War (1756–63). Throughout this period conflict between Britain and its principal imperial rival, France, resulted in significant changes to the balance of power in Europe and with it a reconfiguration in the exercise of European influence overseas. Following the Seven Years War and the signing of the Treaty of Paris (1763), France's position as a major colonial power in North America and the West Indies waned as Britain established primacy in the Americas and began expanding the boundaries of its empire eastward. In particular, important British military victories over France during the Seven Years War enabled a succession of imperial agents and savants to establish British commercial and political authority through much of South Asia and the Pacific.[13] In its search for new markets and resources, the East India Company consolidated its commercial and political foothold in South Asia by assuming the role of territorial power by the second half of the eighteenth century.

In addition to the growing influence of the East India Company, a whole host of new territories were added to what was rapidly becoming

---

[11] S. J. Connolly, *Religion, Law and Power: The Making of Protestant Ireland, 1660–1760* (Oxford University Press, 1992).

[12] J. P. Greene, *Peripheries and Center: Constitutional Development in the Extended Polities of the British Empire and the United States, 1607–1788* (Athens, GA: University of Georgia Press, 1986), p. 2.

[13] For example, see Bayly, *Imperial Meridian*; C. A. Bayly, 'The First Age of Global Imperialism, *c.* 1760 to 1830', *Journal of Imperial and Commonwealth History*, 26 (1998), 28–47.

East India Company, Ireland and the Seven Years War

a 'Second British Empire'.[14] In Southeast Asia the company moved to acquire Penang in 1783 while successive British voyages into the Pacific between 1768 and 1779 resulted in the establishment of another colony in Australia in 1788. This geographical reorientation of empire towards the late eighteenth century was in part financed by the Company's new economic arrangement that it established in Bengal following the conclusion of the Third Carnatic War in 1763. In an attempt to assuage the growing military and economic influence of the East India Company, the Mughal Emperor, Shah Alam, appointed the Company *diwan* (or revenue manager) for Bengal, Bihar and Orissa in 1765. The assumption of the land revenue collecting rights was a pivotal moment in the history of British rule in India – and for that matter, in the history of Ireland and the Empire. On a fundamental level it transformed the East India Company from trading enterprise (albeit an increasingly militarised one) to that of an administrative power. By exercising economic control over Bengal – Mughal India's wealthiest province – the British were able to tap into land revenues estimated at 30 million rupees, while ending their dependence on the importation of bullion to pay for Indian-produced commodities. De facto control of Bengal afforded the Company and its servants a distinct advantage when it came to its dealings with other Indian polities and economies later in the century. With access to a larger revenue base, the Company had the resources to field larger armies than its European or Indian rivals, and thus organise a more efficient state structure. Over the following decades, British territorial expansion throughout India gave way to a gradual reshaping of the Company's administration priorities, as its fundamental motivation changed from trade to dominion.[15] As more factories were built and garrisons sprang up in tandem, British presence and authority in the region was reconfigured to focus on the problems of defending, financing and administrating colonial possessions.

Following the Seven Years War, the issues of imperial defence and finance gathered increasing momentum as British officials and administrators sought to assert the legislative supremacy of the British parliament and tighten the bonds of a rapidly expanding empire. Regulating imperial authority in the 1760s and 1770s was problematic, not least because British involvement in the Seven Years War had caused a

---

[14] V. T. Harlow, *The Founding of the Second British Empire, 1763–93, Vol. I: Discovery and Revolution* (London: Longmans, 1952). See also P. J. Marshall, 'Britain without America: A Second Empire?' in P. J. Marshall (ed.), *The Oxford History of the British Empire: The Eighteenth Century* (Oxford University Press, 1998), pp. 576–95.

[15] For a detailed discussion on the growing administration responsibilities of the East India Company, see H. V. Bowen, '"No Longer Mere Traders"', pp. 19–32.

70 Ireland and the sinews of colonial power

severe drain on the treasury, and the Empire was in serious debt. In an attempt to lessen the financial burden of empire, the British parliament sought, for the first time, to levy taxes on the colonies for the specific purpose of generating much needed additional revenue. The central idea – most famously encapsulated in the 'Townshend Acts' (1767) – was that through increased taxation, the colonies would now be able to pay their own way by meeting the cost of British-appointed governors and judges who would, in turn, be charged with creating a more effective means of enforcing compliance with British trade regulations.

Along with the North American colonies, Ireland was to be brought in line with this fundamental reappraisal of the purpose of empire. During Charles Townshend's Viceroyalty (1767–72), for example, several attempts were made to further circumscribe the power of the Irish parliament for the greater good of the Empire.[16] Upon arrival in Ireland in 1767, Townshend's main concern was with increasing the number of soldiers at the disposal of the Empire to be paid for by Ireland. In an attempt to push this through, Townshend put in place a series of reforms that sought to diminish the influence of Irish political magnates (or 'Undertakers') in the Irish parliament; from 1767 a residential Lord Lieutenant was appointed for Ireland, the principles of Poynings' Law were reaffirmed and the King's hereditary revenue in Ireland was substantially increased. Townshend's understanding of Ireland's relationship with Britain was grounded in an imperialistic vision that had a dramatic effect on the manner in which Ireland was to be governed. In short, Ireland was to be made more responsible for sharing the increased military responsibilities and burden of garrisoning a far-flung Empire.[17]

Although Irish military recruitment to the officer class or ranks of the armed forces of the Crown was reserved for Protestants by law, covert Irish Catholic recruitment (especially into the British navy and the East India Company's army) had been gathering steady momentum from the 1750s.[18] British involvement on several fronts including Europe, North America and South Asia during the Seven Years War resulted in depleted numbers among overseas regiments that gradually led to

[16] See T. Bartlett, 'The Townshend Viceroyalty', in T. Bartlett and D. H. Hayton (eds.), *Penal Era and Golden Age: Essays in Irish History, 1690–1800* (Belfast: Ulster Historical Foundation Publication, 1979), pp. 88–112.

[17] T. Bartlett, 'The Augmentation of the Army in Ireland, 1769–72', *English Historical Review*, XCVI (1981), 540–59.

[18] J. G. Simms, 'The Irish on the Continent, 1691–1800', in T. W. Moody and W. E. Vaughan (eds.), *A New History of Ireland IV: Eighteenth-Century Ireland 1691–1800* (Oxford University Press, 1986), pp. 636–8.

East India Company, Ireland and the Seven Years War 71

greater demands for more soldiers for imperial service. Moreover, given the increasingly militaristic nature of the Company's state in India after 1763, and its need for the provision of more garrisons, British officials were forced to reappraise their stance regarding the recruitment of Irish Roman Catholic soldiers.

Indeed, long before the popularisation of martial race ideology led British recruitment officers to favour Highland Scots, Punjabi Sikhs or Nepalese Gurkhas in the later nineteenth century, Irish Catholics were considered as being physically and morally best adapted for imperial military service.[19] During the late eighteenth century Company medical officers commented on the pre-Famine Irish diet of potatoes and the advantages of rural over urban upbringing as factors contributing to the favourable height of Irish recruits.[20] As a result, East India Company recruitment in Ireland (particularly within its southern Catholic communities) was undertaken with scientific precision. Bodies were measured, weighed and examined for any distinguishing marks denoting membership of outlawed agrarian societies or gangs. Those enlisted were generally drawn from the depressed crafts, were skilled in a trade and enjoyed comparatively high levels of literacy in relation to recruits from England, Scotland and Wales.[21]

From the Irish Catholic point of view, enlistment into the Company's European regiments in India was driven by an obvious economic imperative. Following the social and economic deprivation brought about by successive Tudor and Elizabethan policies of plantation – as well as the related political and religious repression that accompanied it – Irish Catholics had simply fewer opportunities to reap the benefits of Ireland's imperial connection. Unlike emigration to pre-Revolutionary North America, which was predominantly an Ulster Presbyterian phenomenon and involved either paying your own passage or entering into a bond of indentured servitude in the West Indies, joining the ranks of the East India Company cost poorer Irish Catholics relatively little money.[22] This economic incentive was important, especially during the

---

[19] For a discussion on martial race ideology, see H. Streets, *Martial Races: The Military, Race and Masculinity in British Imperial Culture, 1857–1914* (Manchester University Press, 2004).

[20] J. Mokyr and C. Ó Gráda, 'The Height of Irishmen and Englishmen in the 1770s: Some Evidence from the East India Company Army Records', *Eighteenth-Century Ireland*, 4 (1989), 83–92.

[21] J. Mokyr and C. Ó Gráda, 'Height and Health in the United Kingdom 1815–1860: Evidence from the East India Company Army', *Explorations in Economic History*, 13, 2 (1996), 141–68.

[22] K. A. Miller, *Emigrants and Exiles: Ireland and the Irish Exodus to North America* (Oxford University Press, 1988), p. 138.

72   Ireland and the sinews of colonial power

late eighteenth and early nineteenth centuries when the population of Ireland experienced unprecedented levels of growth and was among the fastest growing populations in Europe.[23] In the 1790s the population of Ireland was estimated at five million people. This figure almost doubled by the 1840s when the population rose to 8.5 million.[24] Living standards in late-eighteenth-century Ireland varied considerably, particularly among the various sections of the Irish Protestant and Catholic communities. While Protestants generally dominated the urban-based professions, trading and manufacturing sectors, as well as large farming circles, Catholics were numerically more represented as tenant farmers, landless labourers or artisans reflecting a significant disparity between Irish Catholics and Protestants in terms of income, wealth and status. As the population of Ireland gradually increased during the late eighteenth century, the pressure exerted upon a land already seriously affected by a series of subsistence crises, outbreaks of famine and disease in the 1750s meant that enlistment in volunteer armies became an important outlet for Irish Catholics escaping poverty and hunger at home.[25] This link between military recruitment and cyclical decline in the Irish economy is evidenced in the recruitment figures of the East India Company, where between 12,000 and 25,000 Irish soldiers were recruited to service the Company's 400 newly established Indian garrisons dotted throughout the subcontinent during this period.[26]

The decision to start actively recruiting Catholics in Ireland was mainly influenced by the dwindling numbers of European Protestant soldiers (especially German and Swiss) at the Company's disposal during the Seven Years War.[27] In order to facilitate the increasing demand for troops and to maintain a large military presence in India, the Company began competing with the regular army for the services of all readily available able-bodied Irishmen. As soon as the military reservoir of Irish Protestants dried up, covert enlistment of Irish Catholics into the East India Company's army began and a notable build-up of Irish recruits ensued. Between 1759 and 1763 a total number of 3,796 men were recruited for the Company's service, of whom 695 were

[23] C. Ó Gráda, *Ireland: A New Economic History, 1780–1939* (Oxford: Clarendon Press, 1994), pp. 4–5.
[24] K. H. Connell, *The Population of Ireland 1750–1845* (Oxford: Clarendon Press, 1950), p. 59.
[25] D. Dickson, 'The Gap in Famines: A Useful Myth?' in E. M. Crawford (ed.), *Famine, The Irish Experience 900–1900: Subsistence Crises and Famine in Ireland* (Edinburgh: John Donald, 1989), p. 107.
[26] T. Bartlett and K. Jeffery (eds.), *A Military History of Ireland* (Cambridge University Press, 1996), p. 8.
[27] Home Miscellaneous Series, vol., ci. 343., OIOC, BL.

East India Company, Ireland and the Seven Years War   73

enlisted from Ireland.[28] Following the conclusion of the Seven Years War, the Company's Directors were adamant that the territorial advantages gained by their defeat of French forces in India 'could not be preserved without a respectable military force'.[29] Thus, the total number of troops employed by the East India Company rose dramatically from 55,052 in 1766 to 64,192 in 1771.[30] Although the active recruitment of sepoys (Indian soldiers) accounted for a large proportion of this overall increase, the number of European soldiers, particularly Irish Roman Catholics, also rose, albeit not in similar proportions.

Despite the enthusiasm of recruiting sergeants, there was much opposition from within both the English and Irish parliaments at the time over fears that the enlistment of a large number of Irishmen into the East India Company's European regiments would create a standing army of Catholic soldiers in India, and would thereby pose a threat to British aspiration to establish political hegemony throughout the subcontinent. This was something that prominent Company officials such as Sir George Colebrooke, Charles Wolfran Cornwall and William Pulteney vehemently denied. With the backing of senior political figures including the Secretary of State, Lord Weymouth and Lord Townshend, they argued that recruiting large numbers of Irish Catholics for both the regular British army and the Company's forces in India would keep them 'out' of their enemies' armies, particularly that of the French, who had already begun recruiting a large number of Irish Catholic mercenaries to fight British and Maratha forces during the Carnatic Wars.[31]

As relations between Britain and its North American colonies deteriorated in the 1770s, British fears over Irish Catholic enlistment into French and Spanish armies gradually heightened. Lord Townshend, a keen supporter of the Company's attempts to recruit an entire Irish regiment for its service, wrote to Company Director and prominent member of the Irish Sulivan network in Leadenhall St, Sir George Colebrooke, recalling how during his travels around Ireland he had observed 'multitudes of tall, able-bodied men living most miserably...who have...a constant intercourse with France and Spain...in the recruiting way'. It was 'far better', Townshend informed Colebrooke, 'that the military

---

[28] India Office Library, L/Mil/9/85: Typescript of recruits to the East India Company army, 1759–63; A. N. Gilbert, 'Recruitment and Reform', 89–111.

[29] *Ninth Report from the Committee of Secrecy Appointed to Enquire into the State of the East India Company* (1773), p. 576. The report is reproduced in S. Lambert (ed.), *House of Commons Sessional Papers of the 18th Century*, 147 vols. (Wilmington, DE: Scholarly Resources, 1975), p. cxxxvii.

[30] *Ninth Report*, pp. 506–7.

[31] Mokyr and Ó Gráda, 'The Height of Irishmen and Englishmen', 83–6.

74   Ireland and the sinews of colonial power

inclinations of these people [Irish Catholics] were turned to a national service than smuggled by priests into that [an army] of an enemy'.[32] Robert Clive, an ardent supporter of the Company's attempts to reform its recruiting process, believed that the supposed threat posed by the enlistment of Irish Catholics was greatly exaggerated. Clive was 'confident that in a few months [of Company service] they [Irish Catholics] would have no religion at all'.[33] However, despite public backing from Lord Townshend, the plan met with fervent opposition from within the Irish Parliament.[34] While some Irish Protestants were prepared to turn a blind eye to the enlistment of Irish Catholics, they had no desire to see a regiment of Irish Catholics embodied. In a different capacity the regular British army feared that its own recruitment in Ireland would be severely damaged. Fearing uproar in the Irish parliament, the British government quickly decided to drop its plans.

Nevertheless the recruitment of Irish Catholics into the Company's service rapidly gathered pace in 1775 as war between Britain and its North American colonies broke out.[35] In 1777, the Court of Directors, fearing that the American war would further limit their supply of soldiers, sent a petition to Lord Weymouth, requesting the assistance of the British government in strengthening their forces in India. They argued that despite initiating 'the most effectual means, they could think of, by employing several agents and contractors by offering very high prices for...procuring men, in different parts of the [United] Kingdom and also in Germany' in the past year, they had been able to obtain no more than 728 men. They proposed that the Court be given permission to raise troops in Ireland directly in order to fill their annual quota of troops and satisfy the new administrational priorities of the Company. The Directors implored Weymouth to consider the 'great numbers of stout young men, of the Roman Catholick persuasion, who are without employment in the counties of Galway, Roscommon and Clare, and who would...on proper encouragement, be induced to enlist into the Company's service'. By employing certain 'agents' in Ireland who enjoyed the full 'countenance and support of the [British] administration', the Directors felt confident that they could put in place an effective

[32] Townshend to Sir George Colebrooke, 4 January 1770, Townshend Manuscripts, Letterbook 5, W. L. Clements Library, Ann Arbor, Michigan.
[33] Paper by Clive c.1770–1, Mss. Eur., F128/4. OIOC, BL.
[34] H. V. Bowen, 'The East India Company and Military Recruitment in Britain, 1763–71', *Bulletin of the Institute of Historical Research*, LIX, 139 (1986), 78–90.
[35] See 'A Bill with the Amendments for the More Effectually Raising of a Military Force, for the Protection of the Settlements and Possessions of the East India Company', H/84, 28 April 1777, ff. 787–93. OIOC, BL.

Army of 'idle natives' and 'dissolute mechanics'

system 'to beat up for, and to enlist, a sufficient number of Roman Catholicks in Ireland for their military service in the East Indies'. Irish Catholic soldiers would shore up the 'very great deficiency in the number of men sent...to India' and would enable Britain 'to complete the establishment' in the full knowledge that 'every idea of danger to which our settlement may be liable' would be removed.[36]

Robert Brooke's army of 'idle natives' and 'dissolute mechanics'

The task of enlisting Irish Catholic recruits for India fell to Robert Brooke, a former ensign in the Company's army who had returned to Ireland and established a reputation as a local business entrepreneur. While serving under Clive in Bengal, Brooke had received a large payment from the Company for his part in suppressing a revolt in Corah in 1764. Upon his return to Ireland, he had sought to reinvest this money in a cotton-manufacturing enterprise based in Prosperous, Co. Kildare. Brooke used his Indian savings to purchase eighty-eight acres of land for the purpose of fostering industrial development in Ireland along the lines of the manufacturing revolution that was happening in England. His vision was to create a large textile centre built on cheap land outside Dublin that not only would generate local employment but would help to alleviate what he believed was Ireland's chronic dependence on the land. To put this vision into operation, Brooke petitioned members of the Irish parliament and for a time his venture was partly assisted by the Lord Lieutenant, the Duke of Leinster, and won the support of the Royal Dublin Society. He aimed to follow the successful Manchester model by importing skilled labour and technology from England in the hope that this knowledge and expertise would be passed on to local Irish spinners and weavers.

Despite Brooke's intention to produce low-cost high-quality goods in Ireland, however, his attempts were ultimately unsuccessful. The increased cost of cotton after 1782 and the rise of greater competition from larger manufacturing outlets based in Manchester as well as the flood of cheaply imported English-produced fabrics in Ireland meant that Brooke's business venture in Prosperous quickly ran aground.[37] In

---

[36] Court of Directors to Lord Weymouth, 16 October 1777, Recruitment of Irish Roman Catholics, East India Series 42. IOR/H/134 (1776–1777), ff. 447–9. OIOC, BL.

[37] J. Kelly, 'Prosperous and Irish Industrialisation in the Late Eighteenth Century', *Journal of the County Kildare Archaeological Society*, XVI, 5 (1985/6), 442–67; A. Longfield, 'Prosperous', *Journal of the County Kildare Archaeological Society*, XIV (1964), 212–31.

76   Ireland and the sinews of colonial power

1778, partly out of a desire to fund his business venture in Prosperous, Brooke accepted a commission by the Company to serve as a recruitment agent or 'crimp' for its European battalions in Ireland.[38] His plan was to establish a recruiting office in Naas, Co. Kildare, from where he would use his contacts to drum up local recruits for the East India Company via newspaper advertisements and poster campaigns before expanding the operation into more populous areas based around Co. Dublin. Once enlisted, Irish recruits would then be transported across the Irish Sea and sent to Gravesend where they would be examined and questioned before being shipped to India. Despite Lord Weymouth's support for the Company's recruitment plans in Ireland, however, certain factions within the Irish House of Commons vehemently resisted the Company's attempt to enlist Irish Catholics in their army. One such opponent, Sir Lucius O'Brien, an MP for Clare, raised the issue of Brooke's poster campaign, arguing that it was unconstitutional and that no troops could be legally raised in Ireland unless by the King's order and without prior consent of the Irish parliament. O'Brien was particularly perturbed about the publication of newspaper advertisements concerning a 'rendez-vous to enlist men in the town of Naas'. He insisted that Brooke travel to Dublin to defend his methods and the situation was serious enough to warrant the arrest of the man who was hired to distribute Brooke's posters.

Although the issue was later resolved by the intervention of the Duke of Leinster, Brooke's initial attempts to recruit Irish Catholics for the Company's army outside of Co. Kildare were checked.[39] On several occasions he complained to the Directors that his numbers were low because of continuing opposition from the O'Brien faction in the Irish House of Commons. Fearing a complete ban on the recruitment of Irish Catholics as well as the effects that war with France might have on his plans to ship new recruits from Ireland to England, Brooke proposed that the Company send two chartered ships directly to Cork and Dublin where Irish soldiers could be 'immediately embarked, and all dangers of desertion, passage and press avoided' if they could be transported to India directly. In addition, the Company's Directors were keen to stress to Lord Weymouth the ideological imperatives behind their decision to recruit Catholics in Ireland. They argued that through his actions in

[38] R. Callaghan, *The East India Company and Army Reform 1783–1798* (Cambridge, MA: Harvard University Press, 1972), pp. 5–6.
[39] Brooke to Court of Directors, d. 7 March 1778, Home Miscellaneous Series, IOR/H/139 (East India Series 47). OIOC, BL.

Army of 'idle natives' and 'dissolute mechanics' 77

Ireland, Brooke would 'thereby promote the welfare of the East India Company and render the most essential service to the British nation'.[40] It was only in the current state of 'distress', during the American War, that the Company now 'turned to this kingdom [Ireland] for relief and gladly listened to Captain Brooke's proposal for recruiting their armies from hence'. Moreover, by enlisting large numbers of Irish Catholic soldiers for their army in India, the Directors maintained that they would be providing a great service to the people of Ireland:

> let it be considered that the evils are outweighed by the benefits that will attend this temporary emigration of the natives idle and (f.7) dissolute mechanics will find that employment of which they were deprived at home, and the industrious tradesmen, obtain a greater field for the exertion of his talents the kingdom will no longer wear a face of poverty, the parishes will discharged of a heavy load for the succour of the distrest, and Ireland will be purged of a riotous peasantry, that often pass their lives in beggary, and generally conclude them in a jail.[41]

Britain's troubles in America were thus central to the success of the Company's endeavours in the East for, as the Directors urged, 'now America seems mouldering from our side, it behoves us to have a stricter attention to the welfare of that quarter which may hereafter prove the richest jewell in the British crown'.[42] Ireland was integrally linked to this plan. Between 1778 and 1783 – at the very height of the American War of Independence – almost 1,500 men were sent from Ireland to India by Brooke's agency in Naas, at once affirming the notion that perhaps Britain was resigned to its fate in the Atlantic by this time and was already planning for its re-emergence in the East. These figures multiplied again in the 1780s, as war intensified between Britain and its American colonists and their French and Spanish allies.[43]

During this period the government of Lord North supported the introduction of a measure of Catholic relief in Ireland in return for more Irish Catholic recruits. Although in desperate need of more soldiers, Lord North's decision to grant concessions to Catholics in the 1780s was in part a response to the growing political importance of the Irish Volunteer movement during this period. The Volunteers were

[40] Directors to Lord Weymouth, 18 March 1778, Home Miscellaneous Series, IOR/H/139 (East India Series 47), pp. 1–9, 17–19. OIOC, BL.
[41] Home Miscellaneous Series, 139(1), d. 12 March 1778. OIOC, BL.
[42] Ibid.
[43] A. N. Gilbert has estimated that, in 1778, out of 1,684 men sent to India, roughly 30 per cent were born in Ireland. In 1779, 275, or 35 per cent, were Irish, and in 1780, the percentage of Irish-born recruits rose to nearly 44 per cent before declining to 28 per cent in the following year. L/MIL/9/103, Vol. 7, 1778–84. OIOC, BL; see also Gilbert, 'Recruitment and Reform', 89–111.

78   Ireland and the sinews of colonial power

a part-time militia formed in Ulster in the late 1770s that consisted mainly of Presbyterians but who also enjoyed significant Anglican and Catholic support. They were founded as a means of defending Ireland from a possible French invasion when regular British soldiers were withdrawn from Ireland to fight in the American War of Independence. As the threat of a French incursion gradually faded by the late 1770s, the Volunteers, who numbered almost 70,000 and who became infiltrated by political radicals, became the focal point in the emergence of Irish Protestant nationalism in the late eighteenth century. Against the backdrop of Britain's difficulties in America, the Volunteers soon began demanding political redress in relation to long-standing Irish grievances. Their demands were given voice by the political wing of the movement, the Irish Patriot party, who under the leadership of Henry Grattan sought greater legislative freedom for the Irish parliament and increased Irish access to colonial trade. Facing defeat in America and in desperate need of more soldiers, Lord North acquiesced to the demands of the Irish Patriots and authorised the removal of British restrictions on Irish trade.

Following news of Cornwallis' surrender at Yorktown in 1781, the British government granted further concessions to Ireland by way of recognition of the Irish parliament's legislative independence. Grattan's 'Constitution of 1782', which saw the Declaratory Act repealed and Poynings' Law seriously modified, witnessed the high point of Protestant or 'colonial' nationalism in Ireland. Thereafter, up until 1801, Ireland enjoyed a form of dominion status within the Empire, whereby the power to legislate for Ireland was returned to the executive in the Irish House of Parliament. The granting of legislative independence to Ireland had important implications for the number of Irish Catholic soldiers who now seized the opportunity of employment in the East India Company's army overseas. In 1783, Lord North wrote to the Board of Directors of the East India Company informing them that King George III had given official consent to their idea of carrying out further recruiting in Ireland.[44] However, with the advance of the French Revolution and the Napoleonic Wars, tension between the regular British army and the East India Company arose again over recruiting in Ireland. For much of the 1790s the British army accused the East India Company of stealing its source of recruitment and thus driving up the price of the bounty paid to its recruiting sergeants. In addition, the British army argued that the presence of two armies

---

[44] Lord North to the Directors, 20 May 1783, Home Miscellaneous Series, IOR/H/172 (East India Series 80) – (11), f. 245. OIOC, BL.

Army of 'idle natives' and 'dissolute mechanics' 79

operating in one theatre would eventually lead to disputes among men over pay, promotion and privilege. It was not until the late 1790s that it was agreed that the Company should be allowed to follow the same pattern of recruitment as the Crown's armed forces in Ireland. In 1799, an act was passed permitting the Company to train, array, exercise and discipline recruits in both England and Ireland, and to subject them to martial law prior to embarkation and during the voyage to India. As a result of this act, full-time recruiting officers, each with a staff of NCOs, were stationed in Dublin and Belfast with additional officers at Cork from 1822, and Newry from 1846. Smaller recruiting offices were also established in Limerick and Enniskillen.[45]

The steady increase in the number of Irish soldiers entering imperial service in part reflected the Company's ability to penetrate rural communities in the south of Ireland during the first half of the nineteenth century, in its attempts to enlist more recruits. The majority of these men (and their wives and families who frequently accompanied them) were recruited from several destinations in Leinster (most notably Athlone, Birr, Carlow and Wexford) where it was believed that English was more widely spoken.[46] A particularly striking aspect of the social and cultural background of the Company's Irish recruits during this period was that they were not necessarily an undifferentiated mass of illiterate labourers. Although they were overwhelmingly Catholic in denomination and generally hailed from modest to poor backgrounds, many recruits tended to be skilled in a trade or listed a previous occupation that suggested literacy or numeracy competence. These included carpenters, masons, blacksmiths and coopers but also comparatively high-skill-level occupations such as clerks, scribes and teachers.[47] Company recruiting officers particularly liked soldiers with artisan backgrounds since a practical knowledge of mechanical work set them up better for the handling of arms.[48] Moreover, those with an agricultural background or skilled in a trade generally impressed the Company's medical examiners. Rutherford Alcock, while deploring the poor physical condition of many of the unemployed English and Scottish

---

[45] East India Register and Directory, 1813, p. liii.

[46] The East India Company's Depot Embarkation Lists, giving recruits' ages and occupations, also reveal that wives and children accompanied about one in twenty recruits to India. See L/MIL/9/77–81. OIOC, BL.

[47] J. Mokyr and C. Ó Gráda, 'The Heights of the British and the Irish *c.* 1800–1815: Evidence from Recruits to the East India Company's Army', in J. Komlos (ed.), *Stature, Living Standards and Economic Development: Essays in Anthropometric History* (University of Chicago Press, 1994), pp. 39–59.

[48] H. Strachan, *Wellington's Legacy: The Reform of the British Army, 1830–54* (Manchester University Press, 1984), pp. 50–74.

80 Ireland and the sinews of colonial power

recruits from larger towns and industrial cities, believed that the more rural-based Irish recruits would prove hardier and less susceptible to disease. In his opinion, Irish soldiers 'were physically and morally... best adapted for the service'.[49] It appears Alcock's observations were not entirely unfounded. One recent study examining the heights of English and Irish soldiers recruited by the East India Company between 1800 and 1815 has demonstrated that the Company recruiting officers may have liked the actual physical size of Irish recruits. According to the personal information that the recruiting officers recorded and noted down it appears that the average Irish recruit in India was an inch or two taller than his English, Scottish or Welsh counterpart.[50]

Given the large numbers of Irish men and women who migrated to India – temporarily or otherwise – during this period and the diverse nature of the work in which they became involved, the 'export' of Irish labour to India should be viewed not as an isolated phenomenon but more so as a branch of imperial commerce. In effect, Irish soldiers were essentially valuable commodities, exported as a crucial component of the broader mechanisms of East Indian business and trade. The Company's recruitment of Irish Catholics in the second half of the eighteenth century (however much to the disapproval of certain factions) was a necessity that simply far outweighed any reservations that the British government had in relation to the threat posed by Catholicism. Moreover, as Company Directors and shareholders were influential members of parliament, vested Company interests dominated political machinery in the late eighteenth century as a new phase of Company rule in India witnessed a gradual militarisation of its ruling apparatus. By 1763, British naval and financial superiority had all but removed French presence from India. As the dominant European colonial power in the subcontinent, the Company began work to secure important bonds of dependency between themselves and other powerful Hindu and Muslim rulers outside of Bengal.[51] The establishment of a scheme known as the subsidiary alliance system was central to the Company's quest to secure a fixed frontier for British commercial interests and for the payment of Company soldiers throughout the entire subcontinent. This scheme, initiated by Robert Clive during his campaigns in Bengal in the 1750s, was borrowed from Indian and French

[49] R. Alcock, *Notes on the Medical History and Statistics of the British Legion in Spain* (London: John Churchill, 1838), pp. 4, 6–7.
[50] Mokyr and Ó Gráda, 'The Height of Irishmen and Englishmen in the 1770s'.
[51] M. H. Fisher, *Indirect Rule in India: Residents and Residency System, 1764–1858* (Oxford University Press, 1998).

Union for Ireland, union for Empire 81

powers and was based on the principle of the Company establishing garrisons in Indian territories (as protection against enemies) in return for a 'subsidy' or a lease of productive land that the Company could use for its own commercial interests.[52] Among those drawn into this net of collaboration were the rulers of Arcot, Oudh and Hyderabad. While outwardly these alliances seemed mutually beneficial, in reality they placed an enormous financial strain on fragile Indian states whose rulers struggled to meet the cost of securing Company troops in their domains and gradually fell into debt. As these rulers fell behind in their subsidiary payments, the Company began annexing more and more tracts of land in an attempt to stabilise the precarious finances of numerous Indian regional states. Whether supplying Indian princely rulers with troops or maintaining soldiers in newly acquired territories, the Company required a steady flow of personnel from Ireland as a means of facilitating the expansion of its military state in India. Indeed, recruitment of Irish Catholic soldiers was only gradually offset during the 1790s by the increasing number of sepoy or 'native' regiments at its disposal.[53]

Union for Ireland, union for the Empire

By the mid 1790s, however, the legislative freedom that the Irish parliament had acquired in 1782 once again came under threat. The renewal of hostilities between Britain and Napoleon's Revolutionary France in 1793 presented a formidable threat to the integrity of the British Empire, still reeling from the loss of its thirteen North American colonies in the aftermath of the American War of Independence. In Ireland, agrarian trouble sparked Catholic agitation and ignited the push for more comprehensive reform, while Irish radicals followed what was happening in France with great interest.[54] Throughout the early 1790s Dublin booksellers advertised a wide range of books on contemporary French politics, and pamphleteers provided extensive coverage on the principles of the Revolution for the Irish public.[55] Irish newspapers too were laden with reports on the meetings of the States General, printing in great detail the debates in the successive French representative assemblies and the Jacobin Club.

[52] C. A. Bayly, *Indian Society and the Making of the British Empire* (Cambridge University Press, 1988), pp. 89–95.
[53] S. Alavi, *The Sepoys and the Company: Tradition and Transition in Northern India, 1770–1830* (Oxford University Press, 1995).
[54] S. Small, *Political Thought in Ireland, 1776–1798* (Oxford University Press, 2002), pp. 190–226.
[55] McDowell, *Ireland in the Age of Imperialism and Revolution*, p. 351.

82   Ireland and the sinews of colonial power

Among the intelligentsia, the publication of Edmund Burke's *Reflections on the Revolution in France* (1790) sparked a debate on the significance of the French Revolution in Irish political and intellectual history.[56] It divided opinion so sharply and generated such interest in Ireland that it appeared in eight separate Dublin editions in the first year of its publication. Arguably even more significant in terms of late-eighteenth-century Irish history was the publication of Thomas Paine's *Rights of Man* (1792). Written ostensibly as a reply to Burke's *Reflections*, Paine's work meticulously outlined the faults of the old regime in France as well as drawing attention to the current limitations of the existing order in Great Britain.[57] His appraisal of the new French constitution with its emphasis on the equal and natural rights of man and programme of sensible social reform provided an important degree of intellectual legitimacy for Irish radicals and revolutionaries keen to absorb the core principles and objectives of the Revolution.[58]

In the north of Ireland, Presbyterian radicals, who founded the Society of United Irishmen in 1791, seized the opportunity presented through the renewal of British hostilities with France to extricate themselves from Anglican rule. They were joined by certain dissident elements within the Protestant governing elite (most notably Lord Edward Fitzgerald and Wolfe Tone) and received strong support from Irish Catholics eager to displace the Established Church of Ireland and bring about emancipation.[59] Bearing certain similarities to the American War of Independence, the ensuing 1798 rebellion in Ireland was a Protestant-led secessionist movement whose success ultimately rested on French intervention as well as a determined and unified rebel command. On both counts, the rebellion in Ireland failed. Adequate numbers of French troops ultimately failed to arrive in Ireland to provide much needed support for the rebel forces. Furthermore, unlike the American colonists, Irish rebels lacked a unified leadership and greatly underestimated the determination of Britain and a large proportion of the Irish population to remain loyal to the Crown.[60]

[56] L. Gibbons, *Edmund Burke and Ireland: Aesthetics, Politics and the Colonial Sublime* (Cambridge University Press, 2003), pp. 1–21.
[57] T. Paine, *Rights of Man: Being an Answer to Mr. Burke's Attack on the French Revolution* (Sheffield: J. Crome, 1792).
[58] *Remarks on Mr. Paine's Pamphlet Called the Rights of Man. In a Letter to a Friend* (Dublin: P. Byrne, 1791), pp. 6–7.
[59] M. Elliott, *Partners in Revolution: The United Irishmen and France* (New Haven, CT: Yale University Press, 1990).
[60] See N. J. Curtin, *The United Irishmen: Popular Politics in Ulster and Dublin, 1791–1798* (Oxford: Clarendon, 1998), pp. 282–90.

Throughout the 1790s, in particular, the bonds between Ireland and the Empire were far stronger than they had been in the American colonies in the 1770s, and loyalism (most notably embodied in the foundation of the Orange Order in 1795) played a key role in keeping the rebellion in check.[61] Ireland had assumed an important geographical and strategic role in relation to Britain's plans to consolidate both its position in the West Indies and to expand its influence throughout Asia. Edmund Burke, for one, viewed the problem of Ireland within an imperial framework. He was convinced that Ireland's best interests lay within the wider British Empire, arguing that by emancipating Irish Catholics and easing the restrictions on Irish trade, 'the prosperity arising from an enlarged and liberal system' would improve 'all its objects...better than the monopoly of want and penury'.[62]

By the time the British Prime Minister, William Pitt, proposed a legislative Union between Great Britain and Ireland in the aftermath of the abortive 1798 rebellion, the degree to which empire had entered into Irish political discourse and consciousness was apparent. Although the proposed Union was designed to put an end to Irish secessionist movements, therefore securing British interests on the domestic front, it was the prospect of insinuating Ireland into a broader imperial partnership with Britain – a form of 'Union for Empire' – that captured the imagination of the advocates of the Union the most.[63] On a fundamental level, Unionists believed in the inherent righteousness of their proposal, arguing that a union between Great Britain and Ireland would transcend ordinary political issues at a time when Britain was fighting for 'the protection of the constitution, the religion, the liberties and the social order of the Empire'.[64] Having already lost its colonies in America and at once fighting to preserve the integrity of its remaining overseas possessions, Ireland was deemed to be the weak link in the imperial chain. Too close in proximity to Britain to be left alone, yet too culturally different to be readily assimilated into the metropolitan core, Ireland's hitherto anomalous status within the Empire was now fully exposed. 'Where', the Under Secretary of State, Lord Canning, surmised, 'is the country where the state of society is more adapted to receive, cherish and mature the principles of the French revolution...to

---

[61] C. Kinealy, 'At Home with Empire: The Example of Ireland', in C. Hall and S. Rose (eds.), *At Home with the Empire: Metropolitan Culture and the Imperial World* (Cambridge University Press, 2006), p. 90.

[62] T. W. Copeland (ed.), *The Correspondence of Edmund Burke, Vol. III, July 1774–June 1778* (University of Chicago Press, 1971), p. 426.

[63] McDowell, *Ireland in the Age of Imperialism and Revolution*, pp. 678–704.

[64] *Faulkner's Dublin Journal*, 16 January 1800, p. 17.

84 Ireland and the sinews of colonial power

arm poverty against property, labour against privilege...than a country like Ireland?'[65] Ever mindful of the speed with which Revolutionary France was annexing and democratic America was federating, the future Governor-General of India, Lord Minto, warned his colleagues in parliament that if a union between Great Britain and Ireland was not effected in the near future, 'an Irish democratic republic or rather anarchy' would be established cn Britain's doorstep.[66]

The ideological origins of the Union then lay in a firm belief that a united Great Britain and Ireland would make a significant contribution to imperial strategy and unity.[67] Under the Union, it was hoped that Irish resources and manpower would become more accessible and could be deployed with greater efficiency throughout the Empire. In turn, the Union would transform Ireland from a politically fractious, economically backward country into a dynamic and prosperous region of the United Kingdom. With Irish property and the rights of landowners firmly under the protection of the Crown, the Union, it was argued, would encourage greater capital investment, stimulate economic growth and raise standards of living in Ireland. The industrialist, Sir Robert Peel, hoped that the powerful combination of English capital alongside Victorian technology might 'communicate...British comforts' to Ireland.[68] An 'improved', more prosperous Ireland would play an important role in 'civilising' a discontent and refractory population. Pitt was convinced that the Union would not only help bridge sectarian divides but that it would ultimately 'improve the temper...as well as the understanding of the people of Ireland'.[69] His claims were echoed by the Dean of Gloucester, the Welsh economist and political writer, Josiah Tucker, who argued that under a system of joint legislature and government the Irish people could look forward to a complete 'moral assimilation with Britain'.[70] Pitt's Secretary of State for Foreign Affairs, Lord Grenville, concurred, offering that the only way to remedy the situation in Ireland was 'to meliorate the state of the lower orders...by an infusion of British capital and of British manners'.[71] As

[65] William Cobbett, *The Parliamentary History of England from the Earliest Period to the Year 1803. From Which Last-mentioned Epoch It Is Continued Downwards in the Work Entitled 'Parliamentary Debates'* (London: R. Bagshaw, 1815), xxxiv, p. 236.

[66] Ibid., p. 771.

[67] J. Kelly, 'The Origins of the Act of Union: An Examination of Unionist Opinion in Britain and Ireland, 1650–1800', *Irish Historical Studies*, xxv, 99 (May 1987), 236–63.

[68] *Parliamentary History*, xxxiv, p. 379.

[69] Ibid., p. 481.

[70] T. B. Clarke, *Dean Tucker's Argument on the Propriety of an Union between Great Britain and Ireland: Written Some Years Since, and Now First Published in this Tract upon the Same Subject* (Dublin, 1799), p. 3.

[71] *Parliamentary History*, xxxiv, p. 727.

Fashioning of an Irish imperial identity in India   85

industrious, loyal citizens of a larger United Kingdom, the Secretary of State for War, Henry Dundas, confidently predicted that the voice of Irishmen 'would be heard, not only in Europe but in Asia, Africa and America'.[72]

In the end, the lure of empire and a promise of a greater imperial association with Great Britain proved decisive for the politically involved classes in late-eighteenth-century Ireland. The passing of the Act of Union in 1800 – despite protests from anti-Unionist factions – gave way to a more sustained period of Irish migration (temporary or otherwise) to India. Although the Union would prove over the following century that it was not the panacea for Ireland's economic problems, it did nevertheless provide an important outlet for Irish Catholics and Protestants in terms of greater career and work opportunities afforded to them at home. Certainly the less well connected and those from modest to poor Irish backgrounds made the best of the imperial connection. In the first half of the nineteenth century, for example, Irish recruitment to the East India Company reached its peak. By 1813 the Company had successfully established recruiting offices in Belfast, Dublin, Enniskillen and Limerick that were responsible for supplying almost 50 per cent of the Bengal army's European recruits between 1815 and 1850. Out of 1,982 soldiers recruited between the years 1816 and 1824, an estimated 52 per cent (1,037) were Irish. Similarly, between the years 1828 and 1850 the total number of recruits drawn from Ireland for the Bengal army was 3,639 men, a figure that accounted for 47 per cent of the total intake.[73] In fact, over the following years Irish recruitment continued apace and the numbers steadily rose until the East India Company was disbanded following the Indian Mutiny in 1858.

The fashioning of an Irish imperial identity in India

The rapid increase of Irish Catholic enlistment into the Company's army introduced a particular Gaelic-Irish dimension to Anglo-Indian society. The soldiering networks formed during this time by no means presented an undifferentiated mass of individuals; many came from the same locality in Ireland and were tied together through common bonds of language (many Irish recruits spoke Gaelic), friendship or family ties in India. They referred to each other as 'comrades' or 'townies' – terms

---

[72] Ibid., p. 351.
[73] J. Mokyr and C. Ó Gráda, 'Living Standards in Ireland and Britain 1800–1850: The East India Company Army Data', unpublished papers presented to the Social Science History Meeting, St Louis, October 1986.

86 Ireland and the sinews of colonial power

that implied recognition of shared professional camaraderie, or the obligations of friendship or family, brought about in part by the geopolitical prominence of nineteenth-century Irish garrison towns. The presence of English- and Scottish-born troops within these Irish garrison towns tended to create an atmosphere of 'occupation' and 'colonisation', at once setting Irish inhabitants apart, strengthening ties of loyalty and camaraderie, establishing common ground and instilling a set of shared beliefs and mentalities that they brought with them to India.[74]

Although religion was not necessarily a barrier for Irish people who sought careers in the imperial armed forces after the enactment of the Union, religion nonetheless greatly influenced notions of identity and strongly affected social behaviour and political attitudes among the Irish in India. By focusing on the differences between the 'Irish' and the 'British', nationalist-focused histories have tended to obscure the degree to which both nationalities shared aspects of a common heritage, while simultaneously obfuscating the distinctions between the Irish in the Empire during the nineteenth century. Among the Company's Irish recruits, for example, strong communal bonds of a Roman Catholicism that had survived centuries of persecution tied individuals together into imperial networks centred upon the Church and the activities of Irish military chaplains stationed in British military cantonments on the subcontinent. As Fr Nicholas Barry, an Irish Roman Catholic chaplain stationed at Agra in the 1840s, observed, Irish soldiers and their families formed especially close-knit communities inside the Company's military cantonments in India, at times replicating social norms and patterns of behaviour that they learned growing up in small Irish towns and villages. At the Company's army barracks in Nomelah, Barry noted that every evening, Irish Catholic soldiers and their families would congregate and talk outside the military chapel before entering to say their nightly prayers. Such modes of behaviour, Barry commented, closely resembled what 'the people do in the country parishes in Ireland'.[75] According to Barry, the Company's Irish soldiers 'were persons mostly from the west of Ireland, whose education had been neglected...and spoke nothing but Irish'.[76] He was struck by how readily Irish soldiers exhibited 'the same warm feelings, the same respect and veneration for the clergy, as at home, the same generosity in contributing to works of

[74] H. F. Kearney, *Ireland: Contested Ideas of Nationalism and History* (New York University Press, 2007), p. 99.
[75] Fr Nicholas Barry to Rev. B. Woodcock, d. Nomelah, Agra, 3 July 1848. *First Annual Report of the Missionary College of All Hallows*, 1 November 1848 (Dublin, 1849), p. 43.
[76] Ibid.

Fashioning of an Irish imperial identity in India 87

charity'. The Company's Irish soldiers were, in his opinion, 'the hope of Catholicity in India'.[77]

On another level, class structure among the Company's largely Protestant officer corps played an equally important role as religion in terms of how Irish people defined themselves in an imperial setting. For representatives of the upper and middle classes – who shared the dominant social status as well as economic and political power in nineteenth-century Ireland – class was as important as religion or nationality. Kendal Coghill, son of Protestant landowner from Castletownshend, Co. Cork, attached to the Company's 2nd Bengal Fusiliers, for example, recorded that his station in Agra 'was divided into two classes the upper and the lower current'. In the upper current were those 'who give the crack parties, ride well...and have cliques and admirers...in the lower were those sorts of people met in every station who nobody knows or cares anything about hardly admissible in society'.[78] Even though religion and class structure were important elements in defining various imperial identities among the Irish in India, they were not necessarily competing or incompatible with one another. Owing, in part, to Ireland's strong tradition and history of overseas military service, the Company's Irish recruits had a keen awareness of a distinct military virtue that acted as a unifying factor among the various classes and religions of Irish men and women in India.[79]

In many instances, awareness of an Irish military virtue in India was heightened by the existence of close personal or geographical ties between the Company's officers and their men. Irish provincial towns were small enough for many soldiers to find common ground and in India they tended to form close networks with other men and women from their particular locality or parishes in Ireland. While convalescing in the cantonment town of Landour near Dehradun, Christopher McLoughlin, a former cook from Dublin, employed as a Gunner in one of the Company's European regiments, recalled to his parents in Ireland of striking up a friendship with a man named Ryan: 'a son of Ryan the corn merchant in Stephen's Green...a brother of the House agents that you are acquainted with.'[80] Local news and village gossip circulated among these Irish 'townies' in India where information

---

[77] Ibid.
[78] Lt Kendal Coghill to his brother 'Jos', d. Agra, 6 February 1852, Letters of Lt Kendal Coghill in India (1850–1861), Ms.7112–39–1, National Army Museum, London (hereafter, NAM).
[79] K. Jeffery, 'The Irish Military Tradition and the British Empire', in Jeffery (ed.), 'An Irish Empire'?, pp. 94–122.
[80] Gunner Christopher McLoughlin to his parents, 12 May 1845, in Letters of Sergeant Major William Henry Braithwaite, Ms.7605–75, NAM.

88   Ireland and the sinews of colonial power

spread among their units and filtered down to their friends, tightening bonds of loyalty and friendship between Irishmen of different religions and social origins. Writing to his brother in Cork asking him to inform a neighbouring tenant that her son, Private Dan O'Driscoll, a Catholic labourer from Bearlands who was serving in the 2nd European Bengal Fusiliers, had died during a field operation, Kendal Coghill described how O'Driscoll, 'a plucky young lad', had 'devoted himself to my cause' and had joked how they were both 'townies from Skibbereen'. As opposed to being removed from – or even indifferent to – the welfare of his Catholic Irish counterparts in India, Coghill took an active interest in them. He recorded how his time had been 'chiefly employed in writing dolorous letters reporting to kind parents [in Ireland] the death of their sons' in India. Cahill's reports home on the welfare of Irish troops in the employ of the East India Company were so frequent during the Indian mutiny that he acknowledged that nearly 'every woman in Ireland writes...to know if her son is alive'.[81] Cahill's claims support the idea of the existence of an Irish military virtue that worked to bring the various religions of Ireland closer together in an imperial setting. If the prevalence of a distinct Irish military virtue could work to unify the various religions of Irishmen in India, it could equally serve to break down the various class distinctions. O'Moore Creagh, for instance, son of a Catholic landowner from Co. Clare, spoke of his Irish 'batman' or 'soldier-servant' in India as 'a typical Irishman, a smart soldier...both intelligent and faithful...who came from my own country, knew my family, took the utmost interest in me, and looked upon himself as personally responsible for my welfare. He always spoke of my belongings as "ours" and alluded to my requirements as what "we" wanted'.[82] Creagh reconciled his Catholicism and Gaelic-Irish roots with a career as the Commander-in-Chief in India during the early twentieth century.[83]

Moreover, the example of Creagh as a Catholic Irish officer commissioned in the British army in India was not an isolated phenomenon. His father, a Captain in the Royal Navy, had seven sons, all of whom were attached to 'the services...of the Empire' and who were, according to Creagh, 'typical of those of most of our class in the south and west of Ireland'.[84] Such issues themselves raise pertinent questions regarding

[81] Coghill to his brother 'Jos', 14 March 1858, Ms.7112–38–39, NAM.
[82] G. O'Moore Creagh, *The Autobiography of General Sir O'Moore Creagh, V.C., G.C.B., G.C.S.I.* (London: Hutchinson & Co., 1923), p. 34.
[83] In his autobiography, Creagh recalls no fewer than five members of the Creagh family who were among the prisoners held by Coote and the British forces at Pondicherry in 1760. See ibid., p. 3.
[84] General Creagh had two brothers in the Royal Navy, one in the Punjab Police, one in the Royal Indian Marine and two in the Indian Army. See ibid., p. 4.

Fashioning of an Irish imperial identity in India

the nature of these officials' commitment to Irish identity during this period. Although Irish officers and proconsuls in India were almost entirely drawn from the Anglo-Irish Protestant landowning class, their 'Irishness' was perhaps more culturally prominent (though rarely Gaelic) than is ordinarily perceived. Although much has been made of the unconvincing 'Irishness' of the more celebrated Irish officers in the British army in India such as Arthur Wellesley, to a significant degree both sons of the Irish Catholic gentry and the Anglo-Irish officer class in India during the later nineteenth century could espouse sentiments of 'Irishness', 'Britishness' and even 'Englishness' simultaneously.[85] Born in Ireland to Irish parents, these men carried with them a diverse range of cultural national baggage that encompassed anglicised educations, an innate sense of attachment to English and Irish cultural norms as well as an inherent belief among them that the Empire they were serving was as much Irish as it was British.

Although most of the Irish officers in the East India Company and regular British army in India were Anglo-Irish Protestants and, no doubt, held broadly Unionist political views, there were some notable exceptions. O'Moore Creagh, for example, spoke fondly of his Irish upbringing and took pride in his Gaelic roots while simultaneously occupying the position of Commander-in-Chief of Britain's imperial armed forces in India. As a child growing up on an Irish estate in Co. Clare he recalled the influential story-telling of the *seanachie* (Irish story-tellers), and how 'We ran wild among the peasantry, camping out in the bogs and woods, snaring birds, catching fish and poaching. Our peasant companions filled our heads with legends and stories of the ancient glories of our race, which we firmly believed and so became filled with racial pride'.[86] Equally, though, an Irish background could prove to be a source of rancour and embarrassment for some officers serving in the Company's ranks in India. Apparently it was not just Protestant Ascendancy figures such as Arthur Wellesley who attempted to disavow their Irish roots. As late as the 1860s, Thomas Dennehy, a Catholic, and son of a small landowner from Fermoy, Co. Cork who was serving as Captain of a police military unit at Allahabad, recorded in a letter home to his mother his own personal disdain for everything Irish. Contemplating on returning to Europe on furlough, Dennehy informed his mother:

Ireland is alright as an alternative and as that misty and greenish country had the honour of giving us birth we shall, I suppose, have to visit it briefly; but

[85] See P. Jupp, *The First Duke of Wellington in an Irish Context* (University of Southampton, 1998), p. 4.
[86] O'Moore Creagh, *Autobiography*, p. 9.

90   Ireland and the sinews of colonial power

to live there and subsist on turf smoke, whiskey and potatoes and other native produce, as a form of entertainment on my return from the tropics, no, thank you: I would sooner die now without enduring seasickness, only to travel to that wild and distant country, where the land is all bog and where the potatoes grow in your boots unless you clean them thoroughly twice a day and once at night.[87]

For the wealthy class of Irish men and women, India was a stop-gap measure to a career elsewhere in the Empire. They were what Alan Lester has termed imperial 'careerists' concerned with securing better pay, promotion, working environment and their place in society. As such, an Irish background could be a hindrance, owing to the ambiguity surrounding *Irishness* for an aspiring middle class, for whom Union obfuscated the issue further, leaving them neither central nor peripheral, riddled with financial anxiety and desperate to establish security and respectability in imperial society.

For those from relatively poor or humble origins, the obvious economic imperative of imperial service made issues such as identity and belonging more straightforward. Despite enduring commitment and ties to their religion, most Irish Catholic recruits in the employ of the East India Company seemed to strongly identify with British rule. If anything, identification with the Empire among the poorer classes served to expiate feelings of inferiority associated with modest backgrounds, and many of the Company's Irish Catholic recruits felt pride in the imperial connection. Although lacking awareness of the ideological imperatives behind their presence in India, most Irish recruits acknowledged that the Empire provided them with a unique opportunity to better themselves and the lives of their families. Following the First Anglo-Sikh War, Corporal John Downie told his parents that 'it was a great honour' to receive a medal and to earn the status of an 'old soldier' in the Company's European army.[88] Gunner William Braithwaite (later a Serjeant with the 2/2nd Bengal Horse Artillery), a former carter from Dublin, recorded how his experiences serving in the Company's regiments in India had transformed his life. Writing from his cantonment in Mhow, near Indore, Braithwaite documented how he began to learn to play the flute, sang in the Mhow chapel choir and read almost every day. His experience in the Company's army had changed him from a wild, indisciplined youth into a 'steady' young man. These

[87] 'A Memoir on the Life of Captain Thomas Dennehy' (facsimile of private papers in the personal possession of Professor C. A. Bayly, St Catherine's College, University of Cambridge), f. 3.

[88] B. P. Hughes (ed.), *From Recruit to Staff Serjeant by N. W. Bancroft* [1885] (Hornchurch: Ian Henry Publications, 1979), p. 91.

Fashioning of an Irish imperial identity in India 91

experiences suggest that for many of the Company's Catholic recruits, nineteenth-century Irish identity was to be found as much in the imperial as it was in the national.

Although the Irish from poorer backgrounds to some extent did share a genuine enthusiasm for the Empire – indeed, many believing that Ireland occupied a central role within it – confusion about national roots and imperial loyalties did at times create a degree of conflict among the Irish. Depending on the circumstances of the day, a latent conflict of loyalties among the Irish from humble origins was ever present in the Empire. Many soldiers articulated feelings of exile while in India, often alluding to the bonds of imperial servitude. These feelings were partly brought about as a result of the manner in which Irish recruitment into the Company's army was conducted (especially during periods of cyclical decline in the Irish economy) but also partly because of the lack of feasible alternatives. Gunner John Neary, a labourer from Co. Sligo, recalled how he was 'willing to soldier' only because he had 'no other prospects in life'.[89] Despite the persuasive stories and tales regaled by recruiting sergeants of an exotic and splendorous life that was waiting for recruits in India, the reality was that military life was notoriously difficult. Disease, alcoholism, self-mutilation, crime and suicide were rife in the Company's army, shattering the popular recruiting sergeants' myth that India was a kind of utopia, harbouring relief for nineteenth-century Ireland's poor. As it continued its expansionist policies on the subcontinent during the early nineteenth century, the Company was in almost constant need of mechanically adept manpower, and as a result recruitment was often carried out blindly and attracted a considerable proportion of Irish people who were simply down on their luck. In many instances their education was perfunctory and their ambition essentially personal or familial. The needs of the Empire or an awareness of an imperial mission were secondary, if considered at all. Recalling his attestation in Liverpool in 1829, William Braithwaite told his mother – his 'confessor' – how upon his arrival in India he had 'got among a set of fellows that thought of nothing but drinking...we used to go out on the beach at night [and] take pipes and tobacco and lots of grog...We were...two months before I thought of the life I was leading [in India] getting drunk lying on the damp ground'.[90] Private William Edwards was so dismayed by life in a military barracks in India that he once recalled how 'soldiering and me fell out...the first day I landed in this

[89] *Parliamentary Papers*, Vol. LI (1860), p. 218.
[90] Sgt William Braithwaite to his mother, 29 May 1831, Letters of Sgt Major William Braithwaite, Ms.7605–75. NAM.

92 Ireland and the sinews of colonial power

country'.[91] Another Irishman, Liam Sullivan, claimed that he 'wouldn't be a soldier in this country if I got my weight in gold'.[92]

It was not uncommon for the Company to enlist those who had been rejected from the regular British Army, for example, and many ordinary rank and file Irish were either compelled to join the Company by the authorities or were fleeing the law at home, frequently enlisting under assumed names in the process. Once in India, many men lost contact with their families and friends in Ireland, appearing to vanish in the process. Soldiers' references contain numerous appeals by family members looking for information on their sons' whereabouts. One enquiry from Limerick wanted 'to know' simply if their son was 'dead or alive'.[93] While the Connaught Rangers were notorious for their poor disciplinary record,[94] Order Books of the Portuguese Militia of Bombay dating from 1801 contain multiple accounts of the transactions and proceedings of regimental courts martial involving cases of theft, drunkenness and other 'unsoldierlike' behaviour among Irish recruits stationed in British cantonments.[95] In 1807, twenty men, known to the law as 'thrashers' – a violent agrarian group from counties Mayo and Sligo – chose to enlist in the army rather than receive punishment under the Insurrection Act.[96] Moreover, during the 1830s an estimated two-thirds of all courts martial concerned Irish regiments.[97] To some the Company merely offered an escape route that presented them with an opportunity to better themselves and the lives of their families.

There was much concern voiced over the social backgrounds and political persuasion of Irish recruits who were enlisted into the new European regiments or 'dumpies' during the rebellion in 1858.[98] Apparently the Company Directors' anxiety to expand its European forces during the

---

[91] Testimony of Pte W. Edwards, 2nd BELC, Meerut inquiry, *Parliamentary Papers*, Vol. LI (1860), p. 339.

[92] Ibid, p. 343.

[93] 'Form of inquiry after a soldier', completed in 1860 by the mother of John Young, a Limerick labourer enlisted in 1849. Soldiers' References, Part 2, L/MIL/5/362. OIOC.

[94] H. F. N. Jourdain, *Ranging Memories, by Lieut-Col. H. F. N. Jourdain* (Oxford University Press, 1934).

[95] Ms Order Books of the Portuguese Militia of Bombay. Transcripts of the proceedings of several regimental Courts Martial including the 86th and 88th Regiments of Foot. Ms.8410–144–1/2. NAM.

[96] E. Spiers, 'Army Organisation and Society in the Nineteenth Century', in T. Bartlett and K. Jeffery (eds.), *A Military History of Ireland* (Cambridge University Press, 1996), p. 339.

[97] Sir Hussey Vivian to Sir John MacDonald, 19 October 1834. Ms.7709–6–12, f. 249. NAM.

[98] See Private Patrick Young, 2nd Bombay European Light Infantry, to his family, 31 May 1859, Soldiers' References, Part II, L/MIL/5/362. OIOC.

Fashioning of an Irish imperial identity in India   93

Indian Mutiny resulted in 'almost indiscriminate recruiting' for India. Private Patrick Carroll, a millmaker from Co. Cavan who enlisted for the 2nd Bengal European Light Cavalry in November 1857, described his attestation at Dundee as being chaotic: 'there was about 15 of us in together, and some were smoking and some were cursing and swearing dreadful, and I couldn't hear what was said, and the magistrate was writing away at the table, minding his own business, and I wasn't very sober myself.'[99] Lieutenant Colonel William Butler, an Irish officer serving in southern India in the 1880s, publicly deplored 'the disappearance of the peasant soldier' from Irish regiments and their replacement with what he termed the urban 'riff-raff...of Cork and Dublin'. According to Butler, 'the decent men who want to better their condition do not now think of entering the Army, as was the case before the famine of 1846 and 47–48. This class now emigrates en masse to England, the United States, and the British Colonies in search of work and high wages'.[100] Indeed, for many, soldiering in India was a temporary measure to a better life further east in the colonies of settlement in Australia or New Zealand.[101]

Even though, generally, the Company offered better pay, rations, conditions of service and prospects of promotion, many of the Company's Irish soldiers' accounts of life in India belied the old regular army jibe that the East India Company's initials of 'EIC' were really an abbreviation for 'East India Convicts'. Frequent references to their condition as 'servants' or sardonic remarks made about their 'sentence' in India alluded to the idea that, for many, time spent in India was a nineteenth-century equivalent to a period of indentured servitude in the Caribbean – reconstituted as cheap white labour in the East. Gunner John Hogan, a shoemaker from Clonmel, Tipperary, observed how he had 'sold...[his] body to the Company' when he had taken the oath of allegiance and fidelity to 'serve them', but was certain that 'when there is no Company my body is free'.[102] When the Company's army merged with the regular British army in the aftermath of the Indian Mutiny some compared themselves to 'slaves', complaining that they had been treated like 'Indian stock', 'a herd of camels' or 'a dog or a goat sold in the bazaars' instead of 'free-born' citizens of the Empire.[103]

---

[99] Testimony of Private Patrick Carroll, Meerut Inquiry, *Parliamentary Papers*, Vol. LI (1860), p. 357.
[100] Spiers, 'Army Organisation', p. 340.
[101] Pte James Armstrong, 2nd European Bengal Fusiliers, to his parents, 5 July 1859, Soldiers' References, Part 3, L/MIL/5/362. OIOC.
[102] *Parliamentary Papers*, Vol. LI (1860), p. 206.
[103] Pte Edward Martin, 3rd BER, to the 'Brigadier Commanding', Morar, 12 May 1859, in ibid., pp. 55, 76, 301, 613.

94 Ireland and the sinews of colonial power

Localised networks and patterns of exchange

As to be expected, the networks borne out of Irish military service in India were largely male-oriented. While it was common for many Irish women and children to accompany their spouses to India, barrack life by nature was very much a male-dominated environment. Moreover, the networks created by Irish soldiers in India – and particularly among the Company's Roman Catholics – tended to be based upon ethnic as well as religious affiliation, long before separate Irish regiments came into existence with the amalgamation of the Company's troops with the regular British army in 1859. Within these networks Irish soldiers and their families exchanged an array of information, goods and ideas for a variety of professional or social purposes. Irish imperial networks at the level of rank-and-file military personnel were tightly formed and were by and large sustained over long periods of time. Upon arrival in India, men were assigned a particular unit that they served until either they earned discharge or, more likely, were killed in action. Though part of a larger community consisting of a regiment, each infantry unit was further divided into smaller groups of sub-units or companies containing about 100 men. Gunners, like infantrymen, also lived their lives in India within quite small, compact social units, usually attached to either the Company's horse artillery troop or foot artillery company, where they worked, messed and slept among each other for long periods of time. Their existence and lives were meticulously organised and structured. Each soldier belonged to certain aggregations consisting of rear and front rank pairs who drilled and fought together in battle and who were bound together by ties of camaraderie, duty and obligation.

These specific networks of loyalty, obligation, duty and camaraderie – sometimes, though not always, based upon ethnic or religious affiliation – bound the entire British military structure together. In the context of Irish soldiers, personnel networks were sometimes formed through close personal ties to – or an association with – a particular town or county in Ireland. Corporal Patrick Byrne, a former labourer from Clonmel, Tipperary, was one of ten Irishmen from Clonmel who enlisted in the 1st and 3rd European Bengal Fusiliers in the same year and who took discharge together after the amalgamation of the British army in 1859. Byrne recalled at the time how he had '[met] with a great deal of the Clonmel men of the [Queen's] 89th Regt' in India and how he had received all the local gossip and news from home from 'a chap [of] the name of George Tailborth' who had worked in 'Grubles steam mill'. Through Tailborth, Byrne had heard 'a great deal of yarns about the town girl[s]' from home and how one local woman had asked him to

Localised networks and patterns of exchange 95

accompany her to Australia as soon as he had earned his discharge.[104] Indeed, marriage and domesticity were important social pursuits, conferring status and a degree of respectability for those eager to improve their standing in the army. Kendal Coghill found the women in the Company's army 'different out here...very respectable'.[105] William Braithwaite commented that he hoped to be promoted not 'for ambition...no, it is the wish to be comfortable and settled...the only happiness I can have in this country is by being married'.[106]

The wills and testaments of Irish soldiers name other Irish 'friends' or 'comrades' as beneficiaries. Groups of Irish soldiers agreed to leave their estates to each other, perhaps helping them buy their way out of service in India.[107] Upon death, Irish soldiers overwhelmingly tended to bequeath their property, pay and belongings to other Irish 'comrades' in their regiments and in some instances to those from the same locality in Ireland. These 'worldly belongings' in the majority of cases included all regimental necessaries: bedding, clothing, clothing money, pay, arrears of pay and 'life' savings. Furthermore, from the evidence of these soldiers' wills it seems that there was an acute, almost familial sense among Irish soldiers for the welfare of one another as well as for family members in Ireland. Numerous Irish soldiers' wills contain requests for money to be sent back to Ireland usually for the benefit of mothers and children, but also for local parish priests.[108] Other wills belonging to Irishmen demonstrate a remarkable sensibility towards the welfare of children of deceased comrades. It was not uncommon for Irish soldiers in Bombay in the 1840s, at least, to request that some of their savings should be put into trustee bonds for orphaned Irish or Eurasian children until they reached the legal age at which to claim it. William Corkery of the 1st Battalion of Artillery stationed in Bombay in 1839, for example, bequeathed a sum of money to Margaret Callaghan, daughter of the late Gunner Dennis Callaghan, to go into a savings bank in Bombay until she reached the legal age of sixteen.[109] These ties

[104] Anon. to Byrne, 29 May 1859, Military Consultations, 17 June 1859, No. 585. OIOC, BL.
[105] Kendal Coghill to his brother 'Jos', 19 April 1856. NAM.
[106] William Braithwaite to his mother, 7 March 1837. NAM.
[107] The first 29 volumes of Soldiers' Wills in the Oriental and India Office Collection in the British Library relate to European and other ranks of the East India Company/ Indian Army only and are mostly confined to cases where an ordinary soldier left only his immediate personal effects. Many were written on the point of death, although some do involve larger estates. See Soldiers' Wills, L/AG/34/30. OIOC, BL.
[108] Soldiers' Wills (Bombay), Vol. 1, 1825–42 (mainly 1839–42), L/AG/34/35/23. OIOC, BL.
[109] L/AG/34/35/23, f. 59.OIOC, BL.

96   Ireland and the sinews of colonial power

testify to patterns of obligation binding Irish military networks, also paralleling and replicating an informal system of oaths that was seen as an integral component of Irish culture and society, as it served to unite those engaged in agrarian protest or later in trade unionism in the nineteenth century.[110] Indeed, analysis of remittances, wills and oaths foregrounds an important dimension of the migrant soldier's experience, for these financial flows, connecting imperial service to personal ties of family and country, highlight the migrant's attachment to – and continuing impact upon – the structures of society left behind.

Soldiering networks, in large measure, consisted of men whose primary interest in India was in securing the primacy of their customary rights and economic welfare. This is reflected by the decision of many not to take discharge from the Company at the time of amalgamation between the Company and the British armies. For many, the knowledge of huge unemployment in post-Famine Ireland reinforced their allegiance to the British army; others with Eurasian or Indian wives perhaps may have felt they could not return, aware of the racial sensitivity of contemporary Ireland. Indeed many Irish soldiers married Indian women, had mixed-race families and stayed on to work in the Indian Public Works Department long after they were discharged.[111] Conscious of the periods of subsistence crises or of the long periods of unemployment at home that had prompted them to enlist in the Company's army in the first instance, it appeared Irishmen were less sure of their futures as civilians. Certainly the varying realities of poverty and opportunity in Ireland during this period played a significant role in intensifying the Irishness of Britain's imperial army in India after 1861. Even after the discharged men's departure, nearly half of those remaining in the Bengal Artillery, for example, were of Irish origin.[112]

Nevertheless, the abolition of the East India Company in the wake of the Indian Mutiny in 1858 was to have a significant impact upon the type of Irish recruits entering the British regiments in India during the period 1860–1900. The most central theme during these years was the diminishing proportion of Irish recruits within the ranks. In part, this reflected the decline of all Irish-born, male and female, as a proportion of the British population in India. In 1871, some 16,000 Irish-born (21 per cent) were recorded in the Indian census but by 1911 this

---

[110] M. Beames, *Peasants and Power: The Whiteboy Movements and Their Control in Pre-Famine Ireland* (Brighton: Harvester, 1983), p. 6.
[111] See C. J. Hawes, *Poor Relations: The Making of a Eurasian Community in British India, 1773–1833* (Richmond: Curzon, 1996).
[112] Bengal Artillery MRCR, 1859, L/MIL/10/182. OIOC.

Conclusion 97

number had dropped to around 12,000, or just 10 per cent of the total 'Anglo-Indian' population on the subcontinent. Such figures largely correlate with contemporary regional population estimates. According to the *Report on the Census of Bengal* compiled by H. S. Beverley in 1872, there were 12,317 'Anglo-Indians' recorded as living in Calcutta. From this number, 8,127 were returned as being English-born, 1,857 were Scottish while 2,333 returned themselves as Irish.[113] By 1901, this number had decreased significantly and the number of Irish-born accounted for only 1,648 out of a total number of 11,450 British subjects resident in Calcutta.[114] Moreover, the general decline in the number of Irish recruits entering the British army in the post-Mutiny era can also be attributed in large part to increased mortality rates and migration. The precipitous fall in the Irish population in the later nineteenth century, set in train by Famine mortality and sustained by massive outflows of migrants, reflected the decline in Irish recruitment to the British army, and thence the Irish military presence in India. As the post-Famine Irish population waned and increasing numbers of young men emigrated, the rural basis of recruiting Irishmen for military service in India sharply declined. Indeed it has been suggested that, by 1900, even the Connaught Rangers began to recruit its men not so much from the south and west of Ireland, but more so from the north-eastern counties and particularly from Belfast.[115]

Conclusion

The movement of Irish soldiers to India to facilitate the consolidation of the Second British Empire was critical to the strengthening of the sinews of colonial power. Ireland served as a crucial recruiting ground for the East India Company army, with many young recruits seeking personal and social gain through participation in the imperial project away from the economic straits and deprivations of famine-stricken

---

[113] H. S. Beverley, *Report on the Census of Bengal, 1872* (Calcutta, 1872), pp. 136, 163, 179.

[114] *Report on the Census of India, 1901* (Calcutta, 1901), p. 47. Out of a total number of 45,800 soldiers in the British army during the period 1871–2, some 24.5 per cent were of Irish origin. However, between 1901 and 1902 this number fell to just 28,352, 13 per cent of whom were Irish. Unfortunately, only the total number of British soldiers stationed in India was calculated at this time and separate figures for Irish soldiers serving were not kept. But if one assumes a similar percentage for the Irish serving in British regiments in India during these decades, then the figures show about 16,000 Irish-born soldiers out of a total British garrison of 65,000 in 1870, declining to just over 7,000 out of 77,000 in 1911. See Spiers, 'Army Organisation', p. 337.

[115] See S. Gwynn, 'Irish Soldiers and Irish Brigades', *Cornhill Magazine*, n.s., 53 (1922), 737–49.

Ireland. While many within the British and Irish parliaments opposed the notion of a standing army of Catholic soldiers in India, the counter-argument that imperial military service in India would have the potential to countermand any threat posed by Irish Catholicism gained strength in the context of the expansion of the East India Company's authority over the military and financial administration of the Indian subcontinent. As Irish soldiers travelled to India as imperial servants, they formed networks that were simultaneously voluntary and involuntary, as men compelled by notions of military virtue and expectations of financial gain and social amelioration or simply as men driven by the acute awareness of diminished opportunities and the recognition of obligations to families and parishes at home. While to a certain degree, the bodies of Irish soldiers may be conceived of as commodities, functioning in exchange for remittances home, they also became the pivots of networks spanning out from provincial Irish towns and transposed to Indian barracks and garrisons. The translation of these networks from Ireland to India had the potential to elide religious and class divisions when, as was often the case, a regional identity was shared by subordinate and sergeant alike. However, the increasing desire and demand for the expression of religio-cultural identity in the context of an evangelising empire is one key way in which a study of Irish soldiering networks uncovers the fractures at the heart of the imperial project. These 'subaltern Irish', much like Ireland, were clearly both at the hub yet posed a critical anomaly for the enterprise of empire.

4 From trade to dominion

Introduction

Following the conquest of Bengal and the assumption of the land-revenue management from the Mughal Emperor, Shah Alam, in 1765, the East India Company's position as a trading organisation (albeit an increasingly militarised one) was fundamentally transformed. Hereafter, the Company began to recognise its shifting position as a South Asian territorial power. For the most part, political control in late-eighteenth-century India rested upon the Company's ability to establish a comprehensive network of surveillance and control over the Indian countryside that was based on reports from well-informed Company residents and news-writers based at Indian courts, and intelligence units and spies attached to the Company's army. Complementing this information network was the work of Company-appointed surveyors, botanists, zoologists and geologists whose task it was to amass a dense archive of geographical and scientific data in an attempt to provide the nascent colonial power with sufficient knowledge about the new lands they had conquered. Only through their efforts could the Company truly grasp the complexity of the Indian interior, and hence exert control over its manufactures, population, land and agriculture.

Central to achieving this aim was the role of nineteenth-century Irish scientific institutions and personnel in the process of colonial information-gathering, particularly in relation to surveying and geological exploration in India. Irish people, of both Catholic and Protestant backgrounds, played a critical role in transferring and adapting systems of knowledge and practice from Ireland's 'laboratory' of colonial science to India. From the mid eighteenth century, scientific endeavour in Ireland had been closely bound up with the Irish Ascendancy and landed interest and was directly linked to contemporary British utilitarian ideas of good governance, national security and colonial expansion. In a reflection of the colonial relationship that existed between Irish Protestants and Catholics (under penal law Irish Catholics were barred

99

100   From trade to dominion

from holding commissions in the government and army or owning land), many Irish scientific institutions were designed with a view to enhancing the power of landowners by facilitating the augmentation of tax revenues and the exploitation of Ireland's natural resources. This was a process that involved a high level of collaboration between the military and various different strands of Irish society, albeit in very unequal ways. By the mid nineteenth century, Ireland was arguably the first (and perhaps oldest) of Britain's 'colonies' to have been subjected to a thoroughly comprehensive scientific examination; its towns, villages, hills and mountains had all been surveyed and mapped, its minerals and natural resources identified and put to use in the name of industry and 'improvement'. At the same time, through mass imperial migration, Ireland and Irish people (both Catholic and Protestant) were at the forefront of exporting these systems of scientific knowledge and practice to India where they were adopted and used, albeit in highly modified forms.

Through a scientific network of mutual exchange and influence, one particular constituent of the Empire (Ireland) came to exert a distinctive and unique degree of influence on the intellectual development and growth of another (India). As a growing sub-imperial centre of the Empire in the late eighteenth and early nineteenth centuries, many Irish centres of learning, including Belfast, Cork and Dublin, by-passed important British 'metropolitan' centres in the direct supply of expertise and personnel to British India. Through involvement and deployment of expertise in areas such as mapping and geology in India, Irishmen and Irish institutions (especially universities and learned societies) played a more prominent role in the production of 'colonial knowledge' than previously assumed.

During the 1820s and 1830s the Ordnance Survey of Ireland (OSI) exerted a significant degree of influence upon the organisation and technical structure of the Great Trigonometrical Survey of India (GTS). Established in 1817, the GTS and its associated survey reports and district gazetteers offered colonial administrators a unique insight into the topography, socio-economic structure, historical development and customs of local Indian societies and cultures. While the East India Company borrowed from Irish precedents in its attempts to map India, the transition from amateur to professional status and official support in colonial science on the subcontinent was further aided by a large number of Irish university graduates who competed intensely for places in the various imperial structures of the Crown Raj in the second half of the nineteenth century. The formation and impact of key Irish networks in the context of colonial science in India was particularly visible in the case of Thomas Oldham and his work on the Geological Survey of India (GSI). As superintendent of the GSI for over twenty-five years, Oldham was responsible for cultivating a scientific network based on ethnic affiliation. In contrast to military and civil networks that were largely based on vocation and experience, bonds between members of Irish scientific networks were relatively loose. Within these networks specimens, samples, theories, ideas and agendas (scientific and other) were transmitted across the Empire from Calcutta to London, but also between the colonies themselves. Devoid of cultural dependence upon the metropole, Irish scientific networks promoted the education of Indians and were prominent in forging alliances with other networks eager to promote the autonomy of science in the colonies.

In order to draw attention to some of the nuanced ways in which the different regions of the British and Hibernian Isles contributed to the experience of empire, this chapter focuses on the relationship between Ireland, empire and colonial science during the nineteenth century. By focusing upon Thomas Oldham and his network of Irish geologists who were recruited by the British government to carry out exploration and research on the GSI between 1851 and 1878, the chapter examines the varying degrees of direct Irish involvement that played a significant part in the emerging role of scientific and technological agencies in colonial state-formation and in defining the expanding roles and responsibilities of the modern British state in its Indian environment. Through an examination of Irish involvement in the pursuit of science in nineteenth-century India, the chapter attempts to centre Ireland within the imperial web of connections and global exchange of knowledge that played an important role in the making of modern science. By examining Ireland's engagement with the colonial information order in the geographical construction of British rule in India, particularly in relation to surveying and geological exploration, the chapter views Ireland as an important sub-imperial centre that provided the Empire with a vital repository of manpower, knowledge and skill to draw upon during British attempts to establish primacy in South Asia during the first half of the nineteenth century.

Ireland and the shaping of imperial science

In recent times, both the historiography of the history of science and the history of ideas have lent credence to the idea of the ever-protean and shifting nature of scientific thought and ideological production. The processes of marking boundaries and drawing maps, formulating new methods of legitimising colonial rule and creating histories of

102   From trade to dominion

possession were all constantly shaped and informed by the different geographical locations and cultural encounters involved in the imperial process. Moreover, as G. B. Magee and A. S. Thompson point out in their study of empire and globalisation, it is of primary importance to recognise the contexts in which types of knowledge are produced and the means by which they circulate if we are to understand the cultural dimensions of economic activity such as that generated by the mapping and shaping of colonial space.[1] Correspondingly, David Arnold has placed great emphasis on the multi-centred origins and mobile nature of science during the 'long' nineteenth century, arguing that the history of science in India is not simply a story of 'European discovery' and dissemination, but rather one that recognises how science 'manifests itself across time and cultures in myriad forms, reflecting as much as informing a given society's cultural, economic and political modalities'.[2] Kapil Raj has equally contested the idea of the simple transfer of 'Western' ideas and practices onto receptive and passive colonial societies. In his account of the construction and spread of scientific knowledge in the context of colonial South Asia, Raj has emphasised the reciprocal nature of the processes of circulation and negotiation between coloniser and colonised. Far from being a site where information was uniformly gathered before being transferred and processed in the metropole, South Asia was itself 'an active, though unequal, participant in the emerging world order of knowledge'.[3] Crucially, it was through the 'intercultural encounter' between European and South Asian intellectual and material practices in the 'contact zone' that 'certified knowledges' came into being. Although the unequal power relations engendered by the colonial state in India ensured that these bodies of knowledge followed different paths and trajectories and were appropriated and integrated differently in European and South Asian contexts, they were, nonetheless, born out of the same processes of circulation and exchange. Moreover, that 'place' matters and that geography has a bearing on science has been the subject of extensive treatment in a recent study by David N. Livingstone.[4] Livingstone has argued that the 'where' of scientific activity – 'the sites where experiments are conducted, the places where knowledge is generated, the localities where experiments

---

[1] Magee and Thompson, *Empire and Globalisation*, pp. 1–22.

[2] D. Arnold, *Science, Technology and Medicine in Colonial India*, vol. 3.5 of *The New Cambridge History of India* (Cambridge University Press, 2000), p. 1.

[3] K. Raj, *Relocating Modern Science: Circulation and Construction of Knowledge in South Asia and Europe, 1650–1900* (Basingstoke: Palgrave Macmillan, 2007), p. 13.

[4] D. N. Livingstone, *Putting Science in Its Place: Geographies of Scientific Knowledge* (University of Chicago Press, 2003).

Ireland and the shaping of imperial science

are carried out' – is central to any understanding of how certain sets of ideas, information and practices have impacted upon the world on a global scale. In this regard, scientific activity does not disperse evenly from one space to another. Just as images and ideas are invariably modified as they pass from person to person, from community to community, from culture to culture – subject to different interpretation and meaning within each given context – so scientific activity is persistently shaped and reshaped through its encounters in multiple locations.[5]

Although the historiography of the history of science in South Asia continues to embrace these wider trends in imperial and global history, it has focused almost exclusively to date on Anglo-Indian interactions, thus obscuring an understanding of the substantial involvement of Ireland, Scotland and Wales in this process. Throughout the late eighteenth and nineteenth centuries a wide variety of university graduates from Ireland, England, Scotland and Wales made their way to India via employment with the East India Company. There, as administrators and military men, they honed their skills as 'gentlemanly scholars', frequently amassing private herbariums, housing geological specimens or collecting artefacts of antiquarian value in order to raise their profile and enhance their reputation upon their return home. Later, as doctors, surveyors, botanists and geologists of the Crown Raj, their encounters with their colleagues and indigenous counterparts enabled them to circulate, negotiate and reconfigure their skills in the 'contact zone'. In turn, their skills were absorbed into both the commercial and colonial institutions they represented, impacting not only upon 'metropolitan' science but also on the practice of science globally.

The current lack of literature on the Irish dimension to the twinned relations of science and empire (and the making of geographical knowledge) is surprising given that during the late eighteenth and early nineteenth centuries Irish scientific institutions and Irish people played an increasingly prominent role in Britain's attempts to expand the boundaries of its empire eastward. Following the American War of Independence and the subsequent loss of its thirteen North American colonies, Britain set about consolidating its authority and control on the domestic front, while at the same time looking towards Asia and the Pacific in search of new lands, markets and resources to expand its commercial and political influence overseas. During the late eighteenth century, ongoing hostilities with France encouraged the British to invest heavily in new forms of science in an attempt to gain an advantage over their principal imperial rivals. All of this took place against

[5] Ibid., pp. 4–5.

104   From trade to dominion

the backdrop of the Industrial Revolution in Britain where many innovations in scientific exploration were directly linked to the world-wide marine charting effort undertaken by the Royal Navy and later formalised under the Admiralty's Hydrographic Department.[6] These early coastal reconnaissance missions not only provided openings for many British naturalists such as Charles Darwin, Joseph Hooker and Thomas Huxley to establish their reputations abroad, but also were significant in so far as they represented the first coherent British attempt to codify a diverse body of scientific, strategic and commercial intelligence.[7] Around this time, instruments designed for methodical observation were perfected, map-making techniques harnessed and inquiries into a plethora of native languages, customs, population distribution, production and trade patterns initiated. More significantly still, these early hydrographic endeavours played an important role in the advent of scientific disciplines such as geology, botany and cartography, all of which were integral to British plans to establish colonial rule in India.

At the forefront of these attempts was the East India Company whose rule in India coincided with some of the most critical developments in the history of modern science, from the rise of Enlightenment natural history to the publication of Darwin's *Origin of Species* (1859).[8] As discussed in the previous chapter, Irish involvement in the East India Company began in earnest during the Seven Years War when large numbers of Irish soldiers and officers were recruited into the Company's European regiments.[9] Although early Company interest in the Irish rested on their ability to make up the numbers in the face of alarmingly high mortality rates among British troops in India, this attitude changed towards the end of the eighteenth century as Irish involvement gradually began to inform the recruitment of military personnel in the pursuit of science. This connection between the 'military orientalism' of the Company and Ireland was especially pronounced during the Company's attempts to map India, where from the mid 1820s to the late 1830s, aspects of the organisational and technical structure of the OSI were used to inform the GTS of India. During this period a range of East India Company agents and government officials looked to the example of Ireland in an

---

[6] A. Briggs, *The Age of Improvement, 1783–1867* (Harlow: Longman, 2000), pp. 17–30.

[7] G. S. Ritchie, *The Admiralty Chart: British Naval Hydrography in the Nineteenth Century* (London: Hollis & Carter, 1967).

[8] A. S. Cook, 'Establishing the Sea Routes to India and China: Stages in the Development of Hydrographical Knowledge', in Bowen *et al.* (eds.), *The Worlds of the East India Company*, pp. 119–37.

[9] See Chapter 3; see also T. Bartlett, '"A Weapon of War Yet Untried": Irish Catholics and the Armed Forces of the Crown, 1760–1830', in T. G. Fraser and K. Jeffery (eds.), *Men, Women and War* (Dublin: Lilliput Press, 1993), pp. 66–85.

Ireland and the shaping of imperial science 105

attempt to reinforce the epistemological rationale behind the GTS. In this context, Ireland was considered an important site where new technologies, methods of scientific practice and organisation were being developed and could be used in other parts of the Empire.

Of course, that Ireland was somehow a 'laboratory' for colonial scientific practice in nineteenth-century India is a moot point. The simple one-way transmission of ideas or practices from 'metropole' to 'periphery' has for a long time been open to criticism. This 'diffusionist' model – owed in large measure to George Basalla's much-debated article on 'The Spread of Western Science' (1967) – has been overthrown by recent scholarship in the history of science that has emphasised the mobile nature of scientific ideas during this period, thus debunking the notion of static laboratories and 'receptive' or passive societies.[10] Moreover, Matthew H. Edney's argument that the GTS was a 'flawed ideal' is important in that it draws attention to the ways in which both science and political control were socially mediated processes and that the 'transplantation' of ideas, while high on imperial ambition, was always fragile and incomplete in implementation. In his study of the surveys and maps that the British made in and of South Asia during the late eighteenth and early nineteenth centuries, Edney has argued that what the British achieved was not a 'real' map of India, but rather an image of India 'that they perceived and that they governed'. In failing to experience the many different aspects of India's societies and cultures beyond direct colonial rule, the British 'deluded themselves that their science enabled them to know the "real" India'. Moreover, the establishment of political control in India was never a simple unilateral process involving only the colonisers. Indians, themselves, persistently resisted and negotiated the terms in which the British defined their boundaries and established their hegemony. According to Edney, the surveys and geographical investigations of the GTS were little more than exercises of 'scientistic ideology' designed to create an image of a '*British* India' for the benefit of an expanding empire.[11] Notwithstanding, Irish personnel for the most part supplemented such attempts by the British to establish their authority in India and, as Edney has observed, scientific activity in Ireland (particularly work on the Irish Survey) at times represented 'the epitome of what they hoped to achieve in India'.[12] While not necessarily a 'laboratory' or 'testing-ground' for 'colonial science', Ireland was nevertheless an important reference point in the

[10] G. Basalla, 'The Spread of Western Science', *Science*, 156 (1967), 611–22.
[11] M. H. Edney, *Mapping an Empire: The Geographical Construction of British India, 1765–1843* (University of Chicago Press, 1999), pp. 2–3.
[12] Ibid., p. 35.

106   From trade to dominion

geographical construction of British rule in India, where the ideologies and mechanics of imperial rule were first implemented.

The Irish Ordnance Survey and the Great Trigonometrical Survey of India

In the early nineteenth century the Great Trigonometrical Survey was considered to be one of the greatest sources of scientific knowledge in the Empire, and at once reflected the East India Company's determination to establish the ideological imperatives behind British colonial rule in South Asia. The Indian surveys of the late eighteenth and early nineteenth centuries formed part of a grand utilitarian imperial scheme that sought to locate and extract India's revenues, improve strategic planning and quicken the movement of its armed forces across hazardous terrain.[13] Surveying was also linked to the process of determining accurate maps of the subcontinent. Producing detailed cartographic images was essential in order to locate the precise position of Indian ports as well as determine an accurate outline of India's vast coastal features. This, of course, was closely bound up with the idea of developing the Company's shipping networks in South Asia in an effort to make maritime trade more lucrative.[14]

As the Company slowly began to evolve from commercial enterprise to colonial state during the second half of the eighteenth century, British methods of mapping in India also experienced a gradual transformation. Movement from their initial trading posts on the coast into the Indian interior was soon reflected in the work of Company-appointed surveyors who became less concerned with compiling maritime charts and determining sea routes and more interested in the recording of inland passages, towns and villages. In the aftermath of the British conquest of Bengal and assumption of the land-revenue management in 1765, for example, the geographer James Rennell was commissioned by the Company to compile a series of topographical surveys designed to provide the nascent colonial power with decisive technical information about a hitherto relatively unknown Indian polity.[15] For the most part, these early Company surveys were based on the astronomical

---

[13] Bayly, *Empire and Information*, pp. 6–9, 307–9.
[14] S. Widmalm, 'Accuracy, Rhetoric and Technology: The Paris–Greenwich Triangulation, 1784–88', in T. Frängsmyr, J. L. Heilbron and R. E. Rider (eds.), *The Quantifying Spirit in the 18th Century* (Berkeley: University of California Press, 1990), pp. 201–3.
[15] J. Rennell, *Memoir of a Map of Hindoostan or the Moguls Empire* (London, 1788), pp. iv–xiv.

The OSI and the GTS

observation of lines of latitude and longitude. However, the techniques of Enlightenment mapping were notoriously unreliable and inaccurate, and towards the end of the eighteenth century Company officials began to look to Europe where they believed more effective procedures in mapping and surveying were being carried out. By far the most important development in imperial cartography during the late eighteenth century was the adoption of triangulation as a technical solution to the problem of obtaining more accurate and precise physical geographical knowledge of the Indian countryside. In contrast to maps constructed solely through astronomical observation, triangulation offered the British a newer, more sophisticated technology whereby geographical information could be made certain and comprehensive for the first time.[16]

Central to the introduction of the triangulation method of mapping in India was the work of Valentine Blacker.[17] The Irish-born son of Protestant landowners from Co. Armagh and a prominent military engineer, Blacker was part of a leading group of officials and surveyors who successfully petitioned the East India Company for triangulation to be extended across the whole of India during the 1820s. The very fact that Blacker made a notable contribution to the 'military orientalism' of the East India Company in its attempts to improve military strategy and knowledge is not all that surprising given that Irish life was already firmly rooted within the context of British imperialism and the global personnel networks fashioned by it by the turn of the century. Blacker had first come to India in 1798 after securing a commission in the Madras cavalry through his uncle, Major General Sir Barry Close, and had taken part in British campaigns against Tipu Sultan in Mysore in 1799.[18] Close was a relative of the Acting British Resident of Mysore at the time, Arthur Cole, whose prominent family connections and ties to Enniskillen in Co. Fermanagh had already earned him the patronage of the Governor-General of India, and fellow Irishman, Richard Wellesley. With the help of strong family connections and influential patrons, Blacker secured employment in the quartermaster-general's office at Fort St George in Madras, of which he became head in 1810. In Madras, Blacker was responsible for carrying out various military reconnaissance missions around south India, with the purpose of supplying military intelligence for the Company through compiling detailed

---

[16] Edney, *Mapping an Empire*, p. 19.
[17] Major L. C. M. Blacker, *A History of the Family of Blacker of Carrickblacker in Ireland* (Dublin: Hodges, Figgis & Co., 1901).
[18] G. S. Sardesai (ed.), *Poona Residency Correspondence, Vol. VII, Poona Affairs, 1801–1810* (Bombay, 1940), pp. i–xvi.

108   From trade to dominion

geographical and topographical accounts of the Indian countryside. He earned particular distinction for the scientific work he conducted with the Madras army during British operations in the Deccan in 1815 and soon gained commendation from Company officials in London.

Indeed, the Company's appointment of Blacker as Surveyor-General in India in 1823 was strategic. Although the British had undertaken several substantial surveys in India during the 1780s and 1790s, the GTS did not come into formal existence until 1817. Blacker's appointment as Surveyor-General coincided with the Company's campaign of territorial expansion on the subcontinent in the first quarter of the nineteenth century that sought to consolidate Britain's power base throughout southern India.[19] By the time of his appointment in the early 1820s, political developments on the subcontinent had necessitated that a single, coherent scientific institution be established in order to bring together and make sense of the existing body of geographical data that the Company had accumulated in its various military campaigns against successive Indian princely states and rulers. Moreover, by establishing the headquarters of the GTS in Calcutta under the control of one surveyor-general, the Company was able to keep the disparate activities of the three Presidencies in check and thus exert greater control over the flow of scientific knowledge from India.

This system of Western scientific organisation was first introduced under the governor-generalship of Sir Francis Rawdon-Hastings.[20] Upon taking office Hastings had convinced the Calcutta council that the establishment of the GTS was not only necessary in order to secure the Company's future economic ambitions, but that it was essential if a single cartographic image of India was ever to be constructed. In order to successfully carry this out, Hastings drew upon the vast experience of the personnel at his disposal. Blacker was seen as indispensable to Hastings' vision. By the early 1820s he had earned a considerable reputation among the Court of Directors as an accomplished military engineer and surveyor, whose proven competence in undertaking reconnaissance work and handling the newest surveying technologies was reflected in him being commissioned to write the official military history of the Third Anglo-Maratha War (1817–19).[21] Alongside the survey's superintendent, George Everest, Blacker played an important

---

[19] See Bayly, *Indian Society and the Making of the British Empire*, p. 80, and Bayly, *Imperial Meridian*, p. 106.
[20] Edney, *Mapping an Empire*, p. 199.
[21] V. Blacker, *Memoir of the Operations of the British Army in India during the Mahratta War of 1817, 1818 & 1819* (London: Black, Kingsbury, Parbury & Allen, 1821), p. xix.

The OSI and the GTS

role in taking the Indian surveys onto a new level and in converting the Company to the ideal of an all-India triangulation.[22]

The application of the technique of triangulation on Indian surveys in the 1820s was by no means a new phenomenon. A whole host of Company employees and officials since the 1810s, most notably the survey's previous superintendent, William Lambton, and the Court's military secretary, James Salmond, had advanced its alleged geometrical certainties. Both Lambton and Salmond had based their observations on the work of earlier Indian surveyors such as James Rennell and Colin Mackenzie and had been early advocates for the widespread use of triangulation-based surveys in the southern provinces of the Madras Presidency. As an infantry officer based in New Brunswick following the American War of Independence, Lambton had been involved in surveying the boundary between Canada and the United States. In 1796, he was posted to India where he first perfected the new techniques of geodesy in surveying the region following the Fourth Anglo-Mysore War. While Lambton was integral to the establishment of the GTS on a firm scientific footing in this period, Blacker was charged with the task of devising new ways in which to organise and expand the activities of the GTS. In particular, he was responsible for persuading the Court of Directors to give their full financial backing in support of an all-India triangulation.[23] He wanted the Company to ensure that the entire triangulation process was extended far beyond the coastal series in the east and west of the subcontinent, across the plains to the Himalayas in the north. In persuading the Court to extend the GTS across all of Company-ruled India, Blacker, Everest and Salmond used the example of the Ordinance Survey of Ireland (1824–46) as an important frame of reference for the proposed expansion of the GTS. They hoped to apply the techniques and institutional organisation of the Irish Survey to the Great Trigonometrical Survey of India.[24]

The origins of the Irish Ordnance Survey dated to the early years of the nineteenth century when Irish landowners began to lobby Westminster for the creation of a thoroughly modernised national

---

[22] A. J. Arbuthnot, 'Blacker, Valentine (1778–1823)', rev. James Lunt, *Oxford Dictionary of National Biography* (Oxford University Press, 2004).

[23] Valentine Blacker to William Casement, 11 August 1824, 23, British Military Consultations (hereafter BMC), 23 September 1824, 126, P/30/60. OIOC, BL; F/4/836 22401, 35–231, is a copy of Blacker's letter to the Court of Directors with all enclosures; the letter's text was printed as an appendix to Andrew Scott Waugh, 'Report and Statements on the Operations and Expense of the Great Trigonometrical Survey of India', *British Parliamentary Papers*, 1851 (219) 41:875–936, 899–902.

[24] Edney, *Mapping an Empire*, p. 28.

110   From trade to dominion

survey and land-valuation system for Ireland.[25] As the price of land rose in Ireland in the first quarter of the nineteenth century, Irish landowners became increasingly disillusioned with what they perceived to be antiquated methods of evaluating land taxes. These, they protested, were calculated according to old surveys from the Cromwellian period and were not in scale with current land prices. In 1824, the issue gathered considerable momentum in parliament through the efforts of a Co. Limerick landowner and prominent liberal Irish MP, Thomas Spring-Rice. After publicly denouncing the system for evaluating taxes in Ireland, Spring-Rice duly advised parliament that a new map and cadastral survey of Ireland was needed in order to avoid future disturbances within Ireland's rural communities. After some deliberation, the government acquiesced, legislated accordingly and instructed the military Board of Ordnance to carry out a new national survey of Ireland.

As with the GTS, the OSI had its origins firmly rooted in the ideology of empire. The Spring-Rice report of 1824, which was drafted in response to the government's new initiatives, presented the new survey of Ireland as a 'great national work', motivated by a benevolent utilitarian spirit and charged with the task of 'improving' Ireland.[26] Unsurprisingly, the report emphasised the Irish survey's civil as opposed to military origins and nature. The OSI was to be a grand imperial exercise that involved all sections of nineteenth-century Irish society, particularly its rural communities, where it was hoped that 'native' participation in the scheme would elicit Irish gratitude, bolster imperial authority and would thereby contribute to future political stability on the island.[27] In theory, at least, the work carried out on the OSI would serve to legitimise colonial rule and reinforce Anglophonic views of history. This is a point that has been developed by Ian J. Barrow whose recent work has argued that colonial mapping rendered the Empire a 'concrete territory' that conveyed to others the 'naturalness' of British authority as well as 'a British sense of entitlement to overseas power'. While maps could be used for a range of practical purposes such as the construction of roads or railways, the laying of telegraph cables or the movement of troops and goods, the British sought to exploit the symbolic and intellectual significance of maps as well. According to Barrow,

---

[25] See J. H. Andrews, *A Paper Landscape: The Ordnance Survey in Nineteenth-Century Ireland* (Oxford: Clarendon Press, 1975).

[26] 'Report from the select committee on the survey and valuation of Ireland', H.C. (1824), 445, viii.

[27] G. M. Doherty, *The Irish Ordnance Survey: History, Culture and Memory* (Dublin: Four Courts Press, 2004).

a range of imperial cartographers and surveyors used their maps and representations of territory as a means of legitimising colonial rule. By articulating and manipulating the past by using specific cartographic perspectives and idioms (including the insertion of little vignettes and symbols denoting British imperial culture), they were able 'to demonstrate a history of territory and...to justify the possession of land'.[28]

Surveying and colonial power in Ireland and India

At the centre of the Irish survey's activities was Colonel Thomas Colby, a competent administrator, scientist and inventor who served as director of the Ordnance Survey of Great Britain between 1820 and 1827. Colby, who was also deeply interested in ethnography, was convinced that the trigonometrical survey in Ireland could provide an important 'foundation for statistical, antiquarian, and geological surveys' to be executed in other parts of the British Empire.[29] To this end, Colby instructed all officers employed on the Irish survey that, in addition to the routine work of carrying out measurements and recording results during the course of mapping, they were to record all relevant information pertaining to 'communications by land and water, manufactories, geology, antiquities or other matters connected with the survey' while in Ireland.[30] Both Colby and his assistant, Thomas Larcom, impressed upon the staff of the Irish survey the need to present well-researched and well-written reports that contained valuable ethnographic information on Irish society and culture.[31] As in India, it was believed these reports would offer colonial administrators a unique insight into the topography, socio-economic structure, historical development, customs and languages of local communities.[32]

The ethnographic dimension of the OSI was something that continued apace when Larcom replaced Colby as the survey's director in 1828. Like Colby, Larcom was profoundly interested in the historical and cultural background to the socio-economic conditions that existed

---

[28] I. J. Barrow, *Mapping History, Drawing Territory: British Mapping in India, c.1756–1905* (Oxford University Press, 2003), pp. 2–3.

[29] T. Colby (ed.), *Ordnance Survey of the County of Londonderry, Volume the First: Memoir of the City and Northwestern Liberties of Londonderry, Parish of Templemore* (Dublin: Hodges and Smith, 1837).

[30] Ibid., pp. 7–8.

[31] Ibid., p. 8.

[32] For an example of a civilian assistant's account of his experiences working on the Ordnance Survey, see W. Clare (ed.), *A Young Irishman's Diary (1836–1847): Being Extracts from the Early Journal of John Keegan of Moate* (1928), pp. 13, 23.

112   From trade to dominion

in nineteenth-century Ireland.[33] Under Larcom, engineers on the Irish survey were instructed to investigate the 'natural state' of the landscape, its physical geography and natural sciences (botany, geology and zoology), as well as its 'artificial state' of historical monuments, towns, public buildings, landed estates, industries, mills, infrastructure and communications. Moreover, in order to give a 'full face portrait of the land', Larcom was particularly keen that engineers supplement their statistical reports with detailed information concerning local customs, people, places and the Irish language.[34] By amassing a dense archive of geographical knowledge in Ireland, Colby and Larcom were convinced that their work on the OSI would secure its status as a central reference point for future surveys, to be emulated and copied elsewhere 'in England and wherever England's power is known'.[35]

Lieutenant Denison, a correspondent of Larcom's based in Madras in the 1830s, for example, wanted the scheme to be extended throughout the British Empire, and believed that the Royal Engineers should be used to collect such information wherever they were located.[36] Moreover, the direction of the flow of ideas was not always from Ireland to India. Colby's plans for statistical accounts to accompany maps in Ireland in the early 1820s, for instance, were influenced by earlier Indian endeavours where he employed similar themes and language in the publication of *Heads of Inquiry*. In the context of the GTS, however, Everest, who had replaced Blacker as Surveyor-General in 1826, was quickest to recognise the significance of the work being carried out in Ireland and soon established an important working relationship with Colby. He believed that certain aspects of the organisational structure and technological innovations of the OSI should be replicated on the Indian survey.[37]

By 1827 Blacker and Salmond had succeeded in their attempts to convert the Court of Directors to the idea of supporting an all-India triangulation. In a memorandum to the newly appointed Governor-General of India, Lord William Bentinck (1828–35), the Court outlined

---

[33] Lt T. Larcom, *Heads of Inquiry* (1832): copy in Larcom papers, National Library of Ireland (hereafter NLI), MS 7550.

[34] 'Copy of table of contents to the instructions for the Ordnance Survey memoir of Ireland, showing the subjects embraced in the inquiry, and the order of their arrangements, by Captain Larcom, Royal Engineers', in *Report of the Commissioner Appointed to Inquire into the Facts Relating to the Ordnance Memoir of Ireland*, H.C. (1844) 527, xxx, 87.

[35] Thomas Larcom to George Petrie, 8 December 1837, Larcom papers, NLI, MS 7564.

[36] Lt Denison to Thomas Larcom, 18 January, 20 April 1838, Larcom papers, NLI, MS 7548; Edney, *Mapping an Empire*, p. 280.

[37] Edney, *Mapping an Empire*, p. 280.

Surveying and colonial power in Ireland and India 113

their new cartographic policy for the subcontinent. Central to this new policy was the belief that certain surveying practices common to the OSI could be transplanted to India. Bentinck, for one, was convinced that under Everest, the GTS could be used as an effective means of 'improving' India in the same way Colby's survey was intended to 'improve' Ireland. In September 1827, the Court of Directors wrote to the Calcutta council informing them of their belief that the Irish survey contained 'information or suggestions which may be useful in the prosecution of Indian surveys'.[38] Certainly, the institutional success enjoyed by Colby and Larcom on the OSI seems to have been a factor in persuading the Company to invest in the newest and most precise scientific measuring apparatus for the GTS.[39] Significantly, these innovative mapping instruments had been tested and developed by Colby in Ireland between 1826 and 1828. Impressed by the accuracy and precision of this new instrumentation, the Court donated them to Everest for work on the GTS in 1829.[40] Indeed, during furlough in Europe, Everest spent some time visiting the Irish survey in order to witness what he described as 'the working of the machinery' of Colby's 'beautiful system' in Ireland.[41]

Despite the damp and wet conditions in which surveying in Ireland was being undertaken, Everest was greatly impressed by the institutional structure of the Irish survey.[42] Following discussions with Colby and Henry Kater, a metrologist and former assistant of Lambton's who had since returned from India and had developed close ties with the Ordnance Survey, Everest informed the Court that the Irish survey could act as an important imperial precedent for the Indian survey in terms of the provision of adequate labour and instrumentation. Everest viewed the Irish survey as a sort of 'colonial' prototype, a provider of policy precedent that the Company could draw upon in the geographical construction of British colonial rule in India. In this respect, nineteenth-century Ireland and India were somehow perceived to be similar components of the Empire where ideas and procedures developed in

---

[38] Court of Directors to Bentinck, 26 September 1827, E/4/730, ff. 2–3. OIOC, BL.
[39] Edney, *Mapping an Empire*, p. 246.
[40] G. Everest, 'On the Compensation Measuring Apparatus of the Great Trigonometrical Survey of India', *Asiatic Researches*, 19 (1833), 189–214, 208–9; G. Everest, *An Account of the Measurement of Two Sections of the Meridional Arc of India*, 2 vols. (London: East India Company, 1847); G. Everest, *Account of the Operations of the Great Trigonometrical Survey of India*, 24 vols. (Dehra Dun: Survey of India, 1870–1910), pp. 1–16.
[41] G. Everest, 'Memoir Containing an Account of Some Leading Features of the Irish Survey, and a Comparison of the Same with the System Pursued in India', 20 October 1829, L/MIL/5/402/205, ff. 297–317. OIOC, BL.
[42] Ibid., f. 297.

114   From trade to dominion

one country were frequently employed to influence the formulation of very similar ideas and procedures in another. Following his visit to Colby and Larcom in 1829, Everest confidently informed the Court of Directors that by 'observing' developments on the OSI it could be possible to introduce 'into the Department of Survey in India any improvements which might thence suggest themselves'.[43]

One aspect of the Irish survey that Everest was particularly keen to adopt for the Indian survey was the sub-division of labour and the organisation of its personnel. In this regard, Everest informed the Court that he wished to deploy the formation of an organisation similar to that which had been created by Colby in Ireland.[44] This would involve the employment of military officers, preferably engineers, as suitable overseers of all survey work in India. As on the Irish survey, they would be enticed to work by being offered larger allowances and their appointments would be in an official capacity commensurate with the status of other staff positions. Under this system the calculations of principal baseline triangles was to be reserved for the senior officer on site whom the superintendent was to select on the basis of qualification. The majority of work involving the chain and common theodolite measurements was to be performed by miners and sappers of the Royal Engineers and Royal Artillery Regiment, while much of the ordinary, laborious work undertaken by local Irish civilians, who were recruited variously as labourers, draughtsmen, engravers and collectors of statistics on the Irish survey, could be undertaken by a body of Eurasian civil assistants in India who would have lower expectations of salary and status than army officers.[45] By exposing Indians to scientific practice in a similar way to the experience of Irish Catholics working on the Irish survey, Everest believed the government would promote the development of a loyal and conscientious workforce that was committed to British rule in India and to the benevolent and 'improving' nature of the Empire.

Moreover, the close attention to recording all available ethnographic information by officers on the Irish survey was cited by Everest as being of particular utility to the Indian government. He informed the Court of Directors that the Indian survey could learn much from the 'great pains that are taken [in Ireland] to decide the orthography of the names of the towns and villages'. According to Everest, this was a collaborative initiative where surveyors in Ireland elicited knowledge from

[43] Ibid.
[44] For a full account of the history and organisation of the OSI, see Andrews, *A Paper Landscape*.
[45] Everest, 'Memoir Containing an Account', f. 317.

Surveying and colonial power in Ireland and India 115

Gaelic-speaking locals and other 'various authorities...within reach' in order to properly cite and register the correct mode of spelling of Irish place-names.[46] This initiative was largely attributable to the work carried out on the survey by the Irish antiquarian and archaeologist, George Petrie, who headed up the survey's Topographical Department between 1833 and 1843.[47] Under Petrie, prominent Irish Catholic scholars such as John O'Donovan and Eugene O'Curry were employed on the survey to undertake important place-name research in Ireland's libraries and archives with a view to establishing the correct origin of Ireland's estimated 63,000 townland names.[48]

Despite Everest's obvious admiration for the ethnographic dimensions of the OSI, however, it was the actual institutional organisation of the Irish survey itself that he coveted most. According to Everest, the epistemological rationale for the GTS was being severely undermined by the poor condition of the Indian survey's instruments and equipment. He wanted to see the new theodolites, heliotropes, modern lamps and night-lights all used regularly in Ireland applied for use in India.[49] Unlike the poorly equipped Indian survey, Everest informed the Court that 'the Department [in Ireland] is well and amply supplied with cases of instruments, brass protractors, drawing apparatus, telescopes, levelling instruments and in fact every article that can possibly be required'.[50] If the GTS was to be successfully expanded along the lines proposed by Blacker in 1824, such technologies would have to be procured for India. In response to Everest's proposals, the Court agreed to buy new instruments as well as to increase the number of the GTS' parties. Lord Ellenborough, president of the Board of Control, was particularly receptive to Everest's memoir on the application of the OSI's techniques to India and wrote to Bentinck to inform him that he greatly looked forward to Everest executing a number of similar

---

[46] Ibid., f. 298.

[47] P. Murray, J. Leerssen and T. Dunne, *George Petrie (1790–1866): The Rediscovery of Ireland's Past* (Cork: Gandon Editions for the Crawford Municipal Art Gallery, 2004).

[48] For an example of O'Donovan and O'Curry's antiquarian research while working on the OSI, see J. O'Donovan, *The Antiquities of County Clare: Letters Containing Information Relative to the Antiquities of the County of Clare Collected During the Progress of the Ordnance Survey in 1839; & Letters and Extracts Relative to Ancient Territories in Thomond, 1841* (Ennis: CLASP Press, 2003).

[49] J. E. Insley, '"Instruments of a Very Beautiful Class": George Everest in Europe, 1825–1830', in *Colonel Sir George Everest CB FRS: Proceedings of the Bicentenary Conference at the Royal Geographical Society, 8th November 1990* (London, 1990), pp. 23–30.

[50] Everest, 'Memoir Containing an Account', f. 298.

116   From trade to dominion

surveys focusing on the Indus and the Punjab throughout the 1830s and 1840s.

Everest's desire to transform the British surveys in India into a facsimile of Colby's system in Ireland was later taken up by Thomas Best Jervis, another prominent metrologist who had carried out a survey of the southern Konkan while serving in the Bombay Engineers between 1819 and 1830.[51] Upon furlough from India in 1830, Jervis had divided his time between writing two books on Indian metrology and campaigning for reform to be introduced to the surveys in India using similar lines of argument as previously put forward by Lambton, Blacker and Everest.[52] Born in Ceylon to a father in the Madras Civil Service and a mother who was the daughter of a Royal Engineer, Jervis was an ardent evangelical Christian who was fully committed to promoting Bentinck's 'scientific' ideal for using the GTS as a vehicle for the gradual 'improvement' of India. Between 1836 and 1839 Jervis spent time in London ingratiating himself with the local political and scientific elite as a means of persuading the Company of the benefits of observing and borrowing from similar scientific institutions based in England and Ireland. Jervis was particularly keen on the idea of creating a single survey organisation in India that would incorporate other scientific studies into its domain, most notably those that centred on various geological, tidal and magnetic investigations. As part of this broader initiative, he argued that the Company should adopt a method of organisation for the division of labour on Indian surveys such as that used by Colby in Ireland. By training a body of Indian labourers to carry out much of the repetitive surveying work, Jervis pointed out that not only would this free officers to concentrate on the more important computations and other 'scientific' concerns, but the survey itself would function as a great benign force in India, helping to remove the barriers of caste and integrate the various strata of Indian society into the imperial system as a whole. In order to become familiar with this process, Jervis requested that all future engineer cadets and sappers bound for India would spend some time working under Colby in Ireland first.[53] Jervis,

---

[51] W. P. Jervis, *Thomas Best Jervis, Lt. Col., Christian Soldier, Geographer, and Friend of India, 1796–1857: A Centenary Tribute* (London: Elliot Stock, 1898).

[52] T. B. Jervis, *Records of Ancient Science, Exemplified and Authenticated in the Primitive Universal Standard of Weights and Measures* (Calcutta, 1836); T. B. Jervis, *The Expediency and Facility of Establishing the Metrological and Monetary Systems throughout India, on a Scientific and Permanent Basis, Grounded on an Analytical View of the Weights, Measures and Coins of India, and Their Relative Quantities with Respect to Such as Subsist at Present, or Have Hitherto Subsisted in All Past Ages throughout the World* (Bombay, 1836).

[53] Edney, *Mapping an Empire*, pp. 281–2.

Thomas Oldham and the Geological Survey of India

like Everest, also greatly admired the fine ethnographic detail that accompanied engineers' reports while working on the parish surveys under Colby and Larcom in Ireland and believed that the statistical and historical memoirs that Irish surveyors were instructed to compile could be applied to India, where they could be used to augment future tax revenues.

Thomas Oldham and the Geological Survey of India

While the East India Company clearly borrowed from Irish precedents in its attempts to map India, the transition from amateur to professional status and official support in 'colonial science' in India was aided considerably by a large number of Irish university graduates who competed intensely for places in the various imperial structures of the Crown Raj in the second half of the nineteenth century.[54] During the 1850s the introduction of open competitive examination for entry into the Indian Civil Service by the Secretary of State for India, Sir Charles Wood, allowed many middle-class Irish and Scottish university graduates who lacked important family or business connections to obtain imperial posts otherwise previously denied to them.[55] The large number of successful Irish candidates who obtained employment in India at this time was aided considerably by Irish universities and colleges who were quick to seize this opportunity and subsequently tailored their curriculum to the specific requirements of the entrance examinations.[56] Trinity College Dublin and Queen's College, Belfast, were particularly prominent in their ability to supply the British Empire with a variety of specialised, highly trained professionals. In part, this mirrored a desire among the rising Irish middle classes (both Catholic and Protestant) to obtain careers in the Empire, but it also reflected a strong interest within Irish universities and colleges at the time to promote learning in oriental languages, Indian history, geography, zoology and the natural sciences.[57]

Indeed, the development and impact of key scientific personnel networks based on ethnic affiliation in the Empire can be clearly seen in the example of Thomas Oldham and his work on the GSI. Head-hunted by

---

[54] See S. B. Cook, 'The Irish Raj: Social Origins and Careers of Irishmen in the Indian Civil Service, 1855–1914', *Journal of Social History*, 20, 3 (1987), 507–29.

[55] C. Dewey, 'The Education of a Ruling Caste: The Indian Civil Service in the Era of Competitive Examination', *English Historical Review*, 88 (1973), 262–85.

[56] Cook, 'The Irish Raj', 509–10.

[57] R. B. McDowell and D. A. Webb, *Trinity College, Dublin, 1592–1952: An Academic History* (Cambridge University Press, 1982), pp. 233–4.

118   From trade to dominion

the East India Company in 1851, Oldham and his coterie of Irish geologists (mostly Trinity College Dublin graduates) were responsible for reorganising and restructuring the GSI into a thoroughly modernised scientific institution, and inaugurating the first systematic and sustained approach to the investigation of India's stratigraphy and mineralogy. Under Oldham's directorship, the field of geology shed its amateur status and became an integral branch of the new colonial administration in the 1860s and 1870s. Until his retirement in 1876, Oldham completely transformed the institution, meeting international standards in geological collecting and producing research that was best reflected in its publications, *Memoirs of the GSI*, *Records of the GSI* and the regular *Annual Reports*. In this capacity, both the GSI and the GTS bore witness to the varying degrees of direct Irish involvement that played a significant part in the emerging role of scientific and technological agencies in colonial state-formation and in defining the expanding roles and responsibilities of the modern British state in its Indian environment. Moreover, Oldham's particular education, scientific training and early experiences in Ireland all melded in significant ways to shape his politics and personal responses to both Indians and the colonial authorities who employed him.

As the son of a broker with the Grand Canal Company from Co. Dublin, Oldham attended Trinity College in the mid 1830s before departing briefly for Edinburgh in 1836 to complete his studies in civil engineering.[58] Before accepting the newly created post of Superintendent of the GSI in 1851, Oldham had spent almost ten years working in the trigonometrical branch of the OSI compiling information and drafting reports on the physical aspects, mineralogy and economic products of Ireland. By the time he came to the attention of the East India Company, he was already a distinguished professor of civil engineering and geology at Trinity College Dublin.[59] Upon his arrival in Calcutta in March 1851, Oldham quite literally began setting up the entire GSI on his own. To a significant degree, the lack of adequate manpower and resources placed at Oldham's disposal reflected the Company's limited practical commitment to institutionalised scientific research in India during the early 1850s. Within days of his arrival Oldham wrote to Sir Andrew Ramsay, the Director of the Geological Survey of England and

---

[58] G. L. Herries Davies, *North from the Hook: 150 Years of the Geological Survey of Ireland* (Dublin: Geological Survey of Ireland, 1995), p. 31.

[59] S. Sangwan, 'Reordering the Earth: The Emergence of Geology as a Scientific Discipline in Colonial India', *The Indian Economic and Social History Review*, 31, 3 (1994), 297; T. Oldham, *Annual Report of the Superintendent of the Geological Survey of India and the Museum of Geology* (Calcutta, 1860), p. 5.

Thomas Oldham and the Geological Survey of India 119

Wales, requesting that he investigate the possibility of recruiting some 'well-qualified Irish geologists' whom, he stressed, 'would be more than happy to receive the salary that is on offer [in India]'.[60] Ramsay did not have to use much persuasion. The first of a large personnel network of Irish geologists to join Oldham on the GSI was Joseph Medlicott, son of a Church of Ireland rector from Loughrea, Co. Galway.[61] Indeed, from 1851 to 1920, almost twenty Irish geologists joined the GSI, while during the same time there was only a sixteen-year period when an Irish geologist did not act as the Indian Survey's Director.[62] Most of these men were graduates of Trinity College Dublin, and had previous experience working with one another at various levels on the OSI. In 1854, for example, Joseph Medlicott was joined on the GTS by his brother, Henry Medlicott, after spells on both the Irish and English surveys, while another prominent Indian geologist, Valentine Ball, was a friend and coeval of the Medlicott brothers from their time together in Dublin. William King, the son of a professor of geology at the Queen's College, Galway, joined Oldham's staff shortly afterwards, while Oldham himself secured several appointments for his family members, most notably for his brother Charles and son, Richard Dixon Oldham, who later carried out important early work on the study of seismology and earthquakes in India.[63]

From the outset, geological explorations undertaken by Oldham and his colleagues assumed a direct economic bearing.[64] With the development of steam travel in the 1830s, the economic and military value of geological investigations meant that the search for workable coalmines, in particular, became a priority for Company officials obsessed with balancing books and keeping costs at a minimum.[65] The pursuit of scientific inquiry for solely economic purposes in India, however, quite frequently resulted in increased levels of conflict and tension between Company authorities and sections of its employees during the mid nineteenth century. This can be clearly seen in the experience of Oldham who embroiled himself in several disputes with Company and Crown officials throughout his Indian career, largely because of

---

[60] Thomas Oldham to Sir Andrew Ramsay, d. Calcutta 19 April 1851, Imperial College London Archives (hereafter ICLA), KGA/RAMSAY/8/610/82.

[61] Oldham, *Annual Report*, p. 5.

[62] L. L. Fermor, *First Twenty-Five Years of the Geological Survey of India* (Calcutta, 1976), p. 42.

[63] R. D. Oldham, *A Bibliography of Indian Geology: Being a List of Books and Papers, Relating to the Geology of British India and Adjoining Countries* (Calcutta, 1888).

[64] D. Kumar, *Science and the Raj, 1857–1905* (Delhi: Oxford University Press, 1997), pp. 44–5.

[65] C. S. Fox, 'The Geological Survey of India', *Nature*, 160 (December 1947), 889–91.

120   From trade to dominion

perceived metropolitan interference in – and condescension towards – colonial initiatives, but also partly because of his particular intellectual background and earlier experiences in Ireland. As a middle-class Irish Protestant, Oldham had a particular mindset that was informed by the intellectual milieu long associated with Trinity College Dublin.[66] Having worked with Colby on the Irish survey in the late 1830s and 1840s, Oldham's work on the GSI reflected a strong tradition of Irish antiquarian and historical research that was at times at odds with the utilitarian ethos and evangelical spirit of the East India Company.[67]

During the first half of the nineteenth century, scholarly interest in Irish antiquarian and historical research melded with contemporary investigations by socio-scientific societies into the political and social condition of the Irish people. On the OSI, for example, Colby and Larcom began collecting information for the survey's parish memoirs, intended to provide knowledge about the origins and nature of Ireland's social problems, as well as information necessary to address and resolve them. Having witnessed at first hand conditions in pre-Famine Ireland while undertaking fieldwork, Colby and Larcom were deeply disturbed by the poor state of the Irish peasantry and quickly became involved in Irish political affairs. After studying the literature and participating in debates about possible causes and remedies, they concluded that Ireland's poverty, unemployment and popular discontent were due to the nature of its underdeveloped economy, agriculture and infrastructure, and subsequently accused elites and policy-makers of negligence, ignorance and mismanagement. Colby, in particular, rejected claims that Ireland was responsible for its own problems, that its natural resources were inadequate and that its population was incapable of improvement. He argued, on the contrary, that Ireland's assets were neglected, its potential ignored and its ability thwarted by a combination of bad government and ineffective legislation under the Union.[68]

In part, such views also reflected the beginning of an important shift in outlook within sections of the wider intellectual community towards the second half of the nineteenth century that began moving away from Anglocentric models of socio-economic development of putative universal applicability.[69] In the aftermath of the Great Famine in Ireland

[66] Ballantyne, 'The Sinews of Empire', pp. 151–4.
[67] Oldham's interest in the Irish antiquarian and historical tradition followed him to India where he published an important piece on the origins of encaustic and ornamental tiles used as a pavement for Irish ecclesiastical buildings. See T. Oldham, *Ancient Irish Pavement Tiles* (Dublin: J. Robertson, 1865).
[68] Colby to Larcom, 26 December 1842, Larcom papers, NLI, MS 7553.
[69] C. Dewey, 'Images of the Village Community: A Study in Anglo-Indian Ideology', *Modern Asian Studies*, 6, 3 (1972), 306.

in the 1840s, there was a stark realisation within Britain that the prescriptions of early-nineteenth-century classical political economists had failed to transform Ireland into a diminutive England of improving landlords and prosperous farmers. Throughout the 1850s, the once unwavering belief in the efficacy and applicability of Anglocentric theories that held British structures of land tenure as a 'superior model' for the rest of the civilised and civilising world began to be scrutinised and questioned. Around this time, a range of scholars, most notably sociologists and anthropologists, began adopting new models of inquiry that challenged the normative assumptions of the utilitarians and classical political economists. This scholarship ultimately gave a new theoretical respectability to a set of popular contemporary ideas that sought to preserve and fortify local custom and agrarian structures rather than impose the imprint of British-based concepts, laws and practices onto overseas possessions.[70] In turn, this had an important impact upon the way the Irish middle class (many of whom came from declining landowning backgrounds and had sought employment in the Indian Civil Service after 1855) viewed tenurial relations in India, where they were responsible for influencing a measure of pro-tenant legislation in the second half of the nineteenth century.[71]

Alternative views of history, land and famine impacted upon the careers of Irish administrative and scientific personnel in India alike. Oldham's work compiling individual soil-maps for counties in the south-east and north-west of Ireland on the OSI in the late 1840s coincided with some of the worst instances of famine and pestilence in Irish history. Before departing for Calcutta in 1851, Oldham's correspondence with Sir Andrew Ramsay was laden with several references to the poor working conditions for geological undertakings on the Irish survey, as well as the ongoing plight of the Irish peasantry during the Great Famine.[72] A deep interest in recording and noting down the socio-economic condition of the Indian peasantry was also something that characterised much of Oldham's early writings on geological explorations in Bengal. In the year before the publication of the first volume of the GSI's *Memoirs* in 1859, Oldham was instructed to investigate the economic potential of the iron mines of Cuttack and Talcher in the province of Orissa in Bengal, with a view to opening them out 'to the steady

---

[70] Dewey, 'Celtic Agrarian Legislation and the Celtic Revival'.
[71] See Chapter 7 for discussion of these developments. See also Cook, *Imperial Affinities*, p. 85.
[72] Oldham to Ramsay, d. Gorey, Co. Wexford 26 April 1847. Letters to Sir Andrew Ramsay (1846–8), KGA/RAMSAY/8/610/18. ICLA.

122   From trade to dominion

march of industry'.[73] In his findings Oldham reported to the government that while there were no beds of 'workable coal' to be found in the district, the level of poverty he encountered in many of the iron manufacturing villages greatly concerned him. He stated that the mining of iron ore was a task that seemed to be 'pursued only by a particular caste of the [Talcher] people, who always appear to be among the poorest and the most wretched of the inhabitants'. Oldham maintained that the labour of the poor was being crudely exploited by wealthy Bengali *mahajans* who by a system of advances and payments became the proprietors of the iron-smelting furnaces and fuel. What Oldham referred to as the 'truck system' in operation in Talcher reduced 'the poor workmen to slavery', to the point where they find it almost 'impossible to obtain even a starvation allowance of food of the poorest kind without the aid of the *mahajans*'.[74] Certainly Oldham was not convinced that the government's approach to geological investigations in India was thoroughly appropriate and was critical of the state's handling of the Indian peasantry in general.[75]

Indeed, Oldham's concern for the welfare of indigenous people extended well beyond highlighting the plight of the peasantry to promoting the interests of the Western-educated middle classes, particularly in relation to his efforts to persuade the government to extend scientific education to Indians. In Madras in 1861, for example, assistants of the GSI were utilised by Oldham to deliver a course of lectures on geology at the College of Civil Engineering when fieldwork became impractical during the monsoon months. Keen for officers of the GSI to spread the 'knowledge of geology and its allied pursuits' throughout the subcontinent, Indians as well as Europeans were encouraged to participate; within the first year of its inauguration, Oldham commented to the government that a considerably large number of students had successfully passed and that 'several natives' had performed 'very creditably'.[76] Moved by the paucity of instruction in the natural sciences in the Presidency College in Calcutta, Oldham suggested to the government in 1862 that the GSI itself should become a centre for the study of the applied sciences.[77] The government, however, was

---

[73] T. Oldham, 'Preliminary Notice on the Coal and Iron of Talcheer in the Tributary Mehals of Cuttack', in *Memoirs of the Geological Survey of India*, Vol. I (Calcutta: Geological Survey of India, 1859), p. 10.

[74] Ibid., p. 12.

[75] *Annual Report of the Superintendent of the Geological Survey of India and the Museum of Economic Geology* (London, 1858–9).

[76] *Annual Report of the Superintendent of the Geological Survey of India and the Museum of Economic Geology* (Calcutta, 1862–3), p. 4.

[77] *Calcutta Review*, 39, 78 (1864), 430.

Thomas Oldham and the Geological Survey of India 123

not enthusiastic about Oldham's proposals, fearing that by assuming roles as educators, geological assistants would become distracted from their primary objective of carrying out geological research. In particular, Oldham was keen on the education of young Indians and on several occasions had pleaded with the government for science education to be extended at university level. However, when the government again refused to agree to this proposal, Oldham suggested a remedy by way of introducing a system of geological apprenticeship for Indians through state funding.[78] Instead of increasing levels of pay, Oldham wanted to induce some of the better students of Calcutta University to join the GSI as apprentices by offering them scholarships. This time, however, the Finance Department vetoed his request. In May 1866, the government decided to attract recently qualified young engineering graduates by dividing the assistants into three separate grades, thereby effectively discouraging Indian participation in the GSI.[79]

Nevertheless, by March 1873, Oldham's continual lobbying of the government on this issue succeeded in securing the apprenticeship of Ram Singh, the first Indian to join the GSI, and the first Indian to attend elementary science classes at the Shibpur Engineering School. Two more Indian apprentices, Kishan Singh and Hira Lal, joined the survey in January 1874 where they attended the physical science lectures at the Presidency College in Calcutta. Still, Oldham and the GSI continued to meet official opposition in their drive to extend scientific learning to sections of the Indian community. In particular, their proposals were met with a mixed reaction from the governments of Bengal, Madras and the Punjab. Many believed that the cost of supplying instruction in geology would be financially imprudent given that employment opportunities for Indians in science-related careers were few and far between, and that there was a greater practical demand for instruction in subjects such as physics or botany, knowledge of which were essential for Indians pursuing careers in the subordinate medical services. Moreover, the Director of Public Instruction in the Punjab added that before proper instruction in geology could take place, considerable antecedent knowledge of the applied sciences at base level must first be greatly improved. Although not solely attributable to Oldham's campaigning, the question of scientific education was given a fillip some years later when the government of India decided to readdress the question of providing geological training for Indians and resolved 'to

---

[78] *Records of the Geological Survey of India*, Vol. VII, 1874, p. 8.
[79] *Annual Report of the Superintendent*, 1863–4, p. 10.

124   From trade to dominion

encourage amongst the better educated classes of the native community a scientific habit of mind'.[80]

While the issue of Indian welfare and education was clearly a persistent feature of the tense relations that existed between Oldham and the government in the early years of his career in India, perhaps the greatest point of conflict that arose between members of the GSI and the Crown concerned the gathering and ownership of geological research and intelligence. During the Company period the agenda for geological collecting and research in India had been largely determined by a whole host of metropolitan institutions and scientists based in London. Following the appointment of Oldham and his coterie of Irish geological assistants from the 1850s onward though, the nature of collecting and organisation of geological research changed, especially with the emergence of public museums in India at this time. Through Oldham's influence, the most important of these new museums, the Indian Museum in Calcutta, began to compete with its principal metropolitan equivalent, the British Museum in London, for the possession of Indian geological collections in an effort to establish Calcutta as a centre for scientific collecting and research in its own right. The result was a series of conflicts between the two which was responsible not only for bringing about a fundamental shift in the administration of colonial science on the subcontinent, but also in the position of the 'colonies' themselves in terms of generating and disseminating colonial knowledge throughout the Empire.[81]

Central to this important shift in cultural power in India from the 1860s was the new breed of colonial scientist who arrived towards the end of the Company period and who was prepared to challenge the dominance of the British Museum and its perceived unfair demands and impositions on 'colonial' scientific institutions.[82] Although Oldham's protest was clearly one of a colonial scientist protesting against the domination of the field of geology in India by the metropole, his Irish background and experience was at least partially significant in shaping his expressed political views and objections at the time. Devoid of any sense of cultural dependence upon England or a patriotic desire to shore up the position of London as the Empire's

[80] Proceedings of the Revenue Agriculture Department, Surveys, no. 33, September 1880, quoted in Kumar, *Science and the Raj*, p. 121.
[81] For a detailed account of the politics behind meteorite collecting in India during the 1860s and 1870s, see S. P. Nair, 'Science and the Politics of Colonial Collecting: The Case of Indian Meteorites, 1856–70', *British Journal for the History of Science*, 39, 1 (March 2006), 97–119.
[82] Ibid., 97.

Thomas Oldham and the Geological Survey of India

scientific 'centre', Oldham and several of his Irish assistants publicly challenged the imperial authority of the British Museum in its attempts to create a national geological collection of its own at the expense of the colonies. This involved raising the international profile of the GSI and establishing crucial links with similar scientific institutions abroad. Through a system of exchange of Indian specimens, publications and geological intelligence, for example, Oldham forged a particularly close association with William Haidinger and the Imperial Geological Institute of Vienna with whom he collaborated in compiling a complete series of scientific publications for the geological library in Calcutta.[83]

However, Oldham's efforts to establish Calcutta as an imperial centre for knowledge-making in its own right were initially hindered by the British Museum's antagonistic strategies in controlling and policing the colonial scientific field in India during the 1860s and 1870s. During this period problems arose between the government of India and members of the Indian Museum in Calcutta over the possession of rare meteorological specimens found in Dharamsala and Gorackpore between 1860 and 1861. Dismayed by the British Museum's attempts to influence the government of India to subordinate the activities of the Indian Museum and to acquiesce to their demand that all meteorites found in India be sent to London for more thorough examination, Oldham became embroiled in a dispute with his metropolitan counterpart, Nevil Story Maskelyne. An efficient scientist and administrator, Maskelyne was head of the Mineralogy Department in the British Museum and had been one of the principal catalysts in persuading the government to control and regulate the collection of Indian meteorite specimens. In a blatant attempt to counter this activity, and to demonstrate the GSI's intention of taking control of the collection of Indian meteorites independently of the British Museum, Oldham influenced the government of India to purchase an extensive collection of meteorites from a private dealer based in Manchester in 1865. With the acquisition of this large collection of over 220 meteorite specimens for Calcutta, Oldham succeeded in immediately elevating the status of the collection of aerolites at the Indian Museum on a par with the British Museum in London and the Imperial Geological Institute in Vienna. In 1866, in a direct challenge to the set of instructions issued by Maskelyne to the various official bodies involved in geological investigations in India, Oldham also published his own set of guidelines for collecting, requesting that any future finds be

---

[83] Oldham, *Bibliography of Indian Geology*, p. 5.

126   From trade to dominion

forwarded not to Maskelyne at the British Museum, but sent directly to him and his colleagues at the Indian Museum in Calcutta.[84]

In his attempts to expose the domineering modus operandi of the British Museum and to challenge its right to appropriate Indian scientific knowledge for metropolitan interests, Oldham engaged the GSI in a wider contemporary debate regarding the issue of ownership of intellectual property rights deriving from research and collection conducted in British colonies. His arguments and objections resonated in other scientific fields. During the same period, zoologists and botanists raised similar issues and protested against 'unfair' and 'unwarranted' encroachments by the British Museum and other metropolitan societies on their activities. At the network level, many of these 'colonial' scientists developed close personal links with one another, forging important relationships that worked to satisfy the demands of burgeoning 'national' institutions. Significantly, Oldham's experience as a geologist on the OSI played an important role in the formation of this network. In India, Oldham utilised his extensive web of professional scientific contacts to foster a sound international reputation for the GSI, as well as to establish a forum with other colonial institutions for airing similar grievances throughout the Empire. In Australia, for example, Frederick McCoy of the National Museum of Victoria, an Irish geologist who had worked with Oldham in the Geological Department of the OSI, shared a comparable disposition as a contemporary colonial scientist working within the confines of a metropolitan-dominated field. As with Oldham, McCoy vehemently complained against interference by directors of the British Museum with regard to the organisation of science activity and research in Australia and played an equally important role in promoting cultural interests and intellectual autonomy within Britain's colonial possessions in the late nineteenth century.[85]

Conclusion

This chapter has provided further evidence of the important role that Ireland and Irish people played in the construction of British colonial rule in India during the nineteenth century. Tracing narratives of linkage and reciprocity between nineteenth-century Irish and Indian history is important as it illuminates many overlooked but no less

[84] See Geological Survey of India, *Catalogue of the Meteorites in the Museum of the Geological Survey of India* (Calcutta, 1866).
[85] R. W. Home and S. G. Kohlstedt (eds.), *International Science and National Scientific Identity: Australia between Britain and America* (Dordrecht, Boston and London: Kluwer Academic, 1991), p. 3.

Conclusion 127

significant aspects of Ireland's national development under the Act of Union. Indeed, what emerges implicitly from a historical study concerning the interconnections in 'colonial science' between two very different regions of empire, such as Ireland and India, is a conception that neither place was a specific bounded entity within the context of the nineteenth-century British Empire. Rather, both places constituted what Alan Lester has recently described as an 'imperial space' or 'the sphere of a multiplicity of trajectories'.[86] As a crucial sub-imperial centre of the British Empire, Ireland possessed the ability to by-pass the traditional 'metropolitan' core in the supply of scientific personnel to India. Ireland not only supplied the Empire with key personnel, it also functioned as an important reference point for scientific theory and practice, ultimately paving the way for new legislation and systems of government.

Occupying integral roles within the information systems of the colonial state, Irish people in turn supplied much of the intellectual capital around which British rule in India was constructed. They were part of emerging late-nineteenth-century Irish professional networks that viewed the Empire as a legitimate sphere for work and as an arena in which they could prosper. Many of these men knew each other from their student days at Irish universities, through membership of Irish scientific learned institutions or from their work together on scientific projects in Ireland. Through involvement and deployment of expertise in areas such as surveying and geological research in India, Irishmen and Irish institutions, especially universities and learned societies, were able to act decisively in the development of colonial knowledge, a recognition of which is significant in a field that has been traditionally dominated by Anglo-Indian interactions. On the whole, Irish scientific personnel supplemented British authority in India but there is evidence to suggest that at times they resisted it, bringing with them different ideas of history and science that may well have affected how this knowledge was interpreted and used by both Europeans and South Asians. Moreover, these networks of professional Irish scientists, whose experiences in India confound the 'coloniser/colonised' binary, effectively functioned as Irish 'knowledge communities' or networks of intellectual exchange in their own right, disseminating antiquarian, ethnographic and scientific knowledge throughout the British Empire.

By focusing on the integrative power of various types of networks fashioned through such connections, this chapter has provided further

---

[86] A. Lester, 'Imperial Circuits and Networks: Geographies of the British Empire', *History Compass*, 4, 1 (2006), 124–41.

128   From trade to dominion

evidence to support the view that areas of the world once thought to be distinct and separate have actually been interconnected throughout the course of time and space. This is important because it foregrounds the contention by scholars of globalisation that empires and imperial relations have given rise to the most sustained and pronounced historical periods of social and cultural contact between peoples from different geographical regions. The relationships mapped out in this chapter centre the Irish within the imperial web of connections and global exchange of ideas, technologies and practices during the 'long' nineteenth century and challenge us to rethink how we view imperial relations and accommodate the multiple trajectories and exchanges they gave rise to.

5   Religion, civil society and imperial authority

Introduction

As the Whigs ascended to power and the battle for parliamentary reform raged in Britain during the 1830s and 1840s, the British Empire began to yield further opportunities for the rising Catholic Irish middle classes eager to join their more established Protestant counterparts in imperial service. Under the Whig government, Irish Catholic seminaries and religious institutions began to supply numerous Vicars Apostolic and clergy to attend to the spiritual requirements of the Empire's ever-expanding Irish migrant communities.[1] While Irish Protestants already figured prominently within the British Empire's expanding network of missionary societies and church activity in Africa, Asia and the Pacific by the 1830s, Irish Catholic prelates, too, became deeply embedded in debates concerning religion, civil society and the exercise of imperial authority, especially in India.[2] This chapter examines how during the second half of the nineteenth century, several Irish religious networks came to dominate the administration of Catholic communities in the south and west of India. It argues that following the establishment of a number of Catholic religious institutions in Ireland after Catholic emancipation in 1829, such as All Hallows College, Dublin, whose aim it was to supply the British Empire and North America with priests for its growing number of Catholic migrants, the particular strain of Catholicism practised in Ireland came to exert a notable degree of influence upon many aspects of colonial life in India.[3] In the vicariate of

---

[1] N. Etherington, 'Education and Medicine', in N. Etherington (ed.), *Missions and Empire* (*Oxford History of the British Empire Companion Series*) (Oxford University Press, 2005), p. 262.

[2] A. Porter, *Religion versus Empire? British Protestant Missionaries and Overseas Expansion, 1700–1914* (Manchester University Press, 2004), p. 26.

[3] A. Maher, 'Missionary Links: Past, Present and Future', in M. Holmes and D. Holmes (eds.), *Ireland and India: Connections, Comparisons, Contrasts* (Dublin: Folens, 1997), pp. 29–51.

130   Religion, civil society and imperial authority

Madras, for example, Propaganda Fide, the official Roman Catholic body responsible for overseeing Catholic missionary work overseas, appointed five successive Irish titular bishops, giving rise to a prolonged period of Irish dominance in the Madras vicariate spanning almost eighty years. Although given a mandate to administer the spiritual requirements of their Indian flock, existing communities of Indian Catholics did not always endorse the notions and practices translated to India by these developing Irish Catholic religious networks, particularly when in relation to the contentious issue of caste.

Yet, this chapter also explores how Irish religious interaction with Indian society was not always negative. In addition to the close personal connections forged between Irish Catholic soldiers, military chaplains and Vicars Apostolic in the Presidency Towns of Madras, Bombay and Calcutta, Irish prelates set about introducing reconstructed parochial systems in India – modelled along Irish lines – through the building of churches and other ecclesiastical structures, and promoted the education of (high- and low-caste) Indian and Eurasian children. Within these religious networks, Irish Catholic prelates accumulated substantial bases of revenue from soldiers' wills, donations and monetary contributions. In turn, remittances conveyed through these religious networks also played important roles in reconstructing Catholic infrastructure in Ireland in the wake of emancipation through the education of siblings and building of churches, schools, hospitals and other ecclesiastical structures. Given the tight cultural bonds that existed between Irish Catholic soldiers and Irish military chaplains stationed within the walls of British garrison towns in India, invariably news, ideas and intelligence spread through these religious networks in equal measure.

By the mid nineteenth century, the development of a new language of national politics had given rise to a sense of commonality between sections of the Irish Catholic and Indian Hindu populace. Around this time, the rudiments of a Catholic revolutionary nationalism began to be articulated by members of the Fenian movement in Ireland and North America, who were encouraged by British problems in the Crimea and especially in India during the 1850s. News of suspicion among East India Company officials toward its Irish soldiers' Roman Catholicism quickly spread from military cantonments in Agra or Madras to Cork and Dublin where an expanding imperial press system brought regular news of the Empire onto the printed pages of the *Cork Examiner* and the *Freeman's Journal*.[4] During the second half of the nineteenth

---

[4] See, for example, S. J. Potter (ed.), *Newspapers and Empire in Ireland and Britain: Reporting the British Empire, c. 1857–1921* (Dublin: Four Courts Press, 2004).

The Catholic Church in Ireland after the Union 131

century, for example, Gaelic-speaking Roman Catholic soldiers in India, often supported by influential Irish figures within the Indian Catholic Church's hierarchy, played key roles in debates over the exercise of imperial authority and provided an important reference point for Britain in its attempts to understand and make sense of the indigenous cultures of South Asia.

The Catholic Church in Ireland after the Union

The introduction of Irish Vicars Apostolic and Roman Catholic chaplains in India did not occur until the first half of the nineteenth century. During this period the two interconnecting issues that dominated Irish politics at the time, namely, the nature of the constitutional relationship between Britain and Ireland and the emancipation of Catholics, had already begun to assume a recognisable form by the late 1790s. Throughout the eighteenth century, the political and religious life of Catholics in Ireland and Hindus in India shared certain recognisable traits and shared affinities. Just as Catholics had long been excluded from office, commissions in the British army and even the purchase or mortgage of Protestant land in Ireland, Indians and people of mixed race were excluded from major government and military offices. As Governor-General of India, Lord Cornwallis was convinced that 'native depravity' was the root cause of the problem of corruption that beset British officialdom in India and imperilled the East India Company's finances and security during the 1780s and 1790s.[5] In Cornwallis' view, commerce needed to be separated from the business of government if India was to become a truly integral part of the British Empire. Just as government in Ireland would be brought closer to the executive in London and made more British through the passing of an Act of Union, the introduction of a more viceregal and executive-oriented government would form the basis of a system of colonial rule that would serve to Anglicise large sections of the Indian community while stamping out 'native corruption'.[6] Likewise, in Ireland, it was decided that a legislative union with Great Britain would provide a safer means for addressing the sensitive issue of Catholic enfranchisement and would make government in Ireland more Anglocentric. Central to the design of the Act of Union was the concern by the British government to bolster an

---

[5] See Cornwallis to Dundas, 14 August 1787 about Benares: 'The Raja is a fool, his servant rogues, every native of Hindostan (I really believe) corrupt.' See C. Ross (ed.), *The Correspondence of Charles, First Marquis Cornwallis* (London, 1859), I, p. 206.
[6] McDowell, *Ireland in the Age of Imperialism and Revolution*, pp. 678–9, 699–701.

132   Religion, civil society and imperial authority

unstable Irish constitution made manifest in part by the uniform exclusion of Irish Catholics from representative politics.[7] Within a united parliament of Great Britain and Ireland, Catholics, it was argued, would enjoy full political rights without threatening the essentially Protestant nature of the constitution.[8] Indeed, political union between Great Britain and Ireland in 1801 had a certain resonance in early-nineteenth-century India. As with the classic Indian princely state, ultimate authority in Ireland would remain firmly in the hands of the British, while many of the trappings of local government and native legitimacy remained intact.[9]

In conjunction with union, the liberal and rational tone of Irish Protestantism of the late eighteenth century was widely and swiftly replaced by the growing influence of evangelicalism within the Church of Ireland in the post-Union era. One particular manifestation of this influence was the formation of Irish Protestant national missionary societies, replete with schools, tracts, travelling preachers, Gaelic bibles and scripture readers, aimed at the conversion of Irish Catholics. This marched well with the relative confidence of Irish Protestants in the first quarter of the nineteenth century in so far as it provided them with an alternative means of maintaining various degrees of political and social ascendancy over Catholics. However, Catholicism too had been undergoing a revival (though in a less theological sense) in the post-Union era. While emancipation did not necessarily reinforce Irish Catholic commitment to the Union and to the British government, it did help break down the considerable political and social barriers long restricting Catholic movement both within and outside Ireland. As R. F. Foster has argued, the immediate practical boon of emancipation mattered far less at a time when 'a Catholic middle-class ascendancy, already in the making, was given a vital psychological boost'.[10] Even though emancipation did not necessarily constitute the economic liberation of Irish Catholics, it was the measure by which the prosperity of Catholics began to be converted into social and political recognition.[11] The size of the Catholic population in Ireland by 1835 was itself significant. At a time when the combined population of England and Wales

---

[7] T. Bartlett, *The Fall and Rise of the Irish Nation: The Catholic Question, 1690–1830* (Dublin: Gill and Macmillan, 1992), p. 290.
[8] For a wide-ranging examination of the theme of Union, see J. Kelly, 'The Origins of the Act of Union'.
[9] See B. N. Ramusack, *The Indian Princes and their States*: vol. 3.6 of *The New Cambridge History of India* (Cambridge University Press, 2004), pp. 48–88.
[10] R. F. Foster, *Modern Ireland, 1600–1972* (London: Allen Lane, 1988), p. 302.
[11] See O. MacDonagh, *O'Connell: The Life of Daniel O'Connell, 1775–1847* (London: Weidenfeld & Nicolson, 1991).

The Catholic Church in Ireland after the Union   133

was just under fourteen million people, Irish Catholics alone numbered almost six and a half million, constituting almost 80 per cent of the total population of Ireland in the early nineteenth century.[12] While sheer weight in numbers certainly lent a hand in the struggle to articulate grievances, the social and political recognition of Irish Catholics was further advanced during this period by the accession of the Whigs to power in November 1830, and their subsequent domination of British politics until 1841 (except for the brief interlude of the Peel administration in 1834–5). The ascension of the Whig party to power, who were ostensibly sympathetic to popular Irish demands, ultimately helped anchor the great political reformist Daniel O'Connell at Westminster and played a leading role in the gradual integration of an Irish Catholic middle class into the British imperial system from the 1850s.

Despite the existence of many outstanding issues in relation to the future role of the Catholic Church, including its ill-defined relationship with the Established Church in Ireland, as well as the government's reticence on the question of Catholic education, the early nineteenth century witnessed a newfound spirit of dynamism and freedom within the internal organisation of the Catholic Church as a cadre of new church leaders and institutions evolved. Between 1782 and 1837 there was six major new seminaries founded in Ireland, including Maynooth College in Co. Kildare in 1795. In contrast to the Irish Catholic clergy who had been educated on the European continent during penal times and were influenced by the conservative and reactionary ideas of the *ancien régime*, many early-nineteenth-century Irish Catholic prelates who received their training in the newly established Irish seminaries at Carlow, Maynooth and Dublin were far more proactive, frequently concerning themselves with implementing social and political as well as religious reform.[13]

Indeed, contemporary European observers frequently expressed surprise at how clergy who received their training in the newly founded Irish seminaries were decidedly more radical than their continental counterparts. Gustave de Beaumont and Alexis de Tocqueville who travelled around Ireland in the 1830s, for example, noted how the Irish Catholic bishops and priests with whom they came into contact were decidedly liberal in their outlook, commenting with some alarm that

---

[12] *First Report of the Commissioners of Public Instruction, Parliamentary Papers*, Vol. XXXIII (1835), p. 904.

[13] L. P. Dubois, *Contemporary Ireland* (Dublin: Unwin, 1908), p. 477. In 1852–3, 23 of the 29 Irish Catholic bishops and 1,222 of the 2,291 Catholic clergy had been educated at Maynooth College in Co. Kildare. *Report of HM's Commissioners Appointed to Inquire into the Management of the College of Maynooth, Parliamentary Papers*, Vol. XXII (1854–5), pp. 33–5, 204–31.

134 Religion, civil society and imperial authority

'the feelings they [Irish clergy] expressed [on politics] were extremely democratic'.[14] While the struggle for emancipation in Ireland no doubt played a critical role in the politicisation of the Irish clergy in the 1820s and 1830s, it was one of the most important factors in strengthening the ties and bonds between the majority of the Irish Catholic populace and the Church.[15] In 1835, de Tocqueville expressed his astonishment at what he described as the 'unbelievable unity between the Irish clergy and the Catholic population' founded on the notion that 'all the upper classes are Protestants and enemies'.[16] This notion of unity, based explicitly on religious and class dynamics in early-nineteenth-century Ireland, was to be translated and adapted in the context of the British colonial state in India, impacting upon both Indian society and developing networks of Irish imperial servants.

In Ireland, the years 1830–45 marked the culmination of the first phase of Catholic resurgence. Since the 1790s, the reconstitution of the parochial system, in terms of church building, the education of priests and the establishment of local parish structures, had been gathering pace.[17] Moreover, in the wake of the Great Famine in Ireland in the 1840s, the Catholic Church had become increasingly preoccupied with the question of providing adequate support for the growing number of Irish Catholic communities overseas where an estimated 50,000 to 70,000 Irish men and women were being forced to migrate every year.[18] In 1842, Daniel O'Connell and the rector of the Irish College in Rome, Paul Cullen, succeeded in convincing Propaganda Fide that the opening of a 'foreign missionary seminary' in Ireland was essential in order to maintain the bonds and close affiliation that existed between the Catholic Church and Irish migrants overseas.[19] In November 1842, the first Irish Catholic foreign missionary seminary, All Hallows College, opened in Dublin providing over 120 candidates for the priesthood within the first four years of its inauguration.[20] Although it was originally intended that

[14] A. de Tocqueville, *Journeys to England and Ireland*, trans. G. Lawrence and K. P. Mayer, ed. J. P. Mayer (London: Faber, 1958), p. 130.

[15] O. MacDonagh, 'The Politicization of the Irish Catholic Bishops, 1800–1850', *Historical Journal*, XVIII (1975), 37–53.

[16] Tocqueville, *Journeys*, p. 136.

[17] D. A. Kerr, *Peel, Priests and Politics: Sir Robert Peel's Administration and the Roman Catholic Church in Ireland, 1841–1846* (Oxford: Clarendon Press, 1982), pp. 33, 353.

[18] G. O'Brien, 'New Light on Emigration', *Studies*, XXX (1941), 23; E. J. Coyne, 'Irish Population Problems: Eighty Years A-Growing, 1871–1951', *Studies: An Irish Quarterly Review*, Vol. XLIII, No.170 (1954), 153. By 1871 there were an estimated 1,850,000 Irish men and women in the United States, while there were 200,000 Irish in Australia and 220,000 in Canada.

[19] *All Hallows Annual Report* (Dublin, 1953), p. 22.

[20] K. Condon, *The Missionary College of All Hallows, 1842–91* (Dublin: All Hallows College, 1986), p. 26.

The Catholic Church in Ireland after the Union

All Hallows would provide missionary priests for the large emigrant Irish Catholic communities that had taken root in North America and Australia, its founder, Fr John Hand, was convinced that Ireland, as the principal Catholic country within the British Empire, should serve as the natural centre from which Catholicism should be extended to British colonies in the East.[21] Indeed, the integration of Irish-educated chaplains and prelates into the Indian empire from the 1830s onward had important consequences for the ways in which Catholicism as a religion was practised in India during this period.

The particular strain of Catholicism introduced by Irish prelates in India was noticeably different, for example, from the traditions that had long been practised by Portuguese, French and Italian Catholic missionaries who had come before them. This was something that the East India Company was particularly concerned about. While British authorities tolerated the presence of Irish Catholic chaplains on the subcontinent – where they were effectively introduced to appease the religious concerns of the disproportionate number of Irish Catholics employed by the Company's European regiments – there was considerable tension at the core of the relationship between the two. Fear of the spread of Catholicism and particularly of the influence of 'pernicious' Catholic priests among new settler societies were common factors in reinforcing the Victorian belief that the assertion of Protestant supremacy as well as the imposition of 'English' cultural norms and values overseas was integral to the process of maintaining political control and stability throughout the Empire.[22] This was also true in non-settler colonies such as India where the colonial government in the 1830s was intent on initiating a programme of reform based on the introduction of English workings of law and Western education. Here, the central idea was to create a body of loyal Indians who, in the words of T. B. Macaulay, would become 'English in taste, in opinions, in morals and in intellect'.[23] As the first Law Member of the Governor-General's Council of India, Macaulay was responsible for drafting the famous 'Minute on Education' (1835), a call for Britain to implement an official policy of Anglicisation throughout the subcontinent that would serve to transform 'corrupt' and 'untrustworthy natives' into honest and loyal 'Britons' through the interlinked processes of religion and language. The arrival of Irish Catholic prelates to India during this period was thus seen as potentially

---

[21] Ibid., p. 32.
[22] A. Burton, *Politics and Empire in Victorian Britain: A Reader* (Basingstoke: Palgrave Macmillan, 2001), pp. 17–18.
[23] Macaulay, 'Minute of 2 February 1835 on English Education', in T. B. Macaulay, *Prose and Poetry* (Harvard University Press, 1952), p. 729.

136   Religion, civil society and imperial authority

harmful to the successful implementation of British liberal reform. In particular, the perceived close association between the Catholic Church of Ireland with agrarian unrest and a burgeoning nationalist movement at home was seen as too radical by the British authorities in India that instead favoured the more conservative and established element of the Portuguese *padroado*.[24] Yet, Irish Catholic prelates who arrived in India, not bound to proselytism and largely independent of state control, exercised considerable advances in social services, catechetical instruction and, specifically, Christian education in India.

Roman Catholicism and the East India Company

For much of its existence, the East India Company adopted a policy of non-interference in religious disputes among the subcontinent's many small European ecclesiastical communities. Although wary of Roman Catholicism, as indeed it was of all Christian missionary societies and religious groups whose activity among the people constantly threatened to upset the delicate balance of social conditions necessary to facilitate commercial activity, the East India Company was not necessarily hostile to the presence of Catholic missionaries in India.[25] Prior to the end of the Napoleonic Wars, the Company had expressed genuine concern over the presence of French missionaries whom they believed were infiltrating India in an attempt to overthrow British rule. William Elphinstone, Chairman of the Court of Directors, perhaps best summed up this growing sense of paranoia in a minute written in 1806 when he raised concerns about the activity of French missionaries whom he believed had 'constant intercourse...with the isles of France' and who 'must know everything that passes in Calcutta, and all the news of the country'. Elphinstone was so perturbed about the role of 'able intriguers' among French Catholic missionary societies in precipitating Anglo-French conflict on the subcontinent that he proposed to the government 'to suspend everything', warning in the process that they could not 'be too much on [their]...guard'.[26]

However, British fear of Catholicism did not necessarily translate into discriminatory action. The Company's policy of religious neutrality when it was called upon to intervene in religious disputes was

---

[24] A. Jackson, *Ireland, 1798–1998: War, Peace and Beyond* (Malden, MA; Oxford: Blackwell Publishing, 2010), p. 40.

[25] P. Carson, 'An Imperial Dilemma: The Propagation of Christianity in Early Colonial India', *Journal of Imperial and Commonwealth History*, XVIII (1990), 169–90.

[26] See Elphinstone, minute 'On Missionaries', [1806], William Fullarton Elphinstone Papers, Ms. Eur. F/89, Box 2c, Pt. 5. OIOC, BL.

Roman Catholicism and the East India Company

not always strictly enforced and was certainly not always adhered to. On the contrary, during the eighteenth century the Company actually welcomed and even encouraged Roman Catholic missionaries to the subcontinent. During the 1780s, for example, a time when Britain had forged new commercial links with France, the Company felt it incumbent upon themselves to heed the advice of the London ministry not to neglect the historical ties that England had forged down through the years with Catholic Portugal. As a consequence, the Company took active measures to strengthen the position of both the Archbishop of Goa in Bombay and the Bishop of Mailapur in Madras. Further evidence of the Company's liberal attitude towards the presence of Roman Catholic missionaries in India can be seen in its policy of providing financial assistance to Roman Catholic bishops. Although most Roman Catholic missions in India did not receive any financial assistance from the government, Catholic missionaries acting as chaplains to regiments containing Roman Catholic soldiers were paid small stipends. These stipends varied in amount but did not usually exceed fifty rupees per month. However, some Catholic chaplains at larger military stations such as Dum Dum in Bengal or Fort St George in Madras could receive as much as 200 rupees per month for their efforts. Almost to the end of its reign, the East India Company continued to financially aid Roman Catholic missionaries in India in one way or another.[27] Certainly from the outset, the East India Company was aware of its own status as a secular, foreign institution in India, and its officials, in particular, were extremely conscious of how religious grievances could become a direct catalyst for sparking breaches of peace and revolt. As a consequence, the Company ultimately failed to adopt one specific consistent line of policy that dealt with the plethora of Christian missionary factions in colonial India throughout the late eighteenth and early nineteenth centuries.

Initially, Company officials were far more concerned about the over-reaching aims and proselytising tendencies of the new wave of evangelical Protestant missionaries who began arriving in large numbers in India towards the end of the eighteenth century.[28] Indeed the first Irish religious groups to travel to India were missionaries who came via Irish Protestant societies during the 1820s. The Church Missionary

[27] See K. Ballhatchet, *Caste, Class and Catholicism in India 1789–1914* (Richmond: Curzon, 1998); K. Ballhatchet, *Race, Sex and Class under the Raj: Imperial Attitudes Policies and Their Critics, 1793–1905* (London: Weidenfeld & Nicolson, 1980).

[28] M. A. Laird (ed.), *Bishop Heber in Northern India: Selections from Heber's Journal* (Cambridge University Press, 1971); B. Hilton, *The Age of Atonement: The Influence of Evangelicalism on Social and Economic Thought 1785–1865* (Oxford: Clarendon Press, 1988), p. 287.

138   Religion, civil society and imperial authority

Society, Ireland, formerly known as the Hibernian Auxiliary to the Church Missionary Society for Africa and Asia, was founded as early as 1814 and two of its members became Bishops in the Church of India.[29] By 1837 the British Baptist Mission at Serampore alone maintained permanent stations in nineteen different towns and cities including Calcutta, Benares, Allahabad and Delhi. Central to the Baptist mission was the fundamental belief in Christianising India. This was to be achieved by direct evangelical preaching to Indians who were encouraged to embrace Christianity as a means of ensuring eternal salvation.

The East India Company, however, was particularly wary of the effects of proselytisation on the Indian populace. From the early seventeenth century the Company bore full responsibility for administering its Indian possessions in an orderly and, preferably, profitable manner. The spread of evangelical ideas by Baptist missionaries and of tutoring Indian converts through their literary audience was perceived as a disruptive and potentially damaging influence to the Company's commercial interests.[30] Such fear was not without some justification. Responsibility for inciting mutiny among the Company's sepoys at Vellore in 1806, for example, was widely attributed at the time to the activity of Protestant missionaries, or at least to Indian fears of it.[31] In the aftermath of the Vellore affair, the Company ordered several Baptist missionaries to go back to England, and decreed that the remainder were not to 'interfere with the prejudices of the natives by preaching, dispensing books [Bibles] or pamphlets, or any other mode of instruction, nor permit converted natives to go into the Country to preach'.[32]

Successive Governor-Generals, including Moira and Minto, expressed particular concern over the effects of the Baptists' biblical publications. Evangelical tracts such as the 'Persian Pamphlet' that were distributed in and around Indian towns and British cantonments caused much alarm among the Company's hierarchy. Lord Minto, in particular, believed that such literature berated the religions of the Indian people and would have a disturbing influence upon the stability of Indian society. Rather presciently, he argued that the Vellore Mutiny should act as a warning for what might happen if Indians, and especially India's large Muslim community, became convinced of official British determination to force them to convert to Christianity. As the Baptist Missionary Press was manned by British subjects who were virtually

[29] Maher, 'Missionary Links'.
[30] E. Carey, *Memoir of William Carey* (London: Jackson and Walford, 1836), p. 350.
[31] E. D. Potts, *British Baptist Missionaries in India 1793–1837: The History of Serampore and Its Missions* (Cambridge University Press, 1967), pp. 179–80.
[32] Quoted in ibid., p. 177.

Roman Catholicism and the East India Company

'under the protection and authority of the British Government', the Company feared that Indians might think that published missionary tracts carried official sanction. As Minto warned, 'in the hands of the disaffected or ambitious' the publication of missionary tracts could provide a useful tool for revolt, even 'without the aid of exterior agency [the French]'.[33] In a plea to the Court of Directors in 1812, Minto outlined his objections to the presence of evangelical Protestant missionaries in India:

> The meritorious spirit of religious zeal which animates those respectable persons who deem it their duty to exert their endeavours to diffuse among the misguided natives of India the truths and blessings of the Christian Faith, can seldom be restrained by those maxims of prudence and caution which local knowledge and experience can alone inspire and without which, the labours of the Missionaries become a source of danger, and tend to frustrate, rather than promote, the benevolent object of their attention.[34]

Minto, for one, was convinced that the Court of Directors should discourage all Baptist missionaries from coming to India altogether.

In contrast to its dealings with Evangelical Christians, British concern over the presence of Roman Catholic missionaries in India was alleviated somewhat by the traditional roots which Catholicism had established in India. Goanese and Portuguese priests had been attending to Indian Catholics long before the Company had secured any kind of permanent footing on the subcontinent. The most vigorous attempts by Roman Catholics to proselytise in India had begun with the Portuguese in the sixteenth century. Portuguese Roman Catholic missionaries initially secured many converts in south India. As early as the sixth century, Christian missionaries from the Nestorian church in Syria had been accorded a place of high status among the Hindu population of Kerala, where the church flourished undisturbed for many centuries, marrying within their own communities, keeping aloof from low castes and avoiding attempts to proselytise. Thus, when the Portuguese Roman Catholic missionaries began their work in Kerala there was a long-established body of Syrian Christians already in place who were prepared to convert to Catholicism and accept Papal authority from Rome.

During the early years of European imperial expansion, successive popes had granted the Portuguese monarchy rights of *padroado*, or the rights of patronage and protection over dioceses in the East. Official dispatches and instructions from the Vatican were given the royal bene

---

[33] 'Papers Relating to Missionaries', *Parliamentary Papers*, Vol. VIII (1812–13), p. 46.
[34] Ibid., pp. 46–7.

140   Religion, civil society and imperial authority

placitum before they arrived in Lisbon and thence sent onwards to Goa, the centre of Portuguese missionary life in early colonial India. However, by the beginning of the seventeenth century Portuguese missionary initiatives in India declined and the Vatican decided that another vehicle to sustain and maintain the Catholic missionary momentum was needed. In 1622 the Sacred Congregation de Propaganda Fide was established.[35] This new missionary institution was responsible for sending out its own missionaries of various nationalities to India and in particular to areas beyond Portuguese reach. In order to appease Portuguese concerns that the spirit of the *padroado* was being infringed upon by the new initiatives taken by Propaganda Fide, the men in charge of these new missionaries, the Vicars Apostolic, were given Episcopal rank and assigned the titles of sees in partibus infidelium. This meant that the new Vicars Apostolic in India could only take charge of sees that were essentially redundant. Most of the sees allotted to the new Propaganda Fide missionaries fell into areas that were under Muslim rule and therefore obsolete from a Christian perspective.

From the Vatican's point of view, the establishment of Propaganda Fide and the creation of Vicars Apostolic did not in any way infringe upon the *padroado*. Exploiting the technical wording used to describe their particular office in India, Rome maintained that the new Vicars Apostolic were not bishops in charge of dioceses per se. Of course, the Portuguese did not look upon it in that way and for much of the eighteenth century, official relations between Rome and Lisbon were strained. To further accentuate the fragile relationship that already existed between the Roman Catholic Church and the Portuguese in the eighteenth century, various other tensions were at work. During this period, numerous controversies arose concerning the activities of the missionaries appointed by Propaganda Fide with the intention of operating within the areas that the Portuguese believed belonged to the *padroado* in India. As a consequence of the quarrelling over the rights of jurisdiction between the Portuguese bishops and the Rome-appointed Vicars Apostolic, many sees in India were left vacant. By the end of the eighteenth century there were two distinct and divided camps that came under the umbrella of 'Catholic India'.

From the Company's perspective, they believed that the combined number of Roman Catholics sent out by Propaganda Fide with those

---

[35] C. R. Boxer, *The Portuguese Seaborne Empire 1415–1825* (London: Hutchinson, 1969), pp. 235–6; G. T. MacKenzie, 'History of Christianity of Travancore', in V. Nagum Aiya, *The Travancore State Manual*, 3 vols. (Tribandrum: Travancore Government Press, 1906), I, pp. 188, 191–5.

already operating under the *padroado* regime were more than sufficient to minister to the needs of a relatively small Indian Catholic population. Moreover, Company officials became aware at a very early stage that Catholic missionaries very rarely attempted to proselytise in India. If attempts were made to convert individuals on behalf of Roman Catholic missionaries, Protestants rather than Hindus or Muslims were targeted. Given these circumstances, the Company, therefore, did not initially see Catholic missionaries as being politically dangerous.[36] Throughout the early nineteenth century, several Catholic prelates in India earned the patronage and admiration of the Company's hierarchy. Bishop Luigi in Kerala and Bishop Alcantara in Bombay, for example, both of whom operated under Propaganda Fide, intermittently received generous subsidies and loans from the Bombay government to aid their missions. Similarly, the Italian Carmelite, Fr Francesco Saverio, and the French secular priest from the Missions Étrangères, the Abbé Dubois, were also well-known and widely respected by the Madras establishment. Their ability to supply the Madras authorities with informative local information, and, in particular, the Abbé Dubois' tireless instruction as Superintendent of Vaccination at Mysore, earned both generous grants to fund their missionary work and handsome pensions upon their retirement. Moreover, the Company believed that the presence of Roman Catholic missionaries in India would conveniently serve as a spiritual aid to a large portion of the soldiers in the Company's European army, nearly 50 per cent of whom were Irish Roman Catholics by the early nineteenth century.[37]

Catholic priests and Irish soldiers in India's military cantonments

As the number of Irish Roman Catholic soldiers employed in the regular British and Company's army grew during the second half of the eighteenth century, the British authorities became increasingly nervous of the political implications that a large standing army of Irish Catholics could have upon imperial authority in India. Certainly much of the social and political unrest recorded among the Company and Crown's European soldiers in India during the early years of the nineteenth century concerned Irish Roman Catholics. Foremost among the

[36] See K. Ballhatchet, 'The East India Company and Roman Catholic Missionaries', *Journal of Ecclesiastical History*, 44, 2 (April 1993), 273–88.
[37] See Cadet Papers, 1775–1860: Applications for East India Company Cadetships, L/Mil/9/107–269. OIOC, BL.

142   Religion, civil society and imperial authority

major causes of disaffection among the Company's Irish troops was the demand for English-speaking or, indeed, Gaelic-speaking military chaplains to minister to the spiritual welfare of Irish soldiers in British military cantonments. Throughout the 1820s and 1830s, in particular, French and Italian bishops in India received numerous petitions on behalf of Irish Roman Catholic soldiers seeking assurances from the Pope in Rome that Irish or English priests would be appointed to their cantonments. When Bishop Alcantara of Bombay went to Madras to inspect missionary affairs in 1819, for example, he was presented with both a petition and a memorial to Pope Pius VII by over 850 disaffected Roman Catholic Irish soldiers.[38] While Irish soldiers in the Company's army were largely unaffected by nationalist sentiment in the early years of the nineteenth century, their protests drew on and reflected the communal concerns of those pursuing emancipation at the time and can be viewed as powerful cultural expressions, though not necessarily anti-imperialist in sentiment. One of the first public subscriptions organised by All Hallows College, for example, took place among a group of the Company's Irish soldiers of the Madras Presidency in 1843. This particular petition, which was addressed directly to Rome, alleged that the spiritual needs of Irish Roman Catholic soldiers in India were being neglected by the current set of Christian missionaries in place. Using the medium of missionary priests from All Hallows College, Dublin, the soldiers claimed that they were being

driven out by necessity to this distant part of the world [India], far from our blessed country [Ireland] as well from our dearest relations and parents, living in a continual hardship and incessant labour both of mind and body and stript [sic] of all those blessings which only render the life of a man supportable in this vale of fear.[39]

In addition, the Irish soldiers criticised what they perceived as an elitist approach by Portuguese and French missionaries in administering their communities in India, commenting that these 'preachers of Christian virtues only preach to the rich and well-provided inhabitants and refuse to follow and comfort the distressed in their distress'.[40]

In Ireland, too, there was much public criticism voiced over the Company's inability to supply Gaelic-speaking priests for the large Irish-speaking contingent of soldiers in India during the first half of the nineteenth century. The southern Catholic press, in particular

[38] Memorial to Alcantara, 2 October 1819, Collectanea Sacrae Congregationis (SC) India Orientalis (Ind. Or.) (1811–1819), pp. 596–7; pp. 601–2; quoted in Ballhatchet, *Caste, Class and Catholicism*, p. 18.
[39] Ibid.   [40] Ibid.

Catholic priests and Irish soldiers

The Cork Examiner, printed numerous scathing editorials denouncing the Company's treatment of its Irish Roman Catholic soldiers in the Madras Presidency in the 1850s. One disgruntled Irish journalist condemned what they believed to be 'the haughty bearing of a conqueror who now in her hour of need calls on Catholic, Celtic Ireland to furnish her quota to her legions – and yet she suffers her Catholic soldiers in the Madras Presidency to be persecuted by bigoted commanding officers in the vain efforts to draw them or their children from their faith'.[41] Following the Indian Mutiny and the issue of a proclamation by Queen Victoria promising to uphold the rights and traditions of the Indian princely rulers, many observers among the Irish Catholic press resented what they perceived to be the deference paid by many of the Christian missionaries in India to the practices of Hinduism and Islam while Catholicism, in their opinion, was being severely undermined. One commentator bitterly complained that while the Company was 'profuse in their assurances of respect for the faithful Hindoo and of the Mussulman, the fiercest enemy of the Cross, they treat with cold indifference the claims of the very boldest and bravest of their Christian chivalry – the very soldiers on whose courage they rely for the restoration of power jeopardised by their own parsimoniousness or incompetency'.[42] Another critic who attacked the Company's policy of non-interference in religious matters in India complained that, while 'the Hindu and the Mussulman are to have their religious alarm allayed, their religious jealousy appeased, their religious scruples respected...the Irish soldier, who fights and bleeds in their cause, is unworthy of their consideration'.[43] In India, newspapers such as the *Bengal Catholic Herald* brought the issue of discontent among Catholic Irish soldiers into the public domain, proclaiming that Irish Catholics were 'a moiety in Queen's regiments in this country [India], and therefore it is the bounded duty of the Bishop in whose Vicariate they may be stationed, to see their religious wants properly provided for'.[44] Similarly, the *Bengal Hurkaru*, prompted by the Company's exhausting military campaigns during the 1840s and 1850s, insisted that there were simply not enough chaplains for Irish Roman Catholic soldiers in India.

In the wake of such stinging criticism, the Company, fearing that its popular recruiting stations in Ireland would be hit if something were not done to alleviate the distress of its Roman Catholic Irish soldiers, reluctantly agreed to the provision of English/Gaelic-speaking priests

---

[41] *The Cork Examiner*, 7 September 1857, p. 2.
[42] *The Cork Examiner*, 14 October 1857, p. 2.   [43] Ibid.
[44] *Bengal Catholic Herald*, quoted in ibid.

144   Religion, civil society and imperial authority

for Irish soldiers. As a consequence Irish Catholic priests established themselves in almost every major Indian city and military cantonment where many served as military chaplains during the nineteenth century. The only real concern that Company authorities had with regard to Irish clergy bound for India was that they should not be graduates of Maynooth College, Ireland's national Catholic seminary. During this period, the British authorities believed that Maynooth was inextricably linked to the rise of Irish nationalism and that graduates from there who travelled to India might incite disaffection or unrest among the Company's Irish Roman Catholic troops. Before travelling to India to take up his new position as Vicar Apostolic of Bengal in 1834, for example, Robert St Leger, a former Irish Jesuit Vice-Provincial, was asked to travel to London to meet Charles Grant, the President of the Board of Control. While in London, St Leger was reminded by a Jesuit colleague that his meeting with Grant may not be straightforward, as the 'government have a very great objection to Irish clergymen going to the colonies' and that 'all [Irish clergy] brought up at Maynooth were particularly obnoxious [to the Company] on account of their extreme political opinions'.[45] One such clergyman, Patrick Carew, a former professor of theology at St Patrick's College, Maynooth, who made his way out to India despite the reservations expressed by government officials, frequently exploited the Company's reliance upon Ireland as a crucial military supplier for the imperial armed forces in South Asia. During his tenure as Vicar Apostolic in Bombay, Carew used the Irish press as a platform for raising concerns and issuing demands with a view to negotiating better conditions and pay for his Irish military chaplains and their Catholic co-workers in India. Later still, so-called Irish 'sepoy patriots' used the provincial press system in Ireland to articulate Catholic nationalist grievances and subsequently posted proclamations and manifestos offering support for the Indian mutineers of 1857–8 while inciting Fenian sympathisers to rise against their 'common English oppressors'.

In the context of the East India Company's much debated period of military and political reform in the 1830s, E. T. Stokes has argued that this was a time in which the impact of evangelical and utilitarian ideas of reform became most pronounced on British policy in India.[46] As the Company sought political, economic and social stability during this time, the growing influence of evangelical Protestant officers

[45] See R. Lythgoe, 16 March 1834, London Jesuit Archives (LJA). Archives of English Province, India 1802–1911, f. 205.
[46] E. T. Stokes, *The English Utilitarians and India* (Oxford: Clarendon Press, 1959).

Irish Catholicism and Indian caste 145

was causing some concern among the Company's sepoy regiments. Paradoxically, the reforms introduced by the Company in the 1830s, motivated by the need for economy, led to the spending of large sums of money on the Company's regiments. New waves of evangelical British officers were thus brought in to administer the settlements of invalid soldiers and their families during the 1830s, a process that caused much resentment among the Company's Indian peasant regiments.[47]

Irish protests to Rome were in part also a response to the growing influence of evangelicalism on the subcontinent and demonstrated a desire to participate in the politics of British India, an arena that could be seen to be eroding their cultural and religious sensibilities. Religious networks, formed in Ireland's new seminaries, shaped by the growing confidence of Catholic identity following emancipation and shipped out to minister to the needs of soldiering networks in India, point to a complex and often conflictual web of social, cultural and political needs, demands and desires enacted on the stage of Britain's Eastern Empire within the ranks of the Empire's servants and agents. Moreover, while the politics of religion fermented in India's military cantonments in ways that would connect Ireland and India through new languages of nationalism more fully in the second half of the nineteenth century, the notions and practices of Irish Catholic prelates began to create new tensions between India's Catholic communities and the colonial state through the vexed issue of caste.

Irish Catholicism and Indian caste: Daniel O'Connor and the Madras mission

Of all the topics that have engaged scholars of South Asia in recent years, caste has been one of the most contentious. An elaborate system of stratified social hierarchy that at once distinguished India from all other societies, caste has been discussed in academic debate much in the same way as issues of 'race' in the United States or 'class' in the United Kingdom. Since the days of British rule in India, historians and anthropologists have tended to analyse and view Indian life through the miasma of an all-pervading 'caste-society'. In recent decades, however, scholarship, both within India and abroad, has argued that many of the earlier 'orientalist' accounts of South Asian culture greatly exaggerated the importance of caste in Indian life. Some scholars have even gone so far as to dismiss the idea of a 'caste-society' as nothing more than a colonial construct initiated by data-collecting British administrators and

[47] Alavi, *The Sepoys and the Company*, pp. 95–154.

146   Religion, civil society and imperial authority

their Indian informants.[48] More recent scholarship on the role of caste in Indian society and its effects on Indian politics has demonstrated that, historically, caste played an integral and active part in shaping the political and social structure of Indian life and was not just a mere fabrication of the colonial imagination. Susan Bayly, for example, has shown that caste was engendered, shaped and perpetuated by a complex series of comparatively recent political and social developments on the subcontinent. She has argued that as late as the early eighteenth century, the period encompassing the expansion of British power in India, the institutions and beliefs often described as the elements of 'traditional' caste were only beginning to emerge.[49] In Bayly's view, it was as much the British as the Indians themselves who participated in the process of shaping caste as a stratified 'system' of social hierarchy on the subcontinent.

In this manner, understandings of caste as articulated through the writings of scholar-officials or missionaries during the eighteenth and nineteenth centuries had a considerable effect on Indian life, especially when such views were shaped by contributions from Indians themselves. In many instances, so-called 'orientalists' who depicted low-caste Hindus as the victims of an inflexibly hierarchical and Brahmin-centred value system played a significant part in the shaping of a more class-conscious social order under British rule. For most Christian missionaries working in India during the late eighteenth and early nineteenth centuries, the idea of a caste system was generally acceptable if individual castes were concerned with the formation of social hierarchies, much in the same way as class divisions in Europe. However, if hereditary membership of a caste implied spiritual merit or demerit (as was often the case among Indian Christians), it contradicted certain Western notions of Christianity that all men were equal before God, and thus issues of caste became a point of contention between foreign missionaries and sections of Indian Christian society.[50]

European involvement in the 'shaping' of the Indian caste system began as early as 1682 when the British had welcomed the first French

---

[48] See D. A. Washbrook, 'The Development of Caste Organization in South India', in C. J. Baker and D. A. Washbrook (eds.), *South India: Political Institutions and Political Change 1880–1940* (Delhi: Macmillan, 1975), pp. 150–203.

[49] S. Bayly, *Caste, Society and Politics in India from the Eighteenth Century to the Modern Age*, vol. 4.3 of *The New Cambridge History of India* (Cambridge University Press, 1999); and R. O'Hanlon, *Caste, Conflict and Ideology: Mahatma Jotirao Phule and Low Caste Protest in Nineteenth-Century Western India* (Cambridge University Press, 1985).

[50] S. Bayly, *Saints, Goddesses and Kings: Muslims and Christians in South Indian Society 1700–1900* (Cambridge University Press, 1989), pp. 420–52.

Capuchin missionary to Fort St George, largely in an effort to counter-balance growing Portuguese commercial influence in the Company's new Madras settlement. However, by the 1780s the escalation of Anglo-French rivalry dictated that it was more beneficial for the British to support Portuguese rather than French religious interests in India. During this period the British authorities in Madras, for example, began to favour the Portuguese Bishop of San Thomé in Mylapore rather than the resident French Bishop based in Pondicherry.[51] Aside from the obvious political significance this shift in alliance would bring, supporting Portuguese interests in India meant that the Company would be in a better position to benefit from increased access to Portuguese and Eurasian finance. Here, the bond between the Madras government and Portuguese missionaries was strengthened by powerful Catholic Indian and Eurasian families such as the Di Monte, De Souza and the renowned bankers, the Di Fries brothers, who helped to finance several British ventures in Madras during the 1780s, including the construction of St John's Church.

Among the most important groups of Indian Christians in the Madras Presidency at this time was the Tamil-speaking Parava caste, which was primarily situated in the Rayapuram area and along the Coromandel Coast. For generations, boatmen from the Parava caste were responsible for transporting British merchandise from anchored ships in the bay to and from Madras harbour. As a result, the British looked favourably upon the Paravas and frequently intervened in ecclesiastical disputes on their behalf. As clients and protégés of the Portuguese in the early sixteenth century, the Paravas became professing Roman Catholics in one of the earliest mass conversions to take place in India under the aegis of the colonial state. However, the Paravas retained many of the distinctive features of their earlier social and religious life, while being deeply influenced by the policies and pronouncements of their European priests and missionaries. For the Parava caste, Christianity was not a barrier that separated them from the rest of Indian society. Instead it provided them with a new code of behaviour that Bayly refers to as 'caste lifestyle'. This way of living ordered Parava marriage patterns and domestic ritual practices like that of any other south Indian caste group. Although influenced by the policies of foreign missionaries, the Paravas did not necessarily view their Christian brethren as the sole purveyors of religious truth. As such, the teachings and missionary work by foreign missionaries, including the Irish, were always being

---

[51] See Campbell to Bishop of S. Thomé, Madras Public Proceedings, 3 March 1787, ff. 310–3. OIOC, BL.

148   Religion, civil society and imperial authority

constantly modified by the Paravas to suit the society and indigenous sacred landscape in Madras.[52]

Nor were the Paravas or indeed other Indian Christian castes simply subservient to the will of foreign missionaries. During the early nineteenth century, several Indian Christian communities voiced their concerns over the attitude and behaviour of European missionaries based in Madras. In the 1830s French and Italian Capuchins were accused by low-caste Indian Christians of failing to communicate and interact with the lay community on an equal footing. It was alleged that the aloof behaviour of the Capuchin missionary order in Madras was a result of fear over European priests being replaced by Indian priests, whom sections of the Capuchin mission believed to have immoral lifestyle tendencies. As the majority of Indian Catholics in Madras were of low caste, numerous complaints were made against supposed Capuchin arrogance and unwillingness to cooperate with the local community. In addition, there was grave concern from both the Madras government and Propaganda Fide as to the state of the financial administration of the Capuchin mission. By the 1830s, following a period of sustained criticism directed against French and Italian missionaries in south India, it was decided that the Capuchin mission in Madras was to be replaced. In its investigation into the controversy, Propaganda Fide observed that the British authorities in Madras had largely ignored the mission and refused it help because the Capuchins had so often compromised their relationship with the Portuguese government and Indian society in general, both of which the British could not afford to alienate.

As direct replacements for the Capuchin missionaries in Madras, the Carmelites in Bombay, many of whom by this time were joined by Irish secular priests, were cited as a good example of a Catholic mission who enjoyed the cooperation of the British government.[53] In 1834, following the suspension of diplomatic relations between Rome and Lisbon, Pope Gregory XVI decided to replace the established French Capuchin missionary in Madras with the appointment of Irish secular priests. As the new Vicar Apostolic of Madras, Propaganda Fide appointed Fr Daniel O'Connor, a former Provincial of the Irish Augustinians. In fact, the Vicariate of Madras was to become something of an Irish Catholic stronghold over the next seventy-five years. In total, there were

[52] Bayly, *Saints, Goddesses and Kings*, p. 9.
[53] K. Ballhatchet, 'Roman Catholic Missionaries and Indian Society: The Carmelites in Bombay, 1786–1857', in K. Ballhatchet and J. Harrison (eds.), *East India Company Studies* (Hong Kong: Asian Research Series, 1986), pp. 255–97.

Irish Catholicism and Indian caste 149

five successive Irish Catholic bishops appointed to Madras in the nineteenth century: Daniel O'Connor (1834–40), Patrick Carew (1838–40), John Fennelly (1841–68), Stephen Fennelly (1868–80) and Joseph Colgan (1882–1911).[54] By the time Daniel O'Connor departed from Dublin to south India in 1835, accompanied by five other Irish secular and two student priests from Maynooth College, the condition of the Madras mission was not much improved. Despite formal approaches by O'Connor to the East India Company and the Board of Control in London, he was refused travelling expenses and only through the intervention of the Pope did he manage to secure some form of funding to pay for his passage to the subcontinent.[55] Upon arrival, O'Connor was duly appointed Vicar Apostolic of Madras and was told to take over the Capuchin mission.

Significantly, O'Connor's arrival in Madras coincided with the emergence of O'Connellite constitutional nationalism in the British parliament in the 1830s. In 1833, during the discussions that preceded the renewal of the East India Company's charter, the President of the Board of Control was questioned by O'Connell as to the British government's intention to secure the welfare of the Company's disproportionate number of Irish Roman Catholic soldiers. Mindful of the recent success of mass Catholic agitation in Ireland and the role played by the Irish clergy in political affairs there during the 1820s and 1830s, O'Connor began to challenge the Madras government on its official policies regarding Roman Catholics in India. However, there were strong objections by Protestant missionaries in India to the notion that Roman Catholics should be favoured any more than the Nonconformists. The Whig government, which had been partially sympathetic to Irish grievances, was replaced by the Peel administration during 1834–5 and O'Connor's protestations initially went unheeded. Moreover, influential Protestant Baptist missionaries based at Serampore helped entrench the government's position further by speaking out against the presence of Roman Catholic missionaries in India at the time.[56] From the Baptists' point of view, Roman Catholics were not too dissimilar to the 'heathen Hindoos'.[57] They were critical of Roman Catholic missionaries because Catholics made few attempts to proselytise or to educate the Indian population. They accused the Catholic missionaries of denying access to

---

[54] E. M. Hogan, *The Irish Missionary Movement: A Historical Survey, 1830–1980* (Dublin: Gill and Macmillan, 1990), pp. 26–7.
[55] Ballhatchet, *Caste, Class and Catholicism in India*, p. 99.
[56] Potts, *British Baptist Missionaries in India*, pp. 59–61.
[57] See W. Ward, 'A Protestant's Reasons Why He Will Not Be a Papist' (Singapore: Mission Press, 1802).

150   Religion, civil society and imperial authority

the Bible for converts as well as preaching and conducting their duties in either Latin or Portuguese, thus ignoring the languages of their Indian congregation. Furthermore, the Baptists argued that Roman Catholic missionaries largely ignored Church discipline and protocol and openly practised 'idolatry'. In contrast, British Baptist missionaries only avoided attempts to proselytise Indian or Eurasian Protestants, preferring instead to concentrate their efforts on the conversion of Catholics and Armenian and Greek Christians. The influential Protestant journal, *Friend of India*, thus denounced O'Connor's pleas that the British government should do more for its Irish Roman Catholic soldiers, arguing that the Madras government was already showing great benevolence towards Irish Catholics by providing monthly stipends for priests who acted as military chaplains.[58] Of course, this is not to say that the British authorities in Madras greatly favoured Roman Catholic priests or were prepared to concede ground to them whenever religious disputes arose with other foreign missionaries. In several instances during the late 1830s, the Madras government opted to take a neutral stance regarding ecclesiastical disputes involving Portuguese, Irish or French missionaries. In 1836, for example, when the Portuguese missionary Fr Manoel died, his successor, Dom Antonio Texeira, announced upon his arrival in Madras that he would be functioning as Episcopal Governor until such time as he received official Papal approval recognising him as Bishop; O'Connor's letters of protestation to the Governor-General of Madras, Lord Auckland, were ignored. In this instance, the British authorities maintained that ecclesiastical disputes of this nature should be referred to the law courts.

On balance, however, O'Connor and his Irish priests received perhaps more support than opposition from the British government during this period. In 1835, when the Whig administration returned to power, there were considerable concessions made towards the Irish Catholic mission in Madras. For instance, when O'Connor tried to exert his authority over the rival *padroado* churches in Madras the government was not necessarily averse to his claims. Following a dispute between O'Connor and Fr Manoel de Ave Maria, the Episcopal Governor of Mailapur,[59] over the latter's attempts to regain control of St John's and the Parchery churches, the Madras government gave their support to O'Connor and his Irish priests. In settling the dispute between the rival claims of the Portuguese and Irish missionaries, the government of India commented that it would be preferable if ecclesiastical authority

[58] *Friend of India*, 8 October 1835.
[59] See Ballhatchet, *Caste, Class and Catholicism*, pp. 1–12.

Irish Catholicism and Indian caste 151

over these churches were to be exercised 'by a British-born subject rather than by prelates of foreign extraction'.[60] This was a considerable concession by the British authorities, because although O'Connor acted as Vicar Apostolic of the Capuchin mission, he did not formally exercise any authority over the *padroado* churches.[61] The Company's preference for a 'British-born subject' was significant. Although the East India Company may have favoured the more established and conservative *padroado* element in south India, the recently enfranchised Catholics of Ireland were now officially part of the 'British Empire' and as the struggle for Catholic emancipation had demonstrated, Irish Catholic grievances could not be ignored.

However, despite support from the British government in the 1830s, both O'Connor and his Irish missionaries in Madras were not immune to the criticism that had been levelled at their French predecessors by sections of the Indian Catholic community. During the early years of his tenure in Madras, for example, many of O'Connor's Indian detractors asserted that while Portuguese priests lacked knowledge of Indian languages, they could at least speak Portuguese, which was understood by three-quarters of the congregation of the Capuchin church. Irish priests, Indian Catholics complained, knew neither Tamil nor Portuguese and could only officiate in English or Latin.[62] Moreover, many of O'Connor's Indian parishioners objected to what they perceived as a particular type of Catholicism that the Irish introduced into Madras in the 1830s. It was alleged among a group who described themselves as 'poor Indians' that O'Connor and his Irish priests paid little heed to the proper liturgical practices.[63] The 'native part of the community' were said to be extremely 'displeased and discontented' because of O'Connor's failure to provide High Mass during the week, as well as on Sundays. Furthermore, they alleged that the Irish priests in Madras did not provide novenas for the lay Confraternities, nor did they arrange processions or provide a cross for the pulpit. Other Indian Catholics criticised the Irish clergy's dress code, complaining that they dressed too informally and that they resembled their Protestant counterparts more than Roman Catholic prelates. O'Connor countered such criticism by some of his Indian congregation by stating that he and his

---

[60] Government of India to Madras Government, 19 October 1836, Madras Ecclesiastical Proceedings, November 1836, pp. 507–19.
[61] Elphinstone to Auckland, 12 March 1838, Elphinstone Papers, Ms. Eur. F87/2 G23. OIOC, BL.
[62] See Ballhatchet, 'East India Company and Roman Catholic Missionaries'.
[63] Memorandum of the Funds and other particulars of the Capuchin church, etc., SC Ind. Or. 5, 605–6v; quoted in Ballhatchet, *Caste, Class and Catholicism*, p. 102.

152   Religion, civil society and imperial authority

fellow Irish priests always wore the soutane while saying Mass, and that 'only when he went abroad, like the rest of us, British and Europeans', he wore the same European dress worn by Priests and Bishops in England, Ireland and Scotland. Furthermore, O'Connor maintained that by adopting an informal mode of dress, he and his priests were in a better position to gain access to rural and mountainous regions outside of Madras, insisting that the adoption of informal dress by his Irish priests would enable them to serve the needs of the neglected and would thus 'produce the greatest advantage to the religion'.

Many high-caste Indian Catholics belonging to the Parava caste were not convinced by O'Connor's methods. They complained that the Irish missionaries in Madras spoke no Tamil and devoted much of their time to the Irish Roman Catholic soldiers in the military cantonments. The Irish, they protested, were trying to treat Indian Catholics as if they were Irish and not Indian at all. They did not adhere to Indian customs such as the separation of the sexes during Mass, nor did they take their shoes off before entering the church. In fact, O'Connor made matters worse and continued to incense high-caste Indian sensibilities by separating his 'Cathedral' church in Madras into two distinct sections. In the first section O'Connor assigned seats for Europeans and Indians in European dress, while in the second those wearing Indian dress were put together. As a result, many high-caste Tamils, who resented being mixed together with low-caste Pariahs, began collecting money with a view to building a separate church of their own if something were not done to alleviate the problem. Perhaps what alarmed Indian Catholics most was that it seemed to them as if O'Connor and his Irish priests were somehow trying to blur the lines between high and low caste in Madras. O'Connor, however, was resolute and insisted that his seating arrangement in the Cathedral church dissatisfied only a few high-caste Indians, whom, he observed, were small in number. Despite attempts by O'Connor's Vicar General, the Reverend Moriarty, to sub-divide the Indian section of the church into separate high- and low-caste areas, over eighty high-caste families stopped attending O'Connor's church services altogether and withdrew to the *padroado*.[64]

Such activity as demonstrated by O'Connor and his clergy in India during the 1830s in part reflects the position which a revitalised and reorganised Catholic Church in Ireland held during this period. The emancipation of Catholics gave rise to a lively, fervent, self-confident institution whose strong hold on the loyalty of the Catholic populace

[64] G. M. Sinnappa Pillai to Fr Michel d'Onnion, 25 November 1838, SC Ind. Or. 7, 99–100; see Ballhatchet, *Caste, Class and Catholicism*, p. 104.

Irish Catholicism and Indian caste 153

promoted a confidence and assertiveness among its clergy that was beginning to take recognisable form both within Ireland and among Catholic religious groups throughout the Empire. The relative freedom and newfound authority which Irish Catholic missionaries expressed overseas was predicated largely on the powerful bond that had been created between priest and peasant in Ireland. Throughout the late eighteenth and early nineteenth centuries, regular outbreaks of famine, disease and agrarian unrest contributed to the strengthening of these bonds which often resulted in Catholic priests – who functioned as spokesmen for the poor and disenfranchised – becoming predisposed to the social and economic interests of the Irish landless masses. In many cases, Irish Catholic missionaries took such sensibilities to India with them where they often found themselves aligned to low-caste Indian interests and, of course, to the Company's Irish Catholic soldiers. Being subsidised by Catholic Irish soldiers stationed in British military cantonments, Irish secular priests were inclined to be suspicious of high-caste Hindus and Muslims and were at best indifferent to issues of caste in general.[65]

However, despite the criticism levelled at O'Connor and his Irish missionaries in Madras in the 1830s, the substantial missionary work they undertook and the particular type of Catholicism they introduced to parts of south India did not go unnoticed. In 1838 the Vicar General of Madras, Reverend Moriarty, travelled to Rome in an attempt to defend O'Connor's actions in front of Propaganda Fide. Moriarty argued that the Vicariate of Madras had been considerably destabilised by O'Connor's predecessors, the French and Italian Capuchins, who were responsible for alienating large sections of the Indian Catholic population through internal feuding and controversy. Moriarty argued that Indian dissatisfaction with Propaganda Fide's Madras mission was not simply attributable to O'Connor's actions and those of his Irish priests but had been there for years. The mission, Moriarty claimed, contained many different and opposing factions each trying to secure their own particular interest in south India. In addition, Moriarty pointed out that long before the Irish had arrived in Madras, many Indian Catholics had been paying too much attention to religious pomp and ceremony.

---

[65] See Foreign Missionary Correspondence (India) of Dr Russell, President of Maynooth College (1857–80). Russell Papers 13/43 (Box 13 – Folder 43), St Patrick's College, Russell Library, Maynooth, Co. Kildare. See also K. Ballhatchet, 'French Missionaries and Indian Society: The Jesuit Mission to Maduré, 1837–1902', in M. C. Buxtorf (ed.), *Les Relations Historiques et Culturelles entre la France et l'Inde, XVIIe–XXe Siècle* (Sainte Clotilde: Association Historique Internationale de l'Océan Indien, 1987), pp. 227–48.

154   Religion, civil society and imperial authority

Prior to the arrival of the Irish, not enough attention, he maintained, had been paid to the practical requirements of the Catholic mission such as education, welfare for the poor and the ministering of the sacraments, all of which Moriarty claimed O'Connor was now trying to address in Madras.[66] Though not, of course, necessarily a phenomenon of Irish Catholicism during this period, these were all nevertheless important initiatives undertaken by a reorganised Catholic Church in Ireland during the 1830s and 1840s. In fact, many well-respected figures such as the Pondicherry-based French missionary, Abbé Luquet, praised O'Connor and his Irish priests for their approach to missionary work and interaction with Indian society in general. Luquet asserted that unlike the social conservatism employed by the Jesuits, the Irish paid little deference to high-caste Indians and applauded their adopted stance of neutrality when it came to the issue of caste in general. In Luquet's opinion, the French Jesuits had made a serious error in judgement in their preferential treatment of high-caste Indian Catholics. He maintained that he observed schools and churches established by the Irish missionaries open to all castes, and that Brahman, Pariah and Shudra children mixed freely without any complications whatsoever.[67]

The East India Company and the growth of Irish Catholic networks

Further evidence that Irish missionaries introduced a particular variety of Catholicism that in turn played a part in evolving notions of caste and social organisation in colonial India can be seen by examining the activity of a broader Irish religious network that came to include several Maynooth graduates in the late 1830s. In 1839, John Fennelly, a former Maynooth College bursar, was appointed by Propaganda Fide as O'Connor's direct replacement as Vicar Apostolic of Madras. Shortly before Fennelly's arrival to replace the retiring O'Connor, another Maynooth College graduate and former professor of theology, Patrick Carew, was appointed as interim coadjutor Bishop to O'Connor and given a brief to address some of the problems facing the Madras mission. Upon his arrival in south India in 1839, Carew wrote to Paul Cullen, the Rector of the Irish College in Rome, stating his

---

[66] Moriarty to Propaganda Fide, 8 September 1838, SC Ind. Or. 6, 527–30; Ballhatchet, 'French Missionaries and Indian Society', p. 238.
[67] Luquet to Propaganda Fide, 9 April 1845, AP, Acta 208, 130ff; C. M. de Melo, *The Recruitment and Formation of the Native Clergy in India (16th–19th Century): An Historical-Canonical Study* (Lisbon, 1955), p. 257ff.

The East India Company and Irish Catholic networks 155

determination to put things right in the Catholic mission in Madras.[68] Within six months of his arrival, Carew informed Propaganda Fide that he had succeeded in reconciling some disillusioned high-caste Indians who had left O'Connor's Cathedral church because of the offensive seating arrangements.

However, Carew's tenure in Madras was brief and, shortly before his departure to take up the vacant Vicariate of Calcutta, he too was involved in controversy. Around this time, Fr Doyle, an Irish military chaplain stationed at Bellary in Karnataka, had made an appeal to the Madras government for the supply of prayer books and other Catholic doctrinal works for the Company's Irish Roman Catholic soldiers. Upon referral to the government of India, it was decided that Doyle's request should be turned down on the grounds that the supply of the Bible and the Book of Common Prayer to Protestant soldiers were in accordance with Queen's Regulations and that the demands put forward by the Company's Catholic soldiers were not.[69] When the case was brought to the attention of Carew he was incensed, believing that the decision not to provide adequate prayer books for Irish soldiers was a blatant attempt by the government to exercise tighter control over the Catholic mission in India. Carew was unequivocal in his response. He informed the government that if the spiritual needs of the Company's Roman Catholic soldiers were not met he would appeal to all Irish clergy 'to raise their voices from the thousand altars at which they minister, and dissuade their countrymen from engaging in the military service of India', in the process promising that 'all the wealth of the Honourable Company would not succeed in raising a single regiment in Catholic Ireland'.[70] In response to Carew's very public threat, neither Lord Elphinstone, the Governor of Madras, nor Lord Auckland, the Governor-General, accepted responsibility. They merely denied involvement in the decision taken not to agree to Fr Doyle's request, and made mild assurances that in some special cases provision of Catholic doctrinal material for Roman Catholic soldiers would be possible.[71]

---

[68] Carew to Cullen, n.d., ICRA New Cullen, IV, iv Fi, 9; Ballhatchet, 'French Missionaries and Indian Society', p. 238.

[69] Government of India to Madras Government, 9 December 1840, Madras Ecclesiastical Proceedings, January 1841, 2–3.

[70] Carew to Government of India, 4 January 1841, Madras Ecclesiastical Proceedings, January 1841, 57–65.

[71] Government of India to Madras Government, 9 February 1841, Madras Ecclesiastical Proceedings, 10 February 1841, 14.

156   Religion, civil society and imperial authority

In January 1842, following the appointment of Carew to the Vicariate of Calcutta, John Fennelly arrived in Madras.[72] Shortly afterwards he was joined by his younger brother Stephen Fennelly and a party of Irish priests and students from Maynooth College.[73] From the outset it was obvious to Fennelly that the government of India was distancing itself from Catholic affairs in general, in so far as they preferred to see matters of ecclesiastical dispute going to the law courts. The transferral of Carew and his Vicar-General to Calcutta in 1841 once again destabilised the Catholic mission in Madras. One of Carew's Irish priests, Fr Kennedy, wrote to Fennelly before his arrival in India warning him of the sizeable task that faced him: 'What do you think of us with Madras, St Thomas' Mount, and Poonamalee to attend to, the Seminary, the Nunnery, the Fort and Hospital and Goal, Protestants to silence, preaching in the Cathedral twice every Sunday, Government business, etc.'[74] However, it was not long before Fennelly and his Irish priests in Madras received the necessary institutional support from Ireland in the form of the new missionary college, All Hallows, which had been opened in Dublin in 1842. From the time of his arrival in Madras, Fennelly had been in communication with Fr David Moriarty, the President of All Hallows, urging him to send out as many Irish priests as possible to supplement the mission.[75] In particular, Fennelly was anxious about ministering to the needs of his Indian congregation and that the paucity of existing missionaries at his disposal had meant that 'the natives have hitherto been considerably neglected in our mission, in consequence of the want of priests'.[76] In fact, Fennelly was quite adamant that Irish missionary priests must show greater respect and sensitivity to Indian customs and traditions. Michael Gough, an All Hallows graduate and parish priest in Peringhipooram, for example, wrote to the Vice-President of All Hallows, Bartholomew Woodlock, in 1848 expressing Fennelly's desire that all Irish priests in Madras 'must of course tolerate and respect all their [Indian] innocent usages, even when they appear barbarous in our eyes'.[77] In another letter to Woodlock, one of Fennelly's younger

---

[72] P. J. Corish, *Maynooth College 1795–1995* (Dublin: Gill and Macmillan, 1995), p. 96.
[73] See T. G. Duffy, 'An Irish Missionary Effort: The Brothers Fennelly', *Irish Ecclesiastical Review (IER)*, XVII (May 1921), 464–84; D. Meehan, 'Maynooth and the Missions', *IER*, LXVI (September 1945), 223–8; T. P. Corbett, *Ireland Sends India a Noble Prelate* (Calcutta, 1955).
[74] Kennedy to Fennelly, 8 June 1841, Madras Diocesan Archives. Quoted in Duffy, 'An Irish Missionary Effort', 466.
[75] Condon, *The Missionary College of All Hallows*, pp. 31–4, 103–9.
[76] Fennelly to Moriarty, d. Madras 15 February 1844, FAR, 1 November 1848, f. 3.
[77] Gough to Woodlock, d. Peringhipooram, Madras Vicariate, 22 June 1848, FAR, f. 32.

The East India Company and Irish Catholic networks 157

missionaries, Nathaniel O'Donnell, alleged that Fennelly had encouraged his Irish priests to go as far as adopting the traditional clothing and habits of the region in the expectation that by wearing 'the native Teloogoo dress – white soutane, scarlet silk cap and scarf, no shoes, the long flowing beard etc' and 'by conforming ourselves as far as religion will permit to the customs of this strange people, making ourselves all to all', Irish missionary priests would 'thus be the better enabled...to gain all to Christ'.[78] However, it appears that the one point that Fennelly was not prepared to compromise on concerned the issue of caste. Like O'Connor before him, Fennelly, too, was largely unsympathetic to the concerns of high-caste Indian Catholics. In his correspondence with Propaganda Fide, Fennelly warned on several occasions of the unsuitability of training Indians as priests, where he often cited attachment to caste as being an insurmountable obstacle.[79] Unsurprisingly, Fennelly's reluctance to assuage high-caste sensibilities and champion the ordination of Indian Catholic priests made him and his mission a target for much public criticism and complaint in Madras. A common criticism levelled at Fennelly was that he and his Irish priests mainly concerned themselves with the welfare of the European and Eurasian population and failed to observe the distinctions appropriate to high castes. Other Indians, too, criticised the military, as opposed to religious, style of dress worn by Irish priests. Moreover, the Irish, one notable high-caste Indian Tamil, P. D. Sarouvanitomarayan, remarked, 'ate beef and thought it perfectly fine to drive women in their carriages'.

In Calcutta, Bishop Carew had succeeded the French missionary Mgr Taberd as the new Vicar Apostolic in 1842. During his brief stay in Madras, Carew had earned a reputation as a somewhat tough, uncompromising Maynooth cleric. The Rector of St Xavier's, Fr Moré, remarked to Father-General Roothaan of the Jesuit mission how Carew's zeal and determination had already made him 'the terror of Protestants' in Calcutta.[80] Indeed Carew wasted no time in establishing his authority. In March 1843 he presided over the opening of Seal College, a boys' school established under the auspices of a wealthy Hindu, Moti Lal Seal. Although Seal was adamant that the new school should have no religious instruction, and that he alone should determine admissions on the ground that he was best able to judge who were

---

[78] Nathaniel O'Donnell to Woodlock, d. Cathedral Church, Madras, Feast of the Exaltation of the Holy Cross, 1849, *Second Annual Report of the Missionary College of All Hallows, Dublin*, 1 November 1849 (Dublin, 1850) f. 13.
[79] Fennelly to Moriarty, d. Madras 8 May 1846, in *First Annual Report of the Missionary College of All Hallows* (hereafter, FAR) (Dublin, 1849), p. 12.
[80] Moré to Roothaan, d. 4 July 1842, ARSI, Missio Beng. 1, 1-vi-20.

158   Religion, civil society and imperial authority

'the most respectable Hindus', Carew remained enthusiastic. Control
of the school was to be given to the Rector of St Xavier's, Fr Moré, who
in turn entrusted the day-to-day running to his Jesuit brothers. From
Carew's point of view, the establishment of the non-denominational
Seal College would provide an excellent addition to the existing Jesuit
college of St Xavier's, and would thus provide him with an opportunity to impose greater control over the Catholic mission in Calcutta.
However, attempts to centralise the activities of the regular and secular
clergy soon created tensions between the new Vicar Apostolic and the
more established Jesuit missionaries. Within months of the opening of
Seal College, Moti Lal Seal expressed his desire to Carew to break the
connection between his College and the Jesuits. Seal had alleged that
the Jesuit brothers had 'grossly outraged the religious feelings of the
Hindoos', while intimating that they were not thoroughly committed
to the new project.

After dividing Calcutta into ecclesiastical districts, Carew had busied
himself with the building of a new Catholic church, St Thomas', and
had once again asked the Jesuits to take charge. However, the new
Rector, Henry McCann, an Irishman by birth but raised in the English
Province, was soon writing letters of complaint to Propaganda Fide
arguing that the Jesuits did not have full control over St Thomas'
Church and that their abilities were being wasted solely as teachers
there and in St Xavier's.[81] Sensing that some of the English Jesuits did
not find the Calcutta mission particularly worthwhile, his response was
to withdraw the Jesuits' faculties for all parochial duties concerning St
Thomas'. Carew's suspicions, it appears, were not totally unfounded.
Writing to Fr Lythgoe in 1845, McCann made it clear that being stationed in Calcutta 'for the sake of educating a few Catholic children
mixed with some Protestants, Greeks and Musselmen in a manner...
wholly unsuited to their wants and prospects in life' did not greatly
appeal to him or his colleagues.[82]

Disillusioned with life in Calcutta, McCann suggested to Lythgoe
that if all the Jesuits could not leave Calcutta at once, then perhaps he
could let some leave and gradually introduce secular teachers in their
place. Secular teachers, McCann argued, would provide the school
with a better means of fulfilling the wants and needs of the pupils who
attended. According to McCann:

not half a dozen of them [the pupils] are in circumstances to allow of their
aspiring to anything better than employment as underwriters in government

[81] McCann to Lythgoe, d. 7 October 1845, LJA, India 1802–1911, f. 170.
[82] McCann to Lythgoe, ibid.

The East India Company and Irish Catholic networks 159

offices or clerkships in merchants' counting houses. Several of them are actual paupers, and kept by us gratis or at nominal charge to prevent them from going to the Protestant Free School. What folly to establish for such a class of people the full classical course of Stonyhurst, with instruction in Oriental Languages to boot.[83]

In short, McCann and the Jesuits believed their talents were being wasted in Calcutta and that they could achieve a lot more in England.[84] Although they could not accept Carew's attempts to amalgamate the regular and the secular clergy, this was not a phenomenon unique either to Carew or Calcutta. Many other nineteenth-century Vicars Apostolic had attempted to subordinate regulars, like seculars, to their immediate authority. Despite Father-General Roothaan's pleas to the Jesuits to suspend the dissolution of the College, McCann arranged to sell St Xavier's to the Anglican bishop and reported that some of the English Jesuits were on their way home.[85] However, not all the Jesuits under Bishop Carew in Calcutta disliked their duties. Edward Sinnott, a Jesuit Bother from the Irish Province, wrote to his Prefect Fr Kenny in Dublin expressing satisfaction with Calcutta, an eagerness to learn Bengali and an appreciation for the integrative role of St Xavier's.[86]

Although many graduates of both All Hallows and Maynooth College joined Carew in Calcutta and Fennelly in Madras during the 1840s and 1850s, many too were posted to the Vicariate of Agra in North India.[87] Unlike Madras and Calcutta during this period, Agra was presided over by an Italian Capuchin, Joseph Borghi.[88] In his official duties as Bishop of Agra, Borghi developed a close working relationship

[83] McCann to Lythgoe, d. 2 June 1845, cited in Lythgoe to Roothaan, 6 October 1846, ARSI, Angl. 3iii 27.
[84] See Boulogne to Roothaan, 26 March 1846, 1 May 1846, ARSI, Missio Beng. I, 1-iv-3.
[85] McCann to Lythgoe, d. 7 October 1846, LJA, India 1802–1911, p. 176.
[86] Fr Sinnott to Fr P. Kenny, d. 4 March 1837, Jesuit Archives Dublin.
[87] Twenty-six out of the twenty-nine Roman Catholic priests in Madras in 1851 were Irish. Nine were graduates of All Hallows College. See Condon, *All Hallows*, p. 109. The province of Hyderabad also belonged originally to the Madras vicariate. It was committed to the care of Fr Daniel Murphy by Dr Carew in 1841. In 1851 Hyderabad became an independent vicariate, with Murphy as the Vicar Apostolic. He had four Irish priests. Two All Hallows missionaries, John McIssey and Joseph Dalton, served in Hyderabad. In 1864 Bishop Murphy left India and later became Bishop of Hobart. Calcutta in Bengal and later East Bengal were also heavily influenced by Irish missionaries during the nineteenth century. First under Bishop Carew, then under Carew's Vicar General, Thomas Oliffe. Twelve All Hallows missionaries went out to Bengal between 1844 and 1858. See *FAR* (1851), pp. 9–11.
[88] Borghi (1839–49) was succeeded as Vicar Apostolic of Agra by Cajetan Carli (1849–54) and then Ignatius Perisco (1854–61). Bishop Perisco, in particular, was associated with many missionaries of All Hallows from the time when he was Capuchin administrator of the Agra Vicariate.

160   Religion, civil society and imperial authority

with the Catholic hierarchy in Dublin and the Irish Roman Catholic community in Agra. A vast expansive terrain, the Vicariate of Agra included regions such as the Punjab, the North West Provinces and the great central Indo-Gangetic plain. In particular, Borghi and his missionaries became responsible for the large concentration of British military personnel dispersed throughout these regions. Despite opposition from the government, Borghi and his Irish chaplains fought tirelessly to maintain the regimental schools that provided education for the orphans of Catholic Irish soldiers. In his correspondence with All Hallows, Borghi frequently alluded to the unease he felt over the level of suspicion expressed by the British government towards Catholics in India during the 1840s. Writing to Moriarty in Dublin in 1846, Borghi pleaded with the President for additional missionaries to be sent to Agra to tend to the spiritual needs of his 'beloved Irish soldiers'. Although he had managed to lay the foundations of the new Cathedral church of St Peter's in Agra, Borghi informed Moriarty that 'more than 600 Irish Catholics are obliged to assemble for Devine Service under a kind of shed made of straw'.[89] Moreover, Borghi complained to Moriarty that despite his attempts in establishing a military orphan-house in Agra and Sardhana for the sons and daughters of Irish soldiers, 'nothing at all can be expected from the Government' who were 'supporting Protestants, Hindoos and Mussulmans, but not the Catholics'.[90] Despite some official interference, however, Borghi insisted that the Catholic mission in Agra was flourishing. He told Moriarty how he had foiled a government 'plan to seize all the poor orphans, and to throw them into a Protestant Asylum' and how in the future 'with the help of some good Irish priests, things will go much better'.[91]

It wasn't long before Moriarty responded to Borghi's request. In 1848 two missionaries of All Hallows, Fr Joseph Rooney and Fr Nicholas Barry, arrived in Agra.[92] Their initial duty was to teach some 300 pupils in St Peter's College, most of whom were Eurasian but 'of Irish parents'.[93] Within days of his arrival, Barry wrote to Woodlock in Dublin informing him how 'those in high office are very much prejudiced against us'. He was also very impressed by Borghi whom he referred

---

[89] Borghi to Moriarty, d. Agra, 25 May 1846, *FAR*, 1848, All Hallows College, f. 13.
[90] Ibid.   [91] Ibid.
[92] Two other Irishmen from All Hallows also went to Agra in the 1850s. John McGrane was ordained in Agra in 1852 but died two years later. William Gleeson served as a military chaplain in Agra from 1854 to the early 1860s. In 1870 he became the founding pastor of St Anthony's, Oakland, California and died there in 1903.
[93] Fr Nicholas Barry to Woodlock, d. St Peter's College, Agra, 28 January 1848 (AHC), Annual Report, 1848, f. 37.

The East India Company and Irish Catholic networks 161

to as 'a real Father' and applauded his skills in diplomacy. Not only was Borghi 'fully able for them [Government of India]' but he also succeeded in obtaining salaries for the military chaplains 'of about £120 a year each, notwithstanding all their opposition'.[94] Furthermore, Barry informed Woodlock that Borghi was intent on 'lending his entire strength towards the education of the children' in Agra.

Nevertheless, issues of caste and conflict with Indian Catholics were seemingly as apparent within the Irish Catholic mission in Agra as they were in Madras and Calcutta. In writing to a colleague in Dublin in 1848, for example, Fr Barry made several observations about the caste system from an Irish perspective. In India, Barry alleged that 'the English and Irish live in great splendour...and are far more formal than the people at home. They are more exact about their caste than even the natives themselves. The man who has a few rupees a month more than his neighbour, would scarcely invite that neighbour to his table'.[95] Furthermore, Fr Barry concluded that in St Peter's Cathedral at Agra, it was the English and Irish lay congregation that did not like to sit on the same side of the church as Indians, and that as a result Bishop Borghi had reserved a wing 'for the natives solely'.[96]

Neither Fr Barry nor Fr Rooney, however, was totally restricted to teaching in St Peter's. By April 1848, Bishop Borghi had given Barry charge of a military station at Nomelah just outside Agra whose congregation, according to Barry himself, was 'entirely Irish' and thus 'necessitated an Irish priest to go there'.[97] With a congregation about 500-strong, Barry commented that it was composed chiefly of Irish soldiers and their families, with only a few civilians and 'about ten Catholic families of native Christians'. During Barry's chaplaincy at Nomelah, the military station was in the process of acquiring a new chapel. He noted crucially that the roofing, flooring and plastering of the church had been achieved through the patronage of the Irish soldiers. He enthused to Woodlock in Dublin that

The soldiers [in India] have the same warm feelings, the same respect and veneration for their clergy, as at home, the same generosity in contributing to works of charity. These good fellows handed me at the close of the month sometimes 100 rupees, or thirty pounds sterling, was given for that purpose. I

---

[94] Ibid., f. 38.
[95] Fr Nicholas Barry to Rev. N. O'Donnell, d. St Peter's College, Agra, 1 February 1848 (AHC), *First Annual Report*, 1848, f. 39.
[96] Ibid.
[97] Barry to Woodlock, d. Nomelah, Agra, 3 July 1848 (AHC), Annual Report, 1848, f. 43.

162   Religion, civil society and imperial authority

have known several to give half their monthly pay. The soldiers are indeed the hope of Catholicity in India.[98]

Fr Barry also made revealing comments to Woodlock about the social origins and backgrounds of his Irish congregation at Nomelah. Every evening, he observed, the Irish soldiers and their families would congregate and talk outside the chapel before entering to say their nightly prayers. This behaviour, according to Barry, resembled closely that which 'the people do in the country parishes in Ireland'. What mostly surprised him, however, was the difficulty that he experienced in hearing confessions and preparing some of his Irish congregation for confirmation. 'They were persons mostly from the west of Ireland, whose education had been neglected', he informed Woodlock. 'They often puzzled me', he continued, 'as they spoke nothing but Irish, so I had to get a catechist who understood the language'.[99] Indeed, it appeared that once a Gaelic-speaking priest had been found to instruct native Irish-speaking soldiers in the sacraments, Catholic religious practice in and around the military stations was considered to be quite good.

Moreover, there were indications by the 1850s that Indian Catholics were beginning to respond to the particular type of Irish Catholicism introduced by Irish missionaries. Bernard Sheridan, a young Irish Roman Catholic chaplain in Peringhipooram in the 1850s, for example, informed his Prefect in Dublin that 'Christians in India appear to be much better informed than persons of the same low rank in Ireland. They follow the priest through the different parts of the Mass most accurately, and this without the aid of a book. There are catechists appointed throughout the several villages, who instruct the Christians in the Christian doctrine'. 'The children', Sheridan maintained, 'are particularly attended to, as they constitute the hope of the mission. They are, almost in every village well instructed in the Catholic doctrine'.[100] In addition to active instruction, many Irish priests and Bishops in Madras, Calcutta and Agra took advantage of British reticence in formulating an official policy in dealing with its Irish Catholic missionaries in India and received small stipends in return for keeping records of Catholic activity in Indian towns and villages.

Nathaniel O'Donnell, for example, kept a carefully logged account of all baptisms, holy communions and confirmations registered at

---

[98] Ibid.   [99] Ibid.

[100] Rev. Bernard Sheridan to Woodlock, d. Peringhipooram, Madras, 29 March 1851, *Fourth Annual Report of the Missionary College of All Hallows*, 1 November 1851 (Dublin, 1852), f. 7.

Fenian agitation in India 163

St Mary's Seminary at Cardonagh in Madras between 1848 and 1850.[101] Others devoted themselves to the study of Indian languages, thus countermanding the notion that all Irish priests could not, and were not willing to, preach in either Tamil or Hindi. John MacIssey, an Irish Roman Catholic chaplain in Hyderabad, wrote to Fr James in Dublin in 1855 declaring his intent of mastering the Indian vernacular languages: 'I preach in Hindoostanee as yet which is understood by great numbers of the Christians, as it is the common tongue of the citizens of Hyderabad. Telegoo, however, is the language of the native Hindoos, and I am therefore studying it every leisure moment of time. I hope to be able to preach to them in it before Christmas.'[102] The work of chaplains like MacIssey and O'Donnell counter complaints that Irish Vicars Apostolic, and the secular priests and nuns who accompanied them to India, worked largely to promote the interests of soldiers and their families in military cantonments and failed to properly minister to the wider Indian Catholic community, often ignoring specific caste sensibilities. Indeed, the involvement of religious networks in debates on caste, education and the administration of the church demonstrate the myriad ways in which Irish Catholic religious networks became gradually embedded in Indian society from the 1830s onward. Moreover, co-ethnic Catholic networks, such as that fostered by Bishop Borghi and his Irish priests, often acted in divergence from the colonial state, articulating grievances that informed the debates over the methods used by the East India Company to establish its authority in India. This challenge to order takes a further form as evidence of dissension appears among Irish Catholic soldiers from the 1840s onward, when a more clearly defined language of national sentiment finds stronger articulation.

Fenian agitation in India

In his 1891 short story, 'Namgay Doola', Rudyard Kipling describes the particular ties linking the Irish Catholic soldier to India and, in turn,

[101] O'Donnell estimated a population of 46,500 Roman Catholics in the southern part of the Madras vicariate in 1851. The total number of communicants for the year 1850 was 11,405, of which O'Donnell estimates 9,588 were Indians, the remainder being Europeans and Eurasians. He estimates the total number of confirmations in 1848 being 769. In 1849 that number had arisen to 1,295. The total number of adult baptisms over a period of eleven years O'Donnell estimates at 2,979, of whom 2,080 'were from heathenism, the remainder from Protestantism'. See O'Donnell to Woodlock, d. St Mary's Seminary, Madras, Feast of St Gongall, 1851, *Fourth Annual Report*, 1851 (AHC), 1 November 1851 f. 9.
[102] Rev. John MacIssey to Fr James, d. Hyderabad (Deccan) 27 October 1855. *Ninth Annual Report*, All Hallows, 1 November 1855 (Dublin, 1857), f. 76.

164   Religion, civil society and imperial authority

the bonds between Indians and Catholic Ireland. Visiting a remote house in the hills of Tibet, the narrator finds a strange ménage: children with flaming red hair with their mother, 'a woman from the hills'. The father, now dead, was once a soldier in the East India Company, named 'Timlay Doola':

> The Tibetan woman, his wife, touched him, the visitor on the arm gently. The long parley outside the fort had lasted far into the day. It was now close upon twilight – the hour of the Angelus. Very solemnly the red-haired brats rose from the floor and formed a semi-circle. Namgay Doola, the son, laid his gun against the wall, lighted a little oil lamp, and set it before a recess in the wall. Pulling aside a curtain of dirty cloth, he revealed a worn brass crucifix leaning against the helmet-badge of a long forgotten East India regiment. 'Thus did my father', he said, crossing himself clumsily. The wife and children followed suit. Then all together they struck up the wailing chant that I had heard on the hillside –

> > Dir hane mard-i-yemen dir
> > To were ala gee

> I puzzled no longer. Again and again they crooned as if their hearts would break, their version of the chorus of the *Wearing of the Green*.

> > They're hanging men and women too
> > For the wearing of the Green.

Kipling's story speaks of the unexpected imbrications of Irish Catholic identity in the Indian context in which the worn brass crucifix, the East India Army badge and the creolised words of the eighteenth-century Irish rebel ballad ring out in the new context of colonial India. The complex transnational connections that Kipling implies at the end of the nineteenth century were certainly being forged some decades earlier: while Daniel O'Connell in the 1830s did not appear to have had India on his mind very often, the rising Indian intelligentsia were very much interested in political and religious developments in Ireland. The great reformer, Raja Rammohun Roy, in particular, gave strong moral support to Catholic emancipation and as early as 1822 Indian residents in Calcutta set up a fund to help 'the distressed Irish'.[103] Indian proto-nationalists were keenly aware of nationalist developments in Ireland and correlated struggles were being played out on Indian soil as Irish soldiering and religious networks reinforced each other's concerns within India's military cantonments.

---

[103] D. K. Chattopadhyay, *Dynamics of Social Change in Bengal, 1817–1851* (Calcutta: Punthi Pustak 1990), p. 91; *Bengal Hurkaru*, 5, 17 December 1822.

Fenian agitation in India

In some cases, the presence of Irish Roman Catholic priests in Indian cantonments from the 1840s onward contributed towards influencing the articulation of Irish grievances as well as promoting nationalist fervour among close networks of Irish Roman Catholic troops. Contemporary sources provide examples of disaffection and 'mutinous' behaviour among the Company's Catholic Irish soldiers and more significantly in the regular army's various Irish regiments. Though generally concealed by regimental solidarity, there were numerous incidents that involved Irishmen contravening the standards of subordination expected of them in India. The Queen's 53rd Regiment of Foot (an Irish regiment) had allegedly 'run riot' in Gibraltar during the 1840s.[104] During the Indian Mutiny of 1857, John Blackett, a railway engineer in Agra, recorded reports of the 53rd 'kicking up shines very like mutiny'.[105]

During the 'white mutiny' of 1859, when numerous European officers and soldiers protested at the amalgamation of the Company's and Crown's forces in the aftermath of the Indian mutiny, an Irish Roman Catholic priest attached to the 6th Bengal European Fusiliers was involved in an abortive attempt to persuade the men to strike until their grievances were addressed.[106] Indeed the only European regiment to organise a coherent protest or 'mutiny' during the events of 1859 was the 5th Bengal European Regiment (a predominantly Irish regiment) that was stationed at Berhampore in lower Bengal.[107] For eight days during mid July 1859 over 200 of the 372 men stationed at Berhampore refused duty. In the official court of inquiry into the cause of the European soldiers' protest at Berhampore, Private John Harty, a labourer from Dungourney, Co. Cork, among others, was charged with 'inciting the men...to mutinous conduct' by beating a tin pot and wearing the letters 'EIC' on his ribbon-tailored cap.[108] It was not until 25 June, when the 92nd Highlanders arrived from Calcutta, that the protest of the 5th European Bengal Fusiliers was ended. Significantly, it may be noted that the man called upon by the British authorities to quell the unrest among the Company's 5th European regiment at

---

[104] J. Lang, *Wanderings in India: And Other Sketches of Life in Hindostan* (London, 1859), p. 257.

[105] John Blackett to his mother, 18 October 1857, Letters of John Blackett, 1857–9, Photo.Eur.7, OIOC.

[106] Events in the 6th European Bengal Fusiliers can be reconstructed from the papers reproduced in *Parliamentary Papers*, Vol. LI (1860), pp. 57, 59, 113 and 143–4.

[107] For a full account of the 'white mutiny' of 1859, see P. Stanley, *White Mutiny: British Military Culture in India, 1825–1875* (London: Hurst, 1998), pp. 146–65.

[108] 'Charge submitted against No. 100, Private John Harty', *Parliamentary Papers*, Vol. LI (1860), p. 65.

166   Religion, civil society and imperial authority

Berhampore was Lieutenant Colonel Kenneth MacKenzie. An evangelical Scotsman, MacKenzie had vast experience of military service in Ireland where he was twice stationed, first during a Fenian uprising in 1848, when he captured William Smith O'Brien (one of the leading Fenian insurgents), and, later, during similar Fenian disturbances in Ireland during 1865–6.

Although there is little doubt that the vast majority of the Company's Irish soldiers' participation in the 'white mutiny' in 1859 was carried out primarily in the interest of securing what they believed was 'owed to them' in terms of pay and conditions, it appears there was a deeper cultural and even political element to some Irish soldiers' refusal to take 'the Queen's shilling'. One Irish Bombay artilleryman was sentenced to thirty lashes and two years' hard labour for telling the court in Meerut that 'We will not soldier for the Queen' and 'We will have our just rights... they may go and___ the Queen'.[109] Gunner Kinsella, a man of three-and-a-half years' service with the Company who stayed on to join the Queen's Army, was discharged with ignominy as a result of 'mutinous and seditious language calculated to...excite disaffection'.[110] In Meerut and Berhampore there were rumours circulating that upon being asked to return to duty some Irishmen had called for 'three groans for the Queen'.[111] While at Sealkot, Captain Rotton of the 3rd Brigade Horse Artillery recalled to his Staff Sergeant how four Irishmen, Gunners McCarthy, Turner, Malone and Considine, 'men of bad character', had incited twenty or thirty of his men to 'misbehave themselves'. Rotton was particularly scathing in his comments on the 'ringleader' Gunner McCarthy, whose career, in his opinion, 'had been one of perpetual resistance to legitimate authority' for over five years.[112]

In Ireland during the Indian Mutiny, so-called 'Irish *sepoy* patriots' began to post proclamations and manifestos around parts of Munster and Connaught in an attempt to drum up support for the Indian mutineers as well as to incite Irish Fenians to rise against their 'common English oppressors'. One such example, which was reprinted in the *Belfast Daily Mercury* in November 1857, read:

Men of Carlow. The time of England's downfall is at hand. Ireland awake. Will you be up? Long live Nena [*sic*] Sahib. Down with England. Hurray for liberty. God save the people...

---

[109] 'Proceedings of a European General Court Martial', Mhow, 6 June 1859, Rose Letter book, BL.

[110] Adjutant-General to SGIMD, n.d. August 1862, Military Proceedings, September 1862, No. 711, NAM.

[111] *Delhi Gazette*, 10 May 1859.

[112] *Parliamentary Papers*, Vol. LI (1860), p. 251.

Conclusion 167

Men of Cavan – Glorious news! Our Tyrants are in deep mourning – wailing is heard in every corner – thirteen thousand of our oppressors killed by the *sepoys*. Three cheers for the gallant *sepoys*. Men of Cavan, now is the time to strike; strike for your country and nationality...[113]

While it may be difficult to evaluate the extent of the role played by Catholic Irish priests and the influence of Fenianism among Catholic Irish soldiers during the 'white mutiny' in India in 1859, there is evidence to suggest that there was an early element of Fenianism prevalent among the Catholic Irish soldiery stationed in India during the second half of the nineteenth century. Under the leadership of John O'Leary, then William Francis Roantree and, finally, John Devoy, the Fenian movement sought to infiltrate British regiments through a policy of seeking recruits among trained soldiers with access to British arms and ammunition for the purpose of sowing disaffection.[114] Concentrating upon Irish Catholic soldiers, the Fenians recruited substantial numbers (15,000 according to Devoy) in both Ireland and Britain from 1863 to February 1866.[115] In their subsequent writings following their abortive rising in March 1867, some Fenian leaders later claimed that the British authorities had dealt with these 'crack Fenian regiments' by sending them overseas. In the wake of the Fenian crisis in Dublin during the mid 1860s, for instance, the Commander-in-Chief in Ireland, Sir Hugh Rose, reported to the Duke of Cambridge that the 53rd Foot, who had served during the Indian Mutiny, had become notorious for harbouring nationalists.[116]

Conclusion

The period 1830–1860 thus marked a decisive phase in the relationship between Catholic Ireland and Britain's Eastern Empire. Before 1830 the presence of Irish Roman Catholics had been largely confined to the East India Company's European regiments, while Irish Protestants continued to enjoy a hold over the traditional professions and commissions in the British army. The period encompassing Catholic emancipation in the 1830s witnessed the beginning of a gradual integration of middle-class Irish Catholics into Britain's Indian Empire. With a

---

[113] *Belfast Daily Mercury*, 2 November 1857.
[114] R. F. Foster, *Modern Ireland*, pp. 393–4.
[115] J. Devoy, *Recollections of an Irish Rebel* (Shannon: Irish University Press, 1969 [1929]).
[116] Sir Hugh Rose to the Duke of Cambridge, 1 February 1866, Papers of Sir Hugh Rose; Correspondence with the Duke of Cambridge, 1861–5, Add. Ms.42796, BL. Robert Blatchford, *My Life in the Army* (London, 1910), p. 16.

168   Religion, civil society and imperial authority

renewed confidence, Irish Catholic missionaries promoted the interests of a particular Irish dimension in British India. They ministered to Gaelic-speaking Irish soldiers, set about introducing a reconstructed parochial system modelled along Irish lines through the building of churches and other ecclesiastical structures and promoted the education of (high- and low-caste) Indian and Eurasian Christian children.

By the time the Indian Mutiny broke out in 1857 the beginnings of a change in tone in Ireland and India was becoming apparent. Assumed racial difference began to be supplanted by a sense of common grievance under the yoke of imperialism. Irish Catholic patriots began to discover a bond with India. In the 1850s, Britain's problems in the sub-continent and the Crimea, along with the vaunted resurgence of French power, gave hope to radical Fenians in Ireland and America. In Ulster, the *Belfast Daily Mercury*, a newspaper directed towards conservatively minded Protestant liberals, attacked 'Irish *sepoy* patriots', who used the example of the Indian Mutiny in an attempt to stir up disaffection in the south and west of Ireland. It reprinted proclamations and manifestos posted in these areas calling on all 'true Irishmen' to rise against their English oppressors. The *Mercury* was concerned that such proclamations could lead to violent outbursts against British rule. It dropped its usual impartiality and urged the government to take firm action against persons issuing seditious proclamations, which could find sympathy with a 'large portion of the Celtic population'. These proclamations, however, had little effect (except to antagonise Protestants), as Ireland was relatively passive in 1857 and in no mood for widespread revolt.[117] Indeed, as the mutiny came to a close, large numbers of middle-class Irish Catholics and Protestants and their associated educational institutions were realigning themselves for greater integration into an expanding empire. Alongside the Scottish and English schools, Irish universities, learned societies and scientific institutions served as the great imperial powerhouses of the mid nineteenth century in terms of supplying the civil and medical colonial services with a critical base of personnel, expertise and knowledge around which later colonial rule in India was based.

[117] *Belfast Daily Mercury*, 2 November 1857.

6 From Company to Crown rule

Introduction

From the late 1840s onward, a greater number of Irish Catholics began entering imperial service in India, due in part to the introduction of open-competitive examination in place of the old system of patronage. This influx served to balance the numbers of Irish Protestants who had passed through to India via Trinity College Dublin (TCD), the Royal Belfast Academical Institution and the Universities of Edinburgh and Glasgow. The large number of successful Irish candidates who obtained employment in India at this time was aided considerably by Irish universities and colleges (including the non-denominational Queen's College in Belfast, Cork and Galway established in 1845) who were quick to seize this opportunity, and subsequently tailored their curriculum to the specific requirements of the entrance examinations. In part, this drive mirrored a desire among the rising Irish middle classes to obtain careers in the Empire, but it also reflected a strong interest within Irish universities and colleges at the time to promote learning in oriental languages, Indian history, geography, zoology and the natural sciences. In turn, increased Irish numbers in the civil and medical services (including the subordinate colonial services) gave rise to various Irish knowledge communities and more sophisticated networks of intellectual exchange that contributed to the dissemination of antiquarian, ethnographical and medical knowledge throughout the British Empire.

The Indian Medical Service (IMS) was one of the principal scientific agencies in India in which many educated Irish people sought employment during the latter phase of the Company period and under Crown rule. Company surgeons and their successors provided a large proportion of the botanists, geologists and surveyors who travelled to India. It was partly because of their wide-ranging scientific interests that medical personnel played such a vital role in the European investigation of the Indian environment (including its topography, climate and disease).

170   From Company to Crown rule

In comparison to other areas of scientific enquiry, medicine directly engaged with the social, cultural and material lives of Indian people. While recent studies of the history of colonial medicine in India have concentrated heavily on individual subject areas such as issues of tropical medicine, virtually none of these works have taken into account the wider importance of the medical traditions and practices in regions such as Scotland and Ireland, two of the principal areas of the British Empire where Company surgeons and colonial scientists in India had been born and educated.[1]

During the colonial period a network of significant proportions had been created between Irish doctors and the IMS. Their desire for increased upward social mobility and betterment reflected contemporary changes within Irish educational institutions and universities which began to tailor their curricula towards the practical needs for employment of their graduates within the British Empire. Many Irishmen in the IMS published books, pamphlets and journal articles to present their work in the most favourable light, to defend their research or simply to make their names known to the general public or to the Home governments as a means of career advancement. Moreover, they were protégés of a distinctive Irish school of medicine that was very much apparent in India during the second half of the nineteenth century. This school was in part informed and moulded by the Irish famine experience of the 1840s, but more importantly it was characterised by its enthusiasm for technological, diagnostic and therapeutic innovation as well as an adherence to traditional folk medicine.

To a certain degree, the educations of Irish medical personnel reflected the prominence of Irish antiquarian debates and the influence of the Great Famine, which in turn shaped their collective intellectual pursuits and legislative and politico-economic concerns in India during the same period. The proliferation of hospitals and medical training institutes in Ireland in the mid nineteenth century was partly a result of

---

[1] R. Ramasubban, 'Imperial Health in British India, 1857–1900', in R. McLeod and M. Lewis (eds.), *Disease, Medicine, and Empire: Perspectives on Western Medicine and the Experience of European Expansion* (London: Routledge, 1988), pp. 38–60; D. Arnold, *Colonizing the Body: State Medicine and Epidemic Disease in Nineteenth-Century India* (Berkeley: University of California Press, 1996). On epidemics, see I. Klein, 'Malaria and Mortality in Bengal', *IESHR*, 9 (1972), 639–59; on issues of public health, see M. Harrison, *Public Health in British India: Anglo-Indian Preventative Medicine, 1859–1914* (Cambridge University Press, 1994), A. Kumar, *Medicine and the Raj: British Medical Policy in India, 1835–1911* (New Delhi; London: Sage, 1998); and on the interaction between Western and Indian medicine, see B. Gupta, 'Indigenous Medicine in Nineteenth- and Twentieth-Century Bengal', in C. Leslie (ed.), *Asian Medical Systems: A Comparative Study* (Berkeley: University California Press, 1996), pp. 368–78.

Medicine and the modernising state 171

the crisis in public health brought about by the Great Famine in Ireland in the 1840s. In its wake, a distinctive Irish school of medicine emerged that was characterised by major clinical advances developed in response to increased levels of famine diseases, epidemics and rising mortality rates. Irish doctors perceived themselves differently from their contemporary English and Scottish medical counterparts in so far as they were powerful agents of a modernising imperial state on the one hand, but were also champions of a declining traditional culture and rural way of life on the other. They were a particularly close network of professionals whose concerns overlapped and were often tied into several other scientific activities centred on the Ordnance Survey, the Statistical Society of Ireland and Royal Irish Academy. Many exponents of this school carried these intellectual concerns to India with them and wrote extensively on the epidemiology of famine diseases in Bengal and Madras as well as on their views on *Ayurvedic* (Hindu medicine) and *Unani* (Islamic medicine).

This chapter argues that mid- to late-nineteenth-century Ireland was not only prepared to embrace the British Empire at a time when Irish nationalism and unionism were both compelling ideologies, but that much of its infrastructure, including school and university curricula, and training institutes were sufficiently equipped to meet the demands of imperial service directly. By examining the development of specialisation and tailored curricula within Irish universities and certifying institutions that effectively ensured their evolution into imperial-feeder institutions or academies that furnished the British Empire with its personnel, this chapter develops an understanding of the social background, training and career paths of Irish medical personnel within the Company and Crown's service. The chapter argues that these professional networks fostered in Irish institutions brought a particular vision to bear on the evolution of British rule in India during the second half of the nineteenth century.

Medicine and the modernising state: Ireland and India

The Irish members of the East India Company's medical corps, or the Indian Medical Service as it became known in 1764, represented a small but substantial proportion of the transient population of Irishmen in late-eighteenth- and nineteenth-century India.[2] Until the introduction

[2] Lt-Col. D. G. Crawford, *A History of the Indian Medical Service 1600–1913*, Vol. I (London: W. Thacker & Co., 1914), p. 197. The Irish numbers of IMS recruits (and the percentage of all recruits) were: 1855–69, 145 (24 per cent); 1870–9, 117 (38 per

172   From Company to Crown rule

of competitive examination for entry into the Company's various medical services in 1855, Irish physicians and assistant surgeons on the subcontinent were almost entirely drawn from the Protestant Ascendancy in and around Leinster and Munster as well as from a significant body of Scots-Irish from Ulster. For much of the late eighteenth and first half of the nineteenth century, medical science in Ireland was professional and middle class, Anglican in the southern provinces and Presbyterian in the north.[3] During the second half of the century members of the rising Irish Catholic middle classes, both north and south, infiltrated the medical services of India in large numbers until the end of British colonial rule in 1947.

As with Irish Catholics before the 1830s, Indians had little opportunity to enter the Indian Medical Service, still less to rise to senior positions in the service. Nonetheless, Indians and the Irish, Catholic and Protestant, were essential to the organisation and dissemination of Western medicine in British India. Indeed, certain long-range affinities and interconnections tie the history of medical science in both Ireland and India during this period. In both countries the idea of scientific and medical 'improvement' was inextricably linked to the process of modernising rural societies. In India during the late eighteenth and early nineteenth centuries, scientific and medical institutions were almost entirely dominated by British personnel despite the long existence of vibrant Hindu and Muslim traditions of medical science.[4] In some ways this was similar to late-eighteenth- and early-nineteenth-century Ireland where indigenous Catholic folk traditions in medicine and healing were subordinated through the existence of state-funded, 'modernising' medical institutions dominated by members of the Anglo-Irish Protestant elite.[5] In both Ireland and India, modern 'European' scientific and institutional medical practice was established during the late eighteenth and nineteenth centuries. During this period the essential structures and approaches that characterise modern 'Western' medical practice in Ireland and India were formed.

---

cent); 1880–9, 50 (19 per cent); 1890–9, 34 (11 per cent); and 1900–9, 64 (15 per cent). Compiled from IMS papers, 1881–1914, L/MIL/9/408 and L/MIL/9/413–27, OIOC, BL. These figures are confirmed in Lt-Col. D. G. Crawford, *The Roll of the Indian Medical Service 1615–1930* (London: Thacker & Co., 1930).

[3] J. Bennett, 'Science and Social Policy in Ireland in the Mid-Nineteenth Century', in P. J. Bowler and N. White (eds.), *Science and Society in Ireland: The Social Context of Science and Technology in Ireland 1800–1950* (Belfast: Institute of Irish Studies, Queen's University of Belfast, 1997), p. 38.

[4] Arnold, *Science, Technology and Medicine in Colonial India*, p. 2.

[5] G. Jones and E. Malcolm (eds.), *Medicine, Disease and the State in Ireland, 1650–1940* (Cork University Press, 1999).

Medicine and the modernising state

At the same time, however, one should proceed cautiously before claiming that this period witnessed the 'ascendancy of medical science' in both countries.[6] Recent scholarship in the history of science in Ireland, for instance, has demonstrated that the growth of modern medical practice was stunted during much of the eighteenth century because so much of the population (as in India) had no access to trained medical personnel. Due to the huge regional and social disparities in the distribution and access of modern medicine in late-eighteenth-century rural Ireland and India, traditional folk remedies and the placebos and poisons of 'quacks' remained popular and much of the two populations, rich and poor, remained engaged in self-diagnosis.[7]

However, in both countries, the existence of older and culturally entrenched therapeutic beliefs and practices were subordinated in favour of new European models of medical science. The Tudor conquests in Ireland brought about the destruction of the network of leper hospitals, among others, established during the Middle Ages under the aegis of monastic or religious orders, and fundamentally undermined the capacity of the hereditary Gaelic medical families to exercise their skills.[8] Similarly, it was not until the late eighteenth and early nineteenth centuries that Europeans in India began to demonstrate a tolerance of – or even appreciation for – indigenous Indian medical practice in areas such as *Ayurvedic* and *Unani* medicine. To some extent British physicians in India during this period were engaged in a typically Orientalist exercise, widening the bounds of Western knowledge by interrogating Oriental texts and 'native informants'. In 1814 the Court of Directors of the East India Company identified itself with this quest, noting (on the basis of reports received from India) that there existed in Sanskrit 'many tracts of merit...on the virtues of plants and drugs, and on the applications of them in medicine, the knowledge of which might prove desirable to the European practitioner'.[9]

Until the beginning of the nineteenth century in Ireland when major advances in medical practice were being inaugurated, standard medical care was perhaps highest and mostly widely spread around the metropolitan centres of Dublin, Belfast and Cork. However, poor transport

---

[6] F. W. Powell, *The Politics of Irish Social Policy 1600–1900* (Lampeter: E. Mellen Press, 1992), p. 15.

[7] P. Logan, *Making the Cure: A Look at Irish Folk Medicine* (Dublin: Talbot Press, 1972), pp. 2–5; Bayly, *Empire and Information*, p. 363.

[8] J. F. Fleetwood, *The History of Medicine in Ireland* (2nd edn, Dublin: Skellig Press, 1983), pp. 13, 20–1, 25–6, 48; G. A. Lee, *Leper Hospitals in Medieval Ireland* (Dublin: Four Courts Press, 1996).

[9] See D. Kopf, *British Orientalism and the Bengal Renaissance: The Dynamics of Indian Modernisation, 1773–1835* (Berkeley: California University Press, 1969), p. 152.

174   From Company to Crown rule

conditions and the cost of adequate medical care in the late eighteenth century meant that in many rural districts there was still a great dependency on traditional remedies, wise women, herbalists and faith healers.[10] Indeed, indigenous Irish therapeutic practice played a crucial role in the later development of an Irish school of medicine during the mid nineteenth century, a school of thought that was to have a significant degree of influence upon the development of Anglo-Indian medicine later in the nineteenth century. This was similar in many respects to late-eighteenth-century India, where even the most sceptical British observers came to appreciate that there was much to be learned from indigenous Indian medicine, particularly from its rich *materia medica*, that had been accumulated over centuries of empirical trial and observation by the *vaids* or *hakims* (practitioners of *Ayurvedic* and *Unani* medicine respectively). In 1825, for instance, the editor of the *Transactions of the Medical and Physical Society of Calcutta* observed that, although 'the imperfect science of the *Baids* and *Hakeems* of India' could offer little in way of 'instructive lessons to their better educated brethren of Europe...the progress and condition of science in all ages, and in all climes, must be objects of interest', and the Society, accordingly, welcomed any light that might be thrown on 'the past or present existence of Oriental medicine, by information gathered from authentic sources, or derived from actual observation'.[11] Nevertheless, in both countries, although official government tolerated and even explored varieties of 'native' medical practice, they had little time for the religious sanctions and cultural cosmologies attached to 'indigenous' medicine.[12]

In late-eighteenth- and early-nineteenth-century Ireland, in the absence of regularly trained doctors in remote rural districts, clerics often assumed the role of priest-as-physician. Parishioners frequently sought out the local clergy for pastoral advice as well as advice on issues of medicine. Although this custom incorporated clergy of different denominations it was particularly prevalent among Irish Catholics. Here there was often a less tangible, almost supernatural dimension to the priest–healer nexus, one that embraced the whole panoply of Irish Catholic religious and folk belief, including the cult of the Virgin Mary, the shrines and relics of saints, patterns and holy wells.[13] There

---

[10] Foster, *Modern Ireland*, p. 220.
[11] See *Transactions of the Medical and Physical Society of Calcutta*, I (1825), pp. iii–iv.
[12] L. M. Geary, 'Prince Hohenloe, Signor Pastorini and Miraculous Healing in Early Nineteenth-Century Ireland', in G. Jones and E. Malcolm (eds.), *Medicine, Disease and the State in Ireland, 1650–1940* (Cork University Press, 1999), pp. 40–59.
[13] See M. MacNeill, *The Festivals of Lughnasa: A Study of the Survival of the Celtic Festival at the Beginning of the Harvest* (Oxford University Press, 1962), pp. 261–5, 602–42;

Medicine and the modernising state

was a belief, too, that the priest could act as a medium in procuring cures that appeared beyond the reach of conventional medicine. The strong belief among Irish Catholics in the authenticity of faith-healing during the 1820s and 1830s was a conviction that was shared not only by the Catholic hierarchy and clergy but also by some Irish politicians. Daniel O'Connell was a particularly strong advocate of the supernatural agency of Irish medicine, frequently expressing the opinion that 'miracles' and faith-healing had always been and would continue to be a feature of the Catholic religion.[14]

The Catholic belief that miracles were a providential manifestation of religious favouritism, an indication that God was on the side of the Catholic Irish, however, had obvious, threatening implications for the Established Church in Ireland and for the political and social order. The Irish Protestant response to popular 'miraculous healing' in early-nineteenth-century Ireland was thus determined by these and other complex theological considerations. Many Irish Protestant physicians insisted that reported cases of 'miraculous healing' involved individuals with acute psychological disorders who had simply recovered naturally. Others dismissed the so-called cures as nothing more than a combination of delusion and imposture while those who occupied the more extreme evangelical wing of Protestantism accepted a supernatural involvement but claimed that it was the force of darkness rather than goodness: the devil and not the deity.[15] The perceived 'negative' influence of popular religion on medical science was also a concern of many British and Irish physicians employed by the East India Company on the subcontinent during this period.

In India, following the generation of 'Oriental' scholars that came after Sir William Jones, between 1810 and 1830, scholar-surgeons such as Benjamin Heyne and Whitelaw Ainslie in Madras and H. H. Wilson in Bengal began to study *Ayurvedic* texts and Indian folk medicine as a means of obtaining local therapeutic substitutes for costly imported Western drugs. Although keen to impress the superiority of European

---

S. J. Connolly, *Priests and People in Pre-Famine Ireland* (Dublin: Gill and Macmillan, 1982), pp. 135–49.

[14] M. R. O'Connell (ed.), *The Correspondence of Daniel O'Connell: Vol. 2, 1815–1823* (Shannon: Irish University Press, 1972), pp. 504–5.

[15] Contemporary Irish newspapers such as the *Warder* and the *Dublin Evening Mail* reflected the more extreme Protestant reaction to faith-healing in Ireland during the 1820s. Certain words and phrases recurred in numerous letters, notably: 'imposture', 'delusion', 'superstition', 'blasphemy', 'priestcraft', 'fraud', 'credulity', 'ignorance', 'bigotry', 'monkish imposition', 'popish charlatanry' and 'Jesuitical falsehood'. See, particularly, *Dublin Evening Mail*, 30 June, 18, 25 August, 10, 22 September 1823; the *Warder*, 5 July, 23 August, 6 September, 15 November 1823.

176 From Company to Crown rule

over Indian medicine, such physicians were all too aware that when confronted with outbreaks of epidemic diseases, believed to be endemic on the subcontinent, Western therapeutic methods were not necessarily always effective.[16] In typically early nineteenth-century orientalist fashion, such European scholar-physicians displayed a critical attitude to Hindu medicine that was not too dissimilar to the disparagement of indigenous forms of medicine in contemporary Ireland. While appreciating the obvious range and utility of India's *material medica* and the skills of its physicians, many of these early orientalist writers criticised the way in which Indian medicine had become bound up with religion. In his *Materia Indica*, published in 1826, Whitelaw Ainslie, for example, cited the Hindu belief that *Ayurvedic* medicine was a gift from the gods as being 'a circumstance which has been an insurmountable obstacle to improvement' and one of the main reasons why Indian medicine was 'still sunk in such a state of empirical darkness'.[17]

As Irish doctors began to infiltrate the IMS in increasing numbers from the mid nineteenth century onward, domestic Irish medical practice not only found correlates in India, as both were subject to Britain's modernising impulse, but had a particular bearing upon issues of Western medicine introduced in India. The distinctive contributions of Irish medical networks in India required the harsh training ground of the Famine as well as the opening of opportunities presented by the introduction of open competition in the medical and civil services in 1855. Yet before this date there were already significant ways in which Irish physicians were participating in medical research and enterprise as part of the Company's medical services, which were developing in order to deal with the changing nature of trade, colonial rule and British settlement in India. Late-eighteenth- and early-nineteenth-century Irish medical personnel in India drew upon their knowledge of other outposts of empire in order to chart the new imperial environment of India. Their careers demonstrate the translation and development of nascent knowledge networks as well as the mining of the imperial connection for personal and professional gain, by a variety of middle-class Irishmen, Catholic and Protestant alike.

---

[16] For a discussion of the nineteenth-century interaction between Western and Indian medicine, see Gupta, 'Indigenous Medicine', pp. 368–78; J. C. Hume, 'Rival Traditions: Western Medicine and Yunan-I Tibb in the Punjab, 1849–1889', *Bulletin of the History of Medicine*, 61 (1977), 214–31; P. Bala, *Imperialism and Medicine in Bengal: A Socio-Historical Perspective* (New Delhi; London: Sage, 1991); and Kumar, *Medicine and the Raj*.

[17] W. Ainslie, *Materia Indica*, Vol. II (London, 1826), pp. v, vii.

Irishmen and the East India Company's Medical Services, pre 1840s

Unlike other imperial institutions in British India, the IMS was not based directly upon metropolitan or indigenous models. Rather it arose out of the direct military requirements of early British colonial rule in India. During the early seventeenth century most European medical practitioners endeavouring to find employment in the East were to be found as surgeons or physicians at the Courts of various Indian and other Eastern rulers.[18] However, as the Company began to extend its trading operations and began to establish factories around its three main Presidency towns, Calcutta, Bombay and Madras, the number of European surgeons in India steadily increased.[19] With the expansion of the Company in Bengal and south-east India in the mid eighteenth century, the necessity arose for a permanent land-based establishment to meet the medical needs of Company servants, and especially those of its army. Following successive wars between Britain and France during the Seven Years War against France (1756–63), the presence of a larger and more permanent military presence in India dictated a corresponding need to expand the Company's medical services.

In 1763 the Bengal Medical Service was formed with fixed grades or ranks and definite rules of promotion. The creation of a medical service in Bengal was soon followed by the creation along similar lines of two other medical services in Madras and Bombay.[20] From the outset the Company's medical services in India were almost entirely military in orientation. Under the regulations introduced by Governor-General Lord Cornwallis in 1788, all British and Irish surgeons were required to perform nearly two years of military service before they could be eligible for a civil-surgeoncy. Members of the Company's medical services thus held a double commission, as both medical and military officers, whose military responsibilities (especially in times of war) had to take precedence over civil duties. Decades of warfare and European expansion on the subcontinent further highlighted the need for a permanent

---

[18] See Crawford, *Indian Medical Service*, I, pp. 7–8; N. Manucci, *Storia do Mogor, or Mughal India, 1653–1706*, transl. and ed. W. Irvine, *Indian Text Series*, 4 vols. (London: Folio Society, 1907), Introduction.

[19] Crawford, *Indian Medical Service*, I, pp. 1–6; W. B. Baetson, 'Indian Medical Service: Past and Present', *Asiatic Quarterly Review*, 14 (1902), 272–320.

[20] D. MacDonald, *Surgeons Twoe and a Barber: Being Some Account of the Life and Work of the Indian Medical Service (1600–1947)* (London: William Heinemann Medical Books, 1950).

178   From Company to Crown rule

service to supply a body of medical assistants and orderlies to perform the duties of compounders, dressers and apothecaries in European hospitals. Such work usually involved Indians as well as some European soldiers. In Bengal in the 1760s these subordinate medical-men were reorganised into a Military Subordinate Medical Service (SMS), an initiative that was eventually undertaken in the two other Presidencies during the early nineteenth century.[21] In 1858 when the administration of India was transferred from the East India Company to the Crown, the Indian medical services became the responsibility of the British government. Surgeons in the IMS became commissioned officers, although the Indian military medical service remained distinct from that of the British army, which had its own medical service – the Army Medical Department (after 1898, the Royal Army Medical Corps). In 1896 the three Presidency medical services were amalgamated into a single Indian medical service.[22]

For much of the eighteenth century Irish medical connections with India were made via the strong Irish medical presence aboard many of the Company's East Indiamen where surgeons were frequently assigned to Company ships bound for India. From the second half of the seventeenth century they also served at the Company's principal commercial factories and trading ports and towns. In their accounts of the diseases of seamen, visiting fleets and coastal stations, early medical accounts of India by Irishmen reflected the external, essentially maritime nature of British and Irish contact with India.[23] After about 1800, however, as British rule in India became more established, physicians began to compile more systematic accounts of the diseases of India and to relate them to the experience of the West Indies and other tropical climates. Of particular significance was the early work of John Crawford, who was one of the first medical officers in India to write on how climate influenced disease and the vulnerability of Europeans in the tropics. He was perhaps one of the first Irish-trained physicians to write on the effects of tropical disease and medicine among seamen in India.[24] Born in 1746, Crawford was the second son of an Ulster Presbyterian clergyman who entered TCD in 1763 and began his medical studies before enlisting as an Assistant Surgeon on board the East Indiaman, the *Marquis of Rockingham*. Crawford travelled twice to India and also

---

[21] Crawford, *Indian Medical Service*, II, pp. 243–57.

[22] See Harrison, *Public Health in British India*, pp. 6–35.

[23] J. P. Wade, *A Paper on the Prevention and Treatment of the Disorders of Seamen and Soldiers in Bengal* (London: J. Murray, 1793).

[24] R. N. Doetsch, 'John Crawford and His Contribution to the Doctrine of Contagium Vivum', *Bacteriological Reviews*, 28, 1 (March 1964), 87–96.

East India Company's Medical Services, pre-1840s 179

spent some time in China in the service of the East India Company. He was the first physician to suggest that yellow fever might be transmitted by insects and argued that many tropical diseases were caused by tiny organisms called *animalculae* that multiplied within the bodies of their victims. Crawford held these convictions at a time when it was generally believed that most diseases were 'chemical' in nature and that epidemics spread through the medium of foul vapours or gases. In India, Crawford carried out extensive research on medical topography. His first published book, *An Essay on the Nature, Cause and Cure of a Disease Incident to the Liver* (1772), described an illness which was almost certainly beriberi and one which affected seamen under his care during a voyage between China and St Helena in March 1771.[25] Following his stay in India, Crawford enjoyed brief spells as surgeon to the naval hospital in the West Indies and later as Surgeon Major in Demerara (1790–4).[26] By this time Crawford was applying ideas of medical topography derived initially from Europe and the West Indies to the unfolding knowledge of India's diseases and the manner in which these affected Indians as well as Europeans. It was during this period that he produced a paper entitled 'A Letter Addressed to Lieutenant General Matthew on the Means of Preventing, the Method of Treating and the Origin of Diseases Most Prevalent and Which Prove Most Destructive to the Natives of Cold Climates Visiting or Residing in Warm Countries'.[27] Along with later, more comprehensive accounts of the diseases of Madras and Bengal, such early scholarship by Irish naval surgeons such as Crawford constituted a preliminary mapping of India's disease environment.

Another Irish-trained physician with Indian connections was John Zephaniah Holwell, born in Co. Dublin in 1711 to a wealthy merchant family and who had studied at TCD.[28] Following brief stints in hospitals in Iselmond in the Netherlands and Guy's Hospital, London, Holwell obtained the position of Surgeon's Mate on board an East Indiaman

---

[25] J. Crawford, *An Essay on the Nature, Cause and Cure of a Disease Incident to the Liver: Hitherto but Little Known, Though very Frequent and Fatal in Hot Climates* (London, 1772), p. 4.

[26] E. F. Cordell, 'Sketch of John Crawford', *Johns Hopkins Hospital Bulletin*, 102 (1899), 158.

[27] J. Crawford, 'A Letter Addressed to Lieutenant General Matthew on the Means of Preventing, the Method of Treating and the Origin of Diseases Most Prevalent and Which Prove Most Destructive to the Natives of Cold Climates Visiting or Residing in Warm Countries'. Unpublished manuscript, Medical Faculty Library, University of Maryland, Baltimore.

[28] 'Copy of the seals and titles given to John Zephaniah Holwell, temporary governor of Bengal 1760, by Mir Jafar (1691–1765), Nawab of Bengal 1757–60 and 1763–65, on Holwell's appointment', Eur. Ms. C329, OIOC.

180   From Company to Crown rule

in 1732. During his first two years in India, Holwell received employment as a Company Surgeon at Patna and Dacca before finally settling in Calcutta. Holwell made his name in Calcutta, and between 1736 and 1748 he achieved a relatively high social status in India by acting as Second Surgeon-Major and Alderman. During the period 1752–7 Holwell consolidated his standing in Calcutta by becoming a Member of the Council of Bengal and *zamindar* of the Twenty-four Parganas. In 1757 he took command of Calcutta's defence in the wake of the flight of Governor Drake who faced attack from Suraj-ud-daula and was one of the few survivors of the notorious Black Hole incident.[29]

The various eighteenth-century medical services of the East India Company presented ambitious, career-minded individuals such as Holwell with the chance to demonstrate and develop the skills that they had been taught in their native countries. Irrespective of religious creed and ethnic origin, both Catholic and Protestant middle-class Irishmen forged successful and dynamic careers while in India. In Holwell's case, his Irish background and education did not seem to hamper his career prospects in any way. If anything they provided him with the necessary competence to reach the highest rungs of the medical profession. In 1760, on Robert Clive's departure, Holwell succeeded to the Governorship of Bengal for a brief period before he himself was to leave India. In addition to his medical training, Holwell was also extremely proficient in the Indian vernacular languages. Although he knew no Sanskrit, he certainly acquired a colloquial knowledge of Arabic. The attainment of knowledge of indigenous languages was an essential acquisition for an ambitious young Irish medic in the service of the East India Company in the eighteenth century. Not only did it greatly assist in the day-to-day activities and duties, but also for many Irishmen who lacked adequate patronage, the acquisition of professional qualifications such as languages could provide an extremely effective way of propelling themselves and their future careers in British India.

Both language and writing skills had gained a new administrative importance in the late eighteenth and early nineteenth centuries on the subcontinent.[30] In accordance with the gradual bureaucratisation of the middle levels of British Indian government, language skills were viewed as an indispensable component in establishing a successful and lasting career. Although Company officials in India found that

---

[29] J. Z. Holwell, *A Genuine Narrative of the Deplorable Deaths of the English Gentlemen, and Others, Who Were Suffocated in the Black-Hole in Fort-William, at Calcutta* (London: A. Millar, 1758).

[30] McLaren, *British India and British Scotland*.

East India Company's Medical Services, pre-1840s 181

expertise did not necessarily supersede either patronage or seniority as a guaranteed route towards career advancement, it did, however, provide a possible alternative route for able, ambitious junior medics with inadequate connections. In this sense, educated, ambitious Irishmen seeking employment in India benefited enormously. Holwell was an avid writer as well as a dedicated Company medical officer. His first noted published work, *A Genuine Narrative of the Deplorable Deaths of the English Gentlemen, and Others, Who Were Suffocated in the Black-Hole in Fort-William, at Calcutta* (1758), did as much to render him a courageous hero of considerable sensibility as it did to underline colonial anxiety concerning 'native' power. By the time his second major piece of work, *Interesting Historical Events, Relative to the Provinces of Bengal, and the Empire of Indostan*, was published in the mid 1760s, Holwell was regarded by many as a model of cultural empathy at a time when relationships between Company servants and their Bengal agents were almost exclusively limited to commercial dealings.[31]

The imperial nexus, within which individuals like Crawford and Holwell developed the seeds of significant intellectual knowledge networks, also facilitated the later development of Ireland's medical schools under the aegis of the utilitarian technologising drive of the government of India in the first half of the nineteenth century. Yet, before this time the medical profession in Ireland was structured in a very different way, very much along the lines of its Tudor predecessor. There were three main divisions in late-eighteenth-century Ireland's medical structure: the physician, who treated internal disease; the surgeon, who treated external conditions; and the apothecary, who compounded medications.[32] Each had its own different role in Irish society and its own professional bodies that established diploma examinations to supplement and later replace traditional apprenticeship. Internal coherence and discipline, however, were loose, while training and regulation were haphazard. Only Irish physicians required a university qualification (an MD) but even this did not evidence any uniform medical education because of the variable standards and requirements of the universities.[33]

---

[31] See A. Dow, *The History of Hindostan: Volumes I and II* (London: Routledge, 2000); J. Z. Holwell, *Interesting Historical Events, Relative to the Provinces of Bengal, and the Empire of Indostan*, Parts I and II (London: Routledge, 2000).

[32] Physicians as graduates and 'gentlemen' were the highest social and professional estate in early-nineteenth-century Britain and Ireland and were treated and paid accordingly, even when performing general duties in the armed forces. See N. Cantlie, *A History of the Army Medical Department*, Vol. I (Edinburgh: Churchill Livingstone, 1984), pp. 180–1.

[33] C. Newman, *The Evolution of Medical Education in the Nineteenth Century* (London: Oxford University Press, 1957).

182   From Company to Crown rule

By 1900, however, the medical profession in Ireland had undergone a dramatic transformation. The modern 'unitary' structure was in place with a common undergraduate curriculum and approved licensing bodies (certain professional bodies and universities with medical schools), which held 'qualifying examinations' for degrees and diplomas. The statutory national council, the General Medical Council (GMC), maintained a register of all those qualified to practise medicine in nineteenth-century Ireland and rigidly regulated professional standards and behaviour. While the GMC was responsible for regulating medical education in both Britain and Ireland as one, the genesis and imperatives of each country's supplying institutions were very different. For instance, unlike medical education in Scotland and England during the nineteenth century, Irish government policy was to introduce the principle of non-denominational education into the national system. At tertiary level, the new universities and colleges that came into being in Ireland in the mid nineteenth century therefore had religious and political considerations in mind. The precursor medical schools to the Queen's Colleges (1845–1909) and University College Dublin (1882–1909), the Royal Belfast Academical Institution (1835–49) and the Catholic University Medical School at Cecilia Street, Dublin (1855–1909), were founded to serve the needs of upwardly mobile groups of mainly Ulster Presbyterians and Irish Roman Catholics. However, these institutions were not empowered to award degrees or registerable medical diplomas and could only award 'preparatory' and class certificates.

In the absence of Irish medical degree-awarding institutions during the late eighteenth and early nineteenth centuries (with the exception of the Protestant dominated TCD),[34] most aspiring Irish Catholic and Presbyterian medical students instead developed important educational links with co-religionist Scotland. By 1800, Irish students accounted for a considerable proportion of the overall numbers attending not only the Royal College of Surgeons in Edinburgh but also the Universities of Edinburgh and Glasgow as well as the numerous private medical schools established in Scotland.[35] Between 1790 and 1830 there were 1,347 Irish student enrolments for anatomy at Edinburgh University

---

[34] This is described in D. A. Webb, 'Religious Controversy and Harmony at Trinity College Dublin over Four Centuries', *Hermathena*, Quartercentury Papers (1992), 95–114. The Royal College of Physicians of Ireland offered examined 'licenses' but mainly only to matriculated students of TCD or to holders of a degree in Arts. See J. H. D. Widdess, *An Account of the Schools of Surgery, Royal College of Surgeons, Dublin, 1789–1948* (Edinburgh: Livingstone Ltd., 1949), p. 225.

[35] C. J. Lawrence, 'The Edinburgh Medical School and the End of the "Old Thing", 1790–1830', *History of Universities*, 7 (1988), 265–8.

East India Company's Medical Services, pre-1840s   183

and 1,389 at Glasgow University. While most of these were Irish Presbyterians there was also a considerable number of Irish Catholics as well as Anglo-Irish Protestants represented.[36] Indeed the number of medical degrees awarded to Irish students from Scottish medical institutions between 1776 and 1825 surpassed any other single ethnic group, including English and Scottish. During this period, for example, Edinburgh University awarded 2,738 MDs and Glasgow 456. Of these, 958 (30 per cent) were to Irish students.[37]

However, the number of Irish enrolments at Scottish universities and colleges rapidly decreased after the 1830s when opportunities for registerable medical degrees among the developing Dublin and Belfast schools increased. Certainly before the 1850s, Irish medical practitioners who trained in TCD, the Royal Belfast Academical Institution or at the Scottish university medical schools (Catholic and Protestant) were very much a part of the technologising drive initiated by the government of India under the utilitarian influence and evangelical rule of Lord William Bentinck and his successors.[38] William O'Shaughnessy, son of a Catholic landowner from Co. Limerick, for example, began his medical studies at Edinburgh University in the late 1820s before entering the Bengal Medical Service as an Assistant Surgeon in 1833.[39] In India, O'Shaughnessy quickly rose to the forefront of the IMS and by 1835 was appointed professor of chemistry at the newly formed Medical College in Calcutta.[40] As his career in India demonstrates, O'Shaughnessy's introduction into the scientific establishment of Calcutta was strategic and exemplifies the transition from 'Orientalist' governance to state initiative in science and technology in British India after the 1830s. Progressive-minded professionals such as O'Shaughnessy were seen as invaluable to the new shift in scientific approach that was being created by the British government during this period.

In 1834 O'Shaughnessy was appointed Deputy Assay Master at the Calcutta Mint, one of the most senior scientific positions in Calcutta's

---

[36] From study of sample nominal class lists. P. Froggatt, 'The Irish Connection', in D. A. Dow (ed.), *The Influence of Scottish Medicine* (Park Ridge, NJ: Parthenon, 1988), pp. 63–76.

[37] *Evidence, Oral and Documentary, Taken Before the Commissioners for Visiting the Universities of Scotland* (Glasgow) H. of C. 1837 (93), xxxvi, Appendix, p. 533; (Edinburgh), H. of C. 1837 (92), xxxv, Appendix, pp. 149–50.

[38] Stokes, *English Utilitarians and India*.

[39] D. K. L. Chaudhury, '"Beyond the Reach of Monkeys and Men?" O'Shaughnessy and the Telegraph in India *c.* 1836–1856', *The Indian Economic and Social History Review*, 37, 3 (2000), 334.

[40] Home Department, Public Proceedings, Committee of Public Instruction, 5 August 1835, No. 15: From the Secretary with enclosures, d. 28 July 1835, NAI.

184   From Company to Crown rule

official establishment.[41] In this capacity O'Shaughnessy was able to establish himself as a local intellectual among the Anglo-Indian community in Calcutta, frequently publishing books and articles on innovative aspects of medical science. In particular, he was a keen contributor to the *Journal of the Asiatic Society of Bengal*, which had been founded in 1832. His scientific interests and scope of medical knowledge were outstanding and soon brought him into favour with the Bengal establishment.[42] As physician to Sir Charles Theophilus Metcalfe at Agra and as professor of chemistry in the Medical College at Calcutta in the 1840s, O'Shaughnessy began to explore the potential therapeutic effects of Indian hemp or cannabis.[43] His first series of experiments using Indian hemp on both humans and animals were published in the *Transactions of the Medical and Psychiatric Society of California* in 1842, where they generated considerable interest. In the mid nineteenth century cannabis was virtually unknown as a drug in Europe and North America. Within a few years of O'Shaughnessy's experiments, however, it was being used as a medication to treat a wide range of conditions by many of the leading doctors in Ireland, including Robert Graves and Sir Philip Crampton in Dublin.

Centralisation of government, institutionalisation of scientific enterprise and the hardening of imperial attitude in India in the early nineteenth century provided many opportunities and outlets for educated Irishmen. Despite O'Shaughnessy's Catholic Irish background, the IMS proved to be a fair employer that did not necessarily discriminate against him nor prevent the advancement of his career. As the imperial state increasingly sought to define its role as well as the roles of its personnel in India during the 1830s, its European employees in particular fell into rigidly defined roles.[44] As professor of chemistry in the Calcutta Medical College, O'Shaughnessy was very much a part of the new order being created by Governor-General William Bentinck and T. B. Macaulay. His experiments and competence in the scientific field

---

[41] Chaudhury, '"Beyond the Reach of Monkeys and Men?"', 334.

[42] A list of O'Shaughnessy's monograph articles in the *Journal of the Asiatic Society of Bengal*: JLIII, 145; JLVIII, 147; JLVIII, 714; JLVIII, 732, 838; JLVIII, 351; JLIX, 277; JLX, 6; JLXII, 1066; JLXVI, 177, 577.

[43] W. B. O'Shaughnessy, 'Extract from a Memoir on the Preparations of the Indian Hemp, or Gunjah (Cannabis Indica), Their Effects on the Animal System in Health, and Their Utility in the Treatment of Tetanus and other Convulsive Diseases', *The Journal of the Asiatic Society of Bengal*, ed. James Prinsep, viii, 93 (September 1840).

[44] S. Ghose, 'The Introduction and Advancement of the Electric Telegraph in India', PhD thesis, Jadavpur University, Calcutta, 1974, p. 247. Ghose argues that 'liberal and firm government support induced him [O'Shaughnessy] to come out of the laboratory and launch a grand technological enterprise'.

The Great Famine and the Irish School of Medicine 185

brought him into favour with the establishment, and, by 1847, with the help of substantial public donations, he successfully installed the first experimental telegraph lines in India, eventually connecting Calcutta, Agra, Bombay, Peshawar and Madras.[45]

The collaboration of successful Irish-trained medical personnel in Britain's imperial enterprise in India depended on the fostering of a network of educational and training institutes and facilities that met the growing need for the coherent scientific and technological development of Britain's new imperial resources. Competent Irish personnel like O'Shaughnessy were instrumental in ensuring the favourable outcome of scientific enterprise that underpinned the consolidation of British authority in India, while also disseminating new techniques and knowledge to Ireland via the channels of imperial medical and scientific communities. In turn, in the aftermath of the Great Famine in Ireland in the 1840s and its effect on the conditions, management and ideology of medical practice in Ireland, Irish personnel would bring a distinctive experience-driven contribution to bear on imperial policy dealing with corresponding conditions in India.

The Great Famine and the Irish School of Medicine

Unlike the clinical schools of Paris, Vienna, Edinburgh and London, the medical schools of Ireland, particularly those of Belfast, Cork and Dublin, remain largely unexplored by scholars methodologically informed by the new social and cultural history of medicine and science.[46] In recent years historians of empire have begun to examine a variety of shifting 'metropolitan' influences upon the history of science, technology and medicine in British India.[47] Such research, however, has tended to concentrate too heavily upon 'British' doctors from

---

[45] W. B. O'Shaughnessy, 'Memorandum Relative to Experiments on the Communication of Telegraph Signals by Induced Electricity', *Journal of the Asiatic Society of Bengal*, JLVIII (September 1839), 714–31.

[46] For examples of the new social and cultural history of medicine and science, see R. Porter (ed.), *Patients and Practitioners: Lay Perceptions of Medicine in Pre-Industrial Society* (Cambridge University Press, 1985), pp. 283–314; C. E. Rosenberg and J. Golden, *Framing Disease: Studies in Cultural History* (Brunswick, NJ: Rutgers University Press, 1992); J. V. Pickstone (ed.), *Medical Invention in Historical Perspective* (London, 1992); L. Jordanova, 'Medical Men 1780–1820', in J. Woodall (ed.), *Portraiture: Facing the Subject* (Manchester University Press, 1997), pp. 101–15.

[47] R. M. McLeod and M. Lewis (eds.), *Disease, Medicine and Empire: Perspectives on Western Medicine and the Experience of European Expansion* (London: Routledge, 1988).

186   From Company to Crown rule

medical institutions based in Scotland or in London.[48] Hitherto, too little emphasis has been placed and too little research has been undertaken upon the large influx of Irishmen into the medical services in India during the second half of the nineteenth century. Although it may be argued that during the Company Raj, the Irish doctors who travelled to India were very much by-products of a Scottish 'Enlightenment' educational system, this argument cannot be properly sustained after the 1840s. With the demise of the East India Company and the end of the old patronage system, to which the Irish were at an obvious disadvantage in comparison to the large number of Scots who controlled the majority of lucrative patronage networks in India, Irish-born and -educated doctors represented the largest single number of IMS and Army Medical Service (AMS) recruits enlisted during the first half of Crown rule in India.

These Irishmen were not simply offshoots of a Scottish or London school of medicine. The mid nineteenth century saw unprecedented changes in the structure of the medical profession in Ireland that were quite unique to the British Isles. Indeed it is only recently that scholars have stressed the existence of a distinctive Irish school of medicine during this period that was characterised by major clinical advances developed in the aftermath of the Great Famine in Ireland in the 1840s.[49] Moreover, after the late 1820s, Irish representation among the medical schools of Scotland declined considerably as population growth and burgeoning commercial and industrial prosperity in Ulster gave way to an intellectually challenging, upwardly mobile and predominantly Presbyterian Ulster middle class. Prosperous Ulster deplored what it perceived as the growing exodus of its intellectual sons to mainland Britain, and by 1826 the first steps were taken to establish 'a preparatory [non-degree awarding] school of medicine and surgery, useful and important to the medical youth of Ulster'.[50]

In 1835 the medical school of the Royal Belfast Academical Institution was established, and until its demise with the opening of the Queen's Colleges in 1849 it produced some 500 medical diplomats to succeed in professional body examinations. Clearly, the establishment of the medical school at the Royal Belfast Academical Institution in the 1830s served as an important precedent for the establishment of the Queen's

[48] M. Harrison, *Climates and Constitutions: Health, Race, Environment and British Imperialism in India 1600–1850* (Oxford University Press, 1999).
[49] J. B. Lyons, *Brief Lives of Irish Doctors* (Dublin: Blackwater Press, 1978); K. M. Cahill, 'The Golden Era of Irish Medicine', in *Irish Essays* (New York: John Jay Press, 1980), pp. 77–83; D. Coakley, *Irish Masters of Medicine* (Dublin: Town House, 1992).
[50] (Belfast) *Newsletter*, 7 November 1826.

The Great Famine and the Irish School of Medicine 187

Colleges in Belfast, Cork and Galway in 1849. Both institutions had no religious test for proprietors, managers, students or staff. Indeed no church was involved in the governance of either institution. A liberal Presbyterian ethos dominated (in Belfast), which drew on a pedigree of Scottish Enlightenment principles and Germanic and Napoleonic vocational and utilitarian traditions as applicable to a commercial Christian (though not exclusively Catholic) society. In Belfast there was tolerance in non-scriptural matters and a firm belief that secular education should be taken in common, religious education taken separately, and that the United Irishmen principles of self-improvement, diligence and providence should be the principal virtues of its students.

Just as the Royal Belfast Academical Institution had embraced 'Enlightenment' principles and remained staunchly independent, the Queen's Colleges followed a similar trajectory. Unlike the Catholic University Medical School established in Cecilia Street in Dublin in 1854, whose objectives were to make the Catholic religion the basis of a system of academic education for the rising Irish Catholic middle class, the Queen's Colleges were founded with the hope of providing a united education for both Irish Catholics and Protestants alike. The Colleges, one each in Connaught, Munster and Ulster, were to be free of any religious test, totally non-denominational, even secular in ethos, non-residential and were to have no Episcopal involvement in their governance at all. The scheme received a mixed reception. Speaking in parliament on 8 May 1845, Sir Robert Inglis described the Colleges as 'a gigantic scheme of godless education' and indeed they were soon referred to as 'the godless' colleges.[51] Generally, liberal clergy and much of the laity (including Young Ireland) were in support; the more conservative Catholic prelates, high Tories and orthodox Presbyterian divines were generally opposed to the formation of the Queen's Colleges.[52]

By the middle of the century, the infrastructure of an Irish school of medicine was firmly in place. At the time of the introduction of competitive examination for the IMS in October 1855 there were at least 36 students enrolled at the Catholic University Medical School; 320 students enrolled in the medical faculties of the Queen's Colleges and TCD; 129 on the anatomy lists at the Royal College of Surgeons; and a further 204 at the private medical schools of the Ledwich (Peter

[51] *Hansard* (3rd series), Vol. LXXX, p. 378.
[52] The controversy surrounding the inauguration of the Queen's Colleges in Ireland in 1849 and the opposition of the Irish Catholic Church has been well documented. See A. Macauley, *William Crolly: Archbishop of Armagh 1835–49* (Blackrock: Four Courts Press, 1994).

188   From Company to Crown rule

Street), Carmichael (Richmond Hospital) and Dr Steevens' in Dublin.[53] The foundation of St Vincent's and the Mater Hospitals in the 1830s, two Catholic teaching hospitals with important links to the Catholic University, further boosted the training of Irish Catholic doctors. It was hoped that through these institutions 'a new generation of men fitted for any and every post in the administration of the Empire' would prevail.[54]

To a degree the increased popularity of the medical profession in mid-nineteenth-century Ireland reflected its favourable status as a lucrative, moderately open meritocracy of high social prestige that was free of many of the residual sanctions against Catholics that operated in other professions. While traditionally Catholics and Presbyterians had long sought medical training abroad, there was a growing belief in the middle of the nineteenth century that they could now begin to benefit from the increasing demand with the improving fortunes of their co-religionists. Moreover, there was an extensive and growing national network of dispensaries, infirmaries, fever hospitals and poor law institutions to be staffed during and after the Great Famine in Ireland in the late 1840s. Although the population of Ireland decreased somewhat dramatically in the aftermath of the Famine (from 6.5 million in 1851 to 5.2 million by 1881), the number of Irish university medical students, many of whom were Catholic, actually increased at a significant rate.[55]

To a significant degree the creation of a distinct Irish school of medicine during the mid nineteenth century was moulded and informed by the experience of the Great Famine in Ireland during the 1840s and 1850s. Certainly the experience of such large-scale famine, widespread pestilence and disease among the Irish peasantry was unique to Ireland and Irish medical practitioners during this period.[56] In many respects the man who epitomised and directed the emergence of an Irish school of medicine during the famine years was Sir William Wilde.[57] Born in

---

[53] Figures quoted in C. Cameron, *History of the Royal College of Surgeons in Ireland and the Irish School of Medicine* (Dublin, 1st edn, 1886; 2nd edn, 1916), note 21, Appendix A, p. 696.

[54] *St. Stephen's*, June 1903, p. 251.

[55] P. Froggatt, 'Competing Philosophies: the "Preparatory" Medical Schools of the Royal Belfast Academical Institution and the Catholic University of Ireland, 1835–1909', in G. Jones and E. Malcolm (eds.), *Medicine, Disease and the State in Ireland, 1650–1940* (Cork University Press, 1999), p. 71.

[56] S. J. Connelly, 'Normality and Catastrophe in Irish History', unpublished inaugural lecture as professor of modern Irish history, Queen's University, Belfast, 1997.

[57] The standard biography of William Wilde, father of Oscar Wilde, remains that of T. G. Wilson, *Victorian Doctor* (London: Methuen & Co., 1942). See also J. Sproule, 'Sir William Wilde: Surgeon Oculist to the Queen in Ireland', *Dublin University Magazine*, 85 (1875), 570–89.

The Great Famine and the Irish School of Medicine

1815, Wilde was the son of a Protestant doctor who had a private medical practice in Co. Roscommon in the west of Ireland. He received his medical education at the Royal College of Surgeons, the Park Street private medical school, and trained at Dr Steevens' and the Rotunda hospitals in Dublin. Regarded as a leading specialist of his time, Wilde wrote major works on aural surgery, founded his own specialist teaching hospital, ran the leading Irish medical journal of the period, undertook pioneering research on Irish epidemiology and was a noted antiquarian and ethnographer. As both editor of the *Dublin Quarterly Journal of Medical Science* and a census commissioner for Ireland during the Famine, Wilde was one of the leading public representatives of Irish medical men through the famine years that so distinctively shaped their professional development.

This development involved nineteenth-century Irish doctors embracing the conflicting compulsions of tradition and modernity. For instance, Wilde and his cohorts published extensively on the Famine and its medical implications. Moreover, he was the first of his generation to attempt to infuse the Irish famine experience with writings on unique contributions made by his peers to the understanding of famine diseases and on the traditions and values of 'indigenous' Irish folk medicine.[58] The particular history that Wilde attributed to nineteenth-century Irish medicine was indeed very much akin to the writings of William Whewell on the history and philosophy of science in contemporary Britain.[59] Wilde sought to create a distinct discursive superstructure in which to locate Irish medical history, its people, its places and its moments. In his work 'A Short Account of the Superstitions and Popular Practices Relating to Midwifery, and Some of the Diseases of Women and Children, in Ireland' and in the remnants of his jottings for the unpublished 'History of Irish Medicine and Popular Cures', Wilde portrayed popular medicine as a unique national asset threatened with extinction through the combined effects of famine, education and emigration.[60] To counter its disappearance, Wilde eulogised about rural

[58] For Wilde on folk medicine, see his *Irish Popular Superstitions* (Shannon: Irish University Press, 1852). See also J. F. Wilde, *Ancient Cures, Charms and Usages of Ireland: Contributions to Irish Lore*, 2 vols. (London: Ward and Downey, 1887), much of which is composed of material gathered by William Wilde.

[59] R. Yeo, *Defining Science: William Whewell, Natural Knowledge and Public Debate in Early-Victorian Britain* (Cambridge University Press, 1993), pp. 8–9, 50–2, 70–4, 145–9.

[60] W. R. Wilde, 'A Short Account of the Superstitions and Popular Practices Relating to Midwifery, and Some of the Diseases of Women and Children, in Ireland', *Monthly Journal of Medical Science*, 9, 35 (1849), 711–26; W. R. Wilde, 'History of Irish Medicine and Popular Cures', unpublished and incomplete manuscript (University College Dublin Library, Special Collections, UCD Ms 2). For Wilde on the history of

190   From Company to Crown rule

Irish medical superstitions as a uniquely rich history of medical folklore of which it was the particular responsibility of the Irish country doctor to record for posterity.

What Wilde and his contemporaries sought to do was to give Irish medicine a form of identity, always stressing the creative tension between a professionalising drive towards modern scientific medicine on the one hand and the enchantments of Celticism and the west of Ireland on the other. For Wilde, use of folk medicine and traditional herbal remedies remained an important aspect in defining a distinctive 'Irish school' of medicine from the 1840s onward. Wilde was certainly aware of William O'Shaughnessy's contributions to the medical debates in Calcutta during this period. In the second edition of his book, *Narrative of a Voyage to Madeira, Teneriffe and Along the Shores of the Mediterranean*, published in 1844, Wilde drew attention to O'Shaughnessy's work in India, and particularly to O'Shaughnessy's use of Indian hemp as a cure for tetanus and other convulsive diseases. In some ways O'Shaughnessy's medical work in India was seen as an example by other aspiring Irish medics as to the possibilities presented through a career in the Indian Empire. In 1845 the Irish physician and chemist Michael Donovan began his paper 'On the Physical and Medicinal Qualities of Indian Hemp' in the *Dublin Quarterly Journal of Medical Science* with the following eulogy:

If the history of the *Materia Medica* were to be divided into epochs, each determined by the discovery of some remedy of transcendent power, the period of the introduction of Indian hemp into medicine would be entitled to the distinction of a new era...The [Irish] public and the Profession owe a deep debt of gratitude to Professor O'Shaughnessy.[61]

Donovan's tribute to O'Shaughnessy's seminal work reveals the growth of an intellectual network of ideas and influence linking Ireland and India through the knowledge-making and disseminating activities of an Irish medical personnel.

According to Wilde, a nineteenth-century Irish doctor should form part of a modernising coterie; Wilde himself was closely associated with the *Dublin University Magazine*, the Ordnance Survey, the Statistical Society of Ireland and the Royal Irish Academy. Moreover, he should have a particular idea of metropolitan Dublin as well as an ideological

Irish medicine, see also his 'Lecture on the Early History of Irish Medicine', *London Medical Gazette*, new series, 6 (1848), 301, 429, 478.

[61] M. Donovan, 'On the Physical and Medicinal Qualities of Indian Hemp (Cannabis Indica), with Observations on the Best Mode of Administration, and Cases Illustrative of its Powers', *Dublin Quarterly Journal of Medical Science*, XXVI (1845), 368–402.

The Great Famine and the Irish School of Medicine

investment in the west of Ireland and traditional folk medicine.[62] However, this local interest in tradition was replicated in relation to other imperial contexts and was certainly evident by the intellectual concerns Wilde and his medical coterie displayed through their involvement in the *Dublin University Magazine* and the *Dublin Quarterly Journal of Medical Science*. For instance, Wilde was responsible for editing several articles on contemporary medical practice in India and he was particularly interested in aspects of *Ayurveda* and Indian folk medicine. In reviewing T. A. Wise's *Commentary on the Hindu System of Medicine* (1845) in 1847, Wilde observed how from

a very early age the Hindus had attained a higher degree of civilisation, and have made greater advances in the arts and sciences, than any other people, except the Egyptians...we cannot avoid expressing our admiration; and to all who feel an interest in what may be termed the antiquities of medicine, we feel pleasure in recommending it, as a work from the perusal of which they will derive much gratification.[63]

Essentially Wilde and his peers saw themselves as doctors in the metropolitan context of Dublin and in the wider context of traditional rural Ireland, yet this atavistic intellectual predisposition made this Irish coterie receptive to analogous traditions of the imperial world. They perceived themselves as very much different from their contemporary English and Scottish medical counterparts in so far as they were powerful agents of a modernising imperial state on the one hand, but were also champions of a declining traditional culture and rural way of life on the other.

While Irish doctors demonstrated a concern for the traditions of rural life and popular medicine in Ireland during the second half of the nineteenth century, there is also evidence to suggest that, unlike Scotland or England, an ample, if not thoroughly effective, system of national health care was in place in Ireland following the aftermath of the Great Famine.[64] By the mid 1840s the arrangements for dealing with the sick and poor in famine-ridden Ireland were remarkably far-reaching. The numbers practising medicine during this period proliferated, with some 2,600 qualified medical men (80 per cent physicians or surgeons, and only 20 per cent exclusively apothecaries) and perhaps

---

[62] For Wilde on the west of Ireland, see W. R. Wilde, *Lough Corrib, Its Shores and Islands: With Notices of Lough Mask* (Dublin: M. H. Gill, 1867). For general post-Famine views of the west, see S. Deane, *Strange Country: Modernity and Nationhood in Irish Writing since 1790* (Oxford: Clarendon, 1997), pp. 52, 95.

[63] Quoted in the *Dublin Quarterly Journal of Medical Science*, IV (August–December 1847), 204.

[64] Foster, *Modern Ireland*, p. 327.

192   From Company to Crown rule

1,000 others 'ministering to health'.[65] Many of the diseases brought about by the Great Famine were endemic to both Ireland and India during this period. Typhus, relapsing fevers, smallpox, tuberculosis, dysentery, cholera and malnutrition were all prevalent. Indeed one notable Irish historian has asserted that 'if one takes policy and structure as the criteria, Ireland had one of the most advanced health services in Europe in the early nineteenth century'.[66] While this is perhaps too strong an assertion, given that the county dispensaries and centrally controlled fever hospitals were notoriously unable to cope with the huge demand for poor relief in the west of Ireland in the late 1840s, there is little doubt that the infrastructure itself was comprehensive.[67]

By the autumn of 1846, the start of the second successive potato crop failure, all 130 union workhouses, provided for under the Poor Law, were open. Each workhouse had its own infirmary of sorts and about 40 per cent of them provided isolation units for fever victims.[68] In addition to these infirmaries, some 664 medical dispensaries, an average of 1 per 12,000 of the population, provided a nation-wide service of free medicine and advice by the mid nineteenth century. These dispensaries usually constituted a small house or cabin attended by a doctor and a 'porter' and although there were many deficiencies in its operation, such as lack of inspection and control, rudimentary records, uneven quality of care and the problem of administering large rural districts, the system was a substantial administrative and medical achievement without parallel in Scotland or England. Behind these dispensaries were the fever hospitals, 73 of which were operating in Ireland by 1845.[69] Like the dispensaries, the fever hospitals were part charitable and part rate-supported. They too suffered from the deficiencies of the dispensaries and were overcrowded during times of epidemics. Although these fever hospitals did provide initial relief, it would be erroneous to equate them with a modern infectious-disease hospital. Most fever hospitals in mid-nineteenth-century Ireland were small and poorly equipped, often grossly overcrowded and lacked adequate funding to facilitate expansion or maintenance. The other three categories of medical charity, lunatic asylums, county infirmaries, and general voluntary hospitals,

---

[65] Figures from H. G. Croly, *The Irish Medical Directory* (Dublin: W. Curry. Jun. & Co., 1843 and 1846).

[66] O. MacDonagh, *Ireland: The Union and Its Aftermath* (London: Allen and Unwin, 1977), p. 37.

[67] P. Froggatt, 'The Response of the Medical Profession to the Great Famine', in E. M. Crawford (ed.), *Famine: The Irish Experience 900–1900, Subsistence Crises and Famines in Ireland* (Edinburgh: John Donald, 1989), p. 136.

[68] Ibid.   [69] Ibid., p. 137.

also played a significant role in administering to the sick and educating aspiring young Irish medics during the Famine years.

At the forefront of the hospital system lay the general teaching hospitals. Dublin possessed 12 general teaching hospitals; Limerick, Waterford and Belfast had one each; while Cork housed the naval hospital at Haulbowline. The main importance of these medical institutions, however, was to provide theatres for the work and teachings of the Irish medical doctors. Throughout the Famine, Irish medical practitioners played a prominent role in fighting disease on the ground, disseminating knowledge in their published works and through voluntary service on committees from hospital units up to the Central Board of Health. Thus, relative to the general population, nineteenth-century Ireland produced numerous well-educated medical graduates experienced in famine-related diseases who were well informed and trained in the most modern and innovative medical practice. Given the poor post-Famine economic climate, employment opportunities at home remained scarce. Emigration in nineteenth-century Ireland was common and colonial appointments in the armies of Britain were a desirable option for many eager middle-class Irishmen seeking upward social mobility. However, like many aspects of Irish medicine, Ireland's export of medical personnel and their impact on colonial and tropical medicine remain largely untouched by historians.[70]

Irish doctors and the Crown Raj

For the first time, following the introduction of competitive examinations, the IMS became more accessible for the large numbers of middle-class Irish Catholic doctors that had come through the ranks of the recently established Catholic University Medical College at Cecilia Street, Dublin, and the Queen's Colleges in Cork, Galway and Belfast. Likewise, from the early 1870s, TCD began to admit substantially larger numbers of Irish Catholics into its medical degree programmes. The introduction of large numbers of Irishmen into the medical services in British India coincided with a period of relative harmony between the Irish Catholic Church and the British government. Indeed, one may even go as far as to suggest that the British

---

[70] For occasional references to the careers of Irish colonial doctors, see D. Arnold (ed.), *Imperial Medicine and Indigenous Societies* (Manchester University Press, 1988) and D. Arnold, *Warm Climates and Western Medicine: the Emergence of Tropical Medicine, 1500–1900* (Amsterdam: Rodopi, 1996); P. D. Curtin, *Death by Migration: Europe's Encounter with the Tropical World in the Nineteenth Century* (Cambridge University Press, 1989).

194   From Company to Crown rule

authorities in India during the second half of the nineteenth century actually began to favour Irish Catholics, as a lot of work on the ground, particularly among the Indian and expanding Eurasian population, was being carried out by Irishmen.[71] Moreover, there was a growing belief by the British government in India in the second half of the nineteenth century that the Irish had an acute awareness, perhaps to a greater extent than did English or Scottish professionals, of the peasant problem. Many Irish IMS recruits had first-hand experience of living among a peasant tenantry before and after their education in post-Famine Ireland that may have predisposed them to issues of famine disease such as cholera and malnutrition.

The first competitive examination for the IMS was held in January 1855. Perhaps contrary to the intentions of Sir Charles Wood, the Secretary of State for India during this period, the Irish, as opposed to the Scots or the English in terms of numbers at least, turned out to be the real beneficiaries of Wood's new reforms.[72] Wood was responsible for initiating similar reforms to the recruiting process of the Indian Civil Service (ICS), where, prior to 1855, India's administrators had been selected through a system of patronage exercised by the Company Directors and the President of the Board of Control in London. With the support of Thomas Babington Macaulay and Sir Charles Trevelyan, Wood was convinced that a system of recruitment by open competition would attract a greater number of men who possessed both a high character and intelligence. However, instead of drawing the Oxbridge scholar-gentleman, the exams seemed to have enticed men from 'obscure corners of society, boorish, contemptible and disgusting', that is to say, those put forward by the London crammers and the Irish universities.[73] Mid-Victorian anti-Irish prejudice, however, did not seem to hamper Irish recruitment into the IMS. Between 1855 and 1884 there were at least 180 Irishmen who entered the service of the IMS, more than 25 per cent of the total intake. In contrast, the Scots had fallen from 37 per cent (1804–54) to 19 per cent (1855–84), while the English element slipped from 37 per cent to 25 per cent during the same periods. The remainder were born outside the

---

[71] Hawes, *Poor Relations*; D. Datta, 'Europeans in Calcutta, 1858–1883', unpublished PhD thesis, University of Cambridge, 1996.

[72] R. J. Moore, *Sir Charles Wood's Indian Policy, 1853–66* (Manchester University Press, 1966), pp. 86–107.

[73] Sir Charles Trevelyan to Sir Edward Ryan, 14 January 1863, quoted in J. M. Compton, 'Open Competition and the Indian Civil Service, 1854–76', *English Historical Review*, LXXXIII (1968), 269. In his article on the social origins and careers of Irishmen in the ICS, S. B. Cook examines the recruitment process and demonstrates effectively how Wood and his colleagues sought to restrict the numbers of Irish administrative parvenus entering the ICS: Cook, 'The Irish Raj', 509–13.

Irish doctors and the Crown Raj 195

British Isles, most of them in India or the Caribbean. Between 1865 and 1896, when Ireland's population was one-fifth of the United Kingdom's, Irish universities supplied no less than 20 per cent of the total number of IMS recruits selected during these years.[74]

However, officers in the IMS, before the Medical Registration Act of 1858, in particular, did not enjoy the same social standing and prestige that was attached to those who received commissions in the Company and Crown's European armies in India. The low regard in which the medical profession was held in mid-Victorian Britain was compounded in India by the apparent indifference of the colonial administration. Medical officers were not perceived to be 'gentlemen' by their superiors in the civil and military government, who believed that surgery was still very much a craft and not a profession.[75] Moreover, certain internal divisions within the medical profession itself further diminished the status of medical men in India in the first half of the nineteenth century. Just as there had been very clear distinctions between the traditional divisions of medical practitioners in Britain and Ireland involving physicians, surgeons and apothecaries, new divisions arose in India throughout the late nineteenth century between new IMS recruits and the more established medical officers.[76]

It was perhaps no coincidence that the period that witnessed the greatest number of IMS recruits from Ireland (1855–84) coincided with a period in which professional grievances over promotion, pay and status was particularly acute.[77] During the 1870s and 1880s, over-staffing in the IMS resulted in much official quarrelling between new IMS recruits (almost 20 per cent of whom were Irish) and the British authorities in India. As a result of over-staffing, new IMS recruits were placed on lower rates of pay ('unemployed pay') until suitable posts were found for them. Nevertheless, if conditions of work in the medical services in India were not all that desirable, they did at least offer some form of financial stability. This was an important incentive for many middle-class IMS recruits from Ireland where professional practices

---

[74] Of the 995 men who passed into the IMS from the Bengal, Madras and Bombay Presidencies during the period 1865 to 1896, 207 (or 20 per cent) had been educated in an Irish university: Crawford, *Roll of the Indian Medical Service*, pp. 638–42.
[75] M. J. Peterson, *The Medical Profession in Mid-Victorian London* (Berkeley: University of California Press, 1978), p. 38.
[76] I. Waddington, 'General Practitioners and Consultants in Early Nineteenth-Century England: The Sociology of an Intra-Professional Conflict', in D. Richards and J. Woodward (eds.), *Health Care and Popular Medicine in Nineteenth-Century England* (London, 1977), pp. 164–88.
[77] *Indian Medical Gazette* (October 1865), 342.

196   From Company to Crown rule

and employment opportunities were not as forthcoming as in England or North America.[78]

After 1855, when the old patronage system of appointment was replaced by competitive examinations, the IMS became open to both Indians and Eurasians. However, unlike Irish Catholics who entered the medical services in India in large numbers during this period, few Indians actually joined the service until the end of the nineteenth century. Yet it appears the small presence of Indians as well as the large number of those recruited from some of the fledgling colleges and licensing medical institutions in Ireland was sufficient to lower the status of the IMS in British eyes.

As with Irish recruitment into the ICS, racial prejudice was a significant feature of the medical profession in India during the nineteenth century.[79] The notion of 'gentility' preoccupied the domestic governing body, the British Medical Association, who frequently displayed its reservations concerning the quality of medical graduates from Irish and Indian universities and medical schools.[80] However, prejudice concerning Irish entry into both the ICS and the IMS was not based upon religion.[81] Socially acceptable and well-educated Irish Protestants found themselves as much the victims of anti-Irish prejudice in British India as did Irish Catholics. The papers of both Irish Catholic and Protestant assistant surgeons and surgeons in the IMS recount the concern by most Irish applicants during this period in emphasising their 'gentlemanly character' and 'moral veracity'.[82] James Moran, a Catholic from Drumcolleher, Co. Limerick, who entered the IMS as an assistant surgeon in the 1870s, sought a reference from his parish priest Fr William Fitzgerald to confirm to the British medical authorities that he was indeed 'a gentleman of excellent good moral character'.[83] Even more pronounced were the personal testimonies and character references given in support of an application for entry into the IMS by a Cork-born Protestant, John Greany. After obtaining his MD from Queen's

---

[78] See Crawford, *Indian Medical Service*, I, p. 386.

[79] Cook, 'The Irish Raj'.

[80] For instance, in 1868 an article in the *Indian Medical Gazette*, though not directly alluding to the service's Irish recruits, declared that while the IMS had no concerns admitting the sons of men of 'low birth', it was particularly insistent 'that the sons themselves shall be, not only professionally, but liberally well educated, and that they shall have some notion of the laws of good society': *Indian Medical Gazette* (May 1868), 111.

[81] J. Harris, *Private Lives, Public Spirit: A Social History of Britain 1870–1914* (Oxford University Press, 1993).

[82] Assistant Surgeons and Surgeons Papers, 1804–1914, L/MIL/9/404, OIOC, BL.

[83] Papers of Assistant Surgeon James Moran, L/MIL/9/404 ff.30–36, OIOC, BL.

Irish doctors and the Crown Raj 197

College, Cork in 1874, Greany's application came highly recommended by Cork's most senior physicians and medical educators, who stressed 'his uniform gentlemanly deportment', his 'gentlemanly demeanor and conduct' as well as 'the excellence of his moral character'.[84]

The level of education attained by members of the IMS provided an important indication of the medical profession's standing in Anglo-Indian society during this period, as well as in its ability to compete in the recruitment stakes with other professions. After 1863, all prospective entrants into the IMS had to undertake a one-year 'professional' course of study that included subjects such as surgery, pharmacy, hygiene and botany at the Royal Army Medical College at Netley. At the end of this one-year programme, all potential IMS recruits were required to sit an examination that was similar to the one sat by respective recruits entering the Army Medical Department (which served the medical requirements of the regular British army in India) and the Naval Medical Service.[85] Nevertheless, between 1857 and 1887, a period of intense Irish recruitment into the IMS, the total number of IMS recruits who actually held medical degrees accounted for only 35.4 per cent of the total intake. Such deficiencies in terms of the educational standards of IMS recruits both reflected and compounded the inferior status of the medical services in India.[86]

Although graduates from the London medical schools occupied the largest single element of IMS recruits selected between 1839 and 1914, the combined proportion of officers drawn from Irish and Scottish universities and certifying institutions was considerably higher.[87] During the first part of the nineteenth century, however, Edinburgh University was particularly dominant in terms of producing the highest number of successful candidates that passed into the IMS from medical schools

---

[84] Papers of Assistant Surgeon John Philip Greany, L/MIL/9/404 ff.111–118, OIOC, BL.

[85] *Qualifications and Examination of Candidates for Commissions in the Medical Services of the British and Indian Armies* (London, 1870).

[86] See 'Papers of Surgeons Selected by the Board of Examiners 1882–94', L/MIL/9/413–18; 'Papers of Candidates Selected by the Board of Examiners for the IMS, 1895–1914', L/MIL/9/419–27, OIOC, BL.

[87] Out of the 1,119 officers that passed into the IMS during the period 1839–60, 45 (8.5 per cent) received their medical education in Ireland. This figure grew steadily with the introduction of competitive examination in 1855 and between 1865 and 1896, 196 (18.7 per cent) out of a total of 995 IMS recruits attended an Irish university, college or certifying medical institute. Between 1897 and 1914 the number of IMS recruits who obtained their medical qualifications in Ireland accounted for 91 (10.6 per cent) of the 655 candidates selected during these years. Sources: L/MIL//413–18; L/MIL/9/419–27; L/MIL/9/428–29, OIOC, BL; see also Crawford, *Roll of the Indian Medical Service*, pp. 639–47.

198   From Company to Crown rule

within the British Isles.[88] The success of Scottish medical institutes during the late eighteenth and early nineteenth centuries was in part derived from the traditional connection that existed between members of the Anglo-Irish and Scots-Irish community, north and south, with Edinburgh University.[89] Families' ties with medical training at Edinburgh was popular among many Irish Protestant, professional, middle-class families during this period where it was respected for its rigour and was believed to offer its graduates the best career prospects within the Empire. In contrast, those who obtained qualifications from Irish universities were looked upon less favourably by members of the British medical profession.[90]

This was in part due to the social composition of the Irish members of the IMS during the nineteenth century, where few Irish candidates were of genteel parentage. Irishmen recruited to serve in the medical services in India were by no means uniformly drawn from the Anglo-Irish Protestant landed class. From the total number of recruits that entered the IMS between 1804 and 1896, only 8 per cent possessed parents that were members of the peerage or landed class.[91] Classified by occupation of parentage, middle classes (professional, mercantile, business and farmers) accounted for approximately 60 per cent of the total, while the lower-middle classes (trade and artisans) made less than 8 per cent.[92] Due to the importance of social class in determining professional status, Irishmen hailing from predominantly middle-class, professional backgrounds were perceived as contributing significantly to the medical profession's low standing in metropolitan society at this time.[93]

---

[88] Edinburgh produced 205 (38.6 per cent) of the 1,119 candidates selected for the IMS during the period 1839–60. Hereafter the number of successful candidates educated at Edinburgh University slowly declined to 16.7 per cent of the total selected for the IMS during 1865–96: Crawford, *Roll of the Indian Medical Service*, pp. 639–47.

[89] Froggatt, 'Competing Philosophies'.

[90] Peterson, *Medical Profession*, pp. 66, 80, 125.

[91] Crawford, *Roll of the Indian Medical Service*, p. 651. See also G. E. Burtchaell and T. U. Sadlier (eds.), *Alumni Dublinensus* (London, 1924); L. G. Pine (ed.) *Burke's Landed Gentry of Ireland* (London, Burke's Peerage 1958); E. Walford, *County Families of the United Kingdom* (London: Chatto & Windus, 1920); A. Webb, *A Compendium of Irish Biography* (New York: Lemma Publishing Co., 1978); J. S. Crone, *A Concise Dictionary of Irish Biography* (Dublin: Talbot Press, 1928); *The India Office List* (London: India Office, 1886); C. E. Buckland, *Dictionary of Indian Biography* (London: Swan Sonnenschein, 1906).

[92] Crawford, *Roll of the Indian Medical Service*, p. 651.

[93] E. Freidson, 'The Theory of Professions: State of the Art', in R. Dingwall and P. Lewis (eds.), *The Sociology of the Professions: Lawyers, Doctors and Others* (London: Macmillan, 1985), pp. 19–35.

Irish universities and the growth of professional networks

There is little doubt that even at this early stage, Ireland was well prepared and equipped to meet the challenge of supplying IMS personnel. TCD was Ireland's oldest and most prestigious university, having educated members of the ascendancy class since 1592. It was a particularly wealthy and well-funded institution that rivalled some of the more prestigious colleges in Oxford and Cambridge. It had a strong and lasting tradition in grooming its students to fill the best places in society and government. As early as 1662, TCD had established a Regius Professorship in Physic and by 1711 had facilitated the building of its first pre-clinical departments of medical study.[94] In Dublin alone by 1830 there were, in addition to TCD, no fewer than three professional groups that examined and granted qualifications in medicine. Two of these, the Royal College of Surgeons and the Company of the Apothecaries' Hall, provided teaching and instruction as well. The third, the Royal College of Physicians, which had much the highest social prestige of the three, did not teach directly, but had its right of nominating to the King's Professorship in the School of Physic a major voice in the control of its clinical teaching. In addition to this there were at least six private medical schools in operation in Dublin by 1830. Under James Macartney, professor of anatomy, and Whitley Stokes, professor of physic, the medical school at TCD became a more homogeneous and disciplined centre for the instruction of young Irish medics.

Throughout the 1830s, the dons and administrators of TCD began to change their curricula to enable medical students to compete for positions in the IMS. Along with London University, TCD was the first to assist its students in preparing for the exams. With the increasing need to tailor its curricula to meet the needs of civil and professional employment, TCD amalgamated the loosely organised teaching of medicine into one specific course. Subjects such as chemistry, physics and botany were taught in the first year of study, closely followed by anatomy in the second and ending with instruction in therapeutics and clinical training. In the late 1850s, largely at the behest of two junior fellows, Samuel Haughton and Joseph Galbraith, TCD established chairs in Sanskrit and Arabic and began courses in zoology, knowledge of which were essential in passing the IMS exams. In addition to TCD, the Queen's University in Belfast, along with its constituent colleges in

---

[94] McDowell and Webb, *Trinity College, Dublin*, p. 42.

200 From Company to Crown rule

Cork and Galway, established similar amendments to its curricula. The Indian language programme in Belfast, for example, matched TCD's programme.[95] To a similar extent, Cork equally equipped itself for the instruction of young Irish medics who had aspirations of pursuing a career in India. It offered courses in Indian history and geography, while its Hindu and Muslim law classes were very popular. Indeed less than ten years after the introduction of competitive examination for the IMS, Cork proclaimed with great optimism that 'the attention of parents and guardians is directed to the new arrangements for the East India Company Service, according to which are open to competition at Examinations prescribed by the Board of Control. The courses of lectures at the Queen's College, Cork, are well adapted to prepare candidates for their Examination'.[96] John O'Leary, himself a student of both Cork and Galway during the second half of the nineteenth century, later observed that the authorities of Queen's College, Galway attracted potential Catholic IMS recruits by simply 'widening the area to be operated upon, throwing temptation in the way of a class which had been free from it before'.[97]

However, despite such institutional support, Irish interest in the IMS was not entirely down to the promotional activities of the Irish universities. Many recruits were lured into the IMS because family members had already established themselves in the military or had direct links with India. George Chesnaye, a native of Co. Dublin, entered the IMS as Assistant Surgeon and was assigned to Bengal in 1859. His father had been a Captain in the naval forces before he had considered a career in India. Chesnaye carried out extensive work on the cholera epidemic at Mian Mir and Amritsar in 1861, while he was given medical charge of Lawrence Medical Asylum in Sanawar from 1866 to 1868. In many ways Chesnaye was typical of many Irish recruits drafted into the IMS during this period. While they predominantly carried out their civil duties as doctors, their double commission as officers meant that they were expected to perform military tasks as well. From 1871 for over eight years, Chesnaye served as Residency Surgeon at Kathmandu, Nepal, before partaking in operations at Ali Musjid in Kabul during the Second Afghan War (1878–80).[98] Moreover, for many candidates

[95] S. Haughton, *University Education in Ireland* (London, 1868); Anonymous, 'Spirit of the Universities, TCD', *The University Magazine*, V (1880); and 'Annual Reports of Her Majesty's Civil Service Commissioners' (henceforth, ARCSC): *Parliamentary Papers*, Vol. XX (1863), pp. 392–3.

[96] ARCSC, *Parliamentary Papers*, Vol. XVII (pt. 2) (1863), 7, pp. 13–14.

[97] Ibid., p. 15.

[98] J. F. Riddick, *Who Was Who in British India* (London: Greenwood Press, 1998), p. 70.

Irish universities and professional networks 201

entering the IMS, economic urge was a particularly strong incentive.[99] During the early phase of open recruitment, Ireland's economy had not yet recovered from the devastation of the Great Famine. This fragile economy was particularly susceptible to further swings of depression given the fact that its small industrial base was confined to specific areas of the north-east and Dublin. Whatever the inducements were – good pay, promise of rapid promotion, challenge, adventure, prestige or the satisfaction of leadership – Irish interest in the IMS was keen.

However, despite the large numbers of Irish medical graduates enlisting in the service of the Army Medical Department (AMD) and the Royal Navy, their work, irrespective of their social origins, entailed neither administrative responsibility nor research in tropical pathology. Rather, it demanded a routine military variant of general practice, treating the ailments of soldiers and their families, making frequent sanitary inspections, examining recruits and the medically discharged and compiling medical statistics. The IMS, on the other hand, provided more scope for the ambitious young medical protégé of the Irish school of medicine in which to develop and impress upon the imperial system his skill and training. Alexander Porter, born in 1841, was educated at the Ulster Protestant Queen's University, Belfast. In 1865 he entered the IMS as an Assistant Surgeon and was assigned to Madras. Carrying out his main duties as Civil Surgeon at Akola between 1866 and 1874, Porter frequently assumed the role of Acting Sanitary Commissioner for Berar where his diligence and competence in research soon earned him the position of Surgeon and Professor of the Medical College in Madras. Drawing on his own personal experiences of famine and his medical education in Ireland, Porter dedicated his time and learning towards carrying out extensive research on the pathology of famine diseases in India. During the Madras famine of 1877–8, Porter, in addition to his official duties, was in charge of the sick of a famine-relief camp. Indeed Porter's research on famine diseases, presented in his book entitled *The Diseases of the Madras Famine of 1877–78*, was among the first such published work in its field in nineteenth-century India. Similarly, John French, a Catholic from Ballingar, Co. Galway, received his education at Queen's College, Galway, and later TCD, before joining the IMS as an Assistant Surgeon in Bengal in 1872. As editor of the *Indian Medical Gazette* between 1875 and 1876, French was particularly interested in the study of famine disease and published his first major work in 1873 entitled *Endemic Fever in Lower Bengal*. The careers

---

[99] W. J. Reader, *Professional Men: The Rise of the Professional Classes in Nineteenth-Century England* (London: Weidenfeld & Nicolson, 1964), p. 135.

202   From Company to Crown rule

of Porter and French demonstrate the ways in which Irishmen in the IMS, irrespective of religious creed, found that late-nineteenth-century British India enabled them to enjoy a relatively unrestricted freedom to introduce their own research and ideas, fostered by the burgeoning educational system in Ireland primed to meet the Empire's demand for competent medical personnel, able to transpose specialised medical knowledge from one imperial site to another.

Conclusion

Many Irishmen broke new ground in medical advancement following research in India. The emergence and awareness of tropical medicine and disease in Western Europe and North America can be seen as a direct result of the early initiatives taken by men such as John Crawford. The technique of acquiring specialised knowledge, be it that of languages or familiarisation with specific diseases or of the indigenous culture, necessary for a particular type of appointment, served men such as John Holwell and William O'Shaughnessy better than the more conventional paths to office of seniority and patronage. In an era when most IMS servants were isolated from British centres of power and decision-making, the ability to understand and speak Indian languages, to obtain information and interpret Indian culture, were powerful tools that could play important roles in determining whether or not a professional doctor could achieve an important medical position. Many Irishmen in the IMS published books, pamphlets and journal articles to present their work in the most favourable light; to defend their research, or simply to make their names known to the general public or to the Home governments. Essentially these men were protégés of a very distinctive Irish school of medicine that was very much apparent in India during the second half of the nineteenth century. This school was undoubtedly informed and moulded by the Irish famine experience but more importantly it was characterised by its enthusiasm for technological, diagnostic and therapeutic innovation as well as an adherence to traditional folk medicine. By acting as the conveyors of this revolutionary wave in medical theory and practice, many Irish physicians in India played a large part in the transformation of the Dublin clinical school from what had been in effect an outpost of Edinburgh University to a major influence in its own right on research, teaching and practice in the British Empire.

Moreover, as the careers of some Irish IMS recruits demonstrate, it was indeed possible for nineteenth-century Irishmen to eschew radical politics both at home and abroad. The experiences of men such

Conclusion 203

as the Madras Assistant Surgeon Daniel O'Connell Raye, a nephew of the Irish Catholic emancipationist, Daniel O'Connell, who joined the Bengal Medical Service in 1866, bears testament to the Irish ability to sustain a deep commitment to national liberty and yet to seize the opportunities open to Irishmen to assist an empire that imposed colonial rule on others as well as arguably on themselves. While there is little doubt that O'Connell Raye possessed strong Catholic sympathies, he was nonetheless driven in his career by a strong desire to achieve recognition among his peers and to be seen as an equal partner in the imperial process. Indeed, the careers of those nineteenth-century Irishmen in the IMS reveal that the Irish middle classes were by no means hostile to the British or indeed the imperial connection. Although many Irish recruits were descended from wealthy Protestant backgrounds, the evidence from East India recruitment lists suggests that among the Catholic and less well-to-do sections of the Irish population interest in employment opportunities within the Empire remained strong well into the twentieth century.

Although some historians have been at pains to show that Home Rule and old-fashioned Unionism were incompatible, when transferred from a parochial to an imperial setting, a local and an imperial patriotism could flourish side by side. Although they may have had different reference points, one to a particular bond with Great Britain and the other to a network linking together a global political and economic system, in British India, at least, these two ideologies were not necessarily competing. In pursuing long and successful careers in the imperial services in India, many professional middle-class Irishmen were able to demonstrate that popular nationalism and imperialism were neither inherently radical nor in direct competition with one another. Within an imperial context it was possible for Irish men and women to sustain both a deep commitment to national liberty (and to the Union) as well as to take advantage of the opportunities open to them in Britain's Eastern Empire. Following a successful career in the Indian Medical Service, Patrick Heffernan reminisced upon his experience as an Irishman in the service of the Empire:

Looking back over sixty years to my year in residence at 'the Castle,' I am amazed to recall the liberal and, shall I add the 'West British' atmosphere which prevailed in our common room. We took in all the best of the British reviews and weekly magazines, including *Cosmopolis*, a journal printed in three languages. We all believed in the British Empire, and many of us looked forward to a career in its service...Not that we did not consider ourselves good Irishmen, we did. For those were the days when Fleet street swarmed with Irishmen and T. P. Connor pontificated in the *Weekly Sun*.

204 From Company to Crown rule

Inevitably our eyes looked away from Dublin to London and the Indian Empire overseas.[100]

Once divided by religious and political considerations in Ireland, domiciled Irishmen in India (Anglicans, Catholics and Presbyterians) were drawn together in a common bond. There was a sense among the different strands of Irish medical personnel and civil servants that they were involved in a legitimate sphere of work, and many Irish, in fact, displayed a sense of pride and commitment to the British Empire.

[100] Heffernan, *An Irish Doctor's Memories*, p. 28.

7 Imperial crisis and the age of reform

Introduction

The historiographies of Ireland and India have long recognised parallels between the countries' shared imperial pasts and their struggle for political freedom and national self-determination. As a consequence, scholars have been able to make significant progress in situating this nexus by exploring links between contemporary Irish and Indian elites and how Irish precedents influenced British policy-making in India and vice versa. While scholars have begun to explore the mutual calls for national self-determination and political freedom articulated by contemporary Irish and Indian elites, fewer studies have focused upon the complex social and cultural networks that bound both dependencies together and through which their development was shaped.[1] In part, the paucity of studies in this area reflects much of the wider contemporary writing on Ireland and empire itself. For the most part, debates surrounding the nature of Ireland's historical relationship with the Empire have remained largely centred upon the character of its constitutional and political ties with Britain.[2]

This chapter examines how during the late nineteenth century increased economic decline both in the agricultural south and west of Ireland (though not in the north, where Ulster experienced rapid economic growth during the same period[3]) and in India provided the impetus for a new generation of nationalists, philanthropists and humanitarians to move their ideologies beyond local predicaments and into the wider international domain. The rigorous imposition of free trade (from 1801 in Ireland and from 1834 in India) brought about a sharp decline in the demand for Irish and Indian commodities in

---

[1] Brasted, 'Indian Nationalist Development'; G. Viswanathan, 'Ireland, India and the Poetics of Internationalism', *Journal of World History*, 15 (2004), 7–30.

[2] See, for example, Kenny, *Ireland and the British Empire*, pp. 1–26.

[3] Philip Ollerenshaw, 'Industry, 1820–1914', in Liam Kennedy and Philip Ollerenshaw (eds.), *An Economic History of Ulster, 1820–1939* (Manchester University Press, 1985), pp. 62–109.

206   Imperial crisis and the age of reform

British and European markets and with it increasing calls from early economic nationalists for the introduction of protective measures for home produce in both countries. Within this context, this chapter examines how an elaborate web of contact, dialogue and exchange was fashioned between the nationalist spokesmen of nineteenth-century Ireland and India who, from the 1870s, gradually became aware of each other's calls for economic reform and national self-determination. Related to these concerns were the comparable moral and political issues raised in both countries at the time over the ownership of land and the administration of famine relief, both of which were used by these networks as tools in imperial politicking. Crucially, it was the position of certain Irish individuals within the power structures of the Empire itself and particularly within the echelons of the Indian Civil Service (ICS) that provided much of the initial impetus for these ideologies to spread and gather momentum.

The introduction of open-competitive examination for the ICS in 1855 enabled a significant number of Irish candidates to enter service in India. Between the 1870s and 1920s the writings of several Irish civil servants, as well as those of their missionary and educationalist colleagues, championed a diverse range of conservative popular cultures in late-nineteenth-century India. As amateur anthropologists and ethnographers, their researches into the vocabularies, rural life, artisan traditions and popular religion of the people of the United Provinces and Bihar were part of a late-nineteenth-century shift from a descriptive to a classificatory representation of colonial knowledge in India. The ethnological information supplied by their bilingual Indian subordinates (such as Pandit Ram Gharib Shaube) and represented through their collective writings demonstrated a common anthropological mission among this network which set about preserving the culture of rural Indian life before it disappeared through increased contact and exposure to Western scientific thought and appliances of civilisation.

Irish professional personnel networks of the late nineteenth century were arguably much more politicised than their English, Scottish or Welsh counterparts. Irish civil networks which published work on the British administration of famine relief, the impoverished state of Indian tenants, landless peasants and rack-renting landlords in Bihar acquired the reputation among some British and Indian officials as pro-*raiyat* (tenant) sympathisers. They recorded and circulated revealing views on religious antagonisms and economic and agrarian malformations, and were particularly forceful in their demands for tenancy legislation. Other Irish professional personnel networks worked to further more radical political agendas and ideologies and were motivated by a desire to bring about reform and change within the Empire. These dynamics are particularly evident in the imperial career of Charles O'Donnell who became embroiled in a number of contemporary debates concerning the duties and responsibilities of the Bengal administration towards its Indian subjects in the 1870s and 1880s.

Irish recruitment and the Indian Civil Service, 1855–1900

Throughout the nineteenth century there was a view among the English aristocracy that Indian service was somehow inferior to appointments in the metropolis. Many English members of the aristocracy who considered careers in India, irrespective of talent or promise, were stigmatised and derided by their peers for endangering the natural progression of their political careers in England. The prevalence of this attitude had detrimental effects on the attempts of the government of India to recruit the services of promising Englishmen not only for the regular Covenanted Civil Service but also for special non-civilian appointments, including the viceroyalty. Similarly, members of the English legal and business professions viewed India with as much disfavour as the British ruling elite. Efforts on behalf of the Calcutta government to entice English lawyers or fiscal experts to become legal and financial members of the Viceroy's Executive Council proved strenuous. For many English lawyers the prospect of service in India during the late nineteenth century was associated with professional regression. Sir Alexander Miller, a law member under both Lord Lansdowne and Lord Elgin's viceroyalty, for example, sought unsuccessfully for employment in London upon his return from India only to end up teaching 'in some obscure college in the North of Ireland'.[4]

In an effort to enhance the lowly profile of Indian service in mainland Britain as well as to attract a greater number of high-calibre students from the universities of Cambridge and Oxford, the British government closed the East India Company's training school, Haileybury College, in 1855 and inaugurated a system of competitive examinations in place of the traditional method of patronage. However, the expectation that a highly superior body of efficient English-born administrators would be created for governing India as a result of the reforms instigated by the Secretary of State for India, Sir Charles Wood, was never fully

---

[4] Hamilton to Curzon, 6 August 1905, Hamilton Correspondence, Eur. Mss D510, OIOC, BL.

208   Imperial crisis and the age of reform

realised.[5] Despite widening the scope of the ICS entrance examinations as well as fixing an age limit for candidates sitting the exams (17–22 years of age), Wood and his colleagues, Thomas Babington Macaulay and Sir Charles Trevelyan, found that many candidates from the desired English universities 'after passing [the ICS exams] successfully, found it more to their advantage to throw-up their Indian prospects and remain at home'.[6] Instead of drawing in the Oxbridge gentleman-scholar, Wood had unwittingly paved the way for an influx of ICS candidates from Irish universities. No less than 24 per cent of the total number of candidates recruited by open examination for the ICS between 1855 and 1863 had been educated at an Irish university. This figure was in clear contrast to the estimated 5 per cent of students who attended Haileybury College from 1809 to 1850 who were Irish-born.[7] Moreover, statistics compiled from the annual reports of the Civil Service Commissioners demonstrate that while the corresponding number of Scottish and English recruits was in decline during these years, Irish universities supplied a number of ICS recruits out of proportion to Ireland's population. For instance, in 1857, the second anniversary of the examinations' inception, Irish universities supplied no less than 33 per cent of the total number of recruits selected for the ICS during that year.[8]

Just as the introduction of open competition for entrance into the ICS brought about a shift in the social backgrounds of civil servants, it stimulated much debate about the representation of British authority in India itself. For the first time the physical body became a distinct category within the official discourse of rule as the government discussed whether the new 'competition-wallahs' were suitable representatives of British imperial power in India.[9] This notion, combined with the growing influence of the contemporary pseudo-scientific discourse of

[5] Moore, *Sir Charles Wood's Indian Policy*, pp. 86–107; Dewey, 'Education of a Ruling Caste'; B. Spangenberg, 'The Problem of Recruitment for the Indian Civil Service during the Nineteenth Century', *Journal of Asian Studies*, XXX (1971), 341–60.

[6] Memorandum by C. J. Lyall, d. 17 May 1875, in 'Papers Relating to the Selection and Training of Candidates for the Indian Civil Service': *Parliamentary Papers*, Vol. LV (1876), p. 422.

[7] Cohn, 'Recruitment and Training of British Civil Servants in India', p. 108; and Annual Reports of Her Majesty's Civil Service Commissioners: *Parliamentary Papers* (1859–83).

[8] Papers Regarding the Selection and Training of Candidates for the Indian Civil Service: *Parliamentary Papers*, Vol. LV (1876), p. 31; Compton, 'Open Competition and the Indian Civil Service', 270–1.

[9] H. Yule and A. C. Burnell, *Hobson-Jobson: A Glossary of Colloquial Anglo-Indian Words and Phrases, and of Kindred Terms, Etymological, Historical, Geographical and Discursive* (London: John Murray, 1903), p. 239.

Irish recruitment and the ICS, 1855–1900

race and class, gave way to what E. M. Collingham has described as 'a legitimate Anglo-Indian official body', or the ideal of the sahib.[10] The idea of the superiority of the Anglo-Saxon race was given greater force now that their supposed attainment of a higher level of civilisation, demonstrated most notably by their intellectual and technological triumphs, was seen as the product of their racial predisposition. While the increasing power of the Anglo-Indian bureaucracy was responsible for modernising India, the actual physical body of the sahib itself provided the basis for an ideology of British rule by virtue of promoting the 'manly prowess' of the Anglo-Saxon over the 'weakly constitution' of their Indian or Celtic counterparts.

When the first wave of competition-wallahs began to arrive in India during the mid nineteenth century they became the focus of much criticism. Their physique was perceived to be inadequate by the Indian government who contended that they lacked the 'fresh and undrained energies' of the Old Haileyburians and that they could not ride, a skill which, it was argued, was essential to the execution of their duties. Behind these veiled attacks on the inferior manners, physique and skills of the new ICS recruits lay class prejudices. As George Birdwood stated explicitly in a paper read before the East India Association: 'the government of the country [India] has at last been gotten into the hands of men born outside the hitherto governing families of the land, into hands bred for generations to other work than man government'.[11] Such criticism was pointed at the large influx of middle-class Irish and Scottish recruits into the ICS after 1855. Unable to compete with the middle classes in intellectual competition, the older order resorted to claims of birth and bodily inheritance to protect their position.[12] In Collingham's view, 'by citing the authority of the sahib in the idea that he embodied racial superiority, the competition-wallah debate had transformed the body of the official into one of the essential tools of power'.[13]

Evidently, Irish ICS recruits were found wanting in this respect. In 1864, Sir Charles Wood privately admitted with disgust the unsatisfactory type of recruit he thought was succeeding in the ICS examination. In a letter to the Governor of Madras, Sir William Denison, Wood accepted

---

[10] E. M. Collingham, *Imperial Bodies: The Physical Experience of the Raj, c.1800–1947* (Cambridge: Polity Press, 2002), pp. 117–50.

[11] G. C. M. Birdwood, *Competition and the Indian Civil Service: A Paper Read before the East India Association, Tuesday, May 21, 1872* (London: H. S. King & Co. 1872), p. 16.

[12] P. Bourdieu, 'Sport and Social Class', *Social Science Information*, 17, 6 (1978), 819–40.

[13] Collingham, *Imperial Bodies*, p. 127.

210   Imperial crisis and the age of reform

that 'nothing can keep out a very clever fellow [from the ICS], though he may not be up to the mark in manners and conversation';[14] such clever fellows, he had earlier expressed to Trevelyan, were typically 'well crammed youths from Irish Universities and Commercial Schools'.[15] While almost certainly the combination of a steady improvement in employment prospects for the middle class as well as a rapidly decreasing Irish population in the mid–late nineteenth century conspired to exert a downward pressure on the number of Irish candidates gaining entry into the ICS, it was the adjustments to the recruiting process itself, introduced by Wood, that proved most detrimental to Irish ICS employment.[16]

In 1864 Wood lowered the maximum age at which candidates could compete for ICS examinations from twenty-two to twenty-one years of age and redistributed the number of points attached to particular subjects, such as Sanskrit and Arabic, in which Irish candidates were known to excel. By initiating such reform Wood hoped to discourage all 'undesirable' university candidates while ultimately promoting the interests of an elite, predominantly Oxbridge grouping. Wood informed Trevelyan that the type of recruit he hoped to attract to the ICS would be 'University men who are gentlemen', commenting further that he had decided to add 'more marks for Greek and Latin by way of giving them [Candidates from Public Schools] a turn'.[17]

There was certainly an obvious incongruity between Wood's personal opinions and the public expressions of support he gave to the work being carried out by the Civil Service Commissioners. In the same letter to Trevelyan, Wood conceded that his concerns over the social profile of some successful Irish ICS candidates were almost impossible to voice in the open: 'It is difficult to say this in public, for I should have half a dozen wild Irishmen on my shoulders and as many middle class examination students, but that makes all the more reason for not giving in to anything which might lead to similar results.'[18] Yet in a speech to the House of Commons less than a year later, Wood maintained that the government's objective should be 'to go into the world and get well educated young men wherever they are to be found, no matter where or in what manner their education has been acquired' for Indian service.[19]

---

[14] Sir C. Wood to Sir W. Denison, d. 9 December 1864, Sir Charles Wood Papers, Mss Eur. F78, Letterbook 19, OIOC.

[15] Sir C. Wood to Trevelyan, d. 16 October 1864, Sir Charles Wood Papers, Mss Eur. F78, Letterbook 18, OIOC.

[16] Cook, 'The Irish Raj', 512.

[17] Wood to Trevelyan, d. 16 October 1864, Sir Charles Wood Papers, Mss Eur. F78, Letterbook 18, OIOC.

[18] Ibid.

[19] *Hansard* (3rd series), 1865, clxxix, p. 418.

Social and intellectual origins of Irish civil servants 211

Nevertheless, by 1866, the average percentage of Irish candidates that successfully passed into the ICS accounted for just 10.2 per cent of the total intake; a considerable decrease considering the number had been almost 30 per cent in 1858.[20] Although the genuine fear of attracting the wrong type of recruit combined with unofficial mid-Victorian anti-Irish prejudice to significantly reduce the number of Irishmen entering the ICS in the late 1860s and early 1870s, it was by no means certain that the quality of candidates being put forward by Irish universities was somehow inferior or second-rate to those that had previously passed to India via Haileybury College.

On the contrary, by the late 1860s, returns from the governments of Bengal, Bombay and Madras argued that while it may 'be premature to pronounce conclusively whether or not the Civil Service has on the whole been improved by the present system [of competitive examination]', it could 'be confidently affirmed that the present system is effective to exclude great inefficiency'.[21] Moreover, far from denouncing the 'ungentlemanly-like' character of the new 'competition-wallahs', the provincial governments in India declared in 1867 that 'the young men who enter the Service under the present system are, as a rule, more highly educated than those who found admittance under the former system'.[22] Nevertheless, by the 1880s the number of successful Irish university students who passed into the ICS had fallen to just below 5 per cent of the total intake, and although there was a slight improvement in the 1890s with the introduction of the recruiting reforms of 1892, Irish interest in ICS recruitment had become almost defunct.[23]

Social and intellectual origins of Irish civil servants in British India

As R. F. Foster has argued, 'Gaelic sympathies, Celtic researches, irritation with many of the actions of the British government and

---

[20] B. Spangenberg, *British Bureaucracy in India: Status, Policy and the Indian Civil Service in the Late 19th Century* (New Delhi: South Asia Books, 1976), p. 23.

[21] Accounts and Papers, East India, Session 5 February–21 August 1867: *Parliamentary Papers*, Vol. L (1867), p. 351.

[22] Ibid.

[23] These percentages and the numbers on which they are based were compiled from the Annual Reports of Her Majesty's Civil Service Commissioners (ARCSC): *Parliamentary Papers* 1859–83 and the annual lists of ICS recruits contained in L/P&J/6 series, 1881–1914, OIOC, BL. By 1914 Irish recruitment into the ICS fell away dramatically. Irish civilians, however, did not necessarily return to Ireland after Indian service. Out of 106 Irish civilians who stayed in India after the First World War, only three retired prematurely between 1919 and 1923. Personal reasons appear to have been cited in each case.

212   Imperial crisis and the age of reform

Anglicised educations could all co-exist, and often did, among the Irish Victorian middle-class intelligentsia'.[24] Indeed, in the context of an imperial setting in India, it was particularly possible to synthesise the competing requirements of Irish Catholicism and Protestantism. As part of a wider 'British' community in India in the late nineteenth century, Irish civilians, both Catholics and Protestants, found that their social and cultural origins were neither inherently different nor incomparable to the predominantly middle-class backgrounds of their English, Scottish and Welsh colleagues. Moreover, while the majority of Indians may have found it difficult to distinguish between varieties of Englishmen, Irishmen and Scotsmen, there is evidence to suggest that even among the British and Irish community at large there was difficulty in determining where exactly a particular civilian was from. Sir Michael O'Dwyer, a Catholic from a modest landowning family from Barronstown, Co. Tipperary, for instance, revealed how his two years served as a probationer for the ICS at Balliol College, Oxford, had sufficiently anglicised him to the extent that his fellow countrymen frequently mistook him for an Englishman.[25]

Such blurring of identity was also evident in the case of another Irish ICS recruit, Richardson Evans. As a Protestant with 'evangelical principles' from Co. Cork, Evans once remarked to Sir William Hegarty upon being asked whether or not he was a Cork man: 'Yes, half with pride at being one and half with pride that I had been taken for an Englishman.'[26] In many ways Evans' career fits the profile of a typical Irish ICS candidate who travelled to India in the late nineteenth century. Educated at Queen's College, Cork, in the 1860s, Evans decided to sit the ICS exam in London, for 'more or less as a joke'. While he may have had low expectations of passing the initial recruiting stage, his schooling in Cork had enabled him to finish ninth out of the total number of candidates selected for Indian service in 1871. Following his two-year probationary period in Oxford, Evans was posted as an Assistant Magistrate and Collector at Mirzapur where he worked assiduously on

---

[24] Foster, *Paddy and Mr Punch*, p. 27.

[25] Sir M. O'Dwyer, *India as I Knew It, 1885–1925* (London: Constable & Co., 1925), p. 11. O'Dwyer mentions significantly in his memoirs that

The atmosphere I was brought up in, though essentially Irish, showed no signs of racial or religious feeling...We were always on the most friendly terms with our Protestant neighbours...As regards internal politics, all of his nine sons followed the example of my father, who had a dislike for politics and a distrust for politicians, less rare in an Irishman than is commonly thought.

See pp. 3–5.

[26] Richardson Evans Papers, Ms. E 404, Box 1, f. 354, OIOC, BL.

Social and intellectual origins of Irish civil servants 213

famine relief. As a reward for his work in Bengal, Evans was transferred by the Lieutenant-Governor, Sir William Muir, 'to a healthier district' and was gazetted to Bulandshahar in the North Western Provinces and Oudh to replace Charles Lyall.

Like many of his Irish colleagues in India, Evans was ever mindful of his ethnicity and was never retiring in his evocation of Irishness. Upon arriving at Bulandshahar Evans commented in his memoirs that he had to share a bungalow with a civil surgeon whom, he recalled, 'I took to be a fellow countryman from his fine Tipperary brogue'.[27] However, Evans soon realised that through his acquaintance with this 'fellow country-man' issues of Irish identity, ethnicity and even class were never wholly straightforward or transparent in nineteenth-century India. To Evans' disbelief, the civil surgeon with the 'fine Tipperary brogue' had actu-ally been born in Calcutta to an Irish father (who had been an officer in the East India Company's army) and an Indian mother, and had been educated at a Eurasian college but 'had not visited Ireland or his people there, until he was of man's estate'.[28]

As the testimonies of Evans and O'Dwyer illustrate, there was cer-tainly an element of confusion and ambiguity in nineteenth-century India surrounding the perceived notions of Irishmen and, for that mat-ter, of specific forms of Irish identity. To an extent O'Dwyer's Catholic upbringing in rural Co. Tipperary and Evans' Protestant evangelical roots in Cork City at once mirrored the socio-economic complexity of the late-nineteenth-century Irish civilian. While certainly a significant proportion of Irish ICS recruits were elite Anglo-Irish and Scots-Irish Protestants educated at Trinity College Dublin (TCD), the majority of Irish civilians were neither members of the peerage nor were they scions of the Irish landed gentry. On the contrary, the socio-economic back-ground that classified the majority of Irish civilians in India, arguably more so than the English or the Scots during the nineteenth century, was predominantly middle class.[29] Through schooling in elite upper-middle-class schools such as the prestigious Royal Belfast Academical Institution and the exclusive Jesuit-run college, Clongowes Wood, it was hoped that a fully trained Irish professional elite would emerge to secure the 'good posts in the Home and Indian Civil Service, in the Banks and Commerce, in the Army and the traditional professions'.[30] Indeed, the most recent historian of Clongowes Wood College has argued that 'the imperial connection had become something more than an exotic flavour

---

[27] Ibid., f. 271.   [28] Ibid.

[29] Cook, 'The Irish Raj', 515.

[30] P. Costello, *Clongowes Wood: A History of Clongowes Wood College, 1814–1989* (Dublin: Gill and Macmillan, 1989), p. 61.

214   Imperial crisis and the age of reform

by the end of the [nineteenth] century, something much more substantial and even sustaining' than Irish national historical narratives would concede.[31] To some extent this reflects the notion that the Irish middle classes saw imperial service as a decidedly legitimate sphere of work.

The Royal Belfast Academical Institution, for example, frequently sought to tap its imperial connection in India by petitioning wealthy Ulster expatriates to become benefactors of their school. When the Institution first opened in 1814 one of the school's most generous supporters, Samuel Thompson, suggested that a petition should be sent to Sir Francis Rawdon-Hastings (Lord Moira), then Governor-General of India, to use his Ulster roots to secure subscriptions for the school and send them to Belfast via Alexander & Co., a banking firm in Calcutta also with strong Ulster connections.[32] Later in 1879, Clongowes Wood openly professed its attachment to empire and set about putting in place a system of Catholic education suitable to the professional wants of imperial India. The school's advertisement for that year proclaimed that their 'pupils are prepared for the degrees of the London University, for the examinations under the Intermediate Act, for the Royal Military College of Sandhurst and Woolwich, and for the Indian and other Departments of the Civil Service'.[33] Ambitious Irish Catholics eager to make their mark in the Empire were lured by the civil and imperial vacancies on offer in India. In particular, a position within the ICS was equally appealing to many Irish Catholic educators concerned with creating a professional Catholic elite in Ireland.[34]

Strikingly, Irish candidates who opted to sit the open examination for the ICS in London during the late nineteenth century were predominantly from the same socio-economic classes in Ireland and sometimes from the same families. Sir Michael O'Dwyer's brother, for example, was a member of the Indian Medical Service (IMS), while several of his colleagues from his early school days at St Stanislaus' and later, under the tutorship of Wren, became close contemporary colleagues in India. J. S. Meston, Sir E. D. Maclagan, Sir B. Robertson and Sir H. J. Maynard, for instance, worked alongside O'Dwyer as proconsuls of the

---

[31] Ibid.

[32] J. Jamieson, *The History of The Royal Belfast Academical Institution, 1810–1960* (Belfast: William Mullan, 1959), p. 32.

[33] Costello, *Clongowes Wood*, p. 45.

[34] S. Paseta, *Before the Revolution: Nationalism, Social Change and Ireland's Catholic Elite, 1879–1922* (Cork University Press, 1999), p. 86; see also K. Flanagan, 'The Rise and Fall of the Celtic Ineligible: Competitive Examinations for the Irish and Indian Civil Services in Relation to the Educational and Occupational Structure of Ireland, 1853–1921', unpublished D.Phil. thesis, University of Sussex, 1978, p. 432.

Social and intellectual origins of Irish civil servants 215

United Provinces, the Punjab and the Central Provinces respectively. Others, including Sir F. W. Duke, A. E. Gait and Sir R. H. Craddock, joined O'Dwyer in becoming Lieutenant-Governors of Bengal, Bihar and Orissa, Burma and the Punjab respectively. Others, such as Sir S. M. Fraser, resident at Hyderabad, Sir H. V. Lovett, Head of the UP Revenue Board, and Sir D. H. Twomey, Chief Judge in the Chief Court of Lower Burma, were friends and classmates from Ireland. According to O'Dwyer, these small networks of Irish civilians were 'a more humdrum lot, and perhaps did better in administration than in politics, a comparatively new and exotic cult in India'.[35]

By the mid nineteenth century, Ireland was well prepared and equipped to meet the challenge of directly supplying the Indian Empire with educated and ambitious officials. TCD was Ireland's oldest and most prestigious university and had a long tradition in grooming its students for positions in the church, government and the professions. Throughout the 1830s TCD began to change its curricula to enable its students to compete for positions within the ICS. By the late 1850s the college had established chairs in Sanskrit and Arabic and began courses in zoology, knowledge of which were essential to pass the ICS exams. In a bid to enhance the success rate of their Indian Civil and Medical Service candidates, the TCD authorities employed their first Indian pandit, Mir Alaud Ali, a native of Oudh, in 1866, to give lessons in Hindustani and later Persian when it was introduced in 1873. Three years later, TCD endeavoured to compete with the universities of Oxford and Cambridge in an attempt to gain recognition by the government of India as one of the few official universities that could house successful ICS candidates during their probationary two-year training period.

In 1876, the Registrar Andrew Seale Hart informed the Civil Service Commissioners that Trinity 'either now supplied, or could without difficulty provide instruction in all the studies which the [ICS] candidates would have to pursue [during their probationary two-year training in Dublin]'.[36] Moreover, the college authorities maintained that the periodical exams which all probationary ICS candidates were required to take before leaving for India could be sat without difficulty in Dublin. Depending on which region of India ICS candidates were assigned to, special provision had been put in place for the instruction of the Indian

---

[35] O'Dwyer, *India as I Knew It*, p. 19.
[36] 'A Copy of all Correspondence between the Registrar of Trinity College Dublin and the Secretary of State for India, Relative to Selected Candidates for the Indian Civil Service': *Parliamentary Papers*, Vol. LV (1876), pp. 603–5.

216   Imperial crisis and the age of reform

vernacular languages: Telugu and Tamil (Madras), Bengali and Hindi (Bengal) and Marathi and Gujarati (Bombay).[37] While Trinity was keen to impress upon the Commissioners that special courses could be made for the teaching of Indian law, it was equally eager to promote the advantages that prospective ICS candidates would obtain by studying in a metropolis: 'For taking notes of cases, with a view to the reports required of selected [ICS] candidates, the student would be favourably circumstanced at Dublin, as he could attend the law courts without quitting the place of his ordinary studies, whilst it would be necessary for a student of Oxford or Cambridge to transfer himself to London for the purpose.'[38]

In addition to TCD, the vocationally oriented Queen's University in Belfast, along with its constituent colleges in Cork and Galway, established similar amendments to its curricula. In 1855, Richard Oulton, the Registrar of Queen's College, Belfast, wrote to the Civil Service Commissioners stating that 'this College sanctioned some years back the establishment of special courses for students intending to become candidates for appointment in the Civil Services of India, the Public Services at home, and for Commissions in the Royal Artillery and Engineers'.[39] The Indian-language programme in Belfast, for example, matched that of Trinity's courses in Sanskrit and Arabic, while Cork and Galway offered courses in Indian history and geography as well as classes in Hindu and Muslim law.[40] Even the Catholic University of Ireland publicly stated its desire to organise classes in political economy and oriental languages, 'with a view to preparing students for the competitive examinations required of candidates for commissions in the Royal Artillery and Engineers, or for appointments in the Indian Civil Service'.[41]

Irish 'Orientalists', the Gaelic revival and the Indian Civil Service after 1858

As in the fields of geology, surveying and medicine, the Irish engagement with language and forms of written communication in India

---

[37] Ibid., p. 604.   [38] Ibid., p. 605.

[39] See 'Annual Report of Her Majesty's Civil Service Commissioners': *Parliamentary Papers*, Vol. XX (1863), p. 392: 'The Commissioners will find that with this addition our curriculum is so complete in its character and comprehensive in its details as to embrace fully all the requirements of the public examinations.'

[40] Haughton, *University Education in Ireland*; Anonymous, 'Spirit of the Universities, TCD', and ARCSC, pp. 392–3.

[41] ARCSC, p. 395.

mirrored the changing nature of colonial dominion during the second half of the nineteenth century. The increasing expansion of British military activity in Bengal and south India during the late eighteenth and early nineteenth centuries led to an initial British interest in seeking out antique human knowledge from ancient Sanskrit texts. By the 1840s, under the influence of the British Governor-General of India, Lord William Bentinck, this system of linguistic information-gathering was replaced by the imposition of supposed superior Western knowledge and a drive towards establishing an understanding of the Indian languages and Indian history through the study of empirical fact.[42] However, by the 1860s the process of British interaction with Indian languages and indigenous culture changed again when a new generation of neo-orientalists (among the new 'competition-wallahs') began to develop an understanding of India through the study of popular folklore and regional peculiarities. Central to this shift in British approaches to the understanding of Indian languages and culture throughout this period was the role played by Irish administrators employed by the ICS after 1858. As in India, Irish engagement with 'indigenous' Gaelic culture in Ireland underwent a similar transition that encompassed the work of the late-eighteenth-century Irish antiquarian tradition and culminated in the folklorist traditions of the late nineteenth century.

In both Ireland and India, late-eighteenth-century learned life embraced and celebrated ancient Irish and Indian culture. The Irish and Indian languages, along with Latin and Greek, were found to be among the first and most senior of the Aryan languages. Eighteenth- and nineteenth-century 'Orientalists' such as Colonel Charles Vallancey, Sir William Jones and Francis Wilford devoted long periods of scholarship in tracing convergence and similarities between the religions and social institutions of Ireland, India and mainland Britain. As part of a wider eighteenth-century European interest in Celticism, Vallancey, an English officer in the Royal Engineers stationed in Ireland, purported to show that close links existed between Gaelic and the Phoenician, Chinese and Persian languages.[43] Moreover, Vallancey was convinced that Irish was one of the world's purest and most ancient tongues

---

[42] C. A. Bayly, 'Orientalists, Informants and Critics in Benares, 1790–1860', in J. Malik (ed.), *Perspectives of Mutual Encounters in South Asian History 1760–1860* (Leiden; Boston: Brill, 2000), p. 112.

[43] C. Vallancey, *A Vindication of the Ancient History of Ireland* (Dublin: L. White, 1786); F. Wilford, 'On the Ancient Geography of India', *Journal of the Asiatic Society of Bengal*, XX (1851).

218   Imperial crisis and the age of reform

and through its study held the key to an understanding of all Eastern languages and civilisations.[44]

In tandem, the age of Ossian had produced some stimulating and original work by amateur Irish antiquaries eager to counteract what they perceived as negative outside images of Irish culture by describing the glories of a civilised and sophisticated Celtic past.[45] Gaelic Irish writers such as Geoffrey Keating, Charles O'Connor and Sylvester O'Halloran also concerned themselves with counteracting the barbaric image of Ireland in Britain that had been created by the writings of Giraldus Cambrensis and Edmund Spenser among others. The Ossian debates of the late eighteenth century in Ireland, however, had produced limited scholarly analysis of the texts themselves, compared with Scotland, where the contentious issue of authenticity had given rise to a renewed vigour in Gaelic scholarship.[46] Native Irish writers found that the ancient poems of Ossian could not be used to validate an imagined Gaelic past that was both politically and culturally sophisticated because, in part, their aspirations did not conform to the 'primitivist' paradigm represented by the Ossian texts.[47] Early Irish nationalists, concerned with undermining what they perceived as being the colonial image of a backward and uncivilised Ireland, were reluctant to use the idea of the 'primitive', prevalent throughout the Ossian poetry, for in their minds it was too close to the traditional and disparaging English view of Gaelic Irish culture.

Nevertheless, late-eighteenth-century antiquarian explorations and the age of Ossian succeeded in providing important stimuli for the development of new attitudes in establishing an Irish past by Catholic as well as Protestant Irish intellectuals based at TCD. The work of the Royal Irish Academy (founded in 1786), coupled with contemporary archaeological explorations and investigations into the indigenous folk traditions of Ireland, produced a form of Irish history-writing which sought, as Foster has argued, to 'present a history of the land and its various peoples, rather than a rationalisation of administrative or religious policies in the guise of history'.[48] Moreover, such a stimulus gave way to the introduction of an early and inchoate form of Celticism into the literary and political culture of late-eighteenth-century Ireland.

---

[44] J. T. Leersen, 'On the Edge of Europe: Ireland in Search of Oriental roots, 1650–1850', *Comparative Criticism*, VIII (1986), 91–100.

[45] C. O'Halloran, 'Irish Re-creations of the Gaelic Past: The Challenge of MacPherson's Ossian', *Past and Present*, 124 (1989), 69–95.

[46] K. D. MacDonald, 'The Rev. William Shaw: Pioneer Gaelic Lexicographer', *Transactions of Gaelic Society of Inverness*, 1 (1976–8), 1–2.

[47] O'Halloran, 'Irish Re-creations of the Gaelic Past', 72.

[48] Foster, *Paddy and Mr Punch*, p. 3.

Irish 'Orientalists' and the ICS after 1858

In India, the Royal Asiatic Society of Bengal, which had been founded within a few years of the Royal Irish Academy, had a growing resonance in Ireland. Both intellectual societies, it has been argued, sustained British hegemony while ultimately fostering local patriotisms.[49] In Ireland, the enhanced status of Gaelic, hitherto often considered a barbaric tongue, stimulated a new scholarly interest in the language among many middle-class Irish Protestant writers attached to TCD and the fledgling Royal Irish Academy in the 1780s. Although Irish Protestants were charged by some critics as a particular example of a colonial elite who, once secure in their own position, renewed their interest in the receding indigenous Gaelic culture, they had, in fact, a long and distinguished tradition in Gaelic scholarship. The Old English, descendants of the Anglo-Norman settlers in Ireland from the twelfth century, frequently involved themselves in the study and writing of Gaelic literature and history.[50] The early writings of two Irish Protestant clergymen, Thomas Campbell and Matthew Young, for example, sought to appropriate the popularity of Ossian's works for Ireland's benefit. Campbell, for instance, argued that the songs and poems of the Irish bardic tradition should be collected, printed and translated, along with the extensive range of Irish manuscripts in the library of TCD.[51]

The extent to which cultural nationalism and the 'Gaelic revival' movement in late-nineteenth-century Ireland influenced Indian intellectual life presents interesting connections between Ireland and India. Indeed it has been asserted by one historian that nineteenth-century Bengal orientalism was the matrix of Young India, much in the same way the Anglo-Irish literati provided a proportion of the historical and literary grammar of Young Ireland.[52] Certainly many Irish civilians in India concerned themselves with constructing the notion of the Indian peasant in similar ways to which Irish peasant life and folklore was being reimagined in nineteenth-century Ireland.[53] Many ICS officials

---

[49] O. P. Kerjariwal, *Asiatic Society of Bengal* (Delhi, 1988); Foster, *Paddy and Mr Punch*, pp. 2–5.

[50] See C. Lennon, *Richard Stanihurst: The Dubliner, 1547–1618* (Blackrock: Irish Academic Press, 1981), pp. 88–105. Stanihurst was an example of an Old English writer in the Tudor period that saw his role as an interpreter of the Gaelic world for an English audience: a role which contained inherent tensions arising from the problem of reconciling two contrasting cultural viewpoints.

[51] T. Campbell, *A Philosophical Survey of the South of Ireland* (London: W. Strahan, 1777), pp. 77, 430–1.

[52] Kopf, *British Orientalism and the Bengal Renaissance*.

[53] J. Sheehy, *The Rediscovery of Ireland's Past: The Celtic Revival 1830–1930* (London: Thames & Hudson, 1980).

220   Imperial crisis and the age of reform

educated at TCD spread the concern for folklore and legend to north India, while some of the early writings of W. B. Yeats wove folklore into the national mythology of Ireland.[54] Indeed the Irish contribution to late-nineteenth-century official British 'orientalism' was inextricably linked to the influence of TCD where the realms of language, culture and ethnology had been in the ascendant for generations of Irish intellectuals, many of whom had been groomed for Indian service. The shift in perspective of the 'new orientalism' of the post-Mutiny era was to a large degree influenced by the empirical, pragmatic and visionary dimensions introduced by the new wave of British officials who travelled to India following the introduction of open examination for the ICS in the late 1850s.[55]

Although politically conservative, the ICS became increasingly influenced by the culturally radical temper of many of its Irish members. Likewise, Irish interests and culture came to play a significant part in systems of information collection and diffusion in India. Many Irish-born and -educated Indian philologists, lexicographers and historians displayed similar interests in traditional indigenous Indian culture. William Crooke and George Grierson, for instance, became pioneering enthusiasts in the ethnographic systematisation of colonial knowledge. Both were graduates of TCD who had joined the ICS together in 1871. Son of a Protestant minister from Co. Tipperary, Crooke, as Assistant Magistrate at the east United Provinces district town of Gorakhpur, compiled 'accessible information' by making 'local enquiries' in order to write his *Rural and Agricultural Glossary of the North-Western Provinces and Oudh* in 1879.[56] As an important source of government information, Crooke's glossary concerning the agricultural practices of north Indian peasant life was to be officially circulated within the provincial bureaucracy in order to assist the colonial state in the process of ruling, policing and taxing.[57]

Crooke's scholarship, while involving the ferreting out of indigenous words from readily available gazetteers, settlement reports, extant glossaries and Hindustani dictionaries, can also be viewed as part of

---

[54] See W. Crooke, *Religion and Folklore of Northern India* (Oxford University Press, 1926); W. B. Yeats, *The Celtic Twilight: Myth, Fantasy and Folklore* (Lindfield: Unity, 1990 [1893]).

[55] Bayly, *Empire and Information*, p. 355.

[56] W. Crooke Papers, Correspondence, Notes and Journals, c.1890–1921. Ms. 127, Royal Anthropological Institute of Great Britain and Ireland.

[57] W. Crooke, *Materials for a Rural and Agricultural Glossary of the North-Western Provinces and Oudh* (Allahabad: Government Press, 1879). See also S. Amin (ed.), *W. Crooke, A Glossary of North Indian Peasant Life* (Oxford University Press, 1989), p. xix.

Irish 'Orientalists' and the ICS after 1858

the late-nineteenth-century shift from a descriptive to a classificatory representation of colonial knowledge in India.[58] As a greenhorn *junt-sahib* (the Assistant or Joint Magistrate of local parlance), Crooke's achievement as author of this text lay in his arranging of some 5,000 rustic words or phrases associated with traditional Indian peasant life. Here, Crooke represents the physical environment of the Indian peasantry within a changeless tradition that is principally inhabited by agricultural implements, tools and appliances. While he lists words associated with traditional village Indian life he chooses to exclude borrowed anglicisms and words associated with modernity. From the viewpoint of 'discursive catalogues' of rural life, the significance of Crooke's text lay in its prototypical character and its subsequent appropriation by his fellow Irishman, George Grierson, for his work on the Bihar peasantry and later as Director of the Linguistic Survey of India.[59] As editor of the monthly periodical *Punjab Notes & Queries* at Mirzapur, Crooke could 'search into the minds of a primitive population and into the civilisation of the remoter parts of India' to describe the physical environment of the Indian *raiyats*.[60] Meanwhile, Grierson's relentless photographing of the peasant villages in the Sadr Tahsil of the Patna district left Max Müller expecting to find in *Bihar Peasant Life* 'the houses and carts and utensils of the people very much as they are described in the Vedas'.[61]

In Crooke's *Materials* and Grierson's *Bihar Peasant Life* both Irish civilians had annexed large portions of the intellectual and spiritual worlds of the peasants of northern India as their fields of specialisation. While Grierson concentrated on the popular literature and languages of the eastern United Provinces and Bihar, Crooke spent much of his time examining the religion and ethnography of the tribes and castes of north India.[62] Indeed, it was once asserted that Grierson's true delight 'was to hear of some orally current song or poem, to get it written, to find if possible, an existing manuscript, to trace its tradition or authorship

---

[58] B. S. Cohn, *An Anthropologist among the Historians and Other Essays* (Delhi: Oxford University Press, 1987).

[59] G. A. Grierson, *Bihar Peasant Life: Being a Discursive Catalogue of the Surroundings of the People of that Province, With Many Illustrations from Photographs Taken by the Author* (prepared under the orders of the government of Bengal) (Calcutta, 1885; reprinted Delhi, 1975), pp. 1–2.

[60] R. C. Temple, 'William Crooke, 1848–1923', Obituary Notice, *Proceedings of the British Academy* (London, 1924).

[61] M. Müller to G. A. Grierson, 5 January 1896, Grierson Papers, OIOC, Ms. Eur. E. 226/xi, no. 77(b).

[62] W. Crooke, *An Ethnological Hand-book for the N.W. Provinces and Oudh* (Allahabad: Government Press, 1890); *Religion and Folklore of Northern India*; *Tribes and Castes of the North-Western Provinces and Oudh* (Allahabad: Government Press, 1896).

222   Imperial crisis and the age of reform

and date, and with any available help of local pandits or experts to establish or translate its text'.[63] Similarly, Pandit Ram Gharib Chaube, a prolific ethnographer from the eastern United Provinces, maintained that much of Crooke's writing on the popular religion and folklore of northern India owed much to his consultations with Chaube's grandmother, whom he asserted was 'a living dictionary of all popular beliefs and superstitions' in India.[64]

Grierson and Crooke were responsible for compiling several works of empirical, taxonomising scholarship, as was their colleague Richard Temple. As a Cantonment Magistrate at Ambala in 1883, Temple used some 153 volumes of Punjab Census Records in his quest to compile a dissertation on 'the names of the rustic and urban populations of all parts of the Panjab' so that 'the question of modern Panjabi human nomenclature should be finally set at rest'.[65] Through the aid of his informants, Mir Shibbu and Darogha Chaina Mall, Temple's listings of Punjabi villagers' names sought to contribute to 'the national life, the racial ancestry and the course of civilisation' of the Punjab region. Similarly, Vincent A. Smith, son of the Irish antiquary Aquilla Smith, was also educated at TCD and entered the ICS with Crooke, Grierson and another classmate of theirs, Frederick Growse, in 1871. Smith was also posted to the North Western Provinces and Oudh where he held a wide variety of official appointments, culminating in the chief secretaryship to the government of India, a position that he retired from in 1900. As a settlement officer, Smith directed his early intellectual interests to the study of the antiquities of the Ganges valley, where some of his earliest published work included work on the coinage of the Gupta dynasty and on the Graeco-Roman influence on the civilisation and architecture of ancient India.

In many ways Smith was typical of this group of late-nineteenth-century Irish civilians in that he successfully combined the functions of administrator, antiquarian and conservationist. In January 1896, when another Irish civilian, Sir Anthony MacDonnell, was Lieutenant-Governor of the North Western Provinces, Smith was commissioned to visit the Buddhist remains near Khasia in the Gorakhpur district, with a view to submitting a proposal for the conservation of the monuments

---

[63] R. W. Thomas and R. L. Turner, 'George Abraham Grierson, 1851–1941', Obituary Notice, *Proceedings of the British Academy*, XXVIII (1942), 11.

[64] 'The Domestic Ceremonies of the Eastern Districts of N.W.P. and Oudh', entry under 'Chohri Khilana', Grierson Papers, Ms. Eur. E223, OIOC.

[65] Captain R. Temple, *A Dissertation on the Proper Names of Panjabis, with Special Reference to the Proper Names of Villagers in the Eastern Panjab* (Bombay; London: Education Society's Press; Trübner & Co., 1883), p. 1.

Irish 'Orientalists' and the ICS after 1858

that existed there. Although a 'study of the local facts' in Khasia quickly convinced Smith that the Buddhist remains at Kucanagara clearly did mark the scene of the Buddha's death, he maintained that the 'recommendations for the conservation and further excavation of the extant remains...are nevertheless interesting memorials of the past and well deserving of preservation and thorough exploration'.[66] In complement to his interest in conservation, Smith was also particularly noted for his work on Indian history as well as on Indian and Sinhalese art. In his *A History of Fine Art in India and Ceylon* (1911), Smith purported to extol the virtue of maintaining heritage and the value of indigenous Eastern culture in an age where, he noted 'the ready acceptance of change at expense of tradition lies at the very root of the problem that is modern India'.[67] Similar to late-nineteenth-century Ireland where exponents of the 'Gaelic revival' sought progress and change through maintaining and celebrating indigenous folk culture, Smith urged that '[t]he materialism of to-day is to be checked by Indian Spirituality. Arts and crafts are to flourish everywhere, centred upon the social organisation of the village. India is to arise from the ashes of India'.[68] Like his classmates, Crooke and Grierson, Smith hoped to encourage a form of moral nationalism in north India that would counter the more extreme anti-colonial nationalism of the English-educated upper castes. Smith was certainly wary of the powerful undercurrents of increasing modernisation in north India. In his opinion the way forward was, paradoxically, by looking back.

It is more than significant that Irish civilians such as George Grierson, William Crooke and Vincent A. Smith were all friends and coevals from TCD, while some of their non-TCD Irish contemporaries such as Anthony MacDonnell, William Hoey and Charles McMinn kept in frequent correspondence with them and each other throughout their Indian careers, and were all greatly influenced by aspects of the Irish language and Irish folklorism.[69] Their writings and those of their missionary

[66] V. A. Smith, *The Remains Near Kasia in the Gorakhpur District: The Reputed Site of Kucanagara or Kucinara, the Scene of Buddha's Death* (Allahabad: Government Press, 1896), p. 2.

[67] V. A. Smith, *A History of Fine Art in India and Ceylon: From the Earliest Times to the Present Day*, revised 2nd edn, ed. Karl de Burgh Codrington (New Delhi: Asian Educational Service, 2006), p. 1; V. A. Smith, *The Oxford History of India*, ed. P. Spear (Delhi: Oxford University Press, 1982).

[68] V. A. Smith, *A Report on a Tour of Exploration of the Antiquities in the Turai, Nepal* (Calcutta, 1901), p. 1. Smith writes a preparatory note on the finding of the archaeologist Babu Purna Chandra Mukherji for the Archaeological Survey of India.

[69] W. Crooke Papers, Ms. 123–39, Royal Anthropological Institute of Great Britain and Ireland.

224 Imperial crisis and the age of reform

and educationalist colleagues championed a diverse range of conservative popular cultures in late-nineteenth-century India and vehemently resisted what they perceived as being 'the artificiality of the modern'.[70] The ethnological information supplied by their bilingual Indian subordinates and represented through their collective writings demonstrated a common anthropological mission. In many ways this joint endeavour set about capturing a particular aspect of rural Indian life before, as Denzil Ibbetson asserted, it disappeared 'under the powerful solvent of contact with western thought and appliances of civilisation'.[71]

Sensitive to the social and cultural developments that they had been exposed to in Ireland, the situations that men like Crooke and Grierson encountered and wrote about in the countryside of Bihar during the late nineteenth century were both strengthened and reinforced by their experiences and views of tenurial relationships in both Ireland and India and by their education at TCD.[72] These Irish writers' collective intellectual pursuits seem consistent with the legislative and politico-economic concerns of their fellow Irish civil servants in Bengal during the same period. Whether or not they gave their support for equitable legislation between Indian *raiyat*s and local *zamindar*s (landlords), their work alongside the 'official clique...composing largely of Irishmen' who held 'Irish views of tenant rights' ensured a certain amount of consciousness on their behalf in their attempt to intellectualise the world of the Indian peasant.[73]

Land, tenancy and nationalist thought: Irish and Indian connections

The land problem in both Ireland and India provided an important vector of nationalist thought in both countries. As Clive Dewey and S. B. Cook have demonstrated by focusing upon a network of Irish administrators in Bihar during the late nineteenth century, many Irish Catholic ICS officials, including Anthony MacDonnell and Charles J. O'Donnell, were strong advocates of tenancy legislation and understood north India in a particular Irish context.[74] Son of a small Catholic landowner from rural Connaught, MacDonnell became a leading authority on famine relief and tenure policy at a time when official thinking in

---

[70] Bayly, *Empire and Information*, p. 355.
[71] Amin, *W. Crooke, A Glossary of North Indian Peasant Life*, p. xxviii.
[72] Cook, *Imperial Affinities*.
[73] *The Englishman* quoted in *The Friend of India and Statesman*, 21 November 1882.
[74] Cook, *Imperial Affinities*, pp. 88–94, 103–5.

Land, tenancy and nationalist thought   225

British India favoured men from backgrounds who had an acute awareness of the peasant problem. By the time of his retirement, MacDonnell
had served as the administrative chief of four provinces (Burma, the
Central Provinces, Bengal and the United Provinces). He chaired the
Indian Famine Commission in 1900 and Lord Curzon, the Viceroy
at the end of MacDonnell's tenure in India, was only dissuaded from
keeping him in India (as the governor of Bombay) by the intervention of Edward VII who argued that MacDonnell was needed more in
Ireland.[75]
Frequently drawing upon analogies of the land system in Ireland,
both MacDonnell and O'Donnell carried out their work under the
conviction that north Indian Muslims were not dissimilar from Irish
Protestants in that they had effectively enjoyed a long monopoly over
government office and land ownership.[76] Born in Co. Donegal in 1849,
Charles O'Donnell secured an appointment in the ICS in 1872 after
completing his education at Queen's College, Galway, where he studied English literature, history and political economy.[77] As a junior officer in the Sarun district of Bihar, O'Donnell was officially censured
and temporarily demoted by the government of India for publicly criti-
cising his own provincial administration for its ineffective tenure policies and its mismanagement of famine relief.[78] A few years before the
Bengal tenancy bill was introduced, O'Donnell had ordered a police
investigation of the estates of the Maharaja of Hutwa, a leading Bihar
landowner and one of Britain's more reliable client-*zamindar*s, whom
he described as a 'grievous rack-renter and...a vindictive oppressor
of his tenantry'.[79] MacDonnell, too, was also known for the extreme
benevolence he displayed towards Indian *raiyat*s.[80] Indeed it has been
alleged that throughout his Indian career, MacDonnell was 'haunted'

---

[75] Curzon to MacDonnell, 5 November 1901, Curzon Collection, Eur F111/204,
ff.74–5, OIOC, BL. He was the fifth and last civilian to be ennobled (created Baron
MacDonnell of Swinford in 1908). See G. Wyndham to MacDonnell, 24 February
1903, MacDonnell Papers, Mss. Eng. Hist. e.215, Bodl. Lib., Oxford.

[76] See Letterbook containing copies of letters from MacDonnell as acting Lieutenant-
Governor of Bengal, 14 June–20 November 1893, Mss. Eng. hist. d.235, Bod. Lib.,
Oxford.

[77] Biographical detail for late-nineteenth-century ICS recruits is contained in both the
ARCSC: *Parliamentary Papers*: 1859–1883 and in the annual lists for civilians contained in L/P&J/6 series, 1881–1914, OIOC, BL.

[78] C. J. O'Donnell, *The Ruin of an Indian Province: An Indian Famine Explained* (London:
C. Kegan Paul & Co., 1880); and 'C. J. O'Donnell's protest and censure', L/P&J/3/79
(1349), OIOC, BL.

[79] O'Donnell to Reynolds, 15 March 1880, L/P&J/3/70, no.67 (1389), OIOC, BL.

[80] MacDonnell speech outside the Hotel Metropole, 15 October 1898, MacDonnell
Papers, Mss. Eng. hist. c.395, Bodl. Lib., Oxford.

226   Imperial crisis and the age of reform

by the 'bitter memories of the terrible condition' of the Irish tenantry as he confronted the 'wretched condition of the Indian peasantry'.[81] As Lieutenant-Governor of the United Provinces in 1900, MacDonnell identified with the north Indian Hindus, whom he believed resembled the Catholic peasantry in Ireland. According to MacDonnell, both sets of people urgently required land reform as well as a recognition of their religious and cultural differences.[82] Towards this end, MacDonnell was responsible for allowing the Hindi language in the Devanagari script to be put on an equal footing with Urdu written in the Persian script during the day-to-day transactions within British courts of law in India.[83]

Alongside other Irish colleagues in Bihar, such as Michael Finucane, Peter O'Kinealy, Patrick Nolan and Dennis Fitzpatrick, MacDonnell and O'Donnell formed part of a close-knit Irish administrative network in Bengal which advocated that aspects of Irish land legislation should be applied in modified form to India. Pro-*raiyat* Irish ICS administrators were often bound by social and professional ties, thereby enabling them to form informal alliances with one another. MacDonnell and Finucane, for instance, had collaborated with one another from their early days as freshly recruited 'competition-wallahs' in Darbhangha. In 1880, Nolan, MacDonnell and Finucane jointly suggested a plan to curb illegal rent enhancements in Bihar.[84] In providing the initial impetus for the act, these Irishmen played a critical role in transforming a landlord-enabling bill, the Bengal Tenancy Act of 1885, into a measure conferring tenant protection. In their official reports to the government of India, these Bihar officials pointed to the rapacious nature of leaseholders, the persistence of produce rents, the lack of agricultural improvement and the crushing poverty of local *raiyats*. Such persistent features, they alleged, would continue to weaken the Indian economy and would lead to the eventual political alienation of the rural masses.[85]

---

[81] A. MacDonnell, notes, MacDonnell Papers, Mss. Eng. hist. c.415, Bod. Lib., Oxford; J. L. Hill, 'A. P. MacDonnell and the Changing Nature of British Rule in India, 1885–1901', in R. I. Crane and N. G. Barrier (eds.), *British Imperial Policy in India and Sri Lanka, 1858–1912* (New Delhi: Heritage Publishers 1981), p. 59.

[82] Minute by MacDonnell, October 1901, MacDonnell Papers, Mss. Eng. hist. 350–370, Bod. Lib., Oxford.

[83] See F. Robinson, *Separatism among Indian Muslims: The Politics of the United Provinces' Muslims 1860–1923* (London: Cambridge University Press, 1974), pp. 42–3.

[84] See P. Nolan, 8 November 1880, 'Report of the Government of Bengal on the Proposed Amendment to the Law of...Landlord...and Tenant' (hereafter 'RGBPA'), V/27/312/13, OIOC, BL.

[85] See the opinions of Nolan, MacDonnell and Finucane in 'RGBPA', V/27/312/13, OIOC, BL.

Land, tenancy and nationalist thought

Many Irish civilians, such as O'Donnell, who had published work on the impoverished state of Indian and Irish tenants, landless peasants and rack-renting landlords in Bihar, had acquired the reputation among some British and Indian officials as pro-*raiyat* sympathisers.[86] The Maharaja of Darbhanga, for instance, a member of the Select Committee whose estates consisted of over 2,460 square miles throughout Bihar, once intoned that 'Mr O'Donnell was an Irishman, and Irishmen were generally against landlords'.[87] Similarly, the conservative Bengal newspaper, *The Englishman*, alarmingly declared in 1880 that:

It is remarkable how many Irish civilians have, during the last few years, been located in different parts of Bihar. An Irishman was collector at Darbangah during the 'agitation' in that district in 1877…It was an Irish civilian who first wrote those memorable letters in *The Pioneer* on the evils of the indigo planters and planting, and another Irishman (Patrick Nolan) first reports an 'atrocity' committed by a planter in Shahabad.[88]

Others, including Charles McMinn, a Collector in Tripura and one-time supporter of Anthony MacDonnell's work with the Indian Famine Commission, later admitted that his 'strong sympathy with the people of India…did not find favour with authority'. Writing on the origin, history and etiology of the Indian Famine in 1902, McMinn regretted that because of his unwavering political views on the various abuses being carried out by the *zamindar*s he had been 'punished in various ways, deprived of allowances, refused officiating appointments' and even placed under the authority of his juniors.[89]

While the notion that there was a uniform Irish ideological predisposition towards Indian tenants is fanciful, many Irish civilians, drawn from both the Catholic and Protestant middle classes, however, demonstrated a genuine and real concern for the Indian *raiyats* during the late nineteenth century.[90] Equally, however, though not always, an

---

[86] *Hindoo Patriot*, 28 July 1879, 23 and 30 January 1882; and C. J. O'Donnell, 'The Wants of Behar', *Calcutta Review*, LXIX (1879), 146–66.
[87] *A Full Report of the Public Meeting of the Landholders of Bengal and Behar Regarding the Bengal Tenancy Bill, Held, 29 December 1883* (Calcutta: Indian Daily News Press, 1884).
[88] *The Englishman*, d. 16 September 1880, OIOC, Reel SM 49.
[89] C. W. McMinn, *Famine Truths, Half Truths, Untruths* (Calcutta: Thacker, Spink & Co., 1902), p. 48.
[90] Patrick Nolan, the officiating collector of Sahabad in 1880, was described in a speech by the great landowner, Rajah Shyama Rai Chowdry, as a 'great friend of ryots', while Nolan himself impugned the government's contention that the landlords needed assistance in recovering rents by commenting that 'I can conceive no object more worthy of a statesman than that of securing every ryot in this country in the possession of his holding': Nolan, 'RGBPA'.

228   Imperial crisis and the age of reform

Irishman's social and religious background could determine a particular political disposition that worked in the opposite direction in India. Lord Dufferin, an Ulster Landlord with an Ascendancy background, argued vehemently against Grey's policy of compulsory purchase and redistribution of Irish land in the aftermath of the Fenian troubles in the 1860s and vigorously upheld the fundamental rights of the landowner.[91] As Viceroy in India, Dufferin helped emasculate the Bengal Tenancy Act of 1886. While he supported the idea of introducing social reform to improve the world of the Indian peasant, he strongly held the belief that any interference in the liberty of landowners would seriously undermine the foundations of the government.[92]

Certainly, a complex relationship existed between dissentient Irish members of imperial administrative institutions such as the ICS and the respective Indian and Home governments during the late nineteenth century. Indo-Irish nationalist links permeated traditional points of contact (such as political organisations and the imperial press system) into the very fabric of imperial institutions. Indeed, this relationship must be placed in the context of British sensitivity to perceived threats to the British Empire coming from within the imperial bureaucratic edifice itself. A closer study of the early Indian career of Charles James O'Donnell as a dissentient member of the ICS, and specifically his interventions in issues of famine and land in Bengal between 1872 and 1882, identifies the underlying preoccupations of some Irish Catholic nationalists employed in imperial service, their perception of Victorian ideologies of improvement and their reception in British colonies. In turn, such a focus reveals much about the complex nature of the relationship that existed between Ireland and the British Empire in the late nineteenth century, and may be used to inform hitherto relatively unexplored questions concerning the contested nature of Ireland's status within the Empire, as well as the location of Britain and its Empire in the definition of Irish identities.

L'enfant terrible of the ICS': C. J. O'Donnell and the British administration of Bengal, 1872–82

During his career in India, O'Donnell became embroiled in a number of contemporary debates concerning the duties and responsibilities of

---

[91] C. E. D. Black, *The Marquess of Dufferin and Ava: Diplomatist, Viceroy, Statesman* (London: Hutchinson & Co., 1903), p. 71.
[92] See Dufferin to Lord R. Churchill, d. 30 November 1885, Dufferin Papers, OIOC, Eur Ms. F 130/2. Dufferin refers to the pro-*raiyat* elements of the Bengal Rent Bill as 'the obnoxious clauses introduced into it by the Lieutenant-Governor's wild

'*L'enfant terrible* of the ICS'   229

the Bengal administration towards its Indian subjects; he is perhaps best remembered as the author of two controversial dissenting pamphlets, entitled *The Black Pamphlet of Calcutta* (1876) and *The Ruin of an Indian Province* (1880). Significantly, O'Donnell's introduction into the world of British politics in India followed the decline of the old liberal doctrine of laissez-faire and coincided with the rise of a new historicist tradition in political thought in formulating the laws for governing overseas colonial possessions.[93] Throughout his early career, O'Donnell's views on aspects of British rule in India, particularly in issues relating to land and famine, reflected an important shift in outlook within sections of the British intellectual community in the second half of the nineteenth century which began moving away from Anglocentric models of socio-economic development of putative universal applicability.[94]

During the period 1815–60, the British government had repeatedly given statutory expression to the theories of classical political economists in its attempts to establish an effective system of land tenure in Ireland.[95] However, in the aftermath of the Great Famine, there was a stark realisation within Britain that the prescriptions of these early-nineteenth-century economists had failed to transform Ireland into a diminutive England of improving landlords and prosperous farmers. Around this time, a range of scholars, most notably sociologists and anthropologists, began adopting new models of inquiry that challenged the normative assumptions of utilitarians and classical political economists. This scholarship ultimately gave a new theoretical respectability to a set of popular contemporary ideas that sought to preserve and fortify local custom and agrarian structures rather than impose the imprint of British-based concepts, laws and practices.[96] Informing this new historicist turn in liberal economic thought were evolutionary concepts deriving from Darwinian theory and innovative methodologies that utilised empirical 'scientific' techniques and inductive reasoning rather than a priori paradigms and universal theoretical systems of thought. By the late 1860s, attempts to graft the peculiar British agrarian experience onto both Ireland and India were adjudged by a new generation of political economists, headed by J. S. Mill and J. E. Cairnes, as increasingly

---

Irishmen...!'; see also C. P. Ilbert to Markby, d. 12 September 1884, Ilbert Papers, OIOC, Eur Ms. D 594/12.

[93] Dewey, 'The Education of a Ruling Caste'.

[94] Dewey, 'Images of the Village Community', 306.

[95] G. Ó Tuathaigh, *Ireland before the Famine, 1798–1848* (Dublin: Gill and Macmillan, 1972), p. 115.

[96] Dewey, 'Celtic Agrarian Legislation and the Celtic Revival'.

230   Imperial crisis and the age of reform

arduous if not utterly futile.[97] As conditions in Ireland worsened in the aftermath of the Great Famine, subsequent British legislation aimed at consolidating and enlarging the powers of the landowner in the hope of nurturing a self-regenerating economic order was unable to stem the rising tide of Irish tenant unrest and poverty.[98]

In many of the Irish schools and universities, particularly the fledgling non-denominational Queen's Colleges in Cork and Galway, which had been founded in the mid-1840s and admitted large numbers of Irish Catholics, the historicist reaction against many of the tenets of classical economics gained considerable momentum. In the aftermath of the Great Famine, contemporary political thought in some sections of Ireland became influenced by the latest upsurge of resistance to English ascendancy. However, the process was also closely linked to a wider revival of Celtic culture at the same time. As with the Irish Patriots in the late eighteenth century, the creation of an Irish identity by the burgeoning Irish nationalist movement in the mid nineteenth century was also largely dependent on the recovery of the Celtic past. One aspect of this, in particular, that did more than merely lend momentum to a rising tide of Irish nationalism was what ancient Celtic literature proved, or was at least held to prove. The collation and translation of the Brehon law tracts in 1865 gave an extraordinary impetus both to the new historicist tradition and to Celtic historiography, asserting, as it did, that early Celtic society had from time immemorial enjoyed tenant rights such as those that the contemporary Irish and Scottish tenant and land leagues were demanding. With the publication of the Brehon law tracts, Irish nationalists and tenant-rights campaigners, in particular, were presented with a unique opportunity to present their demands to Britain as an appeal for the restoration of rights only recently, incompletely and unjustly abrogated.

The historicist approach to the Irish agrarian problem, popularised by the publications of the Brehon laws, was significant. On a fundamental level it lent momentum to the Irish nationalist movement by giving tenant rights an intellectual legitimacy for the first time, but it was also important in terms of influencing a certain degree of socialeconomic thought during the Gladstone administration. Both editors of the Brehon law tracts, W. N. Hancock and A. G. Richey, for example, were heavily involved in the formulation of liberal land policy

[97] P. Gray, 'Famine and Land in Ireland and India, 1845–1880: James Caird and the Political Economy of Hunger', *The Historical Journal*, 49 (2006), 193–215.
[98] R. D. C. Black, *Economic Thought and the Irish Question, 1817–1870*, pp. 53–5, 243–5.

'*L'enfant terrible* of the ICS'

and were at least partly responsible for securing Gladstone's commitment to achieving some measure of agrarian amelioration in Ireland in the 1870s. While Richey was accredited with influencing Gladstone to concede compensation to Irish tenants for disturbance and improvement in his Land Act of 1870, his research on ancient Irish land law was known equally to have influenced Gladstone, who cited Richey's work in the House of Commons debates on his second Land Act as proof of the historicist justification for the 'Three Fs' (Fair rent, Free sale, Fixity of Tenure) of the Tenant Land League.

The impact that this intellectual tradition had on the minds of Irish university students in the 1860s and 1870s is of course difficult to gauge, but there is little doubt that such studies of early Celtic society provided important lessons for many in terms of historical relativism. Demonstrating the feasibility and desirability of alternative forms of social organisation to those expressed by the utilitarians in India, was, as S. B. Cook effectively demonstrates, a concern for many young Irish recruits employed by the ICS at the time.[99] However, Cook points out that Irishmen employed by the ICS should not of course be viewed as a homogeneous group that advocated one political or cultural agenda, and stresses that divergent responses to British hegemony by Irish Catholics and Protestants depended by and large on the individual concerned. While the majority of Irish Catholic ICS recruits were able to eschew radical politics and for the most part were able to reconcile a local and an imperial patriotism to satisfy the competing demands of Irish nationalism, British imperialism and Indian welfare, conversely there were examples of quite the opposite being true.

O'Donnell, for one, explicitly employed Irish nationalist tactics as a means of accelerating agrarian reform in Bihar, promoting the idea of a Home Rule India while simultaneously contesting empire from behind the imperial bureaucratic edifice. His passing into the ICS, for example, coincided with the 1874 General Election that brought the Irish Home Rule party into the House of Commons and marked the beginning of the period in the late nineteenth century when Irish nationalists mounted the most direct and serious attack on British imperial authority. Not only this, but O'Donnell's experiences with the authorities in India occurred at the same time that a sympathetic relationship grew up between Irish Home Rulers and India's first generation of political leaders. As Howard Brasted has explored, the years between 1870 and 1886 marked an important stage in Indian nationalist development when moderate nationalists familiarised themselves with most

[99] Cook, *Imperial Affinities*, pp. 2–3.

232   Imperial crisis and the age of reform

facets of the Irish question and drew critically upon the Irish experience in the framing of suitable nationalist objectives and in the formulation of tactics for promoting unity and common cause in India.[100] Here the main channel of discussion and dissemination between Irish and Indian nationalists was through the Irish and Indian press, both English-language and vernacular, though close personal contacts were also sporadically forged through burgeoning nationalist societies, student movements and extra-parliamentary bodies and associations that took root in Dublin, Calcutta and London around the same time.[101] Irish nationalist newspapers such as Patrick Ford's the *Irish World* and A. M. Sullivan's the *Nation* provided content that was endorsed and echoed in several Indian newspapers such as Kristodas Pal's the *Hindoo Patriot* and Subramania Aiyar's the *Hindu* and vice versa. These reports demonstrated that the importance of the connections between Irish and Indian nationalists was not lost on contemporaries and that by acknowledging each other's difficulties under British rule they were allowing one another to recognise the potential for political independence.

Foremost among late-nineteenth-century Irish nationalist MPs who took an avid interest in promoting the cause of Indian nationalism was O'Donnell's brother, Frank Hugh O'Donnell, a somewhat unpredictable character, but nevertheless a highly regarded member of Parnell's party in the late 1870s and early 1880s. The influence of Frank Hugh O'Donnell's nationalist philosophy on his younger brother Charles was important.[102] Along with other notable Irish nationalists such as Alfred Webb, Frank Hugh O'Donnell demonstrated a passionate interest in Indian affairs throughout his political career, during which time he felt obliged to instruct Home Rulers that as pioneers of national freedom they had a duty to uphold and further the principle of nationalism throughout the Empire.[103] Frank Hugh O'Donnell's nationalist philosophy was based on his belief that Ireland's experience of British imperialism was more or less replicated in other parts of the Empire. His ambition was to transform the Empire into a commonwealth of equal partners admitted to membership on the basis of nationality.[104] O'Donnell believed that this coalescence should be achieved by

[100] Brasted, 'Indian Nationalist Development'.
[101] B. B. Majumdar, *Indian Political Associations and Reform of Legislature, 1818–1917* (Calcutta: Firma K. L. Mukhopadhyay, 1965).
[102] F. H. O'Donnell, *A History of the Irish Parliamentary Party*, 2 vols. (London: Longmans, 1910).
[103] I. M. Cumpston, 'Some Early Indian Nationalists and Their Allies in the British Parliament, 1851–1906', *The English Historical Review*, 76 (1961), 279–97.
[104] O'Donnell, *History of the Irish Parliamentary Party*, II, p. 471.

whatever means necessary. Writing in 1878, he advocated the idea that Ireland could take the lead in effecting 'a coalition with the oppressed natives of India', in achieving independence within the Empire by conversion if possible, or by force if necessary. O'Donnell believed that when the British were confronted with the challenge of an extended, cosmopolitan nationalism, they would surrender gracefully and salvage what remained.[105]

Indeed, this vision went well beyond deploying the narrow tactics of obstruction in the House of Commons. His commonwealth ideal was shared by his brother, C. J. O'Donnell, who maintained that only a 'policy of Home Rule All Round, radiating from the centre of a really Imperial Parliament, representative of every race and every Colony', could provide 'hope of a United Empire, and...alone give a sure foundation to a broad and true Imperialism'.[106] Central to O'Donnell's vision of a 'United Empire' and the idea of promoting this 'policy of Home Rule All Round' as he imagined it, was the ability to secure the confidence of the rising urban middle classes in India, who had proved much more receptive to Irish nationalist suggestion than the majority of Indian landowning patrons, many of whom began to distance themselves from the Irish party following the outbreak of the land war in Ireland. With the accession of Parnell as leader of the Home Rule Party in 1877, and his subsequent transformation of it from a mere pressure group to an effective instrument of parliamentary intervention, some of the more advanced sections of the Indian nationalist leadership, such as Surandranth Banerjea and Dadabhai Naoroji, became impressed and stimulated by Irish political strategy.[107] Most of all, they wanted to adopt the Irish policy of alignment with the Liberal Party and hoped India, like Ireland, would become a potent factor in English politics. This was to be achieved, in the main, by bringing about a liaison with the Liberal Party through constitutionalism.[108] However, the effectiveness of the Parnellite model of agrarian disturbance and the activities of the Land League were not lost on Banerjea and the Indian Association of Calcutta, in particular. He argued that parliamentary persuasion could be carried out with greater efficiency and more far-reaching results by

---

[105] F. H. O'Donnell's nationalist principles were outlined in two controversial letters published in Irish newspapers, one in the *Freeman's Journal*, 13 August 1878, and the other in the *Nation*, 24 August 1878.

[106] C. J. O'Donnell, 'Ireland and Conservatism', *Nineteenth Century*, 68 (1910), 194–204.

[107] O'Donnell, *History of the Irish Parliamentary Party*, II, p. 423.

[108] B. C. Pal, *Swadeshi and Swaraj: the Rise of New Patriotism* (Calcutta: Yugayatri Prakashak, 1954), pp. 17–18.

234   Imperial crisis and the age of reform

making common cause with the peasantry and organising determined yet sensible mass agitation. At a time when the government was busy reviewing the system of land revenue and tenurial law in Bengal, it was believed that by establishing linkages with the Bengali peasantry and bringing aggrieved and divided tenants into the national movement, mass Indian discontent could be effectively harnessed to the Home Rule cause.[109]

Critically attuned to these political currents, C. J. O'Donnell, after passing the ICS exams in London, secured a strategic position in charge of the sub-division of Jhenida in the district of Jessore in Lower Bengal and quickly displayed an interest in overseeing tenant rights, particularly by maintaining a judicial control of rents. In 1874, after two years' service, O'Donnell was deputed on famine duty as the District Relief Officer of Birbhum. Here he held the distinction of being the only officer under eight years' service in India placed in charge of the relief operations of an entire district. Having established an initial reputation for probity, in February 1875 he was appointed an assistant to the Director General of Statistics in Calcutta for the purpose of compiling detailed statistical accounts of the outlying districts of Bihar, which had borne the brunt of the famine devastating parts of Lower Bengal between 1873 and 1874. In this capacity, and in his subsequent appointment as Joint Magistrate at the sub-division of Atiya in Mymensingh, O'Donnell carried out a number of inquiries into the administration and handling of famine relief by senior administrative figures such as Sir George Campbell and Sir Richard Temple.[110]

O'Donnell's self-assurance and conviction in his beliefs were striking. Less than three years into his Indian career and with relatively little experience of the socio-economic conditions of Bihar, he published his views in a controversial booklet on the Bengal administration's handling of the Bihar famine in 1873–4, entitled *The Black Pamphlet of Calcutta* (1876).[111] In this pamphlet, which the government of India interpreted as a scathing attack on Temple's Lieutenant-Governorship of Bengal, O'Donnell endeavoured to expose the truth behind what he referred to as the 'shams', 'errors' and 'deceitfulness' of Temple's administration of the humanitarian crisis in Bengal in 1874.[112] There were two main elements to the dissenting views expressed in the *Black Pamphlet*. First,

---

[109] J. C. Bagal, *History of the Indian Association, 1876–1951* (Calcutta: Indian Association, 1953), pp. 50, 53, 70–1, 90.
[110] C. J. O'Donnell file (BL, IOR, L/P&J/3/79).
[111] C. J. O'Donnell, *The Black Pamphlet of Calcutta: The Famine of 1874* (London: William Ridgway, 1876).
[112] Ibid., p. 6.

'*L'enfant terrible* of the ICS'   235

O'Donnell insisted that the Bengal famine should never have occurred and could have been avoided had there been sufficient intervention and policy put in place by the government of India. This, O'Donnell reasoned, owed as much to parliament's shameful unwillingness to investigate Indian matters as it did to the unsuitable laws then governing the subcontinent. He pointed to the British experience of two previous famines in the Lower Provinces in 1770 and 1866 from which both the provincial and the central governments had failed to learn lessons and draw precedents for the future. According to O'Donnell, the mismanagement of the relief effort by Temple rested on the wrongful assumption that the 'so-called famine' in Bihar, in particular, was a result of prolonged periods of drought in the region, ultimately leading to the familiar cycle of crop failure, shortage of food supplies, starvation, disease and death.[113] He rejected this notion and cited as proof the above-average rainfall measurements he collected while on statistical duty during his year visiting some of the worst-affected districts of Bihar, including Purneah, Gya and Sarun.

At a time when the Irish land debate was intensifying and Gladstone was reformulating the party's liberal economic principles in line with a new historical relativism, O'Donnell attacked the Malthusian cynicism and apathy of legislators who failed to take into account the traditional customs and socio-economic realities of Indian peasant life. He argued that it was the alien laws introduced by Britain affecting property and debt – which were not carefully adapted to the position of people in a particular region – that lay behind much of India's famine vulnerability. Intimating that the root cause of the Bengal famine was as much administrative and political as it was economic, O'Donnell stated:

It is true that the apathy of the English people and of the English Peers and Commons in matters of purely Indian interest is a subject of constant complaint, yet we hope, in this instance, that they will not refuse to interfere and to break the long chain of disasters which, disguised under the name of visitations of Providence, have been really the results of bad government and ignorance, when they were not the outcome of a vain and ill-regulated ambition.[114]

He pointed to the wilful ignorance and culpable neglect of the senior government officials involved and delivered a stinging attack on the Indian bureaucracy from the Viceroy down. Among the most serious charges that O'Donnell levelled at some of his colleagues was the lack of knowledge they possessed of the regions they were supposed to be governing. Temple, unsurprisingly, was subjected to some savage criticism.

[113] Ibid., pp. 7–8.   [114] Ibid., pp. 9–14, 79.

236 Imperial crisis and the age of reform

Ridiculing Temple's assertion that diseased rice plants had been the predominant factor in bringing famine to Bengal, O'Donnell wondered whether 'some hazy ideas about swamps and rice-fields seemed to have formed his most accurate idea of the province he was quite ready to govern'. He denounced the administration of relief measures for Bengal as being of 'the most egregious description', citing the examples of the purchase of large quantities of unwanted and unused grain, the grossly inflated wages paid out to labourers employed on relief works and the huge waste of relief money spent on the transport of government grain into allegedly distressed areas.

While reforms might reduce the problems of peasant indebtedness to moneylenders and the spiralling cost of legal cases brought before the district courts, O'Donnell believed that a more fundamental restructuring of British government in India was necessary to prevent further outbreaks of famine and curb spiralling mortality rates. Essentially what began as an assessment of the failings of the Bengal government in 1874 ended up as a critique of British responsibilities to home and empire:

Nor are the circumstances we criticize so exclusively Indian that the self-interest of large classes at home should not be aroused. Little of the waste, indeed, has been derived from English revenues, but English commerce will be burdened, for many a year to come, with taxes which the famine expenditure alone has rendered necessary. This, however, is not the view that England, as a governing country, can allow herself to take. The point she must consider is, whether she can claim to be fulfilling her duty towards this great empire by leaving its finances a prey even to ignorance. The people of India cannot help comparing the swift and severe punishment that descended on an instant's thoughtlessness, and instant's ill-judgement in the case of the 'Vanguard,' with the carelessness with which a loss to India fifty times as great has been disregarded.[115]

Insisting that his only motive for writing the pamphlet was 'to advance the truth' behind the huge loss of life in Bengal, O'Donnell concluded by invoking the memory of the Great Irish Famine and calling on members of the British public and politicians alike to demand the establishment of a Royal Commission to investigate the recurrence of famines in India and that 'weak and shifty thing we now call Government, be it Supreme or be it Provincial, that bullies European gentlemen in Calcutta and wanders thirsting for adulation from Tipera to Bankipure, that substitutes chicane for diplomacy at Baroda, and goes crouching bareheaded and barefooted before the

[115] Ibid., pp. 79–80.

'*L'enfant terrible* of the ICS'

majesty of Burmah, that insults the memory of Mayo and decorates the Faminists'.[116] Significantly, the writing of the *Black Pamphlet* coincided with Frank Hugh O'Donnell's introduction to the House of Commons as a Home Rule MP in 1874. Prior to his brother's statistical tour of famine-racked districts in Lower Bengal in the following year, Frank Hugh O'Donnell had already cited the Irish situation of 1846–7 and its analogy to the Bihar famine of 1873–4 as a means of speaking on behalf of Indian interests.[117] In his maiden parliamentary speech on the subject in April 1874, which was published in the *Times* and attracted considerable attention, O'Donnell confidently asserted that his intelligence on Indian affairs was based on a 'calm assertion of superior information', and that the similarities of the famine experience in both countries had shown him the possibilities of Irish intervention in imperial affairs.[118]

While C. J. O'Donnell's understanding of the Bihar famine was no doubt informed by his experiences in Ireland and the sympathies that motivated him were privately shared, if not as publicly voiced, by others, his publication of the conditions of impoverished tenants, landless peasants, rack-renting landlords and the occurrence of subinfeudation in Bihar during the late 1870s and early 1880s was very unusual for an official of the British Crown during this period.[119] Indeed, the decisive turning point in the relationship between O'Donnell and the Government of India came in 1879, following the publication of another inflammatory article in the *Calcutta Review* entitled 'The Wants of Behar'. While Sub-Divisional Officer of Suran, O'Donnell became embroiled in a bitter dispute with the Maharajah of Hutwa, one of Bihar's leading landowners.[120] The incident began in August 1879 when Richard Pawsey (the Collector of the Sarun district of Bihar) forwarded to Sir Stuart Bayley (Commissioner of the Patna Division and the officiating Lieutenant-Governor of Bengal) correspondence from O'Donnell. This correspondence reported that while on a tour observing suitable land for the construction of the Suran irrigation scheme, in July 1879, large numbers of *raiyats* of the Hutwa Raj had deserted their homes 'owing to flagrant rack-renting and oppression on the part of the *thikadars* or farmers holding land

[116] Ibid., p. 82.
[117] Cumpston, 'Some Early Indian Nationalists', 282; O'Donnell, *History of the Irish Parliamentary Party*, II, pp. 423–4.
[118] O'Donnell, *History of the Irish Parliamentary Party*, II, p. 173.
[119] C. J. O'Donnell, Joint Magistrate and Deputy Collector of Gya to the Magistrate and Collector of Gya, Gya, 1 October 1877 (BL, IOR, V/27/312/12).
[120] O'Donnell, 'The Wants of Behar'.

238   Imperial crisis and the age of reform

under the Maharajah'.[121] As a consequence, O'Donnell employed the local police to enquire into the extent and causes of the alleged desertions, and, by 'adopting their reports implicitly, had submitted to Pawsey very sensational statements as to the state of things throughout the Hutwa properties'.[122] On receipt of these reports, Bayley – 'astonished that the existence of such evils had not before been reported' – directed Pawsey personally to enquire into the matter, and call upon the Maharaja to explain.

Instead of going to the Hutwa estate, Pawsey contented himself by sending O'Donnell, who in turn maintained the correctness of the initial police reports corroborating his overall assessment of the Maharaja's maladministration of his estates.[123] In response, the Maharaja subsequently sent a report of his own to Pawsey, answering all the charges levelled at him by the police inspector and by O'Donnell, together with corresponding ledgers and accounts.[124] After some deliberation, the case was laid before Sir Stuart Bayley in September 1879, who, following a personal tour of Patna Division, concluded that O'Donnell's actions had been injudicious and open to censure, while Pawsey as the Collector and senior officer in charge of Suran, had failed to investigate the incident with 'sufficient discrimination'. Although Bayley was convinced of O'Donnell's 'good faith in the first instance' and that he held 'naturally and justly very strong views as to the depressed condition of the ryots in Behar...and especially to the evils of the existing system of zemindari management in that district', he believed that O'Donnell's strong report against the Maharaja's management was ultimately 'hypothetical' and was based 'on a hasty and insufficient examination of the facts'.[125] He recommended to Sir Ashley Eden, who by then had returned to his post as Lieutenant-Governor of Bengal, that O'Donnell be transferred to Burdwan district in West Bengal and that Pawsey be replaced as Collector of Suran by Anthony Patrick MacDonnell, 'one of the strongest district officers in Behar', and one who, Eden asserted,

---

[121] A. MacKenzie, Secretary to the Government of Bengal to the Secretary to the Government of India, Darjeeling, 30 July 1881 (BL, IOR, L/P&J/3/79).

[122] Ibid.

[123] F. M. Halliday, Commissioner of the Patna Division, to the Secretary to the Government of Bengal, Revenue Department, Bankipore, 4 August 1879 (BL, IOR, L/P&J/3/79).

[124] Maharajah K. P. Sahai, Bahadoor, Hutwa to R. Pawsey, Collector of Sarun, Chupra, 21 July 1879 (BL, IOR, L/P&J/3/79).

[125] Sir S. C. Bayley, Acting Lieutenant Governor of Bengal, to the Commissioner of the Patna Division (BL, IOR, L/P&J/3/79).

'L'enfant terrible of the ICS'

was 'notoriously eager to protect the ryots from oppression of all kinds, whether coming from zemindars or planters'.[126]

MacDonnell, who was another Irish Catholic graduate of Queen's College, Galway, in the 1860s and a well-respected authority on issues of famine and land throughout Bihar, was brought in by the government of Bengal to arbitrate in the dispute and engage in a damage-limitation exercise. Far from aligning himself to his co-religionist and fellow university alumnus, MacDonnell reported to the government that after embarking upon a personal tour of the villages of Katiya on the Hutwa estate during the winter of 1879–80, he was satisfied that the Maharajah had taken all necessary steps to curb illegal activity and punish *thikadars* whenever *raiyats* reported illegal exactions. Moreover, MacDonnell was keen to impress upon the government that while O'Donnell's police reports confirmed 'what no one had ever doubted', that the *thikadars* or farmers under the Maharajah had certainly been guilty of some abuses as was commonly reported on other landed estates throughout Bengal, the Maharajah had 'shown himself most anxious to work with the Collector, and get rid of the system of short farming leases as soon as might be'. Contrary to O'Donnell's allegations of rack-renting against the Maharajah, MacDonnell confirmed to the government that during his visit to Suran, 'not a single case of enhancement of the rates of rent by the present Maharajah had come to his notice'.[127]

O'Donnell's response was immediate. Writing to Andrew MacKenzie, the Secretary to the government of Bengal, he called into question MacDonnell's 'half-hearted defence of the Maharajah' noting that it was 'utterly out of place' with his personal convictions and that for those who knew him, his report must be read 'with pain and a deep regret'.[128] O'Donnell impressed upon MacKenzie the ideological imperatives which he believed went hand in hand with the British imperial mission in India:

What is the great justification of our presence in India but to secure justice between the powerful and the weak, and who more helpless, as has been hundred times proved, than the Behar ryot?...Eight years have passed since the great outbreak of rack-rented misery, miscalled the famine of 1873–4, cost the Empire so many millions. For five years the preparation of a new and

---

[126] A. MacKenzie to the Secretary to the Government of Bengal, 30 July 1881 (BL, IOR, L/P&J/3/79).

[127] A. P. MacDonnell, Collector of Sarun, to the Commissioner of the Patna Division, Moharajgunge, 1 January 1880 (BL, IOR, L/P&J/3/79).

[128] Petition of C. J. O'Donnell to the Secretary to the Government of Bengal, Judicial Department, through the Commissioner, Presidency Division, Jessore, 11 April 1881 (BL, IOR, L/P&J/3/79).

240 Imperial crisis and the age of reform

unnecessary Land Bill has blocked the way of executive reform. The ticca-
dari system lives and thrives, based in practice though on the contemptuous
disregard of the legislature. The landed proprietors still enhance their rents
without reference to our civil courts. The tenants are still refused legal receipts
and quittances for the rents they pay. The extension of indigenous well irrigation, that most certain protection from drought, is almost at a standstill in
consequence of the insecurity of tenures, the most secure and fixed under the
law.[129]

According to O'Donnell, the real problem in Bihar lay not with existing
land legislation in India, which he praised as 'the most equitable land
law in the world', but with the landlords themselves. In his mind, it was
the *zemindari* class that were responsible for abusing power, disobeying
the law and by exacting 'enormous rentals' from their tenants, foment-
ing agrarian unrest. As O'Donnell argued: 'The poor, helpless, discontented men are still, to the dishonour of the Government, driven not
only from village to village by the extortions of underlings, but out from
British territory to the fever-laden jungles of Nepal by the guilty avarice of millionaire Maharajahs.' Although he maintained that the estates
of the Maharajah of Hutwa were by no means 'the worst managed in
Bihar', he was convinced, nevertheless, that the young Maharajah was
'a grievous rack-renter and, when opposed, a vindictive oppressor of his
tenantry'.[130]

Nevertheless, on receipt of MacDonnell's report on the Hutwa episode in February 1880, Eden saw no reason to pay any further attention
to O'Donnell's attempts to reopen the case against the Hutwa Raj and
upheld the original decision by Sir Stuart Bayley to impress upon the
Maharajah the importance of getting rid of *thikadar* short leases and
improving the overall material condition of his *raiyats* in the future,
while at the same time recommending that O'Donnell, as 'a very subordinate, unreliable and inexperienced officer', be removed from Bihar
to avoid any future agitation.[131] However, as Eden prepared to secure
closure on the matter, O'Donnell's relations with the government went
from bad to worse when news reached Calcutta that he had, while on
special leave to Ireland in March 1880, published another inflammatory pamphlet – entitled *The Ruin of an Indian Province* – raging against
the administrations of Bengal and Bombay.[132] O'Donnell, seemingly

---

[129] Ibid.   [130] Ibid.

[131] H. A. Cockerell, Secretary to the Government of Bengal, Judicial and Political
Appointment Departments, to the Secretary to the Government of India, Home
Department, Calcutta, 25 January 1882 (BL, IOR, L/P&J/6/75).

[132] C. J. O'Donnell, *The Ruin of an Indian Province: An Indian Famine Explained. A Letter
to the Marquis of Hartington* (London: C. Kegan Paul & Co., 1880).

'L'enfant terrible of the ICS'

without official sanction from the government, published the pamphlet as a letter addressed directly to the Secretary of State for India, Lord Hartington, outlining the injustice he felt he had received at the hands of Bayley and Eden for merely highlighting the 'evils' that continued to undermine the integrity of British rule in India. In the letter, O'Donnell cited the 'obstinate blindness' of officials 'that refused to recognise that in India a hundred reforms are pressing menacingly for solution, and that the present form of Indian Government is utterly out of tune with the time and its requirements'. According to O'Donnell, a combination of official uninterest and greed was again at the heart of much of the discontent and had eaten away at success achieved by earlier English liberal reform in India:

I have associated too long with English liberals to be ignorant of the thoroughness of their desire to govern India well: but I share the fear, common to most well-wishers of that country, that a sentiment so honourable to England is much too liable to slumber in an ill-founded confidence in high officials... Irishmen, whose memories of British rule are among the darkest in history... can hardly believe what benefits foreign dominion brought to a country torn, as India was last century, by the feuds of a dozen warring races and a dozen militant creeds. Even when Government and the individuals that constitute it get the fullest credit for good intention, it is felt that India is becoming too thoroughly imbued with Western ideas to remain contented with the half-paternal, half-bureaucratic, but most superficially informed system of administration that, from some narrow council-chamber in Calcutta or Simla, governs with more than a despotism of a Caesar...The condition of the agricultural classes in Bombay will immediately present itself to your mind...It may be wonderingly asked, can it be possible that the highly civilised Government of England in the nineteenth century can have reduced a great Indian province to that of the worst extremity of peasant misery which had made the great French social war of the fourteenth century a byword for criminal maladministration.[133]

What was so alarming about O'Donnell's latest critique of British rule in India was not simply its highlighting of the plight of the Indian peasant, but its linking of the combustible elements of inadequate land legislation, peasant unrest and agrarian conflict to Indian nationalist aspirations. Outbreaks of unrest among the agricultural classes in Bombay, O'Donnell reminded Hartington, were attributable to the current inadequate system of land revenue payment in cash by the occupying tenant. Unlike pre-colonial systems of payments in kind, which fluctuated according to the vicissitudes of the harvest, thereby lessening the burden of peasant reliance on moneylenders, alien modes of 'taxation and

[133] Ibid., pp. 6–7.

242   Imperial crisis and the age of reform

over taxation – grinding, merciless, incredible – was [sic] the cause, and almost sole cause' of their discontent.

Given the desperate nature of the circumstances, O'Donnell asked Hartington whether he thought such 'resentment unnatural under these circumstances on the part of the Bombay people, when Government poses as a kind of beneficent Providence interfering to save a lazy and improvident peasantry from the unscrupulous knavery of their brethren of the town?'[134] Moreover, the effects of excessive taxation and rack-renting of tenants by landlords were exacerbated by the presence of a particularly oppressive system of European indigo planting in Bihar that O'Donnell felt was a significant factor in reducing the *raiyats* to a state of poverty and starvation. He believed that as long as government officials maintained a vested interest in indigo planting, *ticcardari*, landlord and indigo oppression would continue unabated. Informing Hartington that it was his 'sincere conviction that the condition of the great province of Behar' was a 'disgrace to the English name', O'Donnell concluded by insisting that 'nothing but the clearly pronounced expression of the will of Parliament can enforce amelioration'.[135]

The fallout over the publication of *The Ruin of an Indian Province* by O'Donnell in 1880 was considerable. O'Donnell not only succeeded in alienating high-level administrators with his accusations of official dishonesty and corruption, but he also earned the wrath of the powerful Bihar Indigo Planters' Association, whose members took umbrage at his allegations of oppression and abuse. They appealed to Lord Hartington directly to censure O'Donnell and 'to take such action in the matter as will satisfy Her Majesty's Government and the public' that they were 'not the selfish oppressors he [O'Donnell] represents us to be'.[136] Anthony Patrick MacDonnell, the Collector of Sarun, who had been responsible for intervening in O'Donnell's dispute with the Maharajah of Hutwa, denounced the pamphlet as an 'anachronism' completely 'out of time with the present state of things' in Bihar. MacDonnell believed that O'Donnell's indictment of *zemindari* mismanagement was an already well-established fact, and said 'nothing which is not extracted from the proceedings of Government and its officers'. Moreover, it completely ignored the fact that reform had already begun in Bihar some years prior to that and that it had been making steady progress since then. These reforms, he maintained, were 'not in indigo matters alone, not

---

[134] Ibid., p. 12.   [135] Ibid., p. 26.

[136] Deputation of the Behar planters by Members of the Behar Indigo-Planters' Association to Sir A. Eden, Lieutenant-Governor of Bengal, 10 August 1880 (BL, IOR, L/P&J/3/79).

'L'enfant terrible of the ICS'

alone in administration of the ward's estates, nor in the management of zemindars' properties – the three heads of Mr O'Donnell's indictment', but in other areas also. MacDonnell assured MacKenzie that

The spread of education and awakening intelligence, may be trusted to secure a more prosperous future to the people of this province; but for the present it is the duty of local officers, doubly armed with the power of good laws, to effectuate the intention of Government. This they can do, not by violent denunciations of stale abuses, but by patient, often wearisome, rarely brilliant rounds of honest daily work.[137]

The Bengal government's response to the publication of the pamphlet was to keep a separate file monitoring O'Donnell's activities. It was suspicious of his motives for continually courting controversy wherever he was placed. From 1881 all materials relating to official disputes in which he became involved were forwarded directly to the Secretary of State for India and the Viceroy in Council with the intention of 'exposing very fully the disingenuous nature of Mr O'Donnell's line of argument' and 'what Mr O'Donnell's services [to the Crown] have really been'. In compiling the file, the Secretary of the government of Bengal, Andrew MacKenzie, commented that O'Donnell was 'an officer in whom the Government has never been able to place the slightest reliance in'. He warned Viceroys Lord Northbrook and Lord Ripon that through his activities O'Donnell had 'repeatedly come unfavourably to notice in the matter of his official duties, while his utter and unprecedented disregard of discipline and want of loyalty to his superiors and to Government have set the worst possible example to the service at large'.[138]

Even before a separate file on O'Donnell was prepared for senior council, suspicion abounded as to the reasons behind his persistently outspoken behaviour. Colman Macaulay, the officiating Secretary to the government of Bengal, had no doubt that O'Donnell was the 'moving spirit' behind the Hutwa dispute in Sarun in 1879. He noted that 'even if rents are too high in these three villages, it may well be asked if this is any excuse for a Government officer travelling entirely beyond his proper sphere, and proceeding to denounce the owner of vast estates, and spread a current of excitement and disaffection among his tenantry'.[139] The editor of the *Indian Mirror* in Calcutta went further, suggesting

---

[137] Memorandum of A. P. MacDonnell, Magistrate-Collector of Sarun, to the Secretary of the Government of Bengal, Judicial Department (BL, IOR, L/P&J/3/79).

[138] MacKenzie to the Secretary to the Home Government, 30 July 1881 (BL, IOR, L/P&J/3/79).

[139] 'Alleged Rack-renting on the Hutwa Estate', C. Macaulay, Officiating Secretary to the Government of Bengal, Revenue Department, Land Revenue, K-W-Miscellaneous Collection X, Nos. 73–79, December 1879 (BL, IOR, L/P&J/79).

244   Imperial crisis and the age of reform

that O'Donnell's motives for publishing the pamphlet lay in his desire to secure a future parliamentary seat for himself in Westminster as an Irish Home Rule MP:

> It is not the alleged maladministration of Bihar, nor the sympathy with the oppressed ryots of the Province, that was the source of inspiration, to which the pamphlet owed its origins. Mr O'Donnell thought that by writing and publishing this violent diatribe against landlords in Behar, he would, at a future election for the place he wished to represent, secure for a man, the votes of all who were qualified to vote.[140]

MacKenzie agreed and commented to the Home government that he believed that O'Donnell was masquerading as a Home Rule informant or spy:

> Mr O'Donnell seems to think that he is in a position to defy all local authority; and it would be affectation to ignore the fact that he conceives himself able to do this solely because of his close relationship to a well-known Irish M.P. [Frank Hugh O'Donnell], who, prompted by him, has no scruple in making repeated and unwarranted attacks upon the Government to which Mr O'Donnell is subordinate.

This was a charge that O'Donnell, of course, strenuously denied. Writing to MacKenzie in April 1880, O'Donnell commented that he had lately 'observed in some non-official criticisms of his conduct the suggestion that his [Irish] nationality has tinged the views he holds in regard to property in land' in India. Rejecting such charges, O'Donnell pointed out to MacKenzie that 'in the struggle he made to secure the benefits of the existing law to the tenantry of the Hutwa Raj, he was working under the orders of a Suffolk Englishman, Mr Pawsey' and that 'he was aided by the advice and sympathy of the Deputy Opium Agent of Sewan, Mr Tytler, a Scottish gentleman who during an equally long service has won a reputation unexcelled by any officer in his department'.[141]

Frank Hugh O'Donnell was also keen to dismiss suggestions appearing in some national newspapers in England that he was in some way in cahoots with his brother, Charles O'Donnell, in plotting nationalist discord in India. In one letter to the *Times* dated 23 August 1880, Frank Hugh O'Donnell requested the editor give publicity to what he referred to as the 'indisputable facts' surrounding his brother's Indian service, in reply to certain 'allegations and semi-insinuations' of disloyalty that had recently appeared in the newspaper. Contrary to attempts to discredit O'Donnell in some sections of the English and Anglo-Indian

---

[140] See *Indian Mirror*, 20 and 27 August, 23 October 1880 and 27 October 1881.
[141] See 'Petition of C. J. O'Donnell', 11 April 1881 (BL, IOR, L/P&J/3/79).

'*L'enfant terrible* of the ICS'

press, Frank Hugh O'Donnell maintained that his brother was 'exceptionally well-informed on the condition of a province in which he spent nearly six years in close investigation of the agrarian question in its various phases'.[142]

Eden, the Lieutenant-Governor of Bengal, with whom O'Donnell had tense relations since the Hutwa episode and his subsequent transfer from Bihar, denounced the publication of *The Ruin of an Indian Province* as an 'ignorant and prejudiced' piece of nationalist propaganda. Writing to Lord Northbrook in October 1880, Eden commented that there was 'not a worse, more useless, officer in the Bengal Civil Service' than O'Donnell and 'not an officer of two years' standing whose opinion on questions of administration would not rank higher than his'. He informed Northbrook that while he was away on the Army Commission in 1879, Sir Stuart Bayley, who was officiating for him as Lieutenant Governor of Bengal, 'was compelled to censure Mr O'Donnell in the severest terms for endeavouring to foment ill feeling between the Maharajah of Hutwa and his ryots'. According to Eden, O'Donnell acted 'as a follower of Parnell and as a brother of Mr Frank Hugh O'Donnell might have been expected to act', making 'statements and assertions which were shown on the report of an officer specially appointed to enquire into the matter [A. P. MacDonnell] to be utterly untrue'. It was because of this, Eden suggested, that Bayley 'felt it his duty to remove him to a district in which his peculiar views would be likely to do less mischief than in Sarun'. Moreover, Eden implied that Charles O'Donnell was acting as an informant of the Irish party and was serving as an intermediary between it and prominent Indian nationalist figures such as Surandraneth Banerjea, whom O'Donnell once referred to as his 'oldest Indian friend'.[143]

Nor was this the first time, Eden informed Northbrook, that O'Donnell had conspired against the government of Bengal in collaboration with Frank Hugh O'Donnell. In the aftermath of the Bihar famine of 1873–4, for example, Eden was convinced that O'Donnell 'with the help of his brother, prepared a grossly libellous pamphlet...which he published in Ireland' with a view to demonstrating 'how wasteful and wicked' Lord Lytton's policy of relief of famine in Bihar had been. He maintained that the 'garbled facts' and 'misquoted figures' used by O'Donnell in this pamphlet to attack the government were allowed to circulate without censure because 'he has a brother who can command

---

[142] *Times*, 23 August 1880.
[143] Letter no. 867-T, Government of Bengal to Government of India, 30 July 1881, para. 13, Vol. 2, 1881 (BL, IOR, L/P&J/3).

246   Imperial crisis and the age of reform

a certain number of votes, and who has therefore to be conciliated; and also because the Viceroy attacked was Lord Lytton, who belongs to the party out of power'. More so than any of his other peers, Eden believed that by not taking O'Donnell 'to book', the government was effectively condoning an 'example of insubordination and contempt for discipline' from within the administrative ranks that was likely to 'form a very awkward precedent' in the future. 'A military man', Eden concluded, 'would have been tried by Court Martial for such conduct'.[144]

Thus, O'Donnell's official interventions in issues of famine and land policy in India in the late nineteenth century proved to be a highly charged and controversial beginning to his career in the ICS. While it is difficult to say that he did act as an unofficial intermediary between the Irish party and early Indian nationalist organisations in plotting nationalist sentiment, evidence suggests that, unlike other Irish Catholic ICS employees with nationalist sympathies, O'Donnell had an unusually high profile. His obvious link to Frank Hugh O'Donnell and his close association with prominent Indian nationalists both in London and Calcutta ensured that his activities were always going to be closely monitored and scrutinised by a government wary of falling victim to the gathering momentum of Victorian domino theory. A more plausible explanation for the reputation O'Donnell earned as the *enfant terrible* of the ICS was, perhaps, that his outspoken comments were made public at a time when a developing critique of British responsibility to its imperial subjects was being formulated by nationalist groups everywhere throughout the Empire. Viewed in this context, O'Donnell's publications, though failing to influence any real measure of future policy in India, drew considerable publicity and attention to the perceived failings of the British administration in Bengal in 1874 and stimulated further nationalist criticism in both Ireland and India.

Emergent Irish and Indian nationalisms

The trajectory of lateral exchanges that linked Ireland and India during the late eighteenth and nineteenth centuries bear further comparison after 1900, not least because many of the lineaments involving elite links and nationalist politics in both countries actually began to be consolidated in the context of interrelated developments within the British imperial system. Along with Egypt, which, it has been argued, provided another important dimension to an increasingly prominent imperial political quadrilateral within the late-nineteenth- and

[144] Eden to Northbrook, 19 October 1880 (BL, Add 43592, vol. 102, ff. 63–70).

Emergent Irish and Indian nationalisms

early-twentieth-century Empire, early nationalist ideology in Ireland and India emerged out of a similar discourse. Scholars of South Asia have perhaps overlooked the importance that the contemporary problems of the British Empire, such as the failure of the Irish Home Rule Bill or Gladstone's occupation of Egypt, played in influencing the early years of Indian nationalism. Strong undercurrents of peasant unrest were not exclusive between emergent Irish and Indian nationalisms within the late-nineteenth-century British Empire. In Egypt, for example, the Arabist movement was underpinned by a strong artisan and peasant following in its struggle with constitutional government.[145] It was in this context, within the broader arena of the British Empire, that tentative links were forged between a new wave of radical Irish and Indian nationalists during the first half of the twentieth century.[146]

Although the Irish had direct experience of India dating back as far as the mid eighteenth century, India's direct experience of Ireland derived largely from sporadic visits by a handful of prominent Indians. During his first visit to England in 1878, the Bengali poet and philosopher Rabindranath Tagore watched the parliament in session, and noting the harassment of Irish members there, found the political conditions in Ireland comparable to those in India.[147] Indeed, some of Tagore's later writings and collaborative works with W. B. Yeats indicate that he found aspects of Irish nationalism inspiring, particularly in its use of language, folklore and mythology.[148] It is interesting to note that the first staging of a play by Tagore outside India, a performance of *Dak Ghar* (The Post Office) held at the Abbey Theatre in Dublin in May 1913, was a benefit performance for Pádraig Pearse's St Enda's College.[149] In London, a new generation of Irish and Indian radicals, such as Michael Davitt (leader of the Irish Land League) and Dadhabhai Naoroji (one of the main advocates of early Indian economic nationalism), converged for the purpose of trying to lay Irish and Indian grievances before the

---

[145] J. R. I. Cole, *Colonialism and Revolution in the Middle East: Social and Cultural Origins of Egypt's Urabi Movement* (Princeton University Press, 1993).

[146] See, for example, Kate O'Malley, *Ireland, India and Empire: Indo-Irish Radical Connections, 1919–1964* (Manchester University Press, 2008).

[147] P. Mukhopadhyay, *Rabindra Jibani (Life of Tagore)*, Vol. I (Calcutta: Visva-Bharati, 1985), p. 93.

[148] Mukhopadhyay, *Rabindra Jibani*, vol. II, pp. 398–9. This also serves to highlight the prominence within both early Indian and Irish nationalist ideologies of mystical ideas of race and nation, revived folklorism and reactive mainline religion: the 'Faith of Our Fathers', in the Irish context, or *sanatam dharma* (ancient religion) in the Indian. See Bayly, 'Ireland, India and Empire', 395.

[149] For a more detailed account of the relationship between Yeats and Tagore, see R. F. Foster, *W. B. Yeats: A Life, Vol. I: The Apprentice's Mage* (Oxford University Press, 1996), pp. 469–73.

248   Imperial crisis and the age of reform

British electorate. As they gradually became aware of each other they began to see similar patterns emerging between the plight of their own countries and of other parts of the British Empire. Supported by English radicals such as Charles Bradlaugh, Davitt began to bring the problems of India and Ireland together in his speeches. Indeed, the place of London was central in the proliferation of a common set of ideas, values and objectives within these networks. Wealthy Indians (including Gyanendra Mohun Tagore and Maharaja Jotendro Mohun Tagore) who lived in London formed political bodies and institutions (such as the British Indian Association) that provided an overarching link and cosmopolitan environment where many of these ideas were allowed to ferment. Within this context, moderate Indian nationalists familiarised themselves with most facets of the 'Irish Question' and drew critically upon the Irish experience in the framing of suitable nationalist objectives and in the formulation of tactics for promoting unity and common cause in India.

At the same time, British Enlightenment ideas of women's equality inspired a new generation of women to disseminate such models throughout the colonial system. In India, the Victorian radical Annie Besant, who was born in England but considered 'three-quarters of her blood and all of her heart Irish' saw Indian issues from an Irish perspective.[150] Besant, who became politically radicalised after witnessing the hanging of three Fenian gunmen in Manchester in 1867, was involved in Irish politics with Michael Davitt and Charles Bradlaugh in London during the 1870s and 1880s before moving to India where she became involved in the Indian Theosophical and Nationalist movements. Throughout her stay in India, Besant's own mystical Irish nationalism melded particularly easily with the neo-Hindu, racial nationalism of some of the early leaders of the Indian National Congress and leading Indian Theosophists.[151] Founded by Helena Petrovna Blavatsky and Henry Steele Olcott in the United States in 1875, the theosophical movement, which had its origins in spiritualism and embraced many aspects of Hinduism, sought to create a brotherhood of man through the promotion of the study of comparative religion and philosophy as well as through the investigation of the mystic powers of man and matter. It was alleged that those who gave their lives to theosophy would in turn have their own lives transformed, while the potential for

---

[150] A. Besant, *Annie Besant: An Autobiography* (London: T. Fisher Unwin, 1908), p. 3.
[151] A. Taylor, *Annie Besant: A Biography* (London: Oxford University Press, 1992), pp. 25–8.

Emergent Irish and Indian nationalisms

doing good in India, which became the movement's headquarters, was immense.[152] Both the spread of theosophy and of Anglo-Celtic radical politics were to have an important impact upon the ideology of the early Indian National Congress which had been established in 1885.

After moving to Benares, in the north of India, Besant played a major part in the emergence of both Indian theosophy and Indian nationalism throughout the 1890s. From November to April each year, beginning in 1893, Besant set herself the task of learning Sanskrit and was responsible for founding the Central Hindu College for boys at Benares. Assisted by a local Brahmin, Babu Bhagavan Das, Besant sought to establish an institution that would combine traditional Hindu values with the infrastructure of an English public school. Within a few years, the Central Hindu College in Benares grew to house over 1,000 boys, whom Besant frequently referred to as 'the natural leaders of young Hinduism'.[153] One of Besant's most enthusiastic supporters was a prominent lawyer and aspiring theosophist from Allahabad, Pandit Motilal Nehru; the father of Jawaharlal Nehru. Indeed from 1899 to 1902 the future prime minister of an independent India was tutored by the theosophist F. T. Brooks, who himself was part-Irish and had been recommended as a tutor by Besant.[154] It is interesting to note that while much of Besant's early activities in India received support from Indian notables such as the Maharaja of Benares and the Maharaja of Kashmir, she was subject to much criticism from British officials, including some prominent Irish Catholics. As Lieutenant-Governor of the United Provinces in 1900, Sir Anthony MacDonnell, for example, denounced Besant's foundation of the Central Hindu College at Benares as a disloyal act towards the Crown. Supported by the Secretary of State for India, Lord George Hamilton, MacDonnell argued that by founding the College Besant was using education as a cloak for the articulation of radical politics.[155]

After the fall of Parnell and the rise in popularity of Arthur Griffith's Sinn Féin party in the years leading up to the First World War, events in Ireland gradually began to have a more pronounced effect on Annie Besant's attitude to Indian politics. In Madras, Besant was responsible for founding several local organisations that supported Indian theosophy and Indian nationalism and that were based on the principles of

---

[152] J. Ransom, *A Short History of the Theosophical Society, 1875–1937* (Adyar: Theosophical Publishing House, 1938).

[153] Taylor, *Annie Besant*, pp. 279–80.   [154] Ibid., p. 279.

[155] MacDonnell Papers (Letters to MacDonnell, 1888–1924), Mss. Eng. hist. c.350, Bod. Lib., Oxford.

250   Imperial crisis and the age of reform

the mass organisations of Irish politics. The establishment of Besant's weekly newspapers, the *Commonweal* and, later, *New India* ('England's need is India's opportunity'), became powerful tools in her public criticism of the British government for their refusal to concede political reform for India during the war. In a letter to the Secretary of State, Austen Chamberlain, in July 1916, Lord Pentland, the Governor of Madras, spoke of his concern regarding Besant's increasing displays of antagonism towards the Raj: 'Indians who know her tell me that she is imperious and even unrestrained in temper, vain, restless, and ambitious', adding as a further matter of official concern that 'she is an Irishwoman'.[156]

Although Pentland was alarmed by Besant's constant attempts to use her position as editor of *New India* to recruit members to the various organisations she founded (such as the Young Men's Indian Association), what worried Pentland most was her employment of the Irish nationalist poet James Cousins to be literary sub-editor of *New India*.[157] Born in Belfast, Cousins resided in Dublin where, as a poet, he joined the Theosophical Society in 1902 and became interested in the idea that Ireland was to play a leading role in the spiritual regeneration of Europe. In India, the Madras government suspected him of having links to the Irish trade union activist James Larkin. Equally disturbing to Pentland and his colleagues was the fact that Cousins' wife Margaret, who accompanied him to Madras in 1915, was a militant suffragette, a veteran of the hunger strike who had spent time in Holloway Gaol for throwing broken flower pots at the windows of 10 Downing Street, and in Mountjoy Prison for a similar assault on Dublin Castle.[158] By May 1916, an article written by James Cousins for *New India* praising the leaders of the Easter Rising in Dublin caused enough outrage among the Madras authorities that Besant was obliged to dismiss him. Such official censure, however, did little to deter Besant and by September 1916 her work in Madras culminated in the founding of the Indian Home Rule Leagues, which were also deliberately modelled along Irish lines.[159]

Conclusion

By the beginning of the First World War, as the Liberal government in Britain attempted to devolve power through a Home Rule Ireland and

---

[156] Pentland to Chamberlain, 7 July 1916, Eur. E. 264/17, OIOC, BL.
[157] Ibid.   [158] Ibid.
[159] Taylor, *Annie Besant*, pp. 301–4.

Conclusion   251

local self-government in India (and Egypt), separatist politics in both
Ireland and India began to take root. In its course, younger leaders of
populist stance replaced the older generation of cultural nationalists
such as Annie Besant and Pádraig Pearse. In India the Home Rule
League of Bal Gangadhar Tilak and later Mahatma Gandhi evolved
into a largely representative Hindu body, while in Ireland, Arthur
Griffith's Sinn Féin party was resolutely more Catholic and exclusion-
ary. By the early decades of the twentieth century explicit connections
were being drawn by figures such as Seán T. O'Ceallaigh, Sinn Féin
TD, who, during a banquet held by the society 'Friends of Freedom for
India' in New York in 1924, declared that the Irish 'are doubly bound to
stand by the cause of India and help her win her way to complete freedom. We owe it to India because India's cause is Ireland's cause'.[160]

It is perhaps one of the greatest ironies of Irish involvement in the
administration of empire in South Asia that although the intellectual
and moral concerns articulated through the writings and official correspondence of Irish civil servants at once stimulated and inspired Indian
nationalism, their very presence working to maintain British rule in
India sought to prevent and deny it. Irish interventions in the debates
over land and famine in India in the 1870s, 1880s and 1890s enabled
Irish parliamentarians to effectively develop and clarify an increasing anti-imperial strand in Irish nationalism, and more importantly to
redefine their roles in contemporary global politics. Their expressed
political views appeared all the more controversial because they were
made public at a time when a developing nationalist critique of British
responsibility to its imperial subjects was being formulated by other
nationalist groups throughout the Empire. Significantly, O'Donnell's
passing into the ICS coincided with the 1874 General Election that
brought the Irish Home Rule Party into the House of Commons and
marked the beginning of the period in the late nineteenth century when
Irish nationalists mounted the most direct and serious attack on British
imperial authority.

O'Donnell's experiences in Bengal during the late 1870s and early
1880s demonstrate explicitly the varying ways in which Irish people
were able to 'play' metropolitan–periphery relations. Given Ireland's
ambivalent position in 'metropolitan Britain', the Empire was not only
a significant arena for the Irish in terms of social mobility and economic betterment, but it also functioned as an important conduit for

---

[160] Eamon de Valera Papers, 676, India File 1399, Franciscan Library, Killiney, Co.
Dublin.

252 Imperial crisis and the age of reform

the spread of Irish ideas, providing opportunities to advertise the particular strain of the nationalist idea and to demonstrate the means of mass political mobilisation. For O'Donnell, a career in the ICS provided a unique opportunity to satisfy the competing demands of Irish nationalism, British imperialism and Indian welfare, demonstrating the Irish ability to simultaneously contest empire and accelerate change from within. During the late nineteenth century Irish imperial servants drew considerable publicity and attention to the perceived failings of the British imperial administration and stimulated further nationalist criticism elsewhere in the twentieth century.

8   Conclusion

In its examination of the colonial connections that bound nineteenth-century Ireland and India together, this book has highlighted the central role played by Ireland and Irish people in the construction and expansion of the 'Second British Empire' during the 'long' nineteenth century. As an alternative to the existing historiography on the Irish diaspora that focuses almost exclusively on Irish settlement and migration to North America and Australasia, it has stressed the ubiquitous influence and distinctiveness of Irish presence in constructing and maintaining almost two centuries of British colonial rule in South Asia. Moreover, the persistence of Irish networks in India throughout this period has demonstrated just how important both Ireland and India were in the discourses and practice of modern British empire-building and 'imperial globalisation'. By examining patterns of Irish migration, social communication and exchange, this study has brought into sharper focus the different coexisting layers of identities of Irish men and women during the late eighteenth and nineteenth centuries, a recognition of which challenges the dialectical formula that so often positions Irish nationalism and unionism as being irreconcilable under the Union. Once divided by religious and political considerations in Ireland, domiciled Irish men and women in India (Anglicans, Catholics and Presbyterians from varying social classes and economic backgrounds) were drawn together in a common imperial bond – a long-standing and multifaceted association that had important implications for the development of British and Irish identity alike.

In describing the multiplicity of Irish connections within the context of Britain's Indian Empire, the book demonstrates how 'imperial networks' (and their resultant relationships) were always subject to constant change and flux – responding to both local and international events – and how they were used by their contemporaries (settlers, migrants and indigenous agents) as mechanisms for the exchange of a whole set of ideas, practices and goods during the colonial era. Moreover, approaches to the study of Ireland's imperial past that

253

254   Conclusion

facilitate such connections allow us to move beyond the old 'coloniser–colonised' debate to address the issue of whether Ireland or the varieties of Irishness of its imperial servants and settlers made a specific difference to the experience of empire. By focusing upon a cross-section of nineteenth-century Irish society in India (Irish elites and the less well connected alike) – and their resultant interconnections – we can reveal much about Ireland's multidirectional involvement in the nineteenth-century British Empire.

For example, the types of connections and movement of people, goods and capital back and forth between Ireland and India – a process that helped tie the wider British world together during the nineteenth century – emphasises the degree to which Irish imperial networks were in fact both transnational and national in nature during this period. Through increased migration these networks at once helped bridge and expand British communities throughout the Empire while simultaneously constituting an ethnic-based web of patronage and support for Irish migrant groups overseas. Built explicitly upon a variety of kinship and friendship structures, religious societies and institutions, cultural, political and intellectual thoughts and practices that connected private, official and provincial interests in Britain, Ireland and India, these networks functioned as the nineteenth-century equivalent of social- and business-related 'virtual networking' applications. This 'software of empire' enabled the operation of a vast system of dialogue and exchange through which ideas and information, trust and contracts, commodities and people ricocheted from one interface to another, in doing so tying disparate parts of the Empire together in a lively and dynamic interconnected zone. While the types of traffic that navigated imperial networks were in part defined by location – and in this sense it is important to recognise the central role of London in the creation and sustenance of many of these networks and how it functioned as a crucial node through which much Irish imperial traffic flowed – this study has argued how a multitude of no less important connections and linkages were often established between the colonies themselves that, at times, enabled Ireland and India to by-pass the metropolitan core entirely, establishing their own complex circuits of exchange in the process.

The interplay between East India Company agents in rural Irish communities during the Seven Years War, for example, facilitated the movement of Irish soldiers to India that ultimately proved critical to the strengthening of the sinews of colonial power as Britain looked to expand the boundaries of its Empire eastward during the second half of the eighteenth century. In this regard, Ireland served as a crucial recruiting ground for the East India Company army, with many young recruits seeking personal and social gain through participation in the imperial project away from the economic straits and deprivations of famine-stricken Ireland. While many within the British and Irish parliaments opposed the notion of a standing army of Catholic soldiers in India, the counter-argument that imperial military service in India would have the potential to countermand any threat posed by Irish Catholicism gained strength in the context of the expansion of the East India Company's authority over the military and financial administration of the Indian subcontinent. As Irish soldiers travelled to India as imperial servants they formed networks that were simultaneously voluntary and involuntary, as men compelled by notions of military virtue and expectations of financial gain and social amelioration or simply as men driven by the acute awareness of diminished opportunities and the recognition of obligations to families and parishes at home. While to a certain degree, the bodies of Irish soldiers may be conceived of as commodities, functioning in exchange for remittances home, they also became the pivots of networks spanning out from provincial Irish towns and transposed to Indian barracks and garrisons. The translation of these networks from Ireland to India had the potential to elide religious and class divisions when, as was often the case, a regional identity was shared by subordinate and sergeant alike. However, the increasing desire and demand for the expression of religio-cultural identity in the context of an evangelising empire is one key way in which a study of Irish soldiering networks uncovers the fractures at the heart of the imperial project. These 'subaltern Irish', like Ireland, were clearly both at the imperial hub yet posed a critical anomaly for the enterprise of empire.

Irish hostility to its link with England and the Union did not, however, extend to Ireland's link with England's Empire, and in particular to the Empire's economic sphere. An examination of the networks born out of a series of business connections between Ireland and India demonstrates the centrality of Ireland in terms of facilitating the commercial expansion of the Empire in Britain's search for new lands, markets and resources in the Indian Ocean region and the Pacific. Irish involvement in colonial trade and commerce in the East was ultimately bound up in the evolving structure and shifting responsibilities of the East India Company over the eighteenth century, a critical period which witnessed a fundamental transition in the Company's organisational structure from trading power to imperial authority on the subcontinent. The gradual transformation of the Company's administrative role and function in India was in part reflected in the nature of much Irish participation at a commercial and business level. Initially,

256   Conclusion

Irish merchants – much like their English, Scottish and Welsh counterparts – were subject to the same restrictions imposed upon private trade by the laws protecting the Company's monopoly and exclusive right to trade in the East. This was mirrored in the relative number of private traders and free merchants from Ireland who attempted to establish legitimate business interests in the Indian Ocean region in defiance of the Company. However, as an increasingly militarised East India Company began extending the boundaries of its political sovereignty in the second half of the eighteenth century, acquiring more and more Indian territory and in doing so developing more sophisticated commercial links both inland and throughout the Indian Ocean region, it began drawing on Irish resources, personnel and experience as an important means of facilitating its new administrative and commercial responsibilities. As the Company evolved into a more complex organisation during the eighteenth century, it was brought into increased contact with a whole host of communities outside of metropolitan London and centres of trade on the Indian subcontinent, particularly in Ireland where it became reliant upon a series of representative agents or business houses in Cork and Limerick to act on its behalf and secure its particular naval and commercial interests in a region. These agencies were established primarily because of the strategic and commercial significance of Ireland in facilitating long-distance trade, but also because of the need to protect the Company's interests during a period of almost constant international conflict. Throughout this period, a whole host of Irish merchants and business entrepreneurs, with prominent links to the principal colonial trading ports and cities of Ireland and India, fashioned a series of commercial and patronage networks between both countries. The powerful Irish Sulivan network with its origins in Cork City, for example, gave rise to important Irish merchant and family business connections in Bombay and Calcutta through its extensive maritime and naval links with the Court of Directors of the East India Company in London. Here, Irish involvement in the Company's commercial expansion on the subcontinent – in terms of patronage, shipping and supplying personnel, maritime expertise and knowledge and commodities, as well as access to Irish ports – further highlights the gradual transition of Ireland from colonial periphery of the Atlantic world to important sub-imperial centre of the 'Second British Empire' by the late eighteenth century. Although the activity of Irish commercial networks in South Asia was considerably checked under the Union, increased migration throughout the Empire – particularly among the Ascendancy and educated Irish Protestant elite centred on Trinity College Dublin – gradually

Conclusion 257

gave rise to a series of important cultural and intellectual links and exchanges between both dependencies. Through its involvement in science – an enterprise that lay at the very heart of the construction of British colonial rule in India – Ireland demonstrated the ability to by-pass the traditional 'metropolitan' core in the supply of scientific personnel to India. Not only did Ireland supply the Indian Empire with key personnel, it also functioned as an important reference point for scientific theory and practice ultimately laying the path for new legislation and systems of government. Occupying integral roles within the information systems of the colonial state, Irish people in turn supplied much of the intellectual capital around which British rule in India was constructed. In scientific fields such as surveying and geology, those who were attached to Irish institutions, especially universities and learned societies, were able to act decisively in the development of colonial knowledge. While Irish scientific personnel on the whole supplemented British authority and contributed to the overall geographical construction of colonial rule in India, there were occasions when Irish personnel worked to resist it, bringing with them different ideas of history and science that affected how colonial knowledge was interpreted and used by both Europeans and South Asians. Moreover, their activities centre Irish people within the broader imperial web of connections and global exchange of ideas, technologies and practices during the early nineteenth century.

The gradual integration of an Irish professional middle class into the Empire during the early nineteenth century quickly gathered pace in the wake of Catholic emancipation in the 1830s. The period 1830–60 specifically marked a decisive phase in the relationship between Ireland and Britain's Eastern Empire that witnessed the gradual integration of a large number of educated Irish Catholics into the imperial system. Before 1830 the presence of Irish Roman Catholics had been largely confined to the East India Company's European regiments, while Irish Protestants continued to be the dominant social group in terms of Irish commerce, the professions and commissions in the British army. Following emancipation, however, Irish missionaries poured out from newly established Catholic seminaries and institutions in Carlow, Maynooth and Dublin intent on ministering to the mass of Irish emigrants overseas. In India, Irish prelates promoted the interests of a particular Catholic Irish dimension in British India. They ministered to Gaelic-speaking Irish soldiers, set about introducing a reconstructed parochial system modelled along Irish lines through the building of churches and other ecclesiastical structures and promoted the education of (high- and low-caste) Indian and Eurasian Christian children.

258   Conclusion

At times at odds with the Protestant ethos of the Company, Irish chaplains and bishops frequently challenged the authority of the colonial power in India. Many Irish protests to Rome during this period, for example, were in part a response to the growing influence of evangelicalism on the subcontinent and demonstrated a desire on behalf of the Irish Catholic clergy to participate in the politics of British India, an arena that could be seen to be eroding their cultural and religious sensibilities. Religious networks, formed in Ireland's new seminaries, shaped by the growing confidence of Catholic identity following emancipation and shipped out to minister to the needs of soldiering networks in India, point to a complex and often conflictual web of social, cultural and political needs, demands and desires enacted on the stage of Britain's Eastern Empire within the ranks of Empire's servants and agents. Moreover, while the politics of religion fermented in India's military cantonments in ways that would connect Ireland and India through new languages of nationalism more fully in the second half of the nineteenth century, the notions and practices of Irish Catholic prelates began to create new tensions between India's Catholic communities and the colonial state through the vexed issue of caste.

From the late 1840s onward, a greater number of Irish Catholics entered imperial service in India, due mainly to the introduction of open-competitive examination in place of the old system of patronage. Alongside the Scottish and English schools, Irish universities, learned societies and scientific institutions served as the great imperial powerhouses of the mid nineteenth century in terms of supplying the civil and medical colonial services with a critical base of personnel, expertise and knowledge on which later colonial rule in India was based. This influx served to balance the numbers of Irish Protestants who had passed through to India via Trinity College Dublin, the Royal Belfast Academical Institution and the Universities of Edinburgh and Glasgow. The large number of successful Irish candidates who obtained employment in India at this time was aided considerably by Irish universities and colleges (including the non-denominational Queen's Colleges in Belfast, Cork and Galway, established in 1845) who were quick to seize this opportunity, and subsequently tailored their curricula to the specific requirements of the entrance examinations. In part, this drive mirrored a desire among the rising Irish middle classes to obtain careers in the Empire, but it also reflected a strong interest within Irish universities and colleges at the time to promote learning in oriental languages, Indian history, geography, zoology and the natural sciences. In turn, increased Irish numbers in the civil and medical services (including the subordinate colonial services) gave rise to various Irish knowledge

Conclusion 259

communities and more sophisticated networks of intellectual exchange that disseminated antiquarian, ethnographical and medical knowledge throughout the Empire.

The Indian Medical Service (IMS) was one of the principal scientific agencies in India during the Company period and later under Crown rule. Company surgeons and their successors provided a large proportion of the botanists, geologists and surveyors who travelled to India. It was partly because of their wide-ranging scientific beliefs that medical personnel played such a vital role in the European investigation of the Indian environment (including its topography, climate and disease). In comparison to other areas of scientific inquiry and matched by few other aspects of technological change, medicine directly engaged with the social, cultural and material lives of the Indian people. While recent studies of the history of colonial medicine in India have concentrated heavily on individual subject areas such as issues of tropical medicine, virtually none of these works have take into account the wider importance of the medical traditions and practice in regions such as Scotland and Ireland, two of the principal areas of the British Empire where Company surgeons and colonial scientists in India were born and educated.

The education of Irish medical personnel reflected the prominence of Irish antiquarian debates and the influence of the Great Famine, which in turn shaped their collective intellectual pursuits in India during the same period. The proliferation of hospitals and medical training institutes in Ireland in the mid nineteenth century was partly a result of the crisis in public health brought about by the Great Famine in the 1840s. In its wake, a distinctive Irish school of medicine emerged that was characterised by major clinical advances developed in response to increased levels of famine diseases, epidemics and rising mortality rates at home in Ireland. During the 1850s, a new body of Irish doctors emerged to service an ailing Empire informed in modern technological, diagnostic and therapeutic innovation but yet mindful of Indian sensibilities and regard for traditional folk medicine. In this sense, Irish doctors perceived themselves differently from their contemporary English and Scottish medical counterparts in so far as they were powerful agents of a modernising imperial state on the one hand, but were also champions of a declining traditional culture and rural way of life on the other. They were a particularly close network of professionals whose concerns overlapped and were often tied into several other scientific activities centred on the Ordnance Survey, the Statistical Society of Ireland and Royal Irish Academy. Many exponents of this school carried these intellectual concerns to India with them and wrote extensively on the epidemiology

260   Conclusion

of famine diseases in Bengal and Madras as well as on their views on *Ayurvedic* and *Unani* medicine.

In doing so, many Irishmen broke new ground in medical advancement following research in India. The emergence and awareness of tropical medicine and disease in Western Europe and North America can be seen as a direct result of the early initiatives taken by men such as John Crawford. The technique of acquiring specialised knowledge, be it that of languages, familiarisation with specific diseases or of the indigenous culture, at times worked to serve Irishmen better than the more conventional paths to office of seniority and patronage. In an era when most IMS servants were isolated from British centres of power and decision-making, the abilities to understand and speak Indian languages, obtain information and interpret Indian culture were powerful tools that could play important roles in determining whether or not a professional doctor could achieve an important medical position. Many Irishmen in the IMS published books, pamphlets and journal articles to present their work in the most favourable light; to defend their research, or simply to make their names known to the general public or to the Home governments. By acting as the conveyors of this revolutionary wave in medical theory and practice, many Irish physicians in India played a large part in the transformation of the Dublin clinical school from what had been in effect an outpost of the Scottish universities to a major influence in its own right on research, teaching and practice in the British Empire.

Towards the late nineteenth century, increased economic decline in both Ireland and India provided the impetus for a new generation of nationalists, philanthropists and humanitarians to move their ideologies beyond local predicaments and into the wider international domain. The rigorous imposition of free trade (from 1801 in Ireland and from 1834 in India) brought about a sharp decline in the demand for Irish and Indian commodities in British and European markets and with it increasing calls from early economic nationalists for the introduction of protective measures for home produce in both countries. Within this context, an elaborate web of contact, dialogue and exchange was formed between the nationalist spokesmen of nineteenth-century Ireland and India who, from the 1870s, gradually became aware of each other's calls for economic reform and national self-determination. Related to these concerns were the comparable moral and political issues raised in both countries at the time over the ownership of land and the administration of famine relief, both of which were used by these networks as tools in imperial politicking. Crucially, it was the position of certain Irish individuals within the power structures of the Empire itself and

Conclusion 261

particularly within the echelons of the Indian Civil Service (ICS) that provided much of the initial impetus for these ideologies to spread and gather momentum.

The introduction of open-competitive examination for the ICS in 1855 enabled a significant number of Irish candidates to enter service in India. Between the 1870s and 1920s the writings of several Irish civil servants as well as those of their missionary and educationalist colleagues championed a diverse range of conservative popular cultures in late-nineteenth-century India. As amateur anthropologists and ethnographers, their researches into the vocabularies, rural life, artisan traditions and popular religion of the people of the United Provinces and Bihar were part of a late-nineteenth-century shift from a descriptive to a classificatory representation of colonial knowledge in India. The ethnological information supplied by their bilingual Indian subordinates and represented through their collective writings demonstrated a common anthropological mission among this network which set about preserving the culture of rural Indian life before it disappeared through increased contact and exposure to Western scientific thought and appliances of civilisation. Irish professional personnel networks of the late nineteenth century were arguably much more politicised than their English, Scottish or Welsh counterparts. Irish civil networks who published work on the British administration of famine relief, the impoverished state of Indian tenants, landless peasants and rack-renting landlords in Bihar, acquired the reputation among some British and Indian officials as pro-*raiyat* (tenant) sympathisers. They recorded and circulated revealing views on religious antagonisms, economic and agrarian malformations and were particularly forceful in their demands for tenancy legislation. Other Irish professional personnel networks worked to further more radical political agendas and ideologies and were motivated by a desire to bring about reform and change within the Empire. In such ways, Irish imperial networks in nineteenth-century India were dynamic and constantly shifting vectors of cultural interaction, rather than frozen channels of an imperial 'centre'. Through increased movement and exchange overseas, Irish imperial networks not only helped mesh a large proportion of the Empire together materially, spiritually and intellectually but encouraged Irish people to think in more transnational and global terms, a process that was temporarily delayed after 1922 as a newly independent Free State committed itself ideologically to the creation of an Irish rural self-identity. This is not to say, of course, that one needs to dispense with the idea of the nation entirely. On the contrary, many important aspects of national histories remain integral to the process of tracing links and reciprocity between

Irish and Indian history. However, if such links are to be more thoroughly examined in the future there is clearly a need to look beyond the limited framework of national histories and boundaries to the broader connections that tied Ireland and India together to a wider imperial system. Only by positing Irish history within the complex global currents fashioned through Ireland's involvement in British imperialism during the 'long' nineteenth century can we understand more fully how Irish national development was shaped during the same period, while simultaneously situating the history of the British Empire in a broader, more dynamic 'four nations' context.

Glossary

Anglo-Indian	Briton living in India.
Aryan	One belonging to, or descended from, the ancient people who spoke the parent Aryan language (sometimes called Indo-European) from which Sanskrit, Greek, Latin, Teutonic, Persian, Celtic and Slavonic (and their modern representatives) are derived; the language spoken by them, and its derivatives; one of those who invaded and conquered India around 1500 BC. From Sanskrit *arya*, 'of noble birth'.
Ayurveda	Hindu medicine.
Babu	A Hindu title of respect, equivalent to Mr or Esq.; an Indian clerk or official who writes in English.
box-wallah	Itinerant salesmen when applied to Indians (it was also used pejoratively to refer to Anglo-Indians in trade).
Brahmin	A member of the first *varna*, traditionally priests and scholars. From Sanskrit *Brahman*, 'prayer' or 'praise'.
caste	Ascribe ritual status in the Indian, especially Hindu, social hierarchy. From Portuguese *casta*, 'race', and Latin *castus*, 'pure' or 'chaste'.
Devanagari	The Sanskrit alphabet, used for modern Hindi.
Dharma	Personal duty or conduct appropriate to one's status; moral obligation; law. From Sanskrit 'decree' or 'custom'.
diwan	The chief civil administrator of an area under the Mughals.
Dravidian	Pertaining to the non-Aryan people of India, or to their languages.
Durbar	The court, public audience or levee of a ruler.
Eurasian	Person of mixed European and Indian parentage.

264   Glossary

Gujar	A Cultivator of northern India.
Guru	Preceptor; religious teacher.
hakim	A physician in the Greek–Islamic tradition.
Hindi	The major Aryan vernacular of northern India, spoken (with many dialects) from the frontiers of Bengal to those of the Punjab and Sind.
Hindustan	'The country of the Hindus'; originally the region of the river Indus; in the colonial period, normally used to denote Upper India (the plain of the Ganges, except Bihar and Bengal); sometimes all of India.
Indo-Irish	Irish man or woman living in India.
jagir	An assignment of government revenue from a district, originally in return for public (especially military) service.
Jagirdar	The holder of a *jagir*.
Jat	A member of the principal cultivating caste of the Punjab and Rajputana.
jyotish	A Hindu astronomer/astrologer.
Khadi	Spinning.
mahajan	Merchant title ('great man').
maulvi	A Muslim cleric.
munshi	A writer; secretary.
nawab	Deputy (to the Mughal Emperor); a quasi-royal title in the eighteenth century; thence 'nabob'.
pandit	A Hindu teacher, often Brahmin with knowledge of classical Hindu scriptures and sciences.
Persian	The literary and government language of the Delhi Sultanate, the Mughal Empire and other pre-modern Indian states.
Purdah	Seclusion or isolation, especially of Muslim women. From Urdu and Persian *pardah*, 'veil' or 'curtain'.
raiyat	Indian peasant.
Raj	Kingdom or principality; rule; often used loosely to denote British rule of India.
Raja	An Indian prince or ruler; a title of nobility.
Rajput	A Kshatriya of the most prominent military and landholding caste-cluster of northern India, distinguished by its martial spirit and aversion to handling the plough.
sepoy	An Indian soldier employed under European, especially British, discipline; an Indian infantry private. From Persian and Urdu *sipahi*, 'soldier' or 'horseman'.

Glossary

shakti	Sanskrit-derived term for activated energy endowing deities, especially goddesses, with power to heal, protect or destroy.
Sikh	A member of the religious sect founded in the Punjab as a branch of Hinduism in the fifteenth century.
swadeshi	An Indian nationalist movement, originating in Bengal, which advocated the support of indigenous industries using home-produced materials (especially cotton). From Sanskrit *sva*, 'one's own' and *desa*, 'country'.
Tamil	The leading Dravidian language of south India; a speaker of that language.
Urdu	The language of the Muslim conquerors of Hindustan, derived from Hindi, but written in the Arabic script, and with a large admixture of Persian and Arabic loanwords. From *zaban-i-urdu*, 'the language of the [royal] camp'. Also called Hindustani.
vaidya	A physician within the Hindu tradition.
Varna	One of the four castes – Brahmins, Kshatriyas, Vaishyas and Shudras – into which all Indian society is ideally divided. From Sanskrit 'colour' or 'class'.
Vedas	India's most ancient classical religious scriptures, compiled *c.*2000 BC.
zamindar	A 'landlord', the person who collects and transmits the revenue or tax claim to the government.

Bibliography

PRIVATE PAPERS

Letters of Sergeant Major William Henry Braithwaite, Ms.7605–75, NAM.
Letters of John Blackett, 1857–59, Photo.Eur.7, OIOC.
Papers of Private Matthew Brown. D.813/24, PRONI.
Papers of Lieutenant Kendal Coghill, Ms. 7112–38–39, NAM.
Papers of Captain Thomas Dennehy, in the personal possession of Professor
  C. A. Bayly, St Catharine's College, University of Cambridge.
Dufferin Papers, Ms. Eur. F. 130.
Richardson Evans Papers, Ms. Eur. E404, OIOC.
Papers of George Grierson, Ms. Eur. E. 226, OIOC.
Papers and Correspondence of Sir James Weir Hogg, Mss. Eur. E342, OIOC.
Papers of Gunner William Hollohan. Mss. Eur. F.133/27, OIOC.
Ilbert Papers, Ms. Eur. D 594, OIOC.
Papers of Sir Lucas White King, Mss. Eur. C852, OIOC.
Papers of Robert Kyd, Mss. Eur. F95, OIOC.
Papers of Lord George Macartney, T.2480, PRONI.
Papers of Sir Anthony Patrick MacDonnell, Mss. Eng. Hist., 350–370, Bod.
  Lib., Oxford.
Papers of Robert Montgomery, Mss. Eur. D1019, OIOC.
Papers of Corporal Henry Smith, Mss. Eur. F/133/51, OIOC.
Sir Charles Wood Papers, Mss Eur. F78, Letterbook 18, OIOC.
Eamon de Valera Papers, 676, India File 1399, Franciscan Library, Killiney,
  Co. Dublin.

OFFICIAL PRIMARY SOURCES – UNPUBLISHED

ORIENTAL AND INDIA OFFICE COLLECTION: BRITISH LIBRARY

Typescript of recruits to the East India Company Army, 1740–53, L/Mil/
  9/89.
Typescript of recruits to the East India Company Army, 1759–63, L/Mil/9/85.
Soldiers' Wills (Bombay), L/AG/34/30.
Home Miscellaneous Series.
East India Register and Directory.
Muster Rolls, L/MIL/10/137–140.

Bibliography 267

Soldiers' References, Part II, L/MIL/5/362.
Cadet Papers (1775–1860), L/Mil/9/107–269.
Applications for East India Company Cadetships, L/Mil/9/85 (1758).
Bombay Public Consultations.
Committee of Correspondence Memoranda.
Cadet Papers, 1775–1860: Applications for East India Company Cadetships, L/Mil/9/107–269.
Madras Public Proceedings.
Madras Ecclesiastical Proceedings.
India Ecclesiastical Proceedings.
Soldiers' Wills (Bombay), Vol. 1, 1825–1842, L/AG/34/35/23.
Indian Medical Service papers, 1881–1914, L/MIL/9/408 and L/MIL/9/413–27.
Assistant Surgeons and Surgeons Papers, 1804–1914, L/MIL/9/404.
British Military Consultations (BMC) 23 September 1824, 126, P/30/60.
George Everest, 'Memoir Containing an Account of some Leading Features of the Irish Survey, and a Comparison of the Same with the System Pursued in India', 20 October 1829, L/MIL/5/402/205, fols. 297–317.
Public and Judicial Files, L/P&J/6 series, 1881–1914.
Report of the Government of Bengal on the Proposed Amendment to the Law of... Landlord...and Tenant, V/27/312/13.

NATIONAL ARMY MUSEUM

Letters of Grenadier John Nicholson Ms. 7605–15.
Ms Typescript of a newspaper or periodical account of the execution of Private O'Hara in the Leinster Regiment at Yerrowda Jail, Poona, 23 April 1894. Ms. 57.
Ms. Order Books of the Portuguese Militia of Bombay. Transcripts of the proceedings of several regimental Courts Martial including the 86th and 88th Regiments of Foot. Ms 8410–144–1/2. NAM.

BODLEIAN LIBRARY, OXFORD

Correspondence, Journals and Papers of Michael Pakenham Edgeworth, Ms. Eng. Misc. d.1299–1307.
Official and Private Correspondence of Sir Anthony Patrick MacDonnell, Mss. Eng. Hist. e.215, c.395, c.415.
Laurence Sulivan's Letterbook, Mss. Eng. Hist. c.269.

ST PATRICK'S COLLEGE, MAYNOOTH

Foreign Missionary Correspondence India, 1857–80, Russell Papers 13/43 (Box 1 – Folder 43).

LONDON UNIVERSITY IMPERIAL COLLEGE ARCHIVES

Letters from Thomas Oldham to Sir Andrew Ramsay (1846–8), KGA/RAMSAY/8/610/18.

268   Bibliography

ARCHIVES OF ROYAL BOTANICAL GARDENS, KEW

Papers of Lieutenant Colonel Edward Madden, Ms. 2574–2582.

UNIVERSITY OF CAMBRIDGE LIBRARY

Whitley Stokes Papers, Philological Papers, Add 7656 (S2338–S2350).

OFFICIAL PRIMARY SOURCES – PUBLISHED

Parliamentary Papers, Vol. VIII (1812–13).
Parliamentary Papers, Vol. XIII (1831–2).
Parliamentary Papers, Vol. XXXIII (1835).
Parliamentary Papers, Vol. XXX (1852–3).
Parliamentary Papers, Vol. XXII (1854–5).
Parliamentary Papers, Vol. XVII (1859).
Parliamentary Papers, Vol. LI (1860).
Parliamentary Papers, Vol. XX (1863).
Parliamentary Papers, Vol. L (1867).
Parliamentary Papers, Vol. LV (1876).
Annual Reports of the Missionary College of All Hallows, Dublin (1848–53).
Report on the Census of Bengal, 1872 (Calcutta, 1872).
Report on the Census of India, 1901 (Calcutta, 1901).
Qualifications and Examination of Candidates for Commissions in the Medical Services of the British and Indian Armies (London, 1870).
Report of the Committee for Investigating the Coal and Mineral Resources of India (Calcutta, 1838).
Annual Report of the Superintendent of the Geological Survey of India and the Museum of Geology (Calcutta, 1862–3).

CONTEMPORARY JOURNALS, MAGAZINES AND NEWSPAPERS

Asiatic Researches
Belfast Daily Mercury
Bengal Hurkaru
Calcutta Review
Delhi Gazette
Dublin Journal of Medical Science
Dublin University Magazine
East India United Service Journal and Military Magazine
English Historical Review
Faulkner's Dublin Journal
Freeman's Journal
Friend of India
Hindoo Patriot
Indian Medical Gazette
Irish Ecclesiastical Review

Bibliography

Journal of the Asiatic Society of Bengal
Journal of Imperial and Commonwealth History
Nature
Past and Present
Proceedings of the Royal Irish Academy
Scientific Proceedings of the Royal Dublin Society
The Cork Examiner
The East India and Colonial Magazine
The Freeman's Journal
The Irish Sword
The Journal of the Royal Asiatic Society of Great Britain and Ireland
The Scientific Proceedings of the Royal Dublin Society
Transactions of the Medical and Physical Society of Calcutta

SECONDARY SOURCES

Acedos, A. B. *The Irish Community in the Basque Country, c.1700–1800* (Dublin: Geography Publications, 2003).

Ainslie, W. *Materia Indica*, II (London, 1826).

Alam, M. *The Crisis of Empire in Mughal North India* (Oxford University Press, 1986).

Alavi, S. *The Sepoys and the Company: Tradition and Transition in Northern India, 1770–1830* (Oxford University Press, 1995).

Alcock, R. *Notes on the Medical History and Statistics of the British Legion in Spain* (London: John Churchill, 1838).

Amin, S. (ed.) *W. Crooke, A Glossary of North Indian Peasant Life* (Oxford University Press, 1989).

Andrews, J. H. *A Paper Landscape: The Ordnance Survey in Nineteenth-Century Ireland* (Oxford: Clarendon Press, 1975).

Anonymous 'Spirit of the Universities, TCD', *The University Magazine*, V (1880).

Appleby, J. C. 'War Politics and Colonization, 1558–1625', in A. Porter (ed.), *The Oxford History of the British Empire: The Nineteenth Century* (Oxford University Press, 1999), pp. 55–79.

Arbuthnot, A. J. 'Blacker, Valentine (1778–1823)', rev. James Lunt, *Oxford Dictionary of National Biography* (Oxford University Press, 2004).

Arnold, D. *Colonizing the Body: State Medicine and Epidemic Disease in Nineteenth-Century India* (Berkeley: University of California Press, 1996).

Science, Technology and Medicine in Colonial India: The New Cambridge History of India, vol. 3.5 (Cambridge University Press, 2000).

Warm Climates and Western Medicine: The Emergence of Tropical Medicine, 1500–1900 (Amsterdam: Rodopi, 1996).

Arnold, D. (ed.) *Imperial Medicine and Indigenous Societies* (Manchester University Press, 1988).

Baetson, W. B. 'Indian Medical Service: Past and Present', *Asiatic Quarterly Review*, 14 (1902), 272–320.

Bagal, J. C. *History of the Indian Association, 1876–1951* (Calcutta: Indian Association, 1953).

270 Bibliography

Bailey, C. 'The Nesbitts of London and their Networks', in D. Dickson, J. Parmentier and J. Ohlmeyer (eds.), *Irish and Scottish Mercantile Networks in Europe and Overseas in the Seventeenth and Eighteenth Centuries* (Gent: Academia Press, 2007), pp. 231–46.

Bala, P. *Imperialism and Medicine in Bengal: A Socio-Historical Perspective* (New Delhi; London: Sage, 1991).

Ballantyne, T. 'Empire, Knowledge and Culture: From Proto-Globalization to Modern Globalization', in A. Hopkins (ed.), *Globalization in World History* (London: Pimlico, 2002), pp. 115–40.

Orientalism and Race: Aryanism in the British Empire (Basingstoke: Palgrave, 2002).

'The Sinews of Empire: Ireland, India and the Construction of British Colonial Knowledge', in T. McDonough (ed.), *Was Ireland a Colony? Economics, Politics and Culture in Nineteenth-Century Ireland* (Dublin: Irish Academic Press, 2005), pp. 145–65.

Ballantyne, T. and A. Burton (eds.) *Bodies in Contact: Rethinking Colonial Encounters in World History* (Durham, NC: Duke University Press, 2005).

Ballhatchet, K. *Caste, Class and Catholicism in India 1789–1914* (Richmond: Curzon, 1998).

'French Missionaries and Indian Society: The Jesuit Mission to Maduré, 1837–1902', in Marie-Claude Buxtorf (ed.), *Les Relations Historiques et Culturelles entre la France et l'Inde, XVIIe–XXe Siècle* (Sainte Clotilde: Association Historique Internationale de l'Océan Indien, 1987), pp. 227–48.

Race, Sex and Class under the Raj: Imperial Attitudes Policies and their Critics, 1793–1905 (London: Weidenfeld & Nicolson, 1980).

'Roman Catholic Missionaries and Indian Society: The Carmelites in Bombay, 1786–1857', in K. Ballhatchet and J. Harrison (eds.), *East India Company Studies* (Hong Kong: Asian Research Series, 1986), pp. 255–97.

'The East India Company and Roman Catholic Missionaries', *Journal of Ecclesiastical History*, 44, 2 (April 1993), 273–88.

Barrow, I. J. *Mapping History, Drawing Territory: British Mapping in India, c.1756–1905* (Oxford University Press, 2003).

Bartlett, T. '"A Weapon of War Yet Untried": Irish Catholics and the Armed Forces of the Crown, 1760–1830', in T. G. Fraser and K. Jeffery (eds.), *Men, Women and War* (Dublin: Lilliput Press, 1993), pp. 66–85.

'Ireland, Empire and Union, 1690–1801', in K. Kenny (ed.), *Ireland and the British Empire: Oxford History of the British Empire Companion Series* (Oxford University Press, 2004), pp. 61–89.

'The Augmentation of the Army in Ireland, 1769–72', *English Historical Review*, XCVI (1981), 540–59.

The Fall and Rise of the Irish Nation: The Catholic Question, 1690–1830 (Dublin: Gill and Macmillan, 1992).

'The Irish Soldier in India', in M. Holmes and D. Holmes (eds.), *Ireland and India: Connections, Comparison and Contrasts* (Dublin: Folens, 1997), pp. 12–29.

'The Townshend Viceroyalty', in T. Bartlett and D.H. Hayton (eds.), *Penal Era and Golden Age: Essays in Irish History, 1690–1800* (Belfast: Ulster Historical Foundation Publication, 1979), pp. 88–112.

Bibliography 271

'"This Famous Island Set in a Virginian Sea": Ireland in the Eighteenth-Century British Empire', in P. Marshall (ed.), *The Oxford History of the British Empire, Vol. 2: The Eighteenth Century* (Oxford University Press, 1998), pp. 254–76.

Bartlett, T. and K. Jeffery (eds.) *A Military History of Ireland* (Cambridge University Press, 1996).

Basalla, G. 'The Spread of Western Science', *Science*, 156 (1967), 611–22.

Bayly, C. A. *Empire and Information: Intelligence Gathering and Social Communication in India, 1780–1870* (Cambridge University Press, 1996).

Imperial Meridian: The British Empire and the World, 1780–1830 (London: Longman, 1989).

Indian Society and the Making of the British Empire (Cambridge University Press, 1988).

'Ireland, India and Empire: 1870–1914', *Transactions of the Royal Historical Society*, X, sixth series (2000), 377–97.

'Orientalists, Informants and Critics in Benares, 1790–1860', in J. Malik (ed.), *Perspectives of Mutual Encounters in South Asian History 1760–1860* (Leiden; Boston: Brill, 2000).

Rulers, Townsmen and Bazaars: North Indian Society in the Age of British Expansion, 1770–1870 (Cambridge University Press, 1983).

The Birth of the Modern World, 1780–1914: Global Connections and Comparisons (Oxford University Press, 2004).

'The First Age of Global Imperialism, *c.* 1760 to 1830', *Journal of Imperial and Commonwealth History*, 26 (1998), 28–47.

Bayly, S. *Caste, Society and Politics in India from the Eighteenth Century to the Modern Age: The New Cambridge History of India*, vol. 4.3 (Cambridge University Press, 1999).

Saints, Goddesses and Kings: Muslims and Christians in South Indian Society 1700–1900 (Cambridge University Press, 1989).

Beames, M. *Peasants and Power: The Whiteboy Movements and Their Control in Pre-Famine Ireland* (Brighton: Harvester, 1983).

Bennett, J. 'Science and Social Policy in Ireland in the Mid-Nineteenth Century', in P. J. Bowler and N. White (eds.), *Science and Society in Ireland: The Social Context of Science and Technology in Ireland 1800–1950* (Belfast: Institute of Irish Studies, Queen's University of Belfast, 1997).

Bennison, A. K. 'Muslim Universalism and Western Globalization', in A. Hopkins (ed.), *Globalization in World History* (London: Pimlico, 2002), pp. 74–98.

Besant, A. *Annie Besant: An Autobiography* (London: T. Fisher Unwin, 1908).

Beverley, H. S. *Report on the Census of Bengal* (Calcutta: Secretarial Press, 1872).

Birdwood, G. C. M. *Competition and the Indian Civil Service: A Paper Read before the East India Association, Tuesday, May 21, 1872* (London: H. S. King & Co. 1872).

Black, C. E. D. *The Marquess of Dufferin and Ava: Diplomatist, Viceroy, Statesman* (London: Hutchinson & Co., 1903).

Black, R. D. C. *Economic Thought and the Irish Question, 1817–1870* (Cambridge University Press, 1960).

272   Bibliography

Blacker, L. C. M. *A History of the Family of Blacker of Carrickblacker in Ireland* (Dublin: Hodges, Figgis & Co., 1901).

Blacker, V. *Memoir of the Operations of the British Army in India during the Mahratta War of 1817, 1818 & 1819* (London: Black, Kingsbury, Parbury & Allen, 1821).

Blatchford, R. *My Life in the Army* (London, 1910).

Bose, S. *Peasant Labour and Colonial Capital: Rural Bengal since 1770* (Cambridge University Press, 1993).

Bourdieu, P. 'Sport and Social Class', *Social Science Information*, 17, 6 (1978), 819–40.

Bourne, J. M. *Patronage and Society in Nineteenth-Century England* (London: Edward Arnold, 1986).

Bowen, H. V. '"No Longer Mere Traders": Continuities and Change in the Metropolitan Development of the East India Company, 1600–1834', in H. V. Bowen, M. Lincoln and N. Rigby (eds.), *The Worlds of the East India Company* (Woodbridge: Boydell, 2002).

The Business of Empire: The East India Company and Imperial Britain, 1756–1833 (Cambridge University Press, 2006).

'The East India Company and Military Recruitment in Britain, 1763–71', *Bulletin of the Institute of Historical Research*, LIX, 139 (May 1986).

Bowen, H. V., M. Lincoln and N. Rigby (eds.) *The Worlds of the East India Company* (Woodbridge: Boydell, 2002).

Boxer, C. R. *The Portuguese Seaborne Empire 1415–1825* (London: Hutchinson, 1969).

Boyle, E. C., Countess of Cork and Orrery (ed.) *The Orrery Papers*, Vols I and II (London: Duckworth & Company, 1903).

Bracken, D. 'Piracy and Poverty: Aspects of the Irish Jacobite Experience in France, 1691–1720', in T. O'Connor (ed.), *The Irish in Europe, 1580–1815* (Dublin: Four Courts Press, 2001), pp. 127–42.

Brady, C. *Interpreting Irish History: The Debate on Historical Revisionism, 1938–1994* (Dublin: Irish Academic Press, 1994).

Brasted, H. V. 'Indian Nationalist Development and the Influence of Irish Home Rule, 1870–1886', *Modern Asia Studies*, 12 (1980), 37–63.

Bridge, C. and K. Fedorowich (eds.). *The British World: Diaspora, Culture and Identity* (London; Portland, OR: F. Cass, 2003).

Briggs, A. *The Age of Improvement, 1783–1867* (Harlow: Longman, 2000).

Buckland, C. E. *Dictionary of Indian Biography* (London: Swan Sonnenschein, 1906).

Burtchaell, G. E. and T. U. Sadlier (eds.) *Alumni Dublinensus* (London, 1924).

Burton, A. *Politics and Empire in Victorian Britain: A Reader* (Basingstoke: Palgrave Macmillan, 2001).

'When Was Britain? Nostalgia for the Nation at the End of the "American Century"', *The Journal of Modern History*, 75, 2 (June 2003), 359–74.

'Who Needs the Nation? Interrogating "British" History', *Journal of Historical Sociology*, 10, 3 (September 1997), 227–48.

Cahill, K. M. 'The Golden Era of Irish Medicine', in *Irish Essays* (New York: John Jay Press, 1980), pp. 77–83.

Bibliography

Cain, P. J. 'Economics and Empire: The Metropolitan Context', in A. Porter (ed.), *The Oxford History of the British Empire, Vol. III: The Nineteenth Century* (Oxford University Press), pp. 31–53.

Callaghan, R. *The East India Company and Army Reform 1783–1798* (Cambridge, MA: Harvard University Press, 1972).

Cameron, C. *History of the Royal College of Surgeons in Ireland and the Irish School of Medicine* (Dublin, 1st edn., 1886; 2nd edn., 1916).

Campbell, T. *A Philosophical Survey of the South of Ireland* (London: W. Strahan, 1777).

Canny, N. *Kingdom and Colony: Ireland in the Atlantic World 1560–1800* (Baltimore: Johns Hopkins University Press, 1988).

Cantlie, N. *A History of the Army Medical Department, Vol. I* (Edinburgh: Churchill Livingstone, 1984).

Carey, E. *Memoir of William Carey* (London: Jackson and Walford, 1836).

Carson, P. 'An Imperial Dilemma: The Propagation of Christianity in Early Colonial India', *Journal of Imperial and Commonwealth History*, XVIII (1990), 169–90.

Chattopadhyay, D. K. *Dynamics of Social Change in Bengal, 1817–1851* (Calcutta: Punthi Pustak, 1990).

Chaudhuri, K. N. *The Trading World of Asia and the English East India Company, 1660–1760* (Cambridge University Press, 1978).

Chaudhury, D. K. L. '"Beyond the Reach of Monkeys and Men?" O'Shaughnessy and the Telegraph in India c. 1836–1856', *The Indian Economic and Social History Review*, 37, 3 (2000).

Clare, W. (ed.) *A Young Irishman's Diary (1836–1847): Being Extracts from the Early Journal of John Keegan of Moate* (1928).

Clarke, T. B. *Dean Tucker's Argument on the Propriety of an Union between Great Britain and Ireland: Written Some Years Since, and Now First Published in This Tract upon the Same Subject* (Dublin, 1799).

Cleary, J. 'Amongst Empires: A Short History of Ireland and Empire Studies in International Context', *Éire-Ireland*, 42, 1–2 (2007), 11–57.

Coakley, D. *Irish Masters of Medicine* (Dublin: Town House, 1992).

Cobbett, W. *The Parliamentary History of England from the Earliest Period to the Year 1803. From Which Last-mentioned Epoch It Is Continued Downwards in the Work Entitled 'Parliamentary Debates'* (London: R. Bagshaw, 1815).

Cohn, B. S. *An Anthropologist among the Historians and Other Essays* (Delhi: Oxford University Press, 1987).

'Recruitment and Training of British Civil Servants in India, 1800–1860', in R. Braibanti (ed.), *Asian Bureaucratic Systems Emergent from the British Imperial Tradition* (Durham, NC: Duke University Press 1966).

Colby, T. (ed.) *Ordnance Survey of the County of Londonderry, Volume the First: Memoir of the City and Northwestern Liberties of Londonderry, Parish of Templemore* (Dublin: Hodges and Smith, 1837).

Cole, J. R. I. *Colonialism and Revolution in the Middle East: Social and Cultural Origins of Egypt's Urabi Movement* (Princeton University Press, 1993).

Colley, L. *Britons: Forging the Nation, 1707–1837* (New Haven, CT: Yale University Press, 1992).

274 Bibliography

Collingham, E. M. *Imperial Bodies: The Physical Experience of the Raj, c.1800–1947* (Cambridge: Polity Press, 2002).

Compton, J. M. 'Open Competition and the Indian Civil Service, 1854–76', *English Historical Review*, LXXXIII (1968).

Condon, K. *The Missionary College of All Hallows, 1842–91* (Dublin: All Hallows College, 1986).

Connell, K. H. *The Population of Ireland 1750–1845* (Oxford: Clarendon Press, 1950).

Connelly, S. J. 'Normality and Catastrophe in Irish History', unpublished inaugural lecture as professor of modern Irish history, Queen's University, Belfast, 1997.

Connolly, S. J. *Priests and People in Pre-Famine Ireland* (Dublin: Gill and Macmillan, 1982).

 Religion, Law and Power: The Making of Protestant Ireland, 1660–1760 (Oxford University Press, 1992).

Cook, A. S. 'Establishing the Sea Routes to India and China: Stages in the Development of Hydrographical Knowledge', in H. V. Bowen, M. Lincoln and N. Rigby (eds.), *The Worlds of the East India Company* (Woodbridge: Boydell, 2002), pp. 119–37.

Cook, S. B. *Imperial Affinities: Nineteenth Century Analogies and Exchanges between India and Ireland* (New Delhi: Oxford University Press, 1993).

 'The Irish Raj: Social Origins and Careers of Irishmen in the Indian Civil Service, 1855–1914', *Journal of Social History*, 20, 3 (1987), 507–29.

Cooper, F. *Colonialism in Question: Theory, Knowledge, History* (Berkeley; London: University of California Press, 2005).

Cooper, F. and A. L. Stoler (eds.) *Tensions of Empire: Colonial Cultures in a Bourgeois World* (Berkeley: University of California Press, 1997).

Copeland, T. W. (ed.) *The Correspondence of Edmund Burke, Vol. III, July 1774–June 1778* (University of Chicago Press, 1971).

Corbett, T. P. *Ireland Sends India a Noble Prelate* (Calcutta, 1955).

Cordell, E. F. 'Sketch of John Crawford', *Johns Hopkins Hospital Bulletin*, 102 (1899).

Corfield, P. J. *Power and the Professions in Britain, 1700–1850* (New York: Routledge, 1995).

Corish, P. J. *Maynooth College 1795–1995* (Dublin: Gill and Macmillan, 1995).

Costello, P. *Clongowes Wood: A History of Clongowes Wood College, 1814–1989* (Dublin: Gill and Macmillan, 1989).

Coyne, E. J. 'Irish Population Problems: Eighty Years A-Growing, 1871–1951', *Studies: An Irish Quarterly Review*, Vol. XLIII, No.170 (1954).

Crawford, D. G. *A History of the Indian Medical Service 1600–1913*, Vol. I (London: W. Thacker & Co., 1914).

 The Roll of the Indian Medical Service 1615–1930, 2 vols. (London: Thacker & Co., 1930).

Crawford, J. *An Essay on the Nature, Cause and Cure of a Disease Incident to the Liver: Hitherto but Little Known, Though very Frequent and Fatal in Hot Climates* (London, 1772).

Croly, H. G. *The Irish Medical Directory* (Dublin: W. Curry. Jun. & Co., 1843 and 1846).

Bibliography 275

Crone, J. S. *A Concise Dictionary of Irish Biography* (Dublin: Talbot Press, 1928).

Crooke, W. *An Ethnological Hand-book for the N.W. Provinces and Oudh* (Allahabad: Government Press, 1890).

Materials for a Rural and Agricultural Glossary of the North-Western Provinces and Oudh (Allahabad: Government Press, 1879).

Religion and Folklore of Northern India; Tribes and Castes of the North-Western Provinces and Oudh (Allahabad: Government Press, 1896).

Religion and Folklore of Northern India (Oxford University Press, 1926).

Cullen, L. M. *Anglo-Irish Trade, 1660–1800* (Manchester University Press, 1968).

'Galway Merchants in the Outside World, 1650–1800', in D. O'Cearbhaill, *Galway, Town and Crown, 1484–1984* (Dublin: Gill and Macmillan, 1984), pp. 63–89.

'The Blackwater Catholics and County Cork Society and Politics in the Eighteenth Century', in P. O'Flanagan and C. G. Buttimer (eds.), *Cork History and Society: Interdisciplinary Essays on the History of an Irish County* (Dublin: Geography Publications, 1993), pp. 535–84.

'The Dublin Merchant Community in the Eighteenth Century', in L. M. Cullen and P. Butel (eds.), *Cities and Merchants: French and Irish Perspectives on Urban Development, 1600–1800* (Dublin: Department of Modern History, Trinity College Dublin, 1986), pp. 195–209.

'The Smuggling Trade in Ireland in the Eighteenth Century', *Proceedings of the Royal Irish Academy*, 67, 5 (1969), 149–75.

Cullen, L. M. and T. M. Smout (eds.) *Comparative Aspects of Scottish and Irish Economic and Social History, 1600–1900* (Edinburgh: J. Donald, 1977).

Cumpston, I. M. 'Some Early Indian Nationalists and Their Allies in the British Parliament, 1851–1906', *The English Historical Review*, 76 (1961), 279–97.

Curtin, N. J. *The United Irishmen: Popular Politics in Ulster and Dublin, 1791–1798* (Oxford: Clarendon, 1998).

Curtin, P. D. *Death by Migration: Europe's Encounter with the Tropical World in the Nineteenth Century* (Cambridge University Press, 1989).

Datta, D. 'Europeans in Calcutta, 1858–1883', unpublished PhD thesis, University of Cambridge, 1996.

Deane, S. *Strange Country: Modernity and Nationhood in Irish Writing since 1790* (Oxford: Clarendon, 1997).

De Melo, C. M. *The Recruitment and Formation of the Native Clergy in India (16th-19th Century): An Historical-Canonical Study* (Lisbon: Agencia-Geral do Ultramar, 1955).

Devine, T. M. *Scotland's Empire, 1600–1815* (London: Allen Lane, 2003).

Devoy, J. *Recollections of an Irish Rebel* (Shannon: Irish University Press, 1969 [1929]).

Dewey, C. 'Celtic Agrarian Legislation and the Celtic Revival: Historicist Implications of Gladstone's Irish and Scottish Land Acts, 1870–1886', *Past and Present*, 64 (1974), 30–70.

'Images of the Village Community: A Study in Anglo-Indian Ideology', *Modern Asian Studies*, 6, 3 (1972).

276 Bibliography

'The Education of a Ruling Caste: The Indian Civil Service in the Era of Competitive Examination', *English Historical Review*, 88 (1973), 262–85.

Dickson, D. 'The Cork Merchant Community in the Eighteenth Century: A Regional Perspective', in P. Butel and L. M. Cullen (eds.), *Négoce et Industrie en France et en Irlande au XVIIIe et XIX siècles* (Paris: Éditions du Centre National de la Recherche Scientifique, 1980), pp. 45–50.

'The Gap in Famines: A Useful Myth?' in E. M. Crawford (ed.), *Famine, The Irish Experience 900–1900: Subsistence Crises and Famine in Ireland* (Edinburgh: John Donald, 1989).

Dickson, D., J. Parmentier and J. Ohlmeyer (eds.). *Irish and Scottish Mercantile Networks in Europe and Overseas in the Seventeenth and Eighteenth Centuries* (Gent: Academia Press, 2007).

Doetsch, R. N. 'John Crawford and His Contribution to the Doctrine of Contagium Vivum', *Bacteriological Reviews*, 28, 1 (March 1964), 87–96.

Doherty, G. M. *The Irish Ordnance Survey: History, Culture and Memory* (Dublin: Four Courts Press, 2004).

Donovan, M. 'On the Physical and Medicinal Qualities of Indian Hemp (Cannabis Indica), with Observations on the Best Mode of Administration, and Cases Illustrative of Its Powers', *Dublin Quarterly Journal of Medical Science*, XXVI (1845), 368–402.

Dow, A. *The History of Hindostan: Volumes I and II* (London: Routledge, 2000).

Drayton, R. *Nature's Government: Science, Imperial Britain and the 'Improvement' of the World* (New Haven, CT; London: Yale University Press, 2000).

'The Collaboration of Labour: Slaves, Empires and Globalizations in the Atlantic World, *c.* 1600–1850', in A. Hopkins (ed.), *Globalization in World History* (London: Pimlico, 2002), pp. 98–115.

Dubois, L. P. *Contemporary Ireland* (Dublin: Unwin, 1908).

Duffy, T. G. 'An Irish Missionary Effort: The Brothers Fennelly', *Irish Ecclesiastical Review*, XVII (May 1921), 464–84.

Edney, M. H. *Mapping an Empire: The Geographical Construction of British India, 1765–1843* (University of Chicago Press, 1999).

Elliott, M. *Partners in Revolution: The United Irishmen and France* (New Haven, CT: Yale University Press, 1990).

Ellis, S. G. *Ireland in the Age of the Tudors, 1447–1603: English Expansion and the End of Gaelic Rule* (London: Longman, 1998).

Etherington, N. 'Education and Medicine', in N. Etherington (ed.), *Missions and Empire, Oxford History of the British Empire Companion Series* (Oxford University Press, 2005).

Everest, G. *Account of the Operations of the Great Trigonometrical Survey of India*, 24 vols. (Dehra Dun: Survey of India, 1870–1910).

An Account of the Measurement of Two Sections of the Meridional Arc of India, 2 vols. (London: East India Company, 1847).

'On the Compensation Measuring Apparatus of the Great Trigonometrical Survey of India', *Asiatic Researches*, 19 (1833), 189–214.

Fenton, S. *Ethnicity* (Cambridge: Polity Press, 2010).

Fermor, L. L. *First Twenty-Five Years of the Geological Survey of India* (Calcutta, 1976).

Bibliography

Fisher, M. H. *Indirect Rule in India: Residents and Residency System, 1764–1858* (Oxford University Press, 1998).

Fitzpatrick, D. 'Ireland and Empire', in *The Oxford History of the British Empire: The Nineteenth Century* (Oxford University Press, 1999), pp. 494–521.

Flanagan, K. 'The Rise and Fall of the Celtic Ineligible: Competitive Examinations for the Irish and Indian Civil Services in Relation to the Educational and Occupational Structure of Ireland, 1853–1921', unpublished D.Phil. thesis, University of Sussex, 1978.

Fleetwood, J. F. *The History of Medicine in Ireland* (2nd edn, Dublin: Skellig Press, 1983).

Foley, T. and M. O'Connor (eds.) *Ireland and India: Colonies, Culture and Empire* (Dublin: Irish Academic Press, 2006).

Foster, R. F. *Paddy and Mr Punch: Connections in Irish and English History* (London: Allen Lane, 1993).

Modern Ireland, 1600–1972 (London: Allen Lane, 1988).

W. B. Yeats: A Life, Vol. I – The Apprentice's Mage (Oxford University Press, 1996), pp. 469–73.

Fox, C. S. 'The Geological Survey of India', *Nature*, 160 (December 1947), 889–91.

Freidson, E. 'The Theory of Professions: State of the Art', in R. Dingwall and P. Lewis (eds.), *The Sociology of the Professions: Lawyers, Doctors and Others* (London: Macmillan, 1985), pp. 19–35.

Froggatt, P. 'Competing Philosophies: the "Preparatory" Medical Schools of the Royal Belfast Academical Institution and the Catholic University of Ireland, 1835–1909', in G. Jones and E. Malcolm (eds.), *Medicine, Disease and the State in Ireland, 1650–1940* (Cork University Press, 1999), pp. 59–85.

'The Irish Connection', in D. A. Dow (ed.), *The Influence of Scottish Medicine* (Park Ridge, NJ: Parthenon, 1988), pp. 63–76.

'The Response of the Medical Profession to the Great Famine', in E. M. Crawford (ed.), *Famine: The Irish Experience 900–1900, Subsistence Crises and Famines in Ireland* (Edinburgh: John Donald, 1989).

Furber, H. *Private Fortunes and Company Profits in the India Trade in the Eighteenth Century*, ed. R. Rocher (Aldershot: Variorum, 1997).

'The East India Directors 1784', *Journal of Modern History*, V (1933).

Geary, L. M. 'Prince Hohenloe, Signor Pastorini and Miraculous Healing in Early Nineteenth-Century Ireland', in G. Jones and E. Malcolm (eds.), *Medicine, Disease and the State in Ireland, 1650–1940* (Cork University Press, 1999).

Geological Survey of India. *Catalogue of the Meteorites in the Museum of the Geological Survey of India* (Calcutta, 1866).

Records of the Geological Survey of India (Calcutta: The Survey).

Ghose, S. 'The Introduction and Advancement of the Electric Telegraph in India', PhD thesis, Jadavpur University, Calcutta, 1974.

Gibbons, L. *Edmund Burke and Ireland: Aesthetics, Politics and the Colonial Sublime* (Cambridge University Press, 2003).

Gilbert, A. N. 'Recruitment and Reform in the East India Company Army, 1760–1800', *Journal of British Studies*, 15, 1 (1975), 89–111.

278 Bibliography

Gray, P. (ed.) 'Famine and Land in Ireland and India, 1845–1880: James Caird and the Political Economy of Hunger', *The Historical Journal*, 49 (2006), 193–215.

    Victoria's Ireland? Irishness and Britishness, 1837–1901 (Dublin: Four Courts Press, 2004).

Greene, J. P. *Peripheries and Center: Constitutional Development in the Extended Polities of the British Empire and the United States, 1607–1788* (Athens, GA: University of Georgia Press, 1986).

Grierson, G. A. *Bihar Peasant Life: Being a Discursive Catalogue of the Surroundings of the People of That Province, With Many Illustrations from Photographs Taken by the Author* (prepared under the orders of the government of Bengal) (Calcutta, 1885; reprinted Delhi, 1975).

Griffin, L. J. *New Methods for Social History* (Cambridge University Press, 1999).

Griffin, P. *The People with No Name: Ireland's Ulster Scots, America's Scots Irish, and the Creation of a British Atlantic World, 1689–1764* (Princeton University Press, 2001).

Guha, R. 'On Some Aspects of the Historiography of Colonial India', in *Subaltern Studies I* (Delhi: Oxford University Press, 1982), pp. 1–8.

Guha, R. and G. Chakravorty Spivak (eds.) *Selected Subaltern Studies* (New York: Oxford University Press, 1988).

Gupta, B. 'Indigenous Medicine in Nineteenth- and Twentieth-Century Bengal', in C. Leslie (ed.) *Asian Medical Systems: A Comparative Study* (Berkeley: University California Press, 1996), pp. 368–78.

Gwynn, S. 'Irish Soldiers and Irish Brigades', *Cornhill Magazine*, n.s., 53 (1922), 737–49.

Hall, C. *Civilising Subjects: Metropole and Colony in the English Imagination 1830–1867* (Cambridge University Press, 2002).

Hancock, D. *Citizens of the World: London Merchants and the Integration of the British Atlantic Community, 1735–1785* (Cambridge University Press, 1995).

Harlow, V. T. *The Founding of the Second British Empire, 1763–93, Vol. I: Discovery and Revolution* (London: Longmans, 1952).

Harris, J. *Private Lives, Public Spirit: A Social History of Britain 1870–1914* (Oxford University Press, 1993).

Harrison, M. *Climates and Constitutions: Health, Race, Environment and British Imperialism in India 1600–1850* (Oxford University Press, 1999).

    Public Health in British India: Anglo-Indian Preventative Medicine, 1859–1914 (Cambridge University Press, 1994).

Haughton, S. *University Education in Ireland* (London, 1868).

Hawes, C. J. *Poor Relations: The Making of a Eurasian Community in British India, 1773–1833* (Richmond: Curzon, 1996).

Heber, R. *Narrative of a Journey through the Upper Provinces of India* (London: John Murray, 1844).

Heffernan, P. *An Irish Doctor's Memories* (Dublin: Clonmore & Reynolds, 1958).

Herries Davies, G. L. *North from the Hook: 150 Years of the Geological Survey of Ireland* (Dublin: Geological Survey of Ireland, 1995).

Bibliography

Hill, J. L. 'A. P. MacDonnell and the Changing Nature of British Rule in India, 1885–1901', in R. I. Crane and N. G. Barrier (eds.), *British Imperial Policy in India and Sri Lanka, 1858–1912* (New Delhi: Heritage Publishers 1981).

Hilton, B. *The Age of Atonement: The Influence of Evangelicalism on Social and Economic Thought 1785–1865* (Oxford: Clarendon Press, 1988).

Hogan, E. M. *The Irish Missionary Movement: A Historical Survey, 1830–1980* (Dublin: Gill and Macmillan, 1990).

Holwell, J. Z. *A Genuine Narrative of the Deplorable Deaths of the English Gentlemen, and Others, Who Were Suffocated in the Black-Hole in Fort-William, at Calcutta* (London: A. Millar, 1758).

Interesting Historical Events, Relative to the Provinces of Bengal, and the Empire of Indostan, Parts I and II (London: Routledge, 2000).

Home, R. W. and S. G. Kohlstedt (eds.) *International Science and National Scientific Identity: Australia between Britain and America* (Dordrecht, Boston and London: Kluwer Academic, 1991).

Hopkins, A. G. 'Back to the Future: From National History to Imperial History', *Past and Present*, 164 (1999), 198–243.

(ed.) *Globalization in World History* (London: Pimlico, 2002).

Howe, S. *Ireland and Empire: Colonial Legacies in Irish History and Culture* (Oxford University Press, 2000).

Hughes, B. P. (ed.) *From Recruit to Staff Serjeant by N. W. Bancroft* (Hornchurch: Ian Henry Publications, 1979 [1885]).

Hull, C. H. (ed.) *The Economic Writings of Sir William Petty, Together with the Observations upon Bills of Mortality, More Probably by Captain John Graunt* (Cambridge University Press, 1899).

Hume, J. C. 'Rival Traditions: Western Medicine and Yunan-I Tibb in the Punjab, 1849–1889', *Bulletin of the History of Medicine*, 61 (1977), 214–31.

Insley, J. E. '"Instruments of a Very Beautiful Class": George Everest in Europe, 1825–1830', in *Colonel Sir George Everest CB FRS: Proceedings of the Bicentenary Conference at the Royal Geographical Society, 8th November 1990* (London, 1990), pp. 23–30.

Jackson, A. *Ireland, 1798–1998: War, Peace and Beyond* (Malden, MA; Oxford: Blackwell Publishing, 2010).

'Ireland, the Union, and the Empire, 1800–1960', in Kevin Kenny (ed.), *Ireland and the British Empire: Oxford History of the British Empire Companion Series* (Oxford University Press, 2004), pp. 123–52.

James, F. G. *Ireland in the Empire, 1688–1770: A History of Ireland from the Williamite Wars to the Eve of the American Revolution* (Cambridge, MA: Harvard University Press, 1973).

'The Irish Lobby in the Early Eighteenth Century', *The English Historical Review*, 82 (July 1966), 543–57.

Jamieson, J. *The History of the Royal Belfast Academical Institution, 1810–1960* (Belfast: William Mullan, 1959).

Jeffery, K. 'The Irish Military Tradition and the British Empire', in Jeffery (ed.), *'An Irish Empire'?*, pp. 94–122.

Jeffery, K. (ed.) *'An Irish Empire'? Aspects of Ireland and the British Empire* (Manchester University Press, 1996).

280   Bibliography

Jervis, T. B. *Records of Ancient Science, Exemplified and Authenticated in the Primitive Universal Standard of Weights and Measures* (Calcutta, 1836).

  The Expediency and Facility of Establishing the Metrological and Monetary Systems throughout India, on a Scientific and Permanent Basis, Grounded on an Analytical View of the Weights, Measures and Coins of India, and Their Relative Quantities with Respect to Such as Subsist at Present, or Have Hitherto Subsisted in All Past Ages throughout the World (Bombay, 1836).

Jervis, W. P. *Thomas Best Jervis, Lt. Col., Christian Soldier, Geographer, and Friend of India, 1796–1857: A Centenary Tribute* (London: Elliot Stock, 1898).

Jones, A. and B. Jones. 'The Welsh World and the British Empire, *c.* 1851–1939: An Exploration', *Journal of Imperial and Commonwealth History*, 31, 2 (May 2003), 57–81.

Jones, G. and E. Malcolm (eds.) *Medicine, Disease and the State in Ireland, 1650–1940* (Cork University Press, 1999).

Jordanova, L. 'Medical Men 1780–1820', in J. Woodall (ed.) *Portraiture: Facing the Subject* (Manchester University Press, 1997), pp. 101–15.

Jourdain, H. F. N. *Ranging Memories, by Lieut-Col. H. F. N. Jourdain* (Oxford University Press, 1934).

Jupp, P. *The First Duke of Wellington in an Irish Context* (University of Southampton, 1998).

Kantak, M. R. *The First Anglo-Maratha War, 1774–1783: A Military Study of Major Battles, 1774–1783* (Bombay: Popular Prakashan 1993).

Kearney, H. *Ireland: Contested Ideas of Nationalism and History* (New York University Press, 2007).

  The British Isles: A History of Four Nations (Cambridge University Press, 1989).

Kelly, J. 'Prosperous and Irish Industrialisation in the Late Eighteenth Century', *Journal of the County Kildare Archaeological Society*, XVI, 5 (1985/6), 442–67.

  'The Origins of the Act of Union: An Examination of Unionist Opinion in Britain and Ireland, 1650–1800', *Irish Historical Studies*, XXV (May 1987), 236–63.

Kenny, K. (ed.) *Ireland and the British Empire: Oxford History of the British Empire Companion Series* (Oxford University Press, 2004).

Kerjariwal, O. P. *Asiatic Society of Bengal* (Delhi, 1988).

Kerr, D. A. *Peel, Priests and Politics: Sir Robert Peel's Administration and the Roman Catholic Church in Ireland, 1841–1846* (Oxford: Clarendon Press, 1982).

Kinealy, C. 'At Home with Empire: The Example of Ireland', in C. Hall and S. Rose (eds.), *At Home with the Empire: Metropolitan Culture and the Imperial World* (Cambridge University Press, 2006), pp. 77–122.

Klein, I. 'Malaria and Mortality in Bengal', *IESHR*, 9 (1972), 639–59.

Kopf, D. *British Orientalism and the Bengal Renaissance: The Dynamics of Indian Modernisation, 1773–1835* (Berkeley: California University Press, 1969).

Kumar, A. *Medicine and the Raj: British Medical Policy in India, 1835–1911* (New Delhi; London: Sage, 1998).

Kumar, D. *Science and the Raj, 1857–1905* (Delhi: Oxford University Press, 1997).

Bibliography

Laidlaw, Z. *Colonial Connections 1815–1845: Patronage, the Information Revolution and Colonial Government* (Manchester University Press, 2005).

Laird, M. A. (ed.) *Bishop Heber in Northern India: Selections from Heber's Journal* (Cambridge University Press, 1971).

Lal, V. 'Subaltern Studies and Its Critics: Debates over Indian History', *History and Theory*, 40, 1 (February 2001), 135–48.

Lambert, S. (ed.) *House of Commons Sessional Papers of the 18th Century*, 147 vols. (Wilmington, DE: Scholarly Resources, 1975).

Lang, J. *Wanderings in India: And Other Sketches of Life in Hindostan* (London, 1859).

Lawrence, C. J. 'The Edinburgh Medical School and the End of the "Old Thing", 1790–1830', *History of Universities*, 7 (1988), 265–8.

Lawson, P. *The East India Company: A History* (London: Longman, 1993).

Lazarus, N. (ed.) *The Cambridge Companion to Postcolonial Literary Studies* (Cambridge University Press, 2004).

Lee, G. A. *Leper Hospitals in Medieval Ireland* (Dublin: Four Courts Press, 1996).

Leersen, J. T. 'On the Edge of Europe: Ireland in Search of Oriental roots, 1650–1850', *Comparative Criticism*, VIII (1986), 91–100.

Lennon, C. *Richard Stanihurst: The Dubliner, 1547–1618* (Blackrock: Irish Academic Press, 1981).

Lester, A. 'Imperial Circuits and Networks: Geographies of the British Empire', *History Compass*, 4, 1 (2006), 124–41.

Imperial Networks: Creating Identities in Nineteenth-Century South Africa and Britain (London: Routledge, 2001).

Livingstone, D. N. *Putting Science in Its Place: Geographies of Scientific Knowledge* (University of Chicago Press, 2003).

Logan, F. A. 'The British East India Company and African Slaves in Bunkulen, Sumatra, 1687–1792', *The Journal of Negro History*, 41, 4 (October 1956), 339–48.

Logan, P. *Making the Cure: A Look at Irish Folk Medicine* (Dublin: Talbot Press, 1972).

Longfield, A. 'Prosperous', *Journal of the County Kildare Archaeological Society*, XIV (1964), 212–31.

Lyons, J. B. *Brief Lives of Irish Doctors* (Dublin: Blackwater Press, 1978).

Macaulay, T. B. 'Minute of 2 February 1835 on English Education', in *Prose and Poetry* (Harvard University Press, 1952), p. 729.

Macauley, A. *William Crolly: Archbishop of Armagh 1835–49* (Blackrock: Four Courts Press, 1994).

MacDonagh, O. *O'Connell: The Life of Daniel O'Connell, 1775–1847* (London: Weidenfeld & Nicolson, 1991).

'The Politicization of the Irish Catholic Bishops, 1800–1850', *Historical Journal*, XVIII (1975), 37–53.

Ireland: The Union and Its Aftermath (London: Allen and Unwin, 1977).

MacDonald, D. *Surgeons Twoe and a Barber: Being Some Account of the Life and Work of the Indian Medical Service (1600–1947)* (London: William Heinemann Medical Books, 1950).

MacDonald, K. D. 'The Rev. William Shaw: Pioneer Gaelic Lexicographer', *Transactions of Gaelic Society of Inverness*, 1 (1976–8), 1–2.

282   Bibliography

McDonough, T. (ed.) *Was Ireland a Colony? Economics, Politics and Culture in Nineteenth-Century Ireland* (Dublin: Irish Academic Press, 2005).

McDowell, R. B. *Ireland in the Age of Imperialism and Revolution, 1760–1801* (Oxford: Clarendon Press, 1979).

McDowell, R. B. and D. A. Webb. *Trinity College, Dublin, 1592–1952: An Academic History* (Cambridge University Press, 1982).

McGeachie, J. 'The Research and Writing of a Biography of the Eye and Ear Surgeon, Antomist and Polymath Sir William Wilde (1815–76)', *Wellcome History*, 1 (1996).

McGilvary, G. K. *Guardian of the East India Company: The Life of Laurence Sulivan* (London: Tauras, 2006).

MacIntyre, S. 'Australia and the Empire', in R. W. Winks (ed.) *The Oxford History of the British Empire, Vol. V: Historiography* (Oxford University Press, 1999), pp. 163–81.

MacKenzie, G. T. 'History of Christianity of Travancore', in V. Nagum Aiya (ed.), *The Travancore State Manual*, 3 vols. (Tribandrum: Travancore Government Press, 1906).

MacKenzie, J. M. 'Irish, Scottish, Welsh and English Worlds? A Four-Nation Approach to the History of the British Empire', *History Compass*, 6/5 (2008), 1244–63.

MacKenzie, J. M. and N. R. Dalziel (eds.) *The Scots in South Africa: Ethnicity, Identity, Gender and Race, 1772–1914* (Manchester University Press, 2007).

McLaren, M. *British India and British Scotland, 1780–1830: Career Building, Empire Building and a Scottish School of Thought on Indian Governance* (Akron, OH: University of Akron Press, 2001).

McLeod, R. M. and M. Lewis (eds.) *Disease, Medicine and Empire: Perspectives on Western Medicine and the Experience of European Expansion* (London: Routledge, 1988).

McMinn, C. W. *Famine Truths, Half Truths, Untruths* (Calcutta: Thacker, Spink & Co., 1902).

MacNeill, M. *The Festivals of Lughnasa: A Study of the Survival of the Celtic Festival at the Beginning of the Harvest* (Oxford University Press, 1962).

Magee, G. B. and A. S. Thompson. *Empire and Globalisation: Networks of People, Goods and Capital in the British World, 1850–1914* (Cambridge University Press, 2010).

Maher, A. 'Missionary Links: Past, Present and Future', in M. Holmes and D. Holmes (eds.), *Ireland and India: Connections, Comparisons, Contrasts* (Dublin: Folens, 1997), pp. 29–51.

Majumdar, B. B. *Indian Political Associations and Reform of Legislature, 1818–1917* (Calcutta: Firma K. L. Mukhopadhyay, 1965).

Mansergh, N. *Commonwealth Perspectives* (London, 1958).

Survey of British Commonwealth Affairs: Problems of Wartime Co-operation and Post-war Change, 1939–1952 (Oxford University Press, 1958).

The Commonwealth Experience (London, 1969).

The Prelude to Partition: Concepts and Aims in Ireland and India (Cambridge University Press, 1978).

Bibliography

283

Manucci, N. *Storia do Mogor, or Mughal India, 1653–1706,* transl. and ed. W. Irvine, *Indian Text Series,* 4 vols. (London: Folio Society, 1907).

Marsden, P. V. and N. Lin (eds.) *Social Structure and Network Analysis* (Beverley Hills, CA: Sage, 1982).

Marshall, P. J. *Bengal: The British Bridgehead – Eastern India, 1740–1828, The New Cambridge History of India,* vol. 2.2 (Cambridge University Press, 1987).

'Britain without America: A Second Empire?' in P. J. Marshall (ed.), *The Oxford History of the British Empire: The Eighteenth Century* (Oxford University Press, 1998), pp. 576–95.

East Indian Fortunes: The British in Bengal in the Eighteenth Century (Oxford: Clarendon Press, 1976).

'Private British Trade in the Indian Ocean before 1800', in A. Das Gupta and M. N. Pearson (eds.), *India and the Indian Ocean, 1500–1800* (Calcutta: Oxford University Press, 1987), pp. 276–300.

Marshall, P. J. (ed.) *The Eighteenth Century in Indian History: Evolution or Revolution?* (New Delhi: Oxford University Press, 2003), pp. 1–49.

Marshman, J. C. *The Life and Times of Carey, Marshman, and Ward: Embracing the History of the Serampore Mission,* 2 vols. (London: Longman and Co., 1859).

Meehan, D. 'Maynooth and the Missions', *Irish Ecclesiastical Review,* LXVI (September 1945), 223–8.

Merriman, R. D. (ed.) *Queen Anne's Navy: Documents Concerning the Administration of the Navy of Queen Anne 1702–1714* (London: Navy Records Society, 1961).

Metcalfe, B. D. and T. R. Metcalfe. *A Concise History of India* (Cambridge University Press, 2002).

Miller, K. A. *Emigrants and Exiles: Ireland and the Irish Exodus to North America* (Oxford University Press, 1988).

Mokyr, J. and C. Ó Gráda. 'Height and Health in the United Kingdom 1815– 1860: Evidence from the East India Company Army', *Explorations in Economic History,* 13, 2 (1996), 141–68.

'Living Standards in Ireland and Britain 1800–1850: The East India Company Army Data', unpublished papers presented to the Social Science History Meeting, St Louis, October 1986.

'The Height of Irishmen and Englishmen in the 1770s: Some Evidence from the East India Company Army Records', *Eighteenth-Century Ireland,* 4 (1989), 83–92.

'The Heights of the British and the Irish *c.* 1800–1815: Evidence from Recruits to the East India Company's Army', in J. Komlos (ed.), *Stature, Living Standards and Economic Development: Essays in Anthropometric History* (Chicago; London: University of Chicago Press, 1994), pp. 39–59.

Moore, R. J. *Sir Charles Wood's Indian Policy, 1853–66* (Manchester University Press, 1966).

Mukhopadhyay, P. K. *Rabindra Jibani (Life of Tagore),* Vol. II (Calcutta: Visva-Bharati, 1985).

Müller, L. 'Scottish and Irish Entrepreneurs in Eighteenth-Century Sweden', in D. Dickson, J. Parmentier and J. Ohlmeyer (eds.), *Irish and Scottish*

284 Bibliography

Mercantile Networks in Europe and Overseas in the Seventeenth and Eighteenth Centuries (Gent: Academia Press, 2007), pp. 147–75.

Murdoch, S. 'Irish Entrepreneurs and Sweden in the First Half of the Eighteenth Century', in T. O'Connor and M. A. Lyons (eds.), *Irish Communities in Early-Modern Europe* (Dublin: Four Courts Press, 2006), pp. 348–66.

Murray, P., J. Leerssen and T. Dunne. *George Petrie (1790–1866): The Rediscovery of Ireland's Past* (Cork: Gandon Editions for the Crawford Municipal Art Gallery, 2004).

Nair, S. P. 'Science and the Politics of Colonial Collecting: The Case of Indian Meteorites, 1856–70', *British Journal for the History of Science*, 39, 1 (March 2006), 97–119.

Nash, R. C. 'Irish Atlantic Trade in the Seventeenth and Eighteenth Centuries', *William & Mary Quarterly*, 3rd series, XLIII (July 1985), 329–56.

Nechtman, T. W. *Nabobs: Empire and Identity in Eighteenth-Century Britain* (Cambridge University Press, 2010).

Newenham, T. *View of the Natural, Political, and Commercial Circumstances of Ireland* (London: T. Cadell and W. Davies, 1809).

Newman, C. *The Evolution of Medical Education in the Nineteenth Century* (London: Oxford University Press, 1957).

O'Brien, G. 'New Light on Emigration', *Studies*, XXX (1941).

O'Connell, M. R. (ed.) *The Correspondence of Daniel O'Connell, Vol. 2: 1815–1823* (Shannon: Irish University Press, 1972).

O'Connor, T. and M. A. Lyons (eds.) *Irish Communities in Early-Modern Europe* (Dublin: Four Courts Press, 2006).

O'Donnell, C. J. 'Ireland and Conservatism', *Nineteenth Century*, 68 (1910), 194–204.

The Black Pamphlet of Calcutta: The Famine of 1874 (London: William Ridgway, 1876).

The Ruin of an Indian Province: An Indian Famine Explained. A Letter to the Marquis of Hartington (London: C. Kegan Paul & Co., 1880).

'The Wants of Behar', *Calcutta Review*, LXIX (1879), 146–66.

O'Donnell, F. H. *A History of the Irish Parliamentary Party*, 2 vols. (London: Longmans, 1910).

O'Donovan, J. *The Antiquities of County Clare: Letters Containing Information Relative to the Antiquities of the County of Clare Collected During the Progress of the Ordnance Survey in 1839; & Letters and Extracts Relative to Ancient Territories in Thomond, 1841* (Ennis: CLASP Press, 2003).

O'Dwyer, M. *India as I Knew It, 1885–1925* (London: Constable & Co., 1925).

Ó Gráda, C. *Ireland: A New Economic History, 1780–1939* (Oxford: Clarendon Press, 1994).

O'Halloran, C. 'Irish Re-creations of the Gaelic Past: The Challenge of MacPherson's Ossian', *Past and Present*, 124 (1989), 69–95.

O'Hanlon, R. *Caste, Conflict and Ideology: Mahatma Jotirao Phule and Low Caste Protest in Nineteenth-Century Western India* (Cambridge University Press, 1985).

Oldham, R. D. *A Bibliography of Indian Geology: Being a List of Books and Papers, Relating to the Geology of British India and Adjoining Countries* (Calcutta, 1888).

Bibliography 285

Oldham, T. *Ancient Irish Pavement Tiles* (Dublin: J. Robertson, 1865).

Annual Report of the Superintendent of the Geological Survey of India and the Museum of Geology (Calcutta, 1860).

'Preliminary Notice on the Coal and Iron of Talcheer in the Tributary Mehals of Cuttack', in *Memoirs of the Geological Survey of India*, Vol. I (Calcutta: Geological Survey of India, 1859).

Ollerenshaw, P. 'Industry, 1820–1914', in L. Kennedy and P. Ollerenshaw (eds.), *An Economic History of Ulster, 1820–1939* (Manchester University Press, 1985).

O'Malley, K. *Ireland, India and Empire: Indo-Irish Radical Connections, 1919–1964* (Manchester University Press, 2008).

O'Moore Creagh, G. *The Autobiography of General Sir O'Moore Creagh, V.C., G.C.B., G.C.S.I.* (London: Hutchinson & Co., 1923).

O'Shaughnessy, W. B. 'Extract from a Memoir on the Preparations of the Indian Hemp, or Gunjah (Cannabis Indica), Their Effects on the Animal System in Health, and their Utility in the Treatment of Tetanus and other Convulsive Diseases', ed. James Prinsep, *The Journal of the Asiatic Society of Bengal*, viii, 93 (September 1840).

'Memorandum Relative to Experiments on the Communication of Telegraph Signals by Induced Electricity', *Journal of the Asiatic Society of Bengal*, JLVIII (September 1839), 714–31.

O'Sullivan, P. *The Economic History of Cork from the Earliest Times to the Act of Union* (Cork University Press, 1937).

Ó Tuathaigh, G. *Ireland before the Famine, 1798–1848* (Dublin: Gill and Macmillan, 1972).

'Religion, Identity, State and Society', in J. Cleary (ed.), *The Cambridge Companion to Modern Irish Culture* (Cambridge University Press, 2004).

Paine, T. *Rights of Man: Being an Answer to Mr. Burke's Attack on the French Revolution* (Sheffield: J. Crome, 1792).

Pal, B. C. *Swadeshi and Swaraj: The Rise of New Patriotism* (Calcutta: Yugayatri Prakashak, 1954).

Parmentier, J. 'The Irish Connection: The Irish Merchant Community in Ostend and Bruges during the Late Seventeenth and Eighteenth Centuries', *Eighteenth-Century Ireland*, 20 (2005), 31–54.

'The Ray Dynasty: Irish Mercantile Empire Builders in Ostend, 1690–1790', in T. O'Connor and M. A. Lyons (eds.), *Irish Communities in Early-Modern Europe* (Dublin: Four Courts Press, 2006), pp. 367–82.

Paseta, S. *Before the Revolution: Nationalism, Social Change and Ireland's Catholic Elite, 1879–1922* (Cork University Press, 1999).

Peterson, M. J. *The Medical Profession in Mid-Victorian London* (Berkeley: University of California Press, 1978).

Pickstone, J. V. (ed.) *Medical Invention in Historical Perspective* (London, 1992).

Pine, L. G. (ed.) *Burke's Genealogical and heraldic history of the Landed Gentry of Ireland*, 4th edn (London: Burke's Peerage, 1954).

Porter, R. 'Empires in the Mind', in P. J. Marshall (ed.), *The Cambridge Illustrated History of the British Empire* (Cambridge University Press, 1996), pp. 185–224.

286   Bibliography

Religion versus Empire? British Protestant Missionaries and Overseas Expansion, 1700–1914 (Manchester University Press, 2004).

(ed.). *Patients and Practitioners: Lay Perceptions of Medicine in Pre-Industrial Society* (Cambridge University Press, 1985).

The Oxford History of the British Empire: Vol. III, The Nineteenth Century (Oxford University Press, 1999).

Potter, S. 'Networks, Webs and Systems: Globalization and the Mass Media in the Nineteenth- and Twentieth-Century British Empire', *Journal of British Studies*, 46 (July 2007), 621–46.

(ed.). *Newspapers and Empire in Ireland and Britain: Reporting the British Empire, c.1857–1921* (Dublin: Four Courts Press, 2004).

Potts, E. D. *British Baptist Missionaries in India 1793–1837: The History of Serampore and Its Missions* (Cambridge University Press, 1967).

Powell, F. W. *The Politics of Irish Social Policy 1600–1900* (Lampeter: E. Mellen Press, 1992).

Prakash, O. *European Commercial Enterprise in Pre-colonial India, The New Cambridge History of India*, vol. 2.5 (Cambridge University Press, 1998).

'The English East India Company and India', in H. V. Bowen, M. Lincoln and N. Rigby (eds.), *The Worlds of the East India Company* (Woodenbridge: The Boydell Press, 2002).

Quinn, D. B. *The Elizabethans and the Irish* (Ithaca, NY: Cornell University Press, 1966).

Raj, K. *Relocating Modern Science: Circulation and Construction of Knowledge in South Asia and Europe, 1650–1900* (Basingstoke: Palgrave Macmillan, 2007).

Ramasubban, R. 'Imperial Health in British India, 1857–1900', in R. McLeod and M. Lewis (eds.), *Disease, Medicine, and Empire: Perspectives on Western Medicine and the Experience of European Expansion* (London: Routledge, 1988), pp. 38–60.

Ramusack, B. N. *The New Cambridge History of India, Vol. 3, Part 6: The Indian Princes and their States* (Cambridge University Press, 2004).

Ransom, J. *A Short History of the Theosophical Society, 1875–1937* (Adyar: Theosophical Publishing House, 1938).

Reader, W. J. *Professional Men: The Rise of the Professional Classes in Nineteenth-Century England* (London: Weidenfeld & Nicolson, 1964).

Rennell, J. *Memoir of a Map of Hindoostan or the Moguls Empire* (London, 1788).

Riddick, J. F. *Who Was Who in British India* (London: Greenwood Press, 1998).

Ritchie, G. S. *The Admiralty Chart: British Naval Hydrography in the Nineteenth Century* (London: Hollis & Carter, 1967).

Robinson, F. *Separatism among Indian Muslims: The Politics of the United Provinces' Muslims 1860–1923* (London: Cambridge University Press, 1974).

Roebuck, P. (ed.) *Macartney of Lisanoure, 1737–1806: Essays in Biography* (Belfast: Ulster Historial Foundation, 1983).

Rosenberg, C. E. and J. Golden. *Framing Disease: Studies in Cultural History* (Brunswick, NJ: Rutgers University Press, 1992).

Bibliography

Ross, C. (ed.) *The Correspondence of Charles, First Marquis Cornwallis* (London, 1859).

Sangwan, S. 'Reordering the Earth: The Emergence of Geology as a Scientific Discipline in Colonial India', *The Indian Economic and Social History Review*, 31, 3 (1994).

Sardesi, G. S. (ed.) *Poona Residency Correspondence, Vol. VII, Poona Affairs, 1801–1810* (Bombay: Government Central Press, 1940).

Schweizer, T. and D. R. White (eds.) *Kinship, Networks and Exchange* (Cambridge University Press, 1998).

Scott, J. *Social Network Analysis: A Handbook* (London: Sage, 2000).

Sheehy, J. *The Rediscovery of Ireland's Past: The Celtic Revival 1830–1930* (London: Thames and Hudson, 1980).

Sheridan, R. B. *Sugar and Slavery: An Economic History of the British West Indies, 1623–1775* (Baltimore: Johns Hopkins University Press, 1974).

Silvestri, M. *Ireland and India: Nationalism, Empire and Memory* (Basingstoke: Palgrave Macmillan, 2009).

Simms, J. G. 'The Irish on the Continent, 1691–1800', in T. W. Moody and W. E. Vaughan (eds.), *A New History of Ireland IV: Eighteenth-Century Ireland 1691–1800* (Oxford University Press, 1986), pp. 636–8.

Small, S. *Political Thought in Ireland, 1776–1798* (Oxford University Press, 2002).

Smith, V. A. *A History of Fine Art in India and Ceylon: From the Earliest Times to the Present Day*, rev. 2nd edn, ed. K. de Burgh Codrington (New Delhi: Asian Educational Service, 2006).

    A Report on a Tour of Exploration of the Antiquities in the Turai, Nepal (Calcutta, 1901).

    The Oxford History of India, ed. P. Spear (Delhi: Oxford University Press 1982).

    The Remains near Kasia in the Gorakhpur District: The Reputed Site of Kucanagara or Kucinara, the Scene of Buddha's Death (Allahabad: Government Press, 1896).

Spangenberg, B. *British Bureaucracy in India: Status, Policy and the Indian Civil Service in the Late 19th Century* (New Delhi: South Asia Books, 1976).

    'The Problem of Recruitment for the Indian Civil Service during the Nineteenth Century', *Journal of Asian Studies*, XXX (1971), 341–60.

Spiers, E. 'Army Organisation and Society in the Nineteenth Century', in T. Bartlett and K. Jeffery (eds.), *A Military History of Ireland* (Cambridge University Press).

Sproule, J. 'Sir William Wilde: Surgeon Oculist to the Queen in Ireland', *Dublin University Magazine*, 85 (1875), 570–89.

Stanley, P. *White Mutiny: British Military Culture in India, 1825–1875* (London: Hurst, 1998).

Stokes, E. T. *The English Utilitarians and India* (Oxford: Clarendon Press, 1959).

Strachan, H. *Wellington's Legacy: The Reform of the British Army, 1830–54* (Manchester University Press, 1984).

Streets, H. *Martial Races: The Military, Race and Masculinity in British Imperial Culture, 1857–1914* (Manchester University Press, 2004).

288 Bibliography

Sulivan, R. J. *An Analysis of the Political History of India* (London, 1779).

Sutherland, L. 'Lord Macartney's Appointment as Governor of Madras, 1780: The Treasury in East India Company Elections', *The English Historical Review*, 90, 356 (July 1975), 523–35.

'Lord Shelburne and East India Company Politics, 1766–9', *The English Historical Review*, 49, 195 (July 1934), 450–86.

The East India Company in Eighteenth-Century Politics (Oxford: Clarendon Press, 1962).

Talbot, I. 'Pakistan's Emergence', in R. W. Winks (ed.), *The Oxford History of the British Empire, Vol. V: Historiography* (Oxford University Press, 1999), pp. 253–63.

Taylor, A. *Annie Besant: A Biography* (London: Oxford University Press, 1992).

Temple, R. C. *A Dissertation on the Proper Names of Panjabis, with Special Reference to the Proper Names of Villagers in the Eastern Panjab* (Bombay; London: Education Society's Press; Trübner & Co., 1883).

'William Crooke, 1848–1923', Obituary Notice, *Proceedings of the British Academy* (London, 1924).

Thomas, J. H. 'East India Company Agency Work in the British Isles, 1700–1800', in H. V. Bowen, M. Lincoln and N. Rigby (eds.), *The Worlds of the East India Company* (Woodbridge: Boydell, 2002), pp. 33–47.

Thomas, R. W. and R. L. Turner. 'George Abraham Grierson, 1851–1941', Obituary Notice, *Proceedings of the British Academy*, XXVIII (1942), 11.

Tocqueville, A. *Journeys to England and Ireland*, trans. George Lawrence and K. P. Mayer, ed. J. P. Mayer (London: Faber, 1958).

Tone, T. W. *The Autobiography of Theobald Wolfe Tone, 1763–1798*, vol. I, ed. R. B. O'Brien (London: T. Fisher Unwin, 1893).

Tone, W. H. *Some Institutions of the Maratha People* (London: D. Lankheet, 1799).

Truxes, T. M. *Irish-American Trade, 1660–1783* (Cambridge University Press, 1988).

'London's Irish Merchant Community and North Atlantic Commerce in the Mid-Eighteenth Century', in D. Dickson, J. Parmentier and J. Ohlmeyer (eds.), *Irish and Scottish Mercantile Networks in Europe and Overseas in the Seventeenth and Eighteenth Centuries* (Gent Academia Press, 2007), pp. 271–309.

'New York City's Irish Merchants and Trade with the Enemy during the Seven Years War', in D. Dickson and C. Ó Gráda (eds.), *Refiguring Ireland: Essays in Honour of L.M. Cullen* (Dublin: Lilliput Press, 2003), pp. 147–64.

Vallancey, C. *A Vindication of the Ancient History of Ireland* (Dublin: L. White, 1786).

van de Ven, H. 'The Onrush of Modern Globalization in China', in A. Hopkins (ed.), *Globalization in World History* (London: Pimlico, 2002), pp. 167–94.

Viswanathan, G. 'Ireland, India and the Poetics of Internationalism', *Journal of World History*, 15 (2004), 7–30.

Bibliography

Waddington, I. 'General Practitioners and Consultants in Early Nineteenth-Century England: The Sociology of an Intra-Professional Conflict', in D. Richards and J. Woodward (eds.), *Health Care and Popular Medicine in Nineteenth-Century England* (London, 1977), pp. 164–88.

Wade, J. P. *A Paper on the Prevention and Treatment of the Disorders of Seamen and Soldiers in Bengal* (London: J. Murray, 1793).

Walford, E. *County Families of the United Kingdom* (London: Chatto and Windus, 1920).

Ward, K. *Networks of Empire: Forced Migration in the Dutch East India Company* (Cambridge University Press, 2009).

Ward, W. *A Protestant's Reasons Why He Will not be a Papist* (Serampore: Mission Press, 1802).

Washbrook, D. A. 'The Development of Caste Organization in South India', in C. J. Baker and D. A. Washbrook (eds.), *South India: Political institutions and Political Change 1880–1940* (Delhi: Macmillan, 1975), pp. 150–203.

'Orients and Occidents: Colonial Discourse Theory and the Historiography of the British Empire', in R. W. Winks (ed.), *The Oxford History of the British Empire, Vol. V: Historiography* (Oxford University Press, 1999), pp. 596–611.

Wasserman, S. *Social Network Analysis: Methods and Applications* (Cambridge University Press, 1997).

Webb, A. *A Compendium of Irish Biography* (New York: Lemma Publishing Co., 1978).

Webb, D. A. 'Religious Controversy and Harmony at Trinity College Dublin over Four Centuries', *Hermathena*, Quartercentury Papers (1992), 95–114.

Wellman, B. and S. D. Berkowitz (eds.) *Social Structures: A Network Approach* (Cambridge University Press, 1988).

Whelan, K. (ed.) *A New Imperial History: Culture, Identity and Modernity in Britain and the Empire, 1660–1840* (Cambridge University Press, 2004).

Widdess, J. H. D. *An Account of the Schools of Surgery, Royal College of Surgeons, Dublin, 1789–1948* (Edinburgh: Livingstone Ltd., 1949).

Widmalm, S. 'Accuracy, Rhetoric and Technology: The Paris–Greenwich Triangulation, 1784–88', in T. Frängsmyr, J. L. Heilbron and R. E. Rider (eds.), *The Quantifying Spirit in the 18th Century* (Berkeley: University of California Press, 1990).

Wilde, J. F. *Ancient Cures, Charms and Usages of Ireland: Contributions to Irish Lore*, 2 vols. (London: Ward and Downey, 1887).

Wilde, W. R. 'A Short Account of the Superstitions and Popular Practices Relating to Midwifery, and Some of the Diseases of Women and Children, in Ireland', *Monthly Journal of Medical Science*, 9, 35 (1849), 711–26.

'History of Irish Medicine and Popular Cures', unpublished and incomplete manuscript (University College Dublin Library, Special Collections, UCD Ms 2).

Irish Popular Superstitions (Shannon: Irish University Press, 1852).

'Lecture on the Early History of Irish Medicine', *London Medical Gazette*, new series, 6 (1848).

290   Bibliography

Lough Corrib, Its Shores and Islands: With Notices of Lough Mask (Dublin: M.H Gill, 1867).

Wilford, F. 'On the Ancient Geography of India', *Journal of the Asiatic Society of Bengal*, XX (1851).

Wilson, T. G. *Victorian Doctor* (London: Methuen & Co., 1942).

Winks, R. W. (ed.) *The Oxford History of the British Empire, Vol. V: Historiography* (Oxford University Press, 1999).

Yeats, W. B. *The Celtic Twilight: Myth, Fantasy and Folklore* (Lindfield: Unity, 1990 [1893]).

Yeo, R. *Defining Science: William Whewell, Natural Knowledge and Public Debate in Early-Victorian Britain* (Cambridge University Press, 1993).

Young, A. 'A Tour in Ireland;...with General Observations...Made in 1776,1777 and 1778 and Brought Down to the End of 1779', in J. Pinkerton (ed.), *A General Collection of the Best and Most Interesting Voyages and Travels in All Parts of the World*, Vol. III (London: Longman, Hurst, Rees and Orme, 1808–14).

Yule, H. and A. C. Burnell. *Hobson-Jobson: A Glossary of Colloquial Anglo-Indian Words and Phrases, and of Kindred Terms, Etymological, Historical, Geographical and Discursive* (London: John Murray, 1903).

Index

Acts of Union (1800), 26–31, 81–85, 131–32
Africa, 14, 33–36
agencies of the East India Company, 25, 42–44
Agra, 159–62
Ainslie, Whitelaw, 175, 176
Alcantara, Peter, Bishop of, 141, 142
Alcock, Rutherford, 79–80
All Hallows College, Dublin, 134–35, 142, 156
American War of Independence, 77
Anglicans, 172
Anglo-Indian, 263
anthropology, 206
antiquities, 222–23
apprenticeships, 123–24
Army Medical Service (AMS), 185–86
Arnold, David, 102
Aryan, 263
Ascendancy, the (Protestant), 64
Atkinson, Richard, 55
Atlantic Empire, 27–30, 33–36, 43, 66–68
Auckland, Lord (George Eden, Earl of Auckland), 155
Australia, 6, 69, 126
ayurvedic medicine, 171, 174, 175–76, 191, 263

Babu, 263
Ball, Valentine, 119
Ballantyne, Tony, 13–15, 17
Banerjea, Surandranath, 233, 245
Baptist missionary work, 138–39, 149–50
Barrow, Ian J., 110–11
Barry, Nicholas, 86–87, 160–62
Bartlett, Thomas, 26
Basalla, George, 105
Bayley, Stuart, 237–39, 245
Bayly, C.A., 7–8, 12, 17
Bayly, Susan, 146, 147

Beaumont, Gustave de, 133–34
Belfast, 186–88, 216–17
Belfast Daily Mercury, 168
Benares, 249–50
Bengal
  Catholic missionary work, 159
  East India Company, 39–40, 69
  land management under British rule, 228, 234–46
  medical services, 177
  socio-economic conditions, 121–22
  surveys of, 106
  trade role, 32
Bengal Tenancy Act (1885), 226, 228
Bennison, Amira K., 12–13
Bentinck, William, 112–13, 184–85, 217
beriberi, 179
Besant, Annie, 248–50
Bihar
  collection of revenues, 40, 69
  land management, criticism of, 225–28, 234–46
Birdwood, George, 209
Black Pamphlet of Calcutta, The (O'Donnell), 229, 234–37
Blacker, Valentine, 107–09, 112
Blackett, John, 165
Blackwood, Frederick Temple Hamilton-Temple- (Lord Dufferin), 228
Blavatsky, Helena Petrovna, 248
Bombay, 44, 45–47, 141, 177
Bombay Faction, 25–26, 48, 51–52
Borghi, Joseph, 159–62
box-wallah, 263
Boyle, Richard, 43
Bradlaugh, Charles, 248
Brahmin, 263
Braithwaite, William, 90, 91, 95
Brasted, Howard, 9, 231
Brehon laws, 230–31

291

292   Index

Britain
Acts of Union (1800), 26–31, 81–85,
131–32
charting of seas and coasts, 103–04
control over Ireland, 66–67, 78
British Army, 70–74, 78–79, 96, 178
British East India Company *see* East
India Company
British Empire
Atlantic Empire, 27–30, 33–36, 43,
66–68
employees' commitment to, 202–04
France, rivalry with, 39–40
history of, 6
Irish imperial networks, 17–23
and Irish national history, 3–11
Irish role in colonial expansion, 1–3
and nationalism, 250–52
networks, 14–17
taxation of colonies, 69–70
see also East India Company;
employment; medicine; military
recruitment; religion; scientific
knowledge; trade
British Museum, London, 124–26
Brooke, Robert, 75–77
Brooks, F.T., 249
Burke, Edmund, 53, 54, 82, 83
Burke, Richard (Collector of Customs,
Grenada), 54
Burke, Richard (solicitor, father of
Edmund), 53
business
agencies of the East India Company,
25, 42–44
Atlantic Empire, 27–30, 33–36, 43,
66–68
business networks in London, 49–51
colonial status, effect of, 26–31
East Indian trade, 30–42
globalisation, 11–14
Irish imperial networks, 17–256
patronage networks, 51–57
private trade with India, 57–62
see also Sulivan, Laurence ('Sulivan
network')
Butler, William, 93
Byrne, Patrick, 94–95

Cairns, J.E., 229
Calcutta, 157–59, 159, 179–80, 183–85
Campbell, Thomas, 219–20
cannabis, 184, 189–90
Canning, George, 83–84
Canny, Nicholas, 8

Capuchin (Franciscan) missionaries,
146–47, 148–49, 159–62
careers, military, 90–93
Carew, Patrick, 144, 148–49, 154–56,
157–59
Caribbean, 27–30, 33–36, 43
Carmelite missionaries, 148
Carmichael (Richmond Hospital) private
medical school, 187–88
Carroll, Patrick, 93
cartography *see* maps
caste, 145–54, 157, 161, 263
Catholic University of Ireland, 187–88,
216
Catholics
agitation by Irish soldiers in India,
163–67
Ascendancy, the (Protestant), effects
of, 64
and caste, 145–54, 157, 161
debarment from commission or
landownership, 99–100
and the East India Company, 64–65,
136–41
emancipation of, 131–36
emigration to North America, 67–68
employment in Ireland, 72
entrance examination for imperial
service, 169
and Hindus, 131–32
in the ICS, 214–15
Irish identity in India, 87, 90–91
Irish imperial networks, 21–22,
129–31, 167–68, 257–58
Irish Volunteer movement, 77–78
in medical services, 171–72, 182–83,
188, 193–98
missionary work, 134–36
networks in India, 94–95, 154–63
population, 132–33
post-Union Catholicism in Ireland,
131–36
priests, 141–45, 174–75
Propaganda Fide, 129–30, 134–35,
140–41, 148–49, 153–54
scientific practice, 99–100
Society of United Irishmen, 82
as soldiers, 70–75, 76–77, 79, 97–98
trade, 33, 44, 50
worship, 161–62
Celtic revival, 230–31
Celticism, 15
Central Hindu College, 249–50
Charles XII of Sweden, 34–35
Chaube, Pandit Ram Gharib, 222

Index

Chennai *see* Madras
Chesnaye, George, 200
children, 95–96, 160–61, 162, 163–64
Church Missionary Society, 137–38
class, social *see* social class
climate, and disease, 178–79
Clive, Robert, 74, 80–81
Clongowes Wood College, 213–14
Close, Barry, 107
coasts, charting, 103–04
Coghill, Kendal, 87, 88, 95
Colby, Thomas, 111–17, 120
Cole, Arthur, 107
Colebrooke, George, 53–54, 73–74
Colgan, Joseph, 148–49
colleges
  ICS, preparation for, 169, 213–14
  IMS, preparation for, 169, 170,
    197–98, 199–200
  Irish imperial networks, 258–59
  medicine, Irish school of, 182–83,
    185–88, 193
  political thought following the Famine,
    230
Colley, Linda, 10
Collingham, E.M., 209
colonies, 3–11
Company of the Apothecaries' Hall, 199
Connaught Rangers, 92, 97
Cook, S.B., 9, 213–14, 224, 231
Cooper, Frederick, 11
Cork
  agency of the East India Company,
    43–44
  Queens College, 186–88, 200, 216–17
  Sulivan network, 44–46
Corkery, William, 95
Cornwall, Charles Wolfran, 73
Cornwallis, Lord (Charles, first
  Marquess Cornwallis), 131, 177
Costello, John A., 1
cotton, 75
Court of Directors
  Great Trigonometrical Survey of India
    (GTS), 109, 113, 115–16
  patronage networks, 51–52
  recruitment of soldiers in Ireland,
    74–75
  role of, 32
  shipping, 25–26
  Sulivan network, 44, 47–48
Court of Proprietors, 25–26, 51–52
Cousins, James, 250–51
Craddock, R.H., 215
Crawford, John, 178–79

Creagh, Sir Garrett O'Moore, 88, 89
Crooke, William, 220–22, 223–24
Cullen, Paul, 134–35
culture, 22, 206, 216–24

Darbhanga, Maharajah of, 227
Davitt, Michael, 247
death, 95–96
Denison, Lieutenant, 112
Dennehy, Thomas, 89–90
Devanagari, 263
Devoy, John, 167
Dewey, Clive, 9, 224
dharma, 263
Dharmasath, Servaji, 47
diseases, 178–79, 192–93
diwan, 263
doctors, 170 *see also* medicine
Downie, John, 90
Dr Steevens Hospital, 187–88, 189
Dravidian, 263
Drayton, Richard, 13
Dubois, Abbé, 141
Dufferin, Lord (Frederick Temple
  Hamilton-Temple-Blackwood), 228
Duke, F.W., 215
Dundas, Henry, 55, 60–61, 84–85
durbar, 263
Dutch East India Company (VOC), 32

East India Company
  abolition of, 96
  agencies in Ireland, 25, 42–44
  agitation by Irish soldiers in India,
    163–67
  and Catholic clergy, 135–36, 142–45
  and Catholicism, 64–65, 136–41
  entrance examination, 169
  Great Trigonometrical Survey of India
    (GTS), 100, 104–17
  growth of, 31–33, 38–42
  imperial science, 104–06
  Irish Catholics, networks of, 94–95,
    154–63
  Irish imperial networks, 17–256
  Irish role, 20–21, 31, 41–42, 62–63
  medical services, 176–85
  patronage networks, 51–57
  private trade between Ireland and
    India, 57–62
  recruitment in Ireland, 64–65, 75–77
  scientific knowledge, use of, 99–101
  soldiers, 39–42, 71–75, 78–81, 97–98
  South Asia, expansion into, 68–69
  subsidiary alliance system, 80–81

294   Index

East India Company (*cont.*)
  Sulivan network, 44–48
Eden, Ashley, 238, 240, 245–46
Eden, George, Earl of Auckland (Lord
    Auckland), 155
Edinburgh University, 197–98
Edney, Matthew H., 105–06
education
  Geological Survey of India (GSI),
    117–19, 122–24
  ICS, preparation for, 169, 213–14
  IMS recruitment, 169–71, 197–98,
    199–200
  of Indians, 122–24
  Irish imperial networks, 22, 258–59
  Irish school of medicine, 169–71,
    182–83, 185–93, 199–200, 202–04
  see also colleges; universities
Edwards, William, 91–92
Egypt, 246
Ellis, Steven G., 8
Elphinstone, William Fullarton, 136, 155
emigration to North America, 67–68, 71
empires
  globalisation effects of, 11–14
  and national history, 3–11
  and networks, 14–17
employment
  in Ireland, 72
  Irish identity in India, 85–93
  Irish role in British colonial project,
    64–66, 97–98
  soldiers' networks in India, 94–96
  union with Britain, effects of, 85
  see also East India Company; Indian
    Civil Service (ICS); Indian Medical
    Service (IMS); soldiers
England, 6, 20, 33
English East India Company *see* East
    India Company
environment, and disease, 178–79
ethnographic surveys, 114–15, 206,
    216–24
Eurasian, 263
Evans, Richardson, 212–13
Everest, George, 112, 113–16
examinations, 207–11

faith healers, 174–75
families, 94–96
Famine, the, 97, 170–71, 188–93, 229–31
Fenian movement, 130–31, 163–67
Fennelly, John, 148–49, 154, 156–57
Fennelly, Stephen, 148–49, 156
5th Bengal European Regiment, 165–66

53rd Regiment of Foot, 165, 167
financial support for families, 95–96
Finucane, Michael, 226–27
folk medicine, 173–74, 189–91
folklore, 216–24
Foster, Roy F., 10, 132, 211–12, 218
France, 39–40, 68, 81–82, 136, 146–47,
    148–49
Fraser, S.M., 215
Frederick I of Sweden, 35
free trade, 57–62
French, John, 201

Gaelic revival, 216–20, 230–31
Gait, A.E., 215
Galway, Queens College, 186–88,
    216–17, 225, 239
Galwey, Andrew, 33–36
Gandhi, Mahatma, 251
General Medical Council (GMC), 182
geological research, ownership of,
    124–26
Geological Survey of India (GSI),
    100–01, 117–26
Gladstone, William E., 230
Gleeson, William, 160
globalisation, 11–14
Godfrey, Edmund, 51
Godfrey, Peter, 51
Godfrey, Thomas, 51
Gough, Michael, 156
Grattan, Henry, 78
Gray, Peter, 10
Greany, John, 196–97
Great Famine, 97, 170–71, 188–93,
    229–31
Great Trigonometrical Survey of India
    (GTS), 100, 104–11
  and the Ordnance Survey of Ireland
    (OSI), 111–17
Grenville, Lord (William Wyndham,
    Baron Grenville), 84
Grierson, George, 220, 221–22, 223–24
Griffiths, Arthur, 251
Gujar, 264
guru, 264

Haggard, A.G., 1–2
hakim, 264
Hancock, W.N., 230
Hand, John, 135
Hart, Andrew Seale, 215
Harty, John, 165
Hastings, Francis Rawdon, 108
Heffernan, Patrick, 1, 203–04

Index

herbalists, 173–74, 189–91
Heyne, Benjamin, 175
Hickey, Joseph, 53–55
Hickey, William, 54–55
Hicky, Thomas, 53
Hindi, 264
Hinduism. promotion of, 249–50
Hindus, 131–32, 143
Hindustan, 264
Hobart, Henry, 61
Hogan, John, 93
Holwell, John Zephaniah, 179–81
Home Rule
  India, 231–34, 250
  Ireland, 228–34, 250–52
Höpken, Baron de, 34
Hopkins, A.G., 11–12, 17
Horne, John, 46, 47, 48
hospitals, 185–88, 193
Hugaetan, Jean Henri, 34
Hutwa, Maharajah of, 225–26,
  237–38
Hyderabad, 81, 159
hydrography, 103–04

Ibbetson, Denzil, 224
ICS (Indian Civil Service) *see* Indian
  Civil Service (ICS)
Imperial Geological Institute of Vienna,
  124–25
imperial science, 101–06
IMS (Indian Medical Service) *see* Indian
  Medical Service (IMS)
India
  agitation by Irish soldiers in India,
    163–67
  Anglicisation of, 135–36
  caste, 145–54, 157, 161, 263
  Catholic church, influence of, 129–31,
    136–41, 167–68
  Catholic clergy in, 131, 141–45
  education, scientific, 122–24
  employment opportunities in colonial
    expansion, 64–66, 196
  Geological Survey of India (GSI),
    100–01, 117–26
  Great Trigonometrical Survey of India
    (GTS), 100, 104–17
  Home Rule, 231–34, 250
  indigenous medicine, 173–74, 191
  Irish Catholics, networks of, 94–95,
    154–63
  Irish imperial identity, 85–93
  Irish imperial networks, 1–3, 17–23,
    253–16

land management, criticism of, 64,
  224–28, 234–46
medicine, modernisation of, 171–76
national history, 6
nationalism networks with Ireland,
  205–07, 246–50
Orientalism as governance discourse,
  15
orientalists' interest in Indian culture,
  216–18, 219–24
private trade with India, 57–62
religious affinities with Ireland, 131–32
socio-economic conditions, 121–24
soldiers' networks, 94–96
subsidiary alliance system, 80–81
Sulivan network, 44–48
surveillance and control of, 99–101
trade, Irish participation in, 20, 30–42,
  62–63
see also East India Company
India Act (1784), 59
Indian Civil Service (ICS)
  background of Irish recruits, 211–16
  Gaelic revival, 216–20
  Irish imperial networks, 22, 258–59,
    260–7
  land management, criticism of,
    224–28, 231–46
  and nationalism, 250–52
  orientalists' interest in Indian culture,
    216–18, 219–24
  professional networks, 206–07
  recruitment, 207–11
Indian hemp (cannabis), 184, 189–90
Indian Medical Service (IMS)
  careers in, 201–02
  incentives for joining, 200–01
  Irish imperial networks, 22, 258–62
  Irishmen in, 177, 185–86, 193–98,
    199–204
  membership, 171–72
  recruitment of Irish doctors, 193–98
  role of, 169–70
  universities, role of, 169–71, 199–200
Indian Mirror, 243
Indian Museum, Calcutta, 124–26
Indian Mutiny (1857), 165, 168
indigenous medicine, 173–74, 189–91
indigo plantations, 242
Indo-Irish, 264
Inglis, Robert, 187
intellectual property rights, 124–26
Ireland
  Acts of Union (1800), 26–31, 81–85,
    131–32

296   Index

Ireland (*cont.*)
  and the Atlantic Empire, 27–30,
    33–36, 43, 66–68
  British control over, 66–67, 78
  business networks, 49–51
  Catholic population, 132–33
  Celticism as governance discourse, 15
  colonial status of, 3–11, 26–31
  the Famine, 97, 170–71, 188–93,
    229–31
  Gaelic revival, 216–20, 230–31
  Home Rule, 228–34, 250–52
  imperial science, 103–06
  Irish identity in India, 85–93
  land system, 64, 224–28
  medicine, school of, 169–71, 182–83,
    185–93, 199–200, 202–04
  migration, 97
  mortality rates, 97
  national health care, 191–93
  national history and empire role, 3–11
  nationalism networks with India,
    205–07, 246–50
  Ordnance Survey of Ireland (OSI),
    100, 104, 109–17
  religious affinities with India, 131–32
  socio-economic conditions, 120–21
  soldiers' networks in India, 94–96
  subaltern Irish, meaning of, 64
  taxation, 69–70
  see also employment; Indian Civil
    Service (ICS); Indian Medical
    Service (IMS); medicine; military
    recruitment; nationalism; religion;
    scientific knowledge; trade
Irish Catholics *see* Catholics
Irish imperial networks
  East India Company, 17–256
  education, 22, 258–59
  and the ICS, 22, 258–59, 260–7
  and the IMS, 22, 258–62
  in India, 1–3, 17–23, 253–16
  medicine, 169–71, 258–62
  nationalism, 22–23, 260–62
  nature of, 253–16
  religion, 21–22, 129–31, 167–68,
    257–58
  scientific knowledge, 21–22, 256–57
  soldiers, 16–17, 20–21
  trade, 17–256
Irish Patriot party, 26, 78
Irish Protestants *see* Protestants
Irish Rebellion (1798), 81–82
'Irish sepoy patriots', 166
Irish Sulivan network *see* Sulivan,
    Laurence ('Sulivan network')

Irish Volunteer movement, 77–78
Irwin, Eyles, 56
Irwin, James, 45–46
Italy, 148–49, 159–62

jagir, 264
Jagirdar, 264
James, F.G., 29–30
Jat, 264
Jeffrey, Keith, 10
Jervis, Thomas Best, 116–17
Jesuits, 158–59
jyotish, 264

Kater, Henry, 113
Keith, Basil, 54
Kennedy, Father, 156
Kenny, Kevin, 8–9
Kerala, 141
khadi, 264
King, William, 119
Kinsale, 42
Kipling, Rudyard, 163–64
Kolkata *see* Calcutta
Kynynmound, Gilbert Elliot Murray,
    first Earl Minto (Lord Minto), 84,
    138–39

Laidlaw, Zoe, 15, 17
Lal, Hira, 123
Lambton, William, 109
land management, criticism of
  India, 64, 224–28, 234–46
  Ireland, 64, 224–28
Lane, Thomas, 48, 51
language
  and career advancement, 180–81
  Catholic missionaries, 152, 163
  Gaelic revival, 216–20
  and the ICS, 210, 215–17
  orientalists' interest in, 216–18,
    219–24
  teaching at Irish Universities, 199–200
Larcom, Thomas, 111–12, 120
Law, Stephen, 46, 47, 48
lawyers, 207, 216
Ledwich (Peter Street) private medical
    school, 187–88
legal profession, 207, 216
Lester, Alan, 14–15, 17, 90, 127
Limerick, 42–43
Livingstone, David N., 102–03
London
  Irish business networks, 16, 49–51
  patronage networks, 51–57
  Sulivan network, 47–48

Index

Lovett, H.V., 215
Luigi, Bishop, 141
Luquet, Abbé, 154

Macartney, George, 54–55
Macaulay, Colman, 243
Macaulay, Thomas Babington, 135, 184–85, 194, 207–08
MacDonnell, Anthony Patrick, 223, 238–40, 242–43, 249–50
MacKenzie, Andrew, 243, 244
MacKenzie, Colin, 109
MacKenzie, Kenneth, 165–66
Maclagan, E.D., 214
Madagascar, 35
Madras
  caste and Catholicism, 146–54
  Irish Catholics, networks of, 154–57
  medical services, 177
  missionary work, 129–30, 141, 148–54, 159
  nationalism, promotion of, 249–50
Magee, Gary B., 15–16, 17, 102
mahajan, 264
Malaysia, 69
Mansergh, Nicholas, 7
maps
  and colonial power, 111–17
  Great Trigonometrical Survey of India (GTS), 100, 104–11
  Ordnance Survey of Ireland (OSI), 100, 104, 109–11
Maratha Confederacy, 40
marine charting, 103–04
marriage, 95, 96, 163–64
Maskelyne, Nevil Story-, 125–26
Mater Misericordiae University Hospital, Dublin, 188
maulvi, 264
Maynard, H.J., 214
Maynooth College, 144, 149, 154–59
McCann, Henry, 158–59
McCoy, Frederick, 126
McGrane, John, 160
McLoughlin, Christopher, 87
McMinn, Charles, 223, 227–28
medical topography, 178–79
medicine
  East India Company medical services, 176–85
  Irish doctors in the IMS, 177, 185–86, 193–98, 199–204
  Irish imperial networks, 169–71, 258–62

Irish school of, 169–71, 182–83, 185–93, 199–200, 202–04
  medical profession in Ireland, 185–93
  modernisation of, 171–76
  national health care in Ireland, 191–93
  participation in Empire though IMS, 202–04
  traditional remedies, 173–74, 189–91
  see also Indian Medical Service (IMS); scientific knowledge
Medlicott, Henry, 119
Medlicott, Joseph, 119
Meston, J.S., 214
migration from Ireland, 97
military recruitment
  Brooke's recruitment business, 75–77
  decline following Indian Mutiny, 96–97
  discharge, 96
  East India Company, 39–42, 71–75, 78–81, 97–98
  following expansion into South Asia, 75–81
  following Seven Years War, 68–75
  Irish identity, 85–93
  Irish imperial networks, 16–17, 20–21
  Irish Volunteer movement, 77–78
  medical services, 177–78
  military life in India, 91–92
  physical condition of soldiers, 79–80
  and religion, 70–75, 76–77, 79, 94–95, 97–98, 141–45, 161–62
  role in British colonial project, 64–66, 97–98
  soldiers' networks in India, 94–96
  union with Britain, effects of, 85
Mill, J.S., 229
Miller, Alexander, 207
Minto, Lord (Gilbert Elliot Murray Kynynmound, first Earl Minto), 84, 138–39
missionary work
  of Catholics, 134–36
  of Protestants, 132, 137–39, 149–50
  Propaganda Fide, 129–30, 134–35, 140–41, 148–49, 153–54
  support for Irish migrants, 134–36
Moran, James, 196
Moré, Father, 157, 158
Morgan, William, 33–36
Moriarty, David (President of All Hallows College), 156, 160
Moriarty, Reverend (Vicar General of Madras), 152, 153–54
Müller, Max, 221–22

298 Index

Mumbai *see* Bombay
munshi, 264
Murphy, Father Daniel, 159
Muslims, 143
Mysore, 40

Naoroji, Dadabhai, 233, 247
national health care in Ireland, 191–93
National Museum of Victoria, 126
nationalism
    agitation by Irish soldiers in India,
        163–67
    and economic hardship, 205–06
    and Empire service, 250–52
    Home Rule movement in Ireland,
        229–34, 250–52
    Irish imperial networks, 22–23,
        260–62
    and land rights, 224–28
    networks between Ireland and India,
        205–07, 246–50
Navigation Acts, 28
nawab, 264
Neary, John, 91
Nehru, Jawaharlal, 249
Nehru, Motilal, 249
Nesbitt, Arnold, 54
networks
    Catholic networks, 94–95, 154–63
    and empires, 14–17
    Irish business networks in London, 16,
        49–51
    Irish identity in India, 85–93
    nationalism in Ireland and India,
        205–07, 246–50
    patronage networks, 51–57
    soldiers in India, 94–96
    see also Irish imperial networks
Newenham, Thomas, 27
newspapers, 232
Nolan, Patrick, 226, 227
Nomelah military station, 161–62
North America, 27–30, 43, 67–68, 71

Ó Tuathaigh, Gearóid, 10
O'Brien, Lucius, 76
O'Ceallaigh, Seán T., 251
O'Connell, Daniel (Irish politician), 133,
    134–35, 149, 164, 175
O'Connell Raye, Daniel, 202–03
O'Connor, Daniel (Vicar Apostolic of
    Madras), 148–54
Odisha *see* Orissa
O'Donnell, Charles J.
    background, 225–27

criticism of policy in Bengal, 207, 224,
    229, 234–46
Home Rule, 231–34
nationalism, promotion of, 251–52
O'Donnell, Frank Hugh, 232–34, 237,
    244, 245
O'Donnell, Nathaniel, 156–57, 162–63
O'Dwyer, Michael, 212, 214
Olcott, Henry Steele, 248
Oldham, Charles, 119
Oldham, Richard Dixon, 119
Oldham, Thomas, 100–01, 117–26
O'Leary, John, 167, 200
Ordnance Survey of Ireland (OSI), 100,
    104, 109–11, 118
    and the Great Trigonometrical Survey
        of India (GTS), 111–17
Orientalism, 15
Orissa, 40, 69, 121–22
O'Shaughnessy, William, 183–85,
    189–90
Ossian, 218–19
Oulton, Richard, 216

padroado (patronage agreement), 139–41,
    150–51
Paine, Thomas, 82
pandit, 264
Parava caste, 147–48, 152
patriot movement, 26, 78
patronage networks, 51–57
Pawsey, Richard, 237–39
Peel, Robert, 84
Penang, 69
Pentland, Lord (John Sinclair, first Baron
    Pentland), 250
Perisco, Bishop, 159
Permanent Settlement Act (1793), 64
Persian, 264
Petrie, George, 115
Petty, William, 28
Pitt, William, 83, 84
Porter, Alexander, 201
Porter, Andrew, 26
Portugal, 137, 139–41, 147–48, 150–51
Presbyterians
    emigration to North America, 67–68,
        71
    Irish Volunteer movement, 77–78
    medical service, 172, 182–83
    Royal Belfast Academical Institution,
        187
    Society of United Irishmen, 82
private trade, 57–62
privateers, 34–35

Index

Propaganda Fide, 129–30, 134–35, 140–41, 148–49, 153–54
Protestants
 business networks, 50
 East Indian trade, 33
 education for imperial service, 169
 faith healing, view of, 175
 Hickey, Joseph, 53
 Irish identity in India, 87
 Irish imperial networks, 129
 medical services, 171–72
 missionary work, 132, 137–39, 149–50
 occupations in Ireland, 72
 patriot movement, 26
 scientific practice, 99–100
 as soldiers, 70, 72
 Sulivan network, 44
published works, 181, 184
Pulteney, William, 73
purdah, 264

Queens Colleges (Belfast, Cork, Galway)
 establishment of, 186–88
 language teaching, 199–200
 MacDonnell, Anthony Patrick, 239
 O'Donnell, Charles J., 225
 political thought following the Famine, 230
 shunned by Catholics, 214–15
 training for the ICS, 216–17
Quinn, D.B., 8

racial prejudice, 196–97
raiyats, 264
Raj, 264
Raj, Kapil, 102
raja, 264
Rajput, 264
Rammohun Roy, Raja, 164
religion
 agitation by Irish Catholics, 163–67
 and caste, 145–54, 157, 161
 Catholic church in Ireland, 131–36
 Catholic networks, 94–95, 154–63
 Catholic priests in India, 135–36, 141–45
 and the East India Company, 136–41
 Irish affinities with India, 131–32
 Irish identity in India, 85–87, 90–91
 Irish imperial networks, 21–22, 129–31, 167–68, 257–58
 and medical services, 171–72
 and the Queens Colleges, 187
 and soldiers, 70–75, 76–77, 79, 94–95, 97–98, 141–45, 161–62

 see also Anglicans; Catholics; Hindus; Jesuits; Muslims; Presbyterians; Protestants
remittances, 65–66, 130
remuneration, 65–66
Rennell, James, 106–11
research, geological, ownership of, 124–26
revolution, Irish movement for, 81–82
Richey, A.G., 230
Roantree, William Francis, 167
Robertson, B., 214
Roman Catholicism, and the East India Company, 136–41 see also Catholics
Rooney, Joseph, 160
Rose, Hugh, 167
Rotton, Captain, 166
Royal Asiatic Society of Bengal, 219
Royal Belfast Academical Institution, 186–87, 214
Royal College of Surgeons, 187–88, 189, 199
Royal Irish Academy, 218–19
Ruin of an Indian province, The (O'Donnell), 229, 240–46

Sacred Congregation de Propaganda Fide, 129–30, 134–35, 140–41, 148–49, 153–54
Salmond, James, 109, 112
Sarouvanitomarayan, P.D., 157
Saverio, Father Francesco, 141
scientific knowledge
 and colonial power, 111–17
 education of Indians, 122–24
 geographical location, influence of, 101–06
 Geological Survey of India (GSI), 100–01, 117–26
 Great Trigonometrical Survey of India (GTS), 100, 104–11
 imperial science, 101–06
 Irish imperial networks, 21–22, 256–57
 Irish role in India, 99–101, 126–28
 Ordnance Survey of Ireland (OSI), 100, 104, 109–11
 research, ownership of, 124–26
 see also medicine
Scotland
 East Indian trade, 33
 IMS, Scots in, 194, 197–98
 medical schools, 182–83
 national history and empire role, 6
 role in British colonial expansion, 4
 trade, colonial, 29

300   Index

Seal, Motilal, 157–58
Seal College, Calcutta, 157–58
seas, charting, 103–04
seminaries, Catholic, 133–34
sepoy, 264
Seven Years War (1756–1763), 68–75
Shakti, 265
Sheridan, Bernard, 162
shipping, 25–26, 46–48
Sikh, 265
Sinclair, John, first Baron Pentland (Lord Pentland), 250
Singh, Kishan, 123
Singh, Ram, 123
Sinn Fein, 251
Sinnott, Edward, 159
6th Bengal European Regiment, 165
slave trade, 33–36
Smith, Vincent A., 222–23
smuggling, 57–62
social class
    in the ICS, 209–11, 213–14
    in the IMS, 195–96, 198
    Irish identity in India, 87–93
social mobility, 25
Society of United Irishmen, 82
socio-economic conditions, 120–24
soldiers
    Brooke's recruitment business, 75–77
    Catholic priests, role of, 141–45
    Catholic worship, 161–62
    discharge, 96
    East India Company, 39–42, 71–75, 78–81, 97–98
    Irish identity in India, 85–93
    Irish imperial networks, 16–17, 20–21
    Irish Volunteer movement, 77–78
    medical services, 177–78
    military life in India, 91–92
    networks in India, 94–96
    physical condition of, 79–80
    recruitment following expansion into South Asia, 75–81
    recruitment following Indian Mutiny, 96–97
    recruitment following Seven Years War, 68–75
    and religion, 70–75, 76–77, 79, 94–95, 97–98, 141–45, 161–62
    role in British colonial project, 64–66, 97–98
    skills of, 79
    union with Britain, effects of, 85
South Asia, 6, 68–69
Spanish Succession, War of the, 43

Spring-Rice, Thomas, 110
St Leger, Robert, 144
St Thomas' church, Calcutta, 158
St Vincent's Hospital, Dublin, 188
St Xavier's Church, Calcutta, 157, 158, 159
Stanihurst, Richard, 219
Stoker, Ann Laura, 11
Stokes, E.T., 144
Story-Maskelyne, Nevil, 125–26
subaltern Irish
    Brooke's recruitment business, 75–77
    discharge, 96
    East India Company, 39–42, 71–75, 78–81, 97–98
    Irish identity in India, 85–93
    Irish imperial networks, 16–17
    Irish role in British colonial project, 64–66, 97–98
    Irish Volunteer movement, 77–78
    meaning of, 64
    medical services, 177–78
    military life in India, 91–92
    networks in India, 94–96
    physical condition of, 79–80
    recruitment following expansion into South Asia, 75–81
    recruitment following Indian Mutiny, 96–97
    recruitment following Seven Years War, 68–75
    and religion, 70–75, 76–77, 79, 94–95, 97–98, 141–45, 161–62
    skills of, 79
    union with Britain, effects of, 85
Subordinate Medical Service (SMS), 177–78
subsidiary alliance system, 80–81
Sulivan, Benjamin (brother of Laurence), 45, 51
Sulivan, Benjamin (nephew of Laurence), 55–56
Sulivan, John (brother of Laurence), 45
Sulivan, John (nephew of Laurence), 55–56
Sulivan, Laurence ('Sulivan network')
    business networks, 49–51
    career of, 44–48
    East India Company, changes in, 57–62
    Irish imperial networks, 256
    origins, 25–26
    patronage, role of, 51–57
    rise of, 25

Index

301

Sulivan, Richard Joseph (nephew of Laurence), 55–56
Sulivan, Stephen (brother of Laurence), 54
Sullivan, Liam, 92
surveys
  and colonial power, 111–17
  Geological Survey of India (GSI), 100–01, 117–26
  Great Trigonometrical Survey of India (GTS), 100, 104–11
  Ordnance Survey of Ireland (OSI), 100, 104, 109–11
swadeshi, 265
Sweden, 33–36
Syria, 139

Tagore, Rabindranath, 247–48
Tamil, 265
taxation, 69–70
telegraph lines, 185
Temple, Richard, 222, 234–37
tenancy, 224–28
theosophy, 248
3rd Brigade Horse Artillery, 166
Thompson, Andrew S., 15–16, 17, 102
Thynne, Thomas, Marquis of Bath (Lord Weymouth), 76
Tilak, Bal Gangadhar, 251
Tocqueville, Alexis de, 133–34
Tone, Wolfe, 58
Townsend, Charles, 70, 73–74
trade
  agencies of the East India Company, 25, 42–44
  Atlantic Empire, 27–30, 33–36, 43, 66–68
  business networks in London, 49–51
  colonial status, effect of, 26–31
  East Indian trade, 30–42, 44–48
  globalisation, 11–14
  Irish imperial networks, 17–256
  patronage networks, 51–57
  private trade with India, 57–62
  see also Sulivan, Laurence ('Sulivan network')
traditional remedies, 173–74, 189–91
Trevelyan, Charles, 194, 207–08
triangulation, use in map-making, 106–09
Trinity College, Dublin
  alumni network in India, 219–24
  ICS, preparation for, 215–16
  IMS, preparation for, 199–200

scientific knowledge, 117–19
shunned by Catholics, 214–215
Tucker, Josiah, 84
Twomey, D.H., 215

Unani medicine, 171, 174
union between Britain and Ireland, 26–31, 81–85, 131–32
universities
  ICS, preparation for, 169, 213–14
  IMS, preparation for, 169, 170, 197–98, 199–200
  Irish imperial networks, 258–59
  medicine, Irish school of, 169–71, 182–83, 185–93, 199–200, 202–04
  political thought following the Famine, 230
Upson, Anthony, 45
Urdu, 265

vaidya, 265
Vallancey, Charles, 217
Van de Ven, Hans, 12–13
Varanasi *see* Benares
varna, 265
Vedas, 265
Vellore mutiny (1806), 138
Vicars Apostolic, 140–41, 148–54

Wake, William, 47
Wales, 6, 33
'Wants of Behar, The' (O'Donnell), 237–40
welfare of residents, 120–24
West Indies, 27–30, 33–36, 43, 71
Weymouth, Lord (Thomas Thynne, Marquis of Bath), 76
Whewell, William, 189
Whig Party, 129, 133
'white mutiny' (1859), 165–66
Wilde, William, 188–91
wills of Irish soldiers, 95–96
Wilson, H.H., 175
women, 248–50
Wood, Charles, 194, 207–08, 209–10
Wyndham, William, Baron Grenville (Lord Grenville), 84

Yeats, W.B., 220, 247–48
Young, Matthew, 219–20

zamindar, meaning of, 265
zamindari land management, 64, 225–26, 237–46

Printed in the United States
By Bookmasters